MUSIC IN THE MEDIEVAL WEST

Western Music in Context: A Norton History

Walter Frisch SERIES EDITOR

Music in the Medieval West, by Margot Fassler

Music in the Renaissance, by Richard Freedman

Music in the Baroque, by Wendy Heller

Music in the Eighteenth Century, by John Rice

Music in the Nineteenth Century, by Walter Frisch

Music in the Twentieth and Twenty-First Centuries, by Joseph Auner

MUSIC IN THE MEDIEVAL WEST

Margot Fassler
University of Notre Dame
and
Yale University

W. W. NORTON AND COMPANY
NEW YORK • LONDON

W. W. Norton & Company has been independent since its founding in 1923, when William Warder Norton and Mary D. Herter Norton first published lectures delivered at the People's Institute, the adult education division of New York City's Cooper Union. The firm soon expanded its program beyond the Institute, publishing books by celebrated academics from America and abroad. By midcentury, the two major pillars of Norton's publishing program—trade books and college texts—were firmly established. In the 1950s, the Norton family transferred control of the company to its employees, and today—with a staff of four hundred and a comparable number of trade, college, and professional titles published each year—W. W. Norton & Company stands as the largest and oldest publishing house owned wholly by its employees.

Printed in the United States of America

Editor: Maribeth Payne
Associate Editor: Justin Hoffman
Editorial Assistant: Michael Fauver
Developmental Editor: Harry Haskell
Manuscript Editor: Jodi Beder
Project Editor: Jack Borrebach
Electronic Media Editor: Steve Hoge
Marketing Manager, Music: Chris Freitag
Production Managers: Ashley Horna and Benjamin Reynolds
Photo Editor: Stephanie Romeo
Permissions Manager: Megan Jackson
Text Design: Jillian Burr
Composition: Jouve International—Brattleboro, VT
Manufacturing: Quad/Graphics—Fairfield, PA

Library of Congress Cataloging-in-Publication Data

Fassler, Margot Elsbeth, author.
Music in the Medieval West/Margot Fassler. — First edition.
pages cm. — (Western music in context : a Norton history)
Includes bibliographical references and index.
ISBN 978-0-393-92915-7 (pbk. : alk. paper) 1. Music—500-1400—History and criticism.
I. Title.
ML172.F37 2014
780.9'02—dc23

2013040325

W. W. Norton & Company, Inc., 500 Fifth Avenue, New York, NY 10110
wwnorton.com

W. W. Norton & Company Ltd., Castle House, 75/76 Wells Street, London W1T 3QT

1 2 3 4 5 6 7 8 9 0

To the memory of László Dobszay, Michel Huglo, Donna Mayer-Martin, Anne Dhu McLucas, Maria Rosa Menocal, and all our wildest dreams . . .

CONTENTS IN BRIEF

CONTENTS

ANTHOLOGY REPERTOIRE

1. Anonymous: *Ave maris stella*
2. Ambrose of Milan: *Eterne rerum conditor*
3. Anonymous: Selected Mass Propers
4. Anonymous: *Ecce apparebit Dominus* and *Laudate Dominum*
5. Fulbert of Chartres: *Stirps Jesse*
6. Anonymous: *Kyrie Cunctipotens genitor* and trope
7. Anonymous and Notker the Stammerer: *Rex omnipotens* and *Sancti Spiritus*
8. Anonymous and Adémar de Chabannes: Tropes for the Introit *Resurrexi*
9. Anonymous: *Congaudentes exsultemus*
10. Anonymous: *The Three Daughters* (opening scenes)
11. Anonymous: *Surrexit Dominus vere* from Winchester
12. Anonymous: *Annus novus*
13. Anonymous: *Stirps Jesse florigeram*
14. Albertus Parisiensis: *Congaudeant catholici*
15. Peter Abelard: *Epithalamica*
16. Marcabru: *L'autrier jost'una sebissa*
17. Bernart de Ventadorn: *Can vei la lauzeta mover*
18. Guiraut de Bornehl: *Reis gloriós*
19. Adam of St. Victor: *Zima vetus*
20. Hildegard of Bingen: *Mathias sanctus*
21. Anonymous: *Laude novella*
22. Anonymous: *Bache bene venies*
23. Thibaut of Champagne: *Chançon ferai que talenz*
24. King Alfonso the Wise (?): *Rosa das rosas*

25. Martin Codax: *Ondas do mare de Vigo*
26. Philip the Chancellor (?): *Sol oritur in sidere*
27. Anonymous: *Stirps Jesse*
28. Anonymous: *Styrps Yesse*
29. School of Pérotin: *Flos Filius eius*
30. Anonymous: *Plus bele que flor/Quant revient/L'autrier joer/Flos Filius; Castrum pudicicie/Virgo viget/Flos Filius*
31. Petrus de Cruce: *S'amours eüst point de poer/Au renouveler/Ecce*
32. Philippe de Vitry: *Tribum/Quoniam/Merito*
33. Guillaume de Machaut: *Dame, de qui toute ma joie; Dame, a vous sans retollir* (from *Remède de Fortune*)
34. Guillaume de Machaut: Kyrie from the *Messe de Nostre Dame*
35. Jacob (Jaquemin) de Senleches: *Je me merveil/J'ay pluseurs fois*
36. Marchetto of Padua: *Ave regina celorum/Mater innocencie/Ite Joseph*
37. Anonymous: *Quando i oselli canta*
38. Francesco Landini: *De sospirar sovente*
39. Antonio Zacara da Teramo: *Cacciando per gustar*
40. Anonymous: *Singularis laudis digna*

SERIES EDITOR'S PREFACE

Western Music in Context: A Norton History starts from the premise that music consists of far more than the notes on a page or the sound heard on a recording. Music is a product of its time and place, of the people and institutions that bring it into being.

Many music history texts focus on musical style and on individual composers. These approaches have been a valuable part of writing about music since the beginnings of modern scholarship in the later nineteenth century. But in the past few decades, scholars have widened their scope in imaginative and illuminating ways to explore the cultural, social, intellectual, and historical contexts for music. This new perspective is reflected in the volumes of Western Music in Context. Among the themes treated across the series are:

- The ways in which music has been commissioned, created, and consumed in public and private spheres
- The role of technology in the creation and transmission of music, from the advent of notation to the digital age
- The role of women as composers, performers, and patrons
- The relationships between music and national or ethnic identity
- The training and education of musicians in both private and institutional settings

All of these topics—and more—animate the pages of Western Music in Context. Written in an engaging style by recognized experts, the series paints vivid pictures of moments, activities, locales, works, and individuals:

- A fourth-century eyewitness report on musical practices in the Holy Land, from a European nun on a pilgrimage
- A lavish wedding at the court of Savoy in the mid-fifteenth century, with music by Guillaume DuFay

- Broadside ballads sung on the streets of London or pasted onto walls, and enjoyed by people from all levels of society
- A choral Magnificat performed at a church in colonial Brazil in the 1770s, accompanied by an organ sent by ship and mule from Portugal
- The barely literate impresario Domenico Barbaia making a tidy fortune at Italian opera houses by simultaneously managing gambling tables and promoting Gioachino Rossini
- A "radio teaching piece" from 1930 by Kurt Weill celebrating the transatlantic flight of Charles Lindbergh

Each volume of Western Music in Context is accompanied by a concise anthology of carefully chosen works. The anthologies offer representative examples of a wide variety of musical genres, styles, and national traditions. Included are excerpts from well-known works like Aaron Copland's *Billy the Kid*, as well as lesser-known gems like Ignacio de Jerusalem's *Matins for the Virgin of Guadalupe*. Commentaries within the anthologies not only provide concise analyses of every work from both formal and stylistic points of view, but also address issues of sources and performance practice.

StudySpace, Norton's online resource for students, features links to recordings of anthology selections that can be streamed from the Naxos Music Library (individual or institutional subscription required), as well as the option to purchase and download recordings from Amazon and iTunes. In addition, students can purchase access to, and instructors can request a free DVD of, the Norton Opera Sampler, which features over two hours of video excerpts from fourteen Metropolitan Opera productions. Finally, for readers wanting to do further research or find more specialized books, articles, or web-based resources, StudySpace offers lists of further readings that supplement those at the end of each chapter in the texts.

Because the books of the Western Music in Context series are relatively compact and reasonably priced, instructors and students might use one or more volumes in a single semester, or several across an academic year. Instructors have the flexibility to supplement the books and the accompanying anthologies with other resources, including Norton Critical Scores and *Strunk's Source Readings in Music History*, as well as other readings, illustrations, scores, films, and recordings.

The contextual approach to music history offers limitless possibilities: an instructor, student, or general reader can extend the context as widely as he or she wishes. Well before the advent of the World Wide Web, the renowned anthropologist Clifford Geertz likened culture to a spider's web of interconnected meanings that humans have spun. Music has been a vital part of such webs throughout the history of the West. Western Music in Context has as its goal to highlight such connections and to invite the instructors and students to continue that exploration on their own.

Walter Frisch
Columbia University

AUTHOR'S PREFACE

The Middle Ages lasted longer by far than any other "period" commonly designated in music history books. To study medieval music is to move from the late antique world of Augustine and Boethius in the late fourth and early fifth centuries all the way to the early fifteenth-century humanistic machinations of Antonio Zacharia da Teramo, whose compositions include many features commonly associated with the Renaissance.

To cover such a vast expanse of time in a short book, I have worked chronologically, avoiding the tendency to treat various repertories as if they were monolithic, appearing at a particular time, and then exiting the stage, untransformed and lifeless. Rather, the composition of monophonic music continued unabated throughout the entire Middle Ages, calling us to know the genius of many melodic strategies. Polyphony was with us from the beginning of music writing in the ninth century, provoking many ideas even at the outset about intervals and the harmonic sense that existed before tempered systems of tuning. Although notation changed, and the most sophisticated repertories changed with it, there was always ex tempore composition, in both sacred and secular realms, however difficult the evidence for these practices may be to uncover. The degree to which instruments were used to accompany secular song in the Middle Ages is ever a subject of debate, and one that calls to the creative imaginations of musicians who play medieval music.

This book—and its accompanying anthology and website—have been created for students, teachers, and, more broadly, for anyone interested in the music of the medieval West and its context. It is a lover's work, inspired not only by sheer personal pleasure in and intellectual engagement with the music itself, but also by a sense of delight—of astonishment, really—in the extraordinary accomplishments of my peers, the scholars who have spent and are spending their professional lives working to understand medieval music and its manifold connections to culture and history. Without attention to music, history is incomplete; by striving to understand the music of the Middle Ages, scholars have not only illuminated the past but also enabled its music to sound new. In *Music in the Medieval West*, I hope to introduce readers to the engaging scholarship that has illuminated this music. For those who would like to go deeper, the notes and end-of-chapter bibliographies suggest avenues for further research; even more sources appear on StudySpace—Norton's online resource for students—and my personal website.

At the same time that there has been so much excellent new scholarship, so many well-informed and lively performances, there has also been an explosion of new resources for the study of medieval manuscripts and the repertories they contain. This book provides gateways to these sources for teaching and learning as well as instructions on how to use them: the Medieval Music Primer that appears in the back of this volume suggests some ways to begin, and my personal website includes lessons based on primary sources.

For students and instructors who wish to delve more deeply into the medieval repertoire, a concise anthology of over 40 works accompanies this text. In the anthology, I have offered commentary and analysis of each work, yet I also have strived to select pieces that have been explored in greater depth by others, offering opportunities to engage with the music on an even deeper level. The works in the anthology also encourage readers to appreciate the many ways that medieval composers and performers created sophisticated soundscapes by relating one piece to another, and another, and another—to experience firsthand the endlessly refracted and re-echoing world of medieval music.

It is the best of times to be a student of medieval music and to learn to hear, sing, and play this music, ever with a spirit of the explorer and the pioneer, entering a world far different from our own, but filled with untold pleasures, treasures, and challenges.

ACKNOWLEDGMENTS

This book is a project that has drawn deeply on the expertise and good will of a great many people (although of course any omissions remain mine). The first thanks goes to Maribeth Payne and Walter Frisch, who have shepherded this series over many years, from its early conceptual development, through writing and editing, to its final publication: their kindness, patience, and encouragement have been foundational to all our efforts. Working with our particular team of series authors, too, has been a joy, through every riotous meeting and email thicket. I am grateful for the wonderful team assembled at Norton for production and editing, to Jodi Beder, Jack Borrebach, Michael Fauver, Harry Haskell, Justin Hoffman, and Marian Johnson. They have made the book so much better, championing consistency and reading with intelligence and sensitivity.

I owe a great deal to my prepublication reviewers—including Susan Boynton, Anna Maria Busse Berger, Michael Long, and Rebecca Maloy—whose every suggestion was gratefully taken. Several scholars read parts of chapters that needed their particular depth of knowledge: Elizabeth Aubrey, Rebecca A. Baltzer, Calvin M. Bower, Susan Boynton, David Ganz, Barbara Haggh-Huglo, Michael Long, Peter Jeffery, Peter Lefferts, and Susan Rankin. The book and the anthology owe them a great deal. Matters of language were discussed with Hildegund Mueller, Isabelle Fabre, and Leofranc Holford-Strevens. Many scholars answered brief questions, and the sense of community within our guild has never ceased to astound me throughout the entire process.

Students at the Medieval Institute at Notre Dame worked with me for several weeks on translations and other aspects of the book and made important contributions to the work; to be singled out are Hailey LaVoy, Nicholas Kamas, and Anna de Bakker. Kate Kennedy Steiner served as a research assistant during one summer and also tried out the book in an early form for a course she taught at NYU; Hillary Sullivan Doerries assisted me in the final stages of production, including work on the glossary; Jeffery Cooper, of Notre Dame's Program in Sacred Music, was ever present to assist with transcriptions and to prepare scores. Professor Michael Anderson of the Eastman School of Music produced recordings of several works in the anthology, lending expertise both musical and musicological. My students at Yale and at Notre Dame tried out many chapters and pieces, and I will forever be thankful to them all.

I am grateful to the staff of the library of the Medieval Institute at Notre Dame, Marina Smyth and Julia Schneider; to Robert Simon, Music Librarian; and to David Gura, curator of Medieval and European Manuscripts, both of the Hesburgh Library, University of Notre Dame. I am thankful as well for the assistance of the staff of the Mendel Music Library at Princeton University, especially to Music Librarian Darwin Scott, and to Suzanne Lovejoy and the staff of the John Herrick Jackson Music Library of Yale University. For the leave time I needed to complete this book, I am most grateful to Yale University, the Institute of Sacred Music, and the University of Notre Dame.

MUSIC IN THE MEDIEVAL WEST

CHAPTER ONE

The Making of the Middle Ages

No one who lived in the Middle Ages knew it. Most medieval people believed themselves to be in an apocalyptic age and watched for signs of a cataclysm that would end time itself. Not until the fourteenth century did some Italian scholars begin to think of European history as divided into three parts: classical antiquity, a middle age, and a modern age. These early humanists were pleased to find a new age dawning with themselves and their friends; this era is the subject of the subsequent volume in the Western Music in Context series, Richard Freedman's *Music in the Renaissance*.

The heroes of the fourteenth-century humanists were the writers (especially), artists, music theorists, and other scholars of ancient Greece and Rome, some of whom we will meet in Chapter 2. The humanists applied the term *medieval* (from the Latin *medium aevum*, or middle age) to the millennium or so between the crumbling of classical Roman civilization in the fourth and fifth centuries of the Common Era (CE) and the first blush of the Italian Renaissance. The poet Petrarch (1304–1374), who was an admirer of the composer Philippe de Vitry (1291–1361), is usually viewed as the father of the movement that became known as humanism. From Italy the enthusiasm for classical antiquity spread throughout Europe, leaving its mark on all aspects of art and music.

Until relatively recently, composers wishing to emulate the music of Greece and Rome had no models to guide them. They had only ancient music theory, the meters and rhythms of poetry, and the sounds described in literary and historical sources. Even today, but little notated music survives from classical antiquity, although evidence of music's importance abounds. That is why this series begins with a volume devoted almost exclusively to the Middle Ages, the first period from which we have a significant written repertory of music.

The ways musicians understand and build on repertories of the past is a theme that runs through this book, and indeed through the entire series. Just as medieval musicians sought to re-create a past that they understood imperfectly, so modern performers approach a piece of medieval music as a mystery inscribed on scraps of parchment, notated in ways that are often difficult to decipher. There is always some dimension of the music that is not well documented or understood, be it pitch, rhythm, the use of instruments, or that most elusive of all musical elements, style. Skilled performers who work with this repertory learn as much as they can about the music's original context and meaning, but at some point their own interpretive ideas can, will, and must take over. Medieval music is, after all, *music.*

Some of the most important evidence for medieval performance practice relates to date, place, and function: the performer should understand when and where a piece was made, remade, or copied, and why some person or group of people put effort into its production and preservation. To this end, historians commonly divide the thousand years constituting the Middle Ages into four epochs: the early Middle Ages (c. 400–750), beginning around the time Rome fell to barbarian warriors in 410; the Carolingian period (c. 750–950), initiated by the demise of the Merovingian kings and the establishment of the lineage of Pippin the Short, father of Charlemagne; the central Middle Ages (c. 950–1200), during which Carolingian kings were replaced by the Capetians in France and the Ottonians in Germany, and the Normans conquered the Anglo-Saxons in England; and the late Middle Ages (c. 1200–1400), ushered in by the signing of the Magna Carta in England and the convening of the Fourth Lateran Council in Rome, both in 1215.

These broad chronological divisions are problematic and exceedingly variable. What was "early" in one region may be "central" in another, and strains of development always coexisted, even within particular geographic areas. As is traditional in the study of European music, *Music in the Medieval West* ends around 1400. We follow this convention for the sake of convenience and not because that or any other particular year constituted an epoch-making watershed in European history. The end points and divisions of our timeline are invented, just as is the concept of the Middle Ages itself.

Although this book focuses on three centuries—the twelfth, thirteenth, and fourteenth—it pays significant attention to late antiquity and prenotational cultures, as well as to the times when notational practices were first developing. To provide continuity over these thousand years—a span of time greater than that covered by the five other volumes in our series combined—several topics have been singled out:

- the organization and exchange of ideas across various geographical, political, social, and artistic boundaries;
- music as an art of memory, especially in regard to the creation of webs of musical meanings;
- music as a documented phenomenon, and the ways and means by which a written record was produced;
- music in time and as a history-making force, especially as related to ceremonial and dramatic reenactments of time;
- understandings of individual women, and of the female in general, as reflected in medieval repertories and in their copying and performance.

A CASE STUDY: *AVE MARIS STELLA*

Themes that run through our discussion all point to the importance of examining the multiple ways musical pieces and repertories of the Middle Ages were interrelated. The hymn text *Ave maris stella*, celebrating the Virgin Mary, is an excellent place to begin our investigation (see Anthology 1). Probably written in the ninth century, this hymn, or sacred song, came to be sung throughout Europe, and many melodies were written for or adapted to this text. Medieval composers used some of these melodies to generate new pieces of music, both monophonic (single-line) and polyphonic (with two or more lines sounding simultaneously).

Ave maris stella is a strophic poem—that is, one based on a repeating unit of poetry with a given number of lines and a particular meter. Each strophe is set to the same melody. The music, when given at all, might be provided for only the first strophe, leaving the performer to fit the text to the repeated melody thereafter.

Example 1.1 shows one of the most widespread melodies sung to the *Ave maris stella* text in two versions, one in "square" notation and the other in modern notation. The former is taken from the *Liber Usualis* (Book for Common Use), a modern book containing the restored melodies of medieval chants organized to provide music for the major feasts of the Christian calendar and for Sunday services throughout the year. (A guide to using the *Liber Usualis* and reading square notation can be found in Primer I.3 and II.1.) This collection offers convenient access to the chant repertory, but it departs, often significantly, from actual medieval manuscripts and must therefore be used with caution. The spellings

Example 1.1: *First strophe of* Ave maris stella, *a Carolingian hymn to the Virgin Mary:* (a) *From the* Liber Usualis

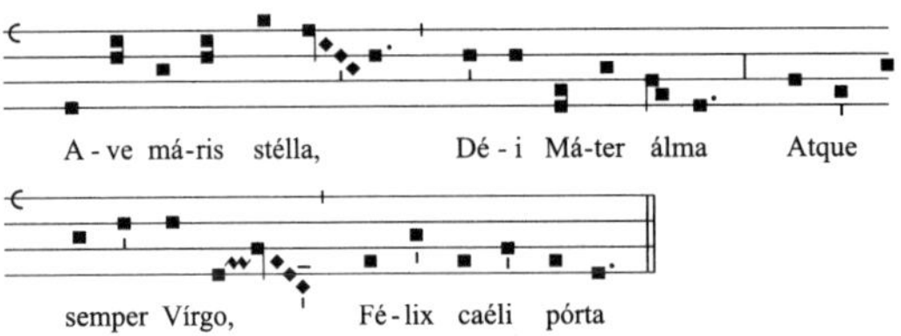

(b) *Pitches in modern notation*

Hail, star of the sea, tender mother of God and ever virgin, happy door of heaven.

of words, and even the letters, are somewhat variable in medieval manuscripts, and a famous text like *Ave maris stella* was set to many different melodies, only some of which are found in the *Liber Usualis*.

INTERTEXTUALITY AND MEDIEVAL VIEWS OF WOMANHOOD

Ave maris stella serves to introduce the concept of intertextuality, which is fundamental to understanding the composition and performance of medieval music. If we take every piece of music—indeed, every work of art—as a "text," capable of being understood and analyzed, we can then speak of the intertextual relationships between and within works of art. In music, examples of intertextuality include phrases taken or adapted from other works, even the use of a particular mode or key that is closely associated with other works that may be familiar to the performer or listener. Within a composition, one section can reference another by repetition, variation, fragmentation. When we deal with the combination of music and text—especially when texts come from liturgy or Scripture—this web of interrelationships becomes that much more complex.

A famous melody such as that of *Ave maris stella* in Example 1.1 offers an especially wide range of possibilities for exploring intertextuality. Even the music repeated for each strophe of the hymn creates an intertextual relationship between the various units of text. As in any strophic piece, poetic images pile up in the memory as the piece is sung and the repeating music relates ideas in one strophe to those in the next. This is one reason that singing *Ave maris stella* is far different from merely reading its words, either silently or aloud.

Another kind of intertextual relationship occurs when a work is created by writing a new text for a preexisting melody. In such cases, the texts of the two pieces play off of each other, sometimes in highly artful ways. The newer work is called a *contrafactum* (from the medieval Latin verb meaning "to imitate" or "counterfeit"). Examples of contrafacta abound in many times and cultures. *My Country, 'Tis of Thee*, for instance, is a contrafactum of an earlier English anthem, *God Save the King*, and the reworking makes a statement about American democracy.

O Maria Deu maire (Ex. 1.2), set to the same melody as *Ave maris stella*, is a twelfth-century poem written in an early relative of the French language called Old Occitan (or Old Provençal). It has the honor of being the only surviving song in this language, either sacred or secular, that was written out in its entirety, strophe by strophe; as such, it provides a rare opportunity to see how a medieval singer might have slightly changed the melody as the text unfolded. (It is also the earliest piece with transcribable music that has come down to us written in the vernacular, rather than in Latin.) Both texts—the hymn and the song—focus on the Virgin Mary, but their contents are quite different. *Ave maris stella* hails the Virgin as the North Star, essential for navigation through life into a safe heavenly port. *O Maria Deu maire*, like its model, praises Mary for lifting the ancient curse placed on Eve, but then takes up other ideas, creating a historical narrative of salvation.

Example 1.2: *First strophe of* O Maria Deu maire, *a twelfth-century Old Occitan song based on* Ave maris stella

Oh Mary, mother of God, God is to you both Son and Father.
Lady, pray for us to your Son, the glorious one.

The view of the female of the species as a paradox, at once damning and saving, is paramount in much medieval art and music (Figs. 1.1 and 1.2). In the biblical Book of Genesis, Eve the temptress is depicted as the prototype of all sinful women. The Virgin Mary, on the other hand, became the greatest saint of all Christendom, in whose honor numberless songs, poems, treatises, and artworks have been created. These contradictory stereotypes were central to the culture that created them. Medieval Christian women thought of themselves as Mary, as Eve, as a host of other women from the Bible, and as saints, as well. Their male counterparts, who were primarily responsible for the music presented in this book, took up these same points of view, exploring the female with a relentless fascination that is sometimes difficult to explain.

Two sides of being female, and of being human, are on display in *Ave maris stella*. "Ave" is the reverse form of "Eva," a deliberate pun suggesting that Mary redressed the evil that the "first mother," Eve, was believed to have engendered. Elsewhere, the Virgin is often compared to her foil, the penitent saint Mary Magdalene. These two powerful figures, one a merciful mother, the other a former prostitute with a heart of gold, are key to understanding conceptions of womanhood through the ages. The deeds of many women—a long and varied cast of characters—are explored in medieval music. It is well to remember this at the outset of a book that will often seem to make little room for women, at least in the acts of composition and performance.

Figure 1.1: *Adam, Eve, and the Snake in the Garden, with the tree morphing into the Cross, from a fifteenth-century Flemish Book of Hours (University of Notre Dame, Hesburgh Library, Cod. Lat. a.1)*

Figure 1.2: *The angel Gabriel holds the text "Ave Maria, gratia plena, Dominus tecum" (Hail Mary, full of grace, the Lord is with you), from a fifteenth-century Flemish book of hours (University of Notre Dame, Hesburgh Library, Cod. Lat. a.2)*

SEQUENCES AND OTHER MUSICAL RESTATEMENTS

Another twelfth-century musical work is also related to *Ave maris stella*, but not only as a contrafactum. *O Maria stella maris* is a sequence, a genre of chant sung as part of the Mass repertory, specifically after the Alleluia, and before the intoning of the Gospel, the major scriptural reading of the day (see Primer IV.2). Sequences served as a kind of commentary upon the meanings of angelic praise and were composed in great numbers from the ninth century forward. *O Maria stella maris* is a sophisticated piece, related not to an Alleluia as might be expected, but rather to a hymn. The composer linked the text of this work directly to the hymn, strophe by strophe. But, unlike hymns, sequences are through-composed—that is, each strophe has different music. The Marian (related to the Virgin Mary) theme of the original hymn tune also permeates the entire fabric of *O Maria stella maris* in a process of constant musical restatement, making a parallel to the development of the text, but in a different medium. The first strophe uses the pitches and ideas of the hymn, but reshapes them to fit another rhyme scheme, adapting the melody accordingly. As can be seen in

Example 1.3, the second strophe is set to a melody that has a freer relationship to the hymn tune. It is no wonder that the melody of the sequence *O Maria stella maris* was set to many poems, six of them in twelfth-century Paris alone, and all related to the many symbolic meanings assigned to the Virgin Mary.

Example 1.3:
(a) *First and second strophes of the twelfth-century sequence* O Maria stella maris, *based on* Ave maris stella *as sung in Paris*

O Mary, star of the sea, uniquely compassionate, with your eye of tenderness

In this valley of tears, nothing is sweet, nothing dear; all things are suspect.

(b) Ave maris stella *as sung in Paris*

Hail, star of the sea, tender mother of God and ever virgin, happy door of heaven.

Example 1.4: *Opening of the thirteenth-century motet* Ave beatissima/Ave Maria/Ave maris stella, *with hymn melody in tenor voice*

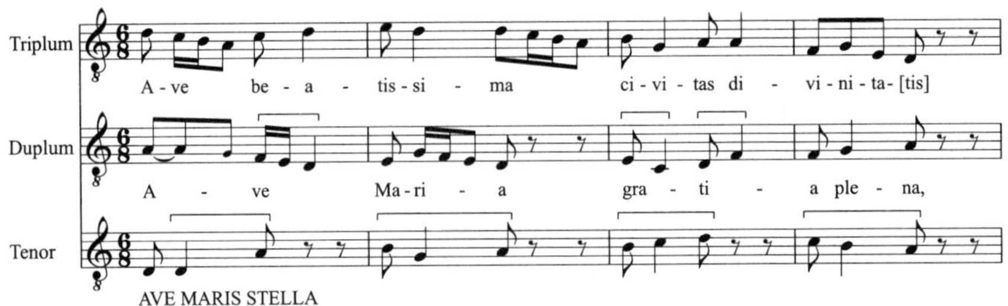

Triplum: Hail, most blessed city of divinity
Duplum: Hail, Mary, full of grace
Tenor: Hail, star of the sea

Ave beatissima/Ave Maria/Ave maris stella (Ex. 1.4), a thirteenth-century polytextual motet (a texted vocal composition, from the French word *mot*, meaning word), shows how the hymn melody could be used to provide a theological, rhythmic, and melodic foundation for other voices. Here the hymn tune is found in the tenor, a slower-moving voice that offers a well-known point of reference for the voices that unfold around it. In another setting, from the fourteenth century, the hymn melody is found in the top voice, with the lower two voices providing a simple harmonic accompaniment of a sort that might easily have been improvised by singers who understood the practice (Ex. 1.5). Yet another, more loosely dependent version of the hymn can be found with Italian words: *Laude novella*, a fourteenth-century popular religious song about the Virgin Mary, uses a refrain that echoes *Ave maris stella* and references it in music for the verses (see Chapter 8 and Anthology 21).

Our story does not end with the Middle Ages: a setting of *Ave maris stella* in an early-fifteenth-century instrumental collection is one of numerous organ versions in later periods (Ex. 1.6). Among the hundreds of choral settings of

Example 1.5: *Opening of a three-voice setting of* Ave maris stella *from the fourteenth century, with hymn tune in the cantus voice*

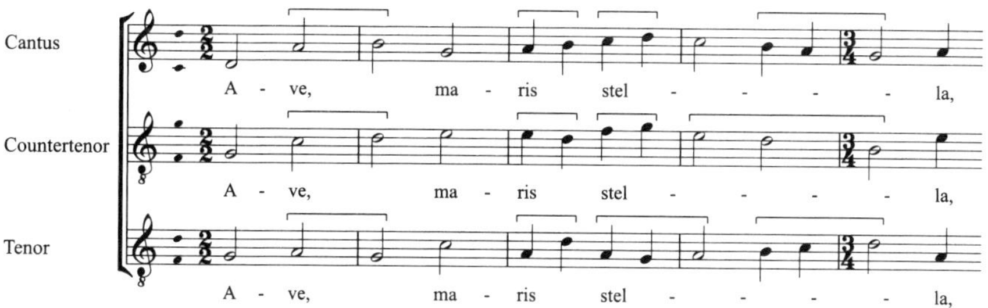

Hail, star of the sea

Example 1.6: *Opening of a setting of* Ave maris stella *for keyboard, from the early-fifteenth-century Faenza Codex, with melody in the lower voice*

this hymn are works by the fifteenth-century masters Guillaume Du Fay and Josquin des Prez. A lush version created by Claudio Monteverdi for his Vespers of 1610 offers a different setting of voices and instruments for each strophe of the hymn, probing into the dramatic meanings of the poem. A well-known Hungarian singer has used the hymn for a jazz recording accompanied by the saxophone. Like an image in a house of mirrors, the medieval hymn tune has produced an endless array of sonic refractions, each different, each related to the time and place in which it was made.

MEDIEVAL BOOKS AND THE SPREAD OF CHRISTIANITY

In the first through the fourth centuries CE, changes took place in the Greco-Roman world that would dramatically affect the art of music and its transcription. Parchment was slowly replacing papyrus as a medium for recording information, and the codex, or book, was taking over from the scroll. There were many reasons for this. Books could be readily accessed by chapters, so texts could be compared with ease. Their titles could be written on their spines, and a writer or reader did not need two hands to use or copy from them. Compared to scrolls, books were easy to carry, easy to consult, and above all, more economical than scrolls because both sides of a page could be used.

These technological developments coincided with the spread of Christianity, and the new religion preferred the new medium of the book. Indeed, Christians became the world's first great book producers. Even before music was written down, various Christian cultures were becoming particularly skilled at using the technology of the book; eventually, this would affect the ways in which repertories of music were stored and transmitted throughout western Europe.

The earliest surviving fragments of codices are made of papyrus, come from Egypt, and date from the late first or early second century. By the early fourth century, the codex had gained wide acceptance as a format throughout the late antique world. Over much of the next four centuries, Christian monks copied manuscripts in scriptoria (rooms set aside for the making of codices) or in cloisters as part of their lives of work and prayer; the bulk of surviving Greek and Roman literature was preserved in this way. Medieval books were made of dried animal skins, or parchment, and a whole flock of sheep might have to be slaughtered to produce just one part of a major codex—a book of the Bible, for example. Consequently, books were expensive and libraries were small by modern standards.

Tangible evidence for the writing down of music begins generally in medieval Europe in the second half of the ninth and early tenth centuries (see Chapter 3), although the practice may well have been established in one form or another significantly earlier. Even long after the beginnings of notation, only a few experts knew how to interpret it. The notation systems were dependent on melodies and musical formulas that most musicians were taught to know from memory. Even when scores became more common in the eleventh century, musicians and their audiences could not acquire them easily. The Catholic Church had a virtual monopoly on book production until the thirteenth century, when independent scribes came to play an increasingly important role and secular as well as sacred works began to be copied (see Chapters 8 and 9). Most medieval musicians worked exclusively by memory, and they were less likely to remember new music that was alien to what they already had stored in their minds. People knew music from what they heard from others and then could remember sufficiently to reimagine, sing, or play themselves.

THE ART OF MEMORY

All medieval knowledge, including musical knowledge, was transmitted along the pathways laid down in the mind by an art of memory. The more a piece of music fit into a preexistent framework, the better it was received. Even the most innovative medieval musicians built on what was already familiar, making old things new and new things old. If new music couldn't conjure up sounds, images, and textures that listeners already knew, it would be meaningless. Utter novelty was bizarre to the mind conditioned to think of knowledge as that which was remembered and memorized; variations on the familiar, on the other hand, were deeply pleasurable. This helps explain why the concept of intertextuality is fundamental to medieval music: it is intrinsic to the art of memory that sustained all musical practices.

As we saw with *Ave maris stella,* medieval music is often powerfully associated with particular images. When a singer "stored" such a melody in the mind, a range of Marian images and texts were stored along with it. Depending upon talent, training, age, and regionality, a musician's memory bank could include vast quantities of such information. Extracting these interrelated melodies, texts, and images through memory and conditioning, often in accordance with sets of preconceived rules or formulas, was fundamental to what it meant to be a musician.

It is important to bear in mind that there were no intellectual property rights in the Middle Ages. People who could afford it commonly bequeathed money or property to pay for musicians to sing at services commemorating them or their family members, but they did not own the music itself. Medieval legal documents consider rights to lands and agricultural products, to mills, bridges, and waterways, but there are no mentions of rights to the ideas in a book, to new ways of instruction, to the arrangements of facts in a chronicle, or to the melodies of a song. In the age before copyrights, borrowers freely helped themselves to whatever interested them, with no shame attached.

The many and varied settings of *Ave maris stella* point to what is perhaps the most important difference between us and our forebears in the Middle Ages. Contemporary heads are relatively empty: printed sources and machines tend to do the remembering for us. Medieval minds, on the other hand, were crammed with all kinds of facts and information. People needed to know when to plant their crops or their families would starve; books for the hours of prayer that we will discuss in Chapter 4 would have been useless to singers who didn't know the psalm tones by heart and how to adapt texts to them. The thousands of bits of musical information that a trained musician possessed necessitated a means of storage and organization, so that one idea could lead to another. Every melody was a remembered strategy for composing other melodies or for storing closely related music and texts in the mind. There were (as there are now) relationships between many bodies of musical materials, and those that resemble each other closely were more powerfully interdependent. Every person possessed a web of information that spun out the intertextuality of any number of pieces.

Ave maris stella was a "piece" only in the most general sense of the word. There were many copies of the work, but no definitive original. Yet the different melodies sung to this text were inscribed in oral traditions, so that by the twelfth century a chant in Paris (*Ave maris stella*) and a song in southern France (*O Maria Deu maire*) were composed to a variation of the same tune. Every musical work belonged to a larger family of pieces that operated though an art of memory, each working in unique ways depending upon musical genre, region, and era. Even the most carefully written and sophisticated pieces were parts of sonic webs that resounded within the intertextual mansions of the medieval imagination. So it is that medieval music insists upon the exploration of interrelationships and only makes sense when the barren rooms of contemporary minds are restocked with tunes.

In the following chapters we will explore many interrelationships between various groups of melodies and modes of music-making. We will examine these in light of the contextual study that has taken hold of scholarship in recent decades, emphasizing the ways in which historical and musical understandings go hand in hand. We also give special consideration to the steadily developing technologies that allowed musicians not only to remember music but also to record it. The desire to capture time, stop it, and then allow it to unfold again, minute by minute, has long been central to human endeavor. Medieval musicians were radically innovative in this pursuit. How, when, and why they discovered new technologies for carrying out their work is one of the most important and fascinating aspects of our story.

FOR FURTHER READING

Busse Berger, Anna Maria, *Medieval Music and the Art of Memory* (Berkeley: University of California Press, 2005)

Carruthers, Mary J., and Jan Ziolkowski, eds., *The Medieval Craft of Memory: An Anthology of Texts and Pictures* (Philadelphia: University of Pennsylvania Press, 2004)

Everist, Mark, "The Miller's Mule: Writing the History of Medieval Music," *Music and Letters* 74 (1993): 44–53

Milsom, John, "'Imitatio,' 'Intertextuality,' and Early Music," in S. Clarke and E. E. Leach, eds., *Citation and Authority in Medieval and Renaissance Musical Culture: Learning from the Learned* (Rochester, NY: Boydell, 2005), 141–51

Peraino, Judith, "Re-Placing Medieval Music," *Journal of the American Musicological Society* 54 (2001): 209–64

Rubin, Miri, *Mary the Mother of God: A History of the Virgin Mary* (New Haven: Yale University Press, 2009)

PART I

Founders and Foundations of Western Music

In the late fourth and early fifth centuries, a number of distinguished scholars steeped in the world of classical antiquity and late Latin learning reshaped the way works of that period were understood, through new modes of study and translation. As we will see in Chapter 2, Jerome (SR 11:126–28; 2/3:16–18) translated into Latin the 150 Hebrew poems known as the Book of Psalms, which became the primary source of texts for early medieval chant repertories. Augustine (SR 13:132–33; 2/5:22–23), through his commentaries on the psalms, pointed the way toward the development of later repertories of music, including tropes, sequences, and prosulae. Boethius (SR 14:137–43; 2/6:27–33) transmitted Greek music theory to the West, his writings forming the essential music textbook for centuries.

Various compendia or encyclopedias produced in the late antique and early medieval periods also facilitated the survival of classical learning and musical understanding. Calcidius commented on Plato's *Timaeus*, a text central to musical learning, especially regarding music and speculative thinking (SR 2:19–23; 1/2:19–23); Martianus Capella surveyed music and the other liberal arts in *The Marriage of Philology and Mercury;* Cassiodorus (SR 15:143–48; 2/7:33–38) wrote the *Institutions*, which laid out a program of monastic learning based on the liberal arts; and the great encyclopedist Isidore of Seville (SR 16:149–55; 2/8:39–45) defined music and musicians.

From Egypt and Ethiopia to Spain and Ireland, the legacy of the classical civilizations of Greece and of Rome was preserved through the care and copying of Christian monks. The survival of classical learning was central to the development of the so-called Carolingian Renaissance, which takes its name from Charlemagne (Charles the Great), who died in 814. In addition to encouraging the liberal arts and the study of the Bible, he promoted the shaping of a "correct" musical repertory for religious services, as discussed in Chapter 3. Both of Charlemagne's biographers testify to his insistence on musical excellence. Einhard reports that Charlemagne "corrected the discipline of reading and singing most carefully, for he was skilled in both." According to Notker the Stammerer (SR 22:181–83; 2/14:71–73), Charlemagne would point out the person he wanted to read in the service and then clear his throat when he wanted the singer to stop. Charlemagne's choir, which apparently traveled with the king when he moved his court, achieved a high level of musical proficiency.

As we will learn in Chapters 3 and 4, the Mass and the Divine Office were the major ritual celebrations in the medieval Church. The Carolingian Mass liturgy centers on the Christian Eucharist, a symbolic meal representative of the Last Supper. The first half of the service consists of prayers and readings separated by chants; the second half commemorates the meal itself through the use of music and ceremonial action. The Office, on the other hand, consists of eight daily hours of prayer, each of which is dominated by the chanting of psalms. During the time of Charlemagne, the Office was standardized and the sixth-century *Rule of St. Benedict* (SR 17:159–64; 2/9:49–54), which contains a plan for

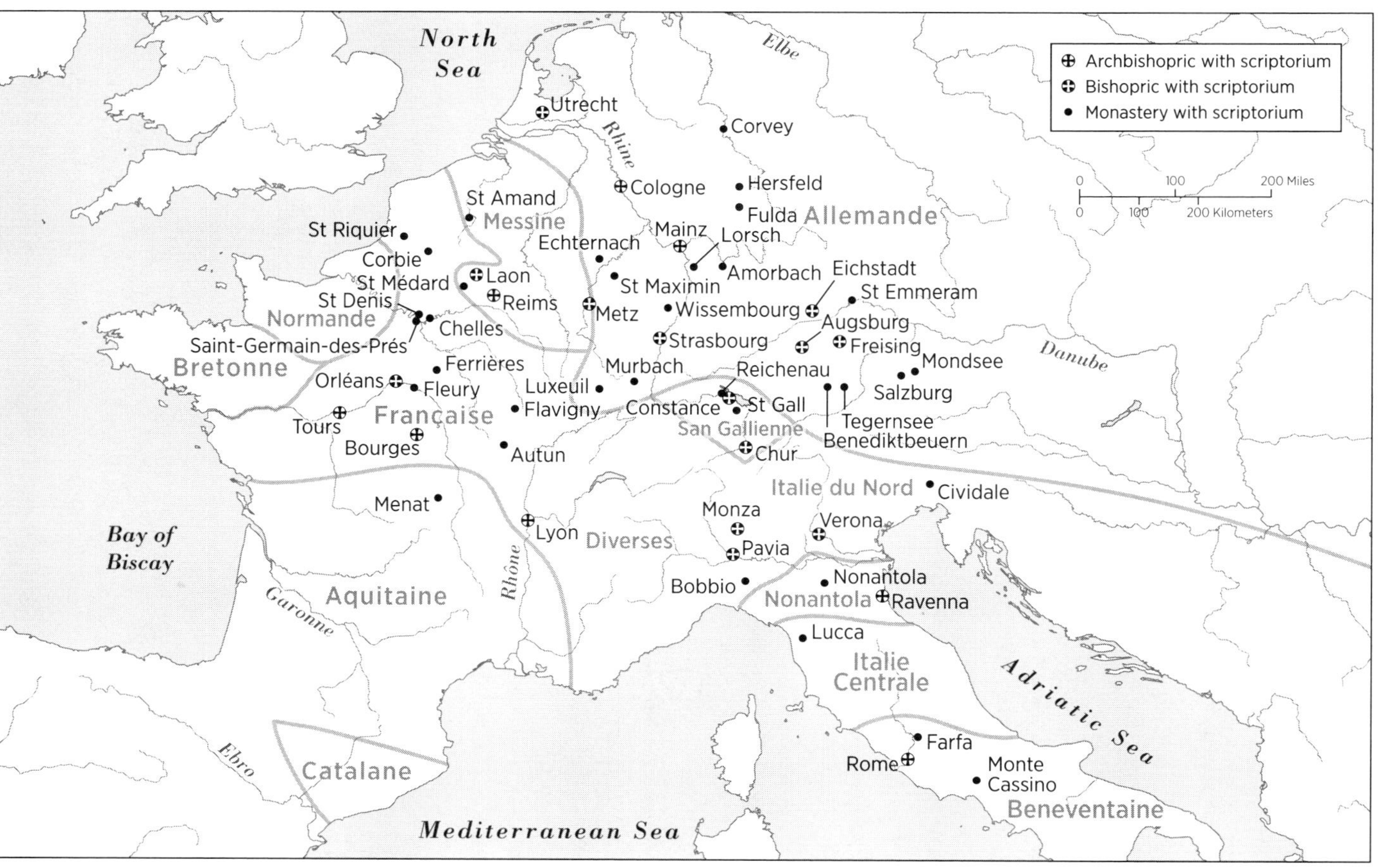

The Carolingian Renaissance

singing all 150 psalms in the course of the week, was slowly adopted throughout the Carolingian Empire.

The music associated with the Mass and the Office must be studied in its chronological layers. The chant remains like a bedrock with other genres of musical sediment lying on top of it, shifting with the winds of time. Mass chants are divided into two categories, Proper and Ordinary—that is, those that change their texts and music every day in accordance with the themes of the feast or season (Proper), and those whose texts remain the same throughout the year (Ordinary). We begin our discussion in Chapter 3 with the Proper chants of the Mass repertory, whose texts were already being copied in collections in the late eighth century. The music set to these texts represents the first layer of existing Western music that survives in written form. Because these chants were established before the splitting of Charlemagne's kingdom in the mid-ninth century, they are fairly well standardized throughout much of northern Europe.

The chants of the Mass Ordinary are generally somewhat later than the Proper chants, many of them composed in the second half of the ninth and the early tenth centuries (see Chapter 4). Chants of the Office are generally somewhat later than those of the Mass Propers, and although the ordering of the hours of prayer and their components are fixed, much music for the Office has a local character, particularly when it comes to the veneration of the saints. Musical repertory was crucial for creating identity, and the particularization found in the Office chant repertory was central to the ways that communities of song were sustained.

Many aspects of the musical traditions now functioning in the Western world originated in the Carolingian Renaissance and its immediate aftermath: the alphabet used for our texts is essentially Carolingian minuscule; the system of tonality we use evolved from that created by medieval composers and theorists; and our dependence upon notation developed from practices established in the ninth through the eleventh centuries. In the chant repertories of the Carolingians, we get our first experience of soloistic singing that required great virtuosity, of a choral repertory sung by a trained choir, and, at the same time, of music that was very simple and could be sung by large groups of untrained voices.

CHAPTER TWO

Medieval Musical Traditions

Before the Written Evidence

The earth is a far smaller place now than it was in late antiquity or the Middle Ages. Today anyone with sufficient funds and freedom to travel can get almost anywhere efficiently. But most people in the ancient and medieval worlds never visited faraway lands; if they did, they were likely to see them once and not live to tell the tale. Hence understandings and memories of distant places had to be carefully cultivated, even in periods of crusade and conquest (see Chapter 6).

What was history to the people of early medieval Europe, even those who could read and write? It was, in most cases, the Bible, commentary upon it, and, for Christians, the historic deeds of biblical figures and saints as reenacted in the liturgy or expressed in related media. This history depended upon the arts, especially music, as its lifeblood. Our art forged crucial connections with places, stories, and characters that most people would never know, except through sung rituals of remembrance.

The characters we will meet in this chapter represent the geographical diversity and the many attitudes toward music encountered in the late antique and Merovingian periods (300–750). Music is fluid, running through the veins of time, giving life and energy to historical understanding. Yet before the development of notation, music survived only in oral traditions throughout western Europe, with the strength of its flow depending upon human relationships to create the necessary channels. We have virtually no music to study from the fourth through the ninth centuries because, with few exceptions, it was not written down. Isidore of Seville (c. 560–636) said that "unless sounds are remembered by man, they perish, for they cannot be written down" (SR 16:149; 2/8:39).

Isidore could not have known that the ancient Greeks or people in other classical civilizations throughout the world once knew how to notate music. Upwards of 50 fragments of Greek music have come down to us from the third century BCE to the third century CE. Many of them survive on broken stone tablets or fragile papyri, and can be reconstructed with varying degrees of success. One of the most famous fragments was found in the early twentieth century near Oxyrhynchus, a city in upper Egypt where thousands of imperfectly preserved ancient texts written on papyrus have been uncovered, some of which can now be read by means of multispectral imaging processes. The so-called Oxyrhynchus Hymn was hurriedly scrawled in the late third century on the back of a list of grain deliveries. It and a group of other fragments prove that musicians in Greco-Roman Egypt were still using letter notation to write down melodies (Ex. 2.1). Roman aristocrats in the provinces were entertained by Greek musicians who possessed skills and musical understanding they did not; the Greeks had a musical heritage that was far advanced over that of Rome, and the phrase of music reproduced here is from the only surviving taste of this late antique repertory.

Another papyrus fragment from the sixth century attests to the use of modes, or scales, in Christian Egypt. (We'll have more to say about the church modes below.) Christianity came early to Egypt, and the Byzantine Church was well established there at the time of the Arab conquest of 639. Many of the advances associated with Western music had their origins among Greek-speaking Christians, and the role of Jerusalem in these developments was fundamental. It is in this historic and holy city that we encounter our most acute firsthand observer of music in late antiquity.

Example 2.1: *Excerpt from the third-century Oxyrhynchus Hymn*

Let all powers proclaim: Amen, amen.

EGERIA IN JERUSALEM: A PILGRIM'S VIEW

The longings for the Holy Land that many early European Christians experienced were expressed in the life of the fourth-century nun Egeria. A pilgrim from the part of the Roman Empire encompassing modern-day southern

France, she transmitted her amazing journey back home through a journal that survives in a single precious manuscript. Egeria was an adventuresome, inquisitive woman who imagined biblical history with help from many people she met on her travels. The Jerusalem she describes had recently been Christianized and later was the fountain of liturgical development for Byzantine churches as well as for churches in the Latin-speaking West (see below). In the fourth, fifth, and sixth centuries, it was the major tourist site for religious pilgrims, as well as the place where the theoretical foundations of medieval European music were established. Liturgies commemorating Jerusalem evolved and spread, taking on different characters in every region, but each drinking deeply from the source. Eventually, every town in Europe would use music and motion, architecture and the arts to re-create some replica of Jerusalem. We will encounter several of these "New Jerusalems" in the following chapters.

Constantine (c. 274–337), the first Christian Roman emperor, shifted the balance of power throughout the late antique world and ushered in the so-called Byzantine era in the history of Jerusalem. His mother, Helena, was a pilgrim to Jerusalem, where, later legends report, she discovered what was believed to have been the True Cross, a wooden relic that would become highly venerated throughout Christendom. Music associated with this relic eventually became emblematic of its meanings, capable of creating palpable relationships with its materiality.

Egeria would have been told all about Helena and the magnificent church that Constantine built in Jerusalem. The builders incorporated what was believed to have been the tomb of Jesus and the place of the crucifixion, creating a setting that would be copied all over Europe. The complex of buildings is laid out like a large temple, possibly modeled on the idealized temple described in the biblical book of the prophet Ezekiel (Chapters 40–48), or on the large basilicas that Constantine knew in Rome. The basilica on Golgotha (Fig. 2.1) included the supposed tomb of Jesus, where there was a major altar, and the area around it, known as the Anastasis. These architectural features represented the Holy of Holies in the Jewish Temple, while also pinpointing the actual location of the tomb of the Christian messiah.

Such an architectural site would have been packed with meaning for pilgrims. The communion meal offered to Christians in Egeria's time was held in the Anastasis; for centuries Christian altars in churches throughout Europe were conceived as replicas of what was once seen there. The plan of a long nave with an apse at the east end became standard throughout medieval Christendom, and the historic meanings of this structure in Jerusalem would be transferred to these buildings, their altars, and their rituals. Music composed for these ceremonies would serve to cement these blocks of understanding, linking worshipping Christians throughout the Western world to their biblical past in the Holy Land.

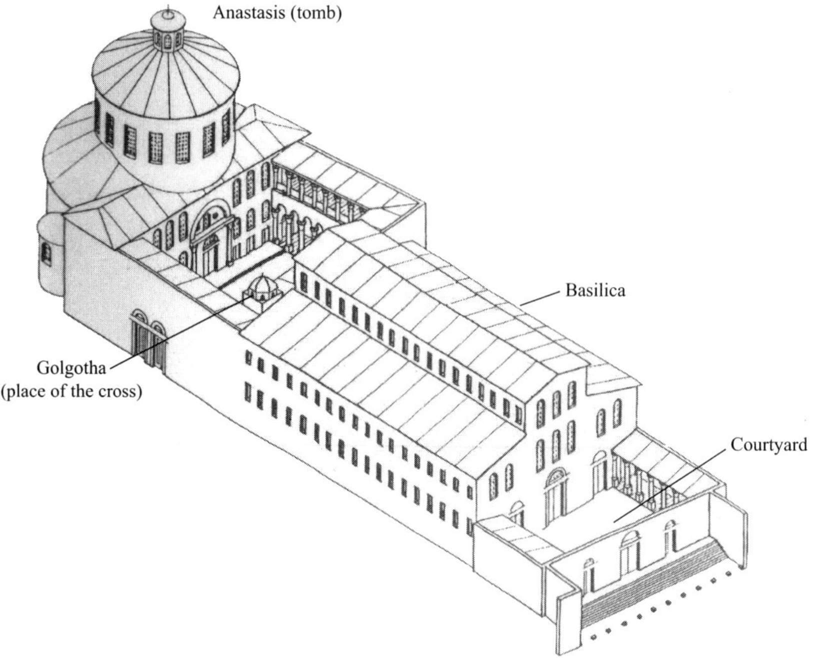

Figure 2.1: *Artist's reconstruction of Constantine's building complex in Jerusalem.*

EGERIA AND THE SINGING OF PSALMS

The 150 psalms found in the Hebrew Bible, or, in its Christian versions, the Old Testament, constitute a large body of texts for singing. Taken over by Christians from the very beginning, the poems are quoted throughout the New Testament and became the essential songbook of the Christian Church. Egeria demonstrates how important psalm singing (psalmody) was to Christian celebration in the fourth century. In the most famous passages from her journal, she describes huge crowds of people singing psalms in Greek and praying as they processed with the bishop, monks, and singers through holy places in Jerusalem, especially during the days and hours leading up to the Easter celebration and the display of the empty tomb in the Anastasis that formed the focal point of Constantine's church.

Early on Easter morning, Egeria says, "the first cock crows, and at that the bishop enters and goes into the cave in the Anastasis." The nun was awestruck by the enclosed area in the complex surrounding the supposed tomb of Jesus. It would have included what people believed was the stone that had sealed the mouth, upon which the angel had sat to announce the mystery of the empty tomb. All the doors opened, Egeria writes, and the entire church was made to "blaze with light" while three psalms were sung and prayers were said. After the bishop read the account of the resurrection from the Gospel, all processed to the Cross (Golgotha). Then some went home to sleep, while others stayed as the monks sang psalms and antiphons (chants with prose texts) until daybreak, separated by prayers in which the people joined.

It is clear from Egeria's descriptions that special hours of the day were set aside for prayer—in the early morning, at various points throughout the day, at dusk, and at night. The presence of the bishop and his entourage, monks, and large numbers of laity suggests the kinds of musical practices Egeria experienced; they would be fundamental to the development of the Office (hours of prayer) in the West (see Chapter 4). The monks sang psalms in a liturgically prescribed order, working through them *seriatim*. But the laity appreciated linking the texts to specific times of the day when they were present, so particular psalms were selected and sung at times that reflected their presence and participation. Some psalms were sung in processions, some in fixed areas of churches; sometimes groups of singers responded to each other (antiphonal singing), and sometimes soloists alternated with the full choir (responsorial singing). The psalms and hymns Egeria heard would have been in Greek; the word *hymn* comes from the Greek *hymnos*, meaning a poem for a god.

Throughout the Holy Land, holy men, monks, and sometimes bishops or other clergy instructed Egeria about the places she visited. Equally interested in the Hebrew Bible (as translated into Latin) and the Greek (Christian) New Testament, she traveled from site to site praying, reading Scripture, and singing psalms appropriate to the place and to events believed to have occurred there. The idea of a station or designated place for prayer, which later spread throughout the Latin-speaking West, informs Egeria's description of her stop near Mount Nebo (in present-day Jordan), where she describes what she saw and heard about Moses and his actions.

Egeria was thrilled to worship in the places where figures she knew from the Bible had walked, talked, and sung the psalms. The sense of place and people she experienced in the Holy Land is central to surviving medieval music: almost all of it was composed to help listeners feel connected to particular events and persons. In an age before written records and other media made the past easier to recall, music and its texts invited crowds of people to remember, observe, and participate in events of long ago. Liturgical reenactment with appropriate biblical texts proclaimed through song helped give people, literate and illiterate, a shared sense of history.

Although no music survives from fourth-century Jerusalem, descriptions are comparatively plentiful. In addition, the liturgy of Christian Jerusalem spread to other areas; early liturgical books witness its spread to Armenia and Georgia, for example. These sources give us a sense of what kinds of pieces were sung on which occasions, and even in what tonal area. In fact, in the centuries immediately after the time of Egeria, the chant of this venerable city was organized into a system of eight modes that formed the basis for the oldest monophonic chants in the Catholic Church. (For an overview of the church modes and psalm tones, see Primer III.2 and III.3.)

JERUSALEM IN THE SIXTH AND SEVENTH CENTURIES

The world of prayer and praise that Egeria experienced in Jerusalem was doomed: it depended on the strength of the Roman Empire, which was slowly melting under the twin suns of various barbarian tribes and its own internal weaknesses. It was also splitting into two spheres, one Latin and one Greek, marked by theological as well as linguistic differences (hence the terms "Latin West," or "Latin Middle Ages," as opposed to areas of Europe without a Roman and Latin heritage). Justinian (527–565), master of both eastern and western Christian lands, was the last Roman emperor to build in Jerusalem in the late antique period. The enormous church he constructed in honor of the Virgin Mary complemented his Hagia Sophia in Constantinople, the capital of the Byzantine (eastern Roman) world, as well as the monastic fortresses of St. Catherine's in Sinai and St. Saba in Palestine, also built by him.

The fate of Jews living in the Roman Empire was insecure. Although Empress Eudocia had permitted Jews to live in Jerusalem from the early fifth century forward, they were often treated as pagans or persecuted as heretics within the dominant Christian culture. The smaller percentage of Jews in what remained of the Persian Empire were treated better. When the Persians conquered Jerusalem in 614, they were aided by contingents of Jews and tens of thousands of Christians were killed, their churches ruined, and the Holy Cross confiscated. Payback time came in 629, when the Byzantines recaptured the city under Emperor Heraclius (r. 610–641), who recovered the Cross and returned it to Jerusalem in 629–30.

In the waning years of the Persian Empire, new winds of faith blew toward Jerusalem. By the time Muhammad (570–632) and his followers conquered Mecca in 630, Islam was firmly established throughout the Arabian peninsula. In 638, under Caliph Umar, Jerusalem was taken from the Byzantines, apparently without strife. By the end of the seventh century, Jerusalem had become central to the religious tradition of Muslims, too, through the story of Muhammad the Prophet rising to God at night from the Temple Mount, with the angel Gabriel as his escort. In 687–91 Caliph Abd al-Malik hired Byzantine architects to construct a new building, the Dome of the Rock, on the site of the two ancient Jewish Temples, to commemorate Muhammad's rising.

The Dome of the Rock (which survives, although heavily restored) is a composite, just as are its holy foundations: it lies atop the most sacred place of Jews; it was constructed by architects from the Christian East, who incorporated architectural remains from Christian churches destroyed in 614; and it commemorates part of the final journey of the Prophet Muhammad to God. Its construction points to one of the most troubling aspects of triumphalism: when one group conquerors another, it often deliberately annihilates its cultural treasures, rituals, and libraries and other buildings in an attempt to destroy its memories or to reshape them into something that belongs to the conquering group. Constant reprisals in this holiest of cities mean that much has been destroyed. Yet in spite of this upheaval, Jerusalem remained the cradle of the music, texts, and liturgical practices of the medieval West, and of key components of Western music theory as well.

The dream of restoring Jerusalem to Christendom would live on in western Europe, inspiring many musical works and theological treatises throughout the Middle Ages. In 1099 the city was recaptured, only to be surrendered (in 1187), the medieval Western Christian political presence in the Near East ending with the fall of Acre in 1291. During the thirteenth century alone no fewer than ten crusades were undertaken, most of them for the ostensible purpose of reestablishing Christian Jerusalem.

PSALMS AND HYMNS: TRANSLATIONS, INTERPRETATIONS, AND FORMS

Because so many traditions of singing and worship coexisted in Jerusalem, the psalms are an especially important subject. The psalms are poems that depend on parallelism—that is, on saying one thing and then saying it again in a different way, in verse after verse. An advantage of this poetic form is that it translates fairly readily from the original Hebrew into all other languages. Rephrasing ideas has nothing to do with devices such as meter and rhythm, and so can be readily duplicated as a poetic strategy in any language. Although the words and phrases lose much in translation, an elemental sense of the original poetry remains.

According to Egeria—who references the psalms repeatedly throughout her diary—the Christian liturgy in Jerusalem was trilingual, being conducted in Greek, Syriac, and Latin. The psalms, believed to have been the songbook of the ancient Jewish Temple, were first translated by Hellenistic Jewish scholars as part of the Septuagint (the Hebrew Bible in Greek). Subsequently, they were translated into all the major languages of Christian antiquity. As the most important texts for worship in the Western world, the psalms have provided the fundamental repertory of poetic images used to express religious ideas in song for many centuries.

Jerome (c. 340–420), born in what is today Croatia, was a younger contemporary of Egeria and one of the most highly trained linguists of his time. He made translations of the trilingual tradition of the Old Testament (Hebrew, Greek, and earlier Latin versions) into a more eloquent Latin. Jerome studied in Rome and then moved to the Holy Land, spending the last decades of his life in Bethlehem, on the outskirts of Jerusalem, where he worked with

Jewish scholars to improve his Hebrew and his understanding of texts in that language. The so-called Vulgate Bible, Jerome's translation, is heavily Christianized and owes much to the Greek Septuagint for its Psalter; throughout this book we quote from the Douay-Reims translation, the English translation that was prepared by Catholic scholars who fled from England to the Continent in the sixteenth century.

Jerome also wrote commentaries on many books of the Bible (see, for example, SR 11:126–28; 1/3:16–18). His highly influential interpretations, which were often read in the Divine Office (see Chapter 4) in medieval monasteries and cathedrals, are fundamental to understanding the texts and contexts of much medieval chant.

Of Jerome's three translations of the Psalter, it is the second one, the so-called Psalterium Gallicanum (Gallican Psalter), that was used for the psalms of the Divine Office in the Latin West. Many early chant texts are from Latin versions of the psalms that predate Jerome, but Jerome's authoritative text is often used for the best scholarly editions of the medieval texts today. Once such a text or collection of musical pieces caught on and became institutionalized, it tended to push out other versions; we will see this happen frequently with various segments of medieval musical repertory as well.

AUGUSTINE AND AMBROSE

Except for the Asiatic Huns led by Attila, the late-fourth- and fifth-century barbarian armies that crossed the permeable borders of the Roman Empire and sometimes attacked major cities (including Rome itself in 410 and in 455) were mostly Germanic. Many members of these invading Germanic tribes were Christians, the intermarriage of Roman women with mercenary soldiers from the north having promoted conversion more readily than the work of clerics ever could. In the Arian Christianity that predominated among the Germanic tribes, however, Christ was more of an intermediary between God and human beings than truly and fully God and coeternal with God the father. As a result of such doctrinal differences, various church councils were convened to resolve disputes concerning the nature of the Trinity, Christology, and the role of the Virgin Mary in salvation history. Creeds were issued to proclaim the resolutions, that of Nicaea in 325 being the most famous.

The fashioning of an orthodox Christian doctrine to be transmitted to the West, and a body of writings that expressed it, was the primary work of the theologian and bishop Augustine of Hippo (354–430), whose early life as a pagan and heretical Christian gave him firsthand knowledge of the opposition (see SR 13:132–33; 1/5:22–23).

Augustine was born in Tagaste (in modern-day northeastern Algeria) and educated in local schools and at Carthage; his father was a pagan and his mother a devout Christian. His career path led to Milan, where he held a chair of rhetoric (secured in part through the support of powerful Manicheans, the heretical group he had joined in his young adulthood). He read widely in Christian texts and was baptized by Ambrose (c. 339–397), bishop of Milan, at the Easter Vigil in 387, subsequently returning to northern Africa and becoming a bishop himself.

Augustine wrote a treatise on music, a Neo-Platonic investigation of rhythmic poetry and the importance of number and proportion in verse. The power at work in Christian hymnody can be observed by studying this work in conjunction with the kinds of texts being written in the fifth century. Most important, Augustine wrote commentaries on the psalms and sermons for major Christian feasts. His words were fundamental for the ways these texts were received, set to music, and sung in the liturgy throughout the Western world during the entire Middle Ages. Virtually every library in the Latin West would have included a copy of Augustine's commentaries on the psalms.

Ambrose, Augustine's mentor, is known as the father of Latin hymnody. Although only a handful of hymns can be securely attributed to him, many more were thought to be by Ambrose in the Middle Ages. The style in which he wrote became classic: eight four-line strophes in iambic tetrameter (lines consisting of four metrical units stressed short-long). Ambrose's *Eterne rerum conditor,* a concise statement about time and eternity, is filled with both comfort and challenge (see Anthology 2).

As the genre developed, what came to matter most were the numbers of syllables (eight per line) and the rhyming ends of lines. The textual lines "harmonize" through their syllable count, accentual patterns, and rhymes. The latter are reinforced by the upward motion of the cadential pattern at the end of each line. Translating heavily accentual or metrical verse is far more difficult than translating poetry based on parallel meanings, like the psalms, as the following example from a seventh-century hymn in the Ambrosian style reveals. Here John M. Neale (1818–1866) sacrificed meanings as he attempted to account not only for the number of syllables, but also for accent and rhyme. (In Anthology 2 a literal translation is used, one that does not try to mirror these poetic devices.)

Condí/tor ál/me sí/derúm	*Creator of the stars of night,*
aetér/na lúx/credén/tiúm,	*Thy people's everlasting light,*
Christé,/redémp/tor óm/niúm,	*Christe, Redeemer, save us all,*
exáu/di pré/ces súp/plicúm.	*and hear Thy servants when they call.*

BOETHIUS AND THE GREEKS: A SCHOLAR'S VIEW OF ANTIQUE MUSIC

Of all the characters to be encountered in this book, perhaps none had an early life that promised such brilliance and yet met with such a sorrowful end as Boethius (c. 480–c. 524), who was imprisoned and then brutally executed after he fell from favor with the Arian King Theodoric (454–526). As a member of a cultivated and prominent family, Boethius possessed great wealth, played a major role in late Roman politics, and was given sufficient leisure for his scholarship. Exceedingly learned in a period when scholarship was in decline, he knew Greek and the classics of antiquity very well. He set himself the monumental task of translating the most essential works from Greek to Latin. In his commentaries he hoped to reconcile Plato to Aristotle, that is, the idealistic dreamer to the pragmatic scientist (it has never been done).

In his short life Boethius penned many works, including a translation of and commentary on ancient Greek theoretical writings about music called *De institutione musica* (Fundamentals of Music), which would become the standard textbook on music for well over 1,000 years (SR 14:137–43; 2/6:27–33). In addition, his treatise *De institutione arithmetica* (Fundamentals of Arithmetic), based on the work of the Greek Nicomachus, transmitted Pythagorean number theory (see below) to the Latin West. Moreover, his translations of Aristotle's *Categories* and *On Interpretation* and Porphyry's *Isagoge* constituted the basic materials for the study of logic until the twelfth century. Boethius's masterful *Consolation of Philosophy*, written while he languished in prison, resolves philosophical and theological difficulties with free will and predestination; it introduces Lady Philosophy and Lady Fortune, the one a wise and trustworthy counselor, the other as fickle as time itself. (We will meet Lady Fortune again in Chapter 10.)

Boethius's treatise on music is both mathematical and ethical, drawing upon Plato and other ancients. Music is seen as rooted in the principles of mathematics, but its purposes are to improve those who understand the ratios and systems of proportions that govern the sounds. According to Plato's *Republic* (SR 1:9–19; 1/1:9–19), music is related to good governance. In his *Timaeus*, the body and soul are joined harmoniously, and their joining reflects the workings of the cosmos (SR 2:22; 1/2:22). Plato's disciple Aristotle further developed ideas about music and ethics in his fragmentary *Politics* (SR 3:23–34; 1/3:23–34); music was so powerful because those who controlled it shaped people's modes of action. Boethius says:

> Discipline has no more open pathway to the mind than through the ear; when rhythms and modes gain access to the mind by this path, it is evident that they affect it and cause it to conform to their nature. . . . Hence Plato holds that music which is carefully and modestly composed, so that it is chaste, simple, and masculine, not effeminate, savage, and inconsistent, is a great guardian of the commonwealth. (SR 14:138–39; 2/6:28–29)

Boethius promises to return to the considerations with which he opens his treatise, especially those having to do with the ways music conjoins body and soul, but he never does. Instead, he marches the reader through five books of mathematics, some of it fairly complex, and in doing so lays the groundwork for the theory of Western music and its dependence upon particular formulas and ways of thinking. We will encounter the subjects Boethius broaches throughout this book: the nature of pitches and of the relationships between them; the Greek tonal system and ways of measuring it using a single-stringed instrument called the monochord; scales and the genera of tetrachords (groupings of four consecutive pitches); and the speculative and mathematical nature of musical study and its role in the definition of the word *musician*.

Boethius explains that there are three kinds of music: celestial, which relates to the motions of the planets and of the seasons; corporeal, which has to do with the harmony between reason and the body; and instrumental, music that is produced by the actual sounding of voices or instruments. There are also three kinds of musicians: performers on instruments; those who write songs (for him, the poets, since lyrical poetry was sung); and those who can weigh rhythms and melodies, and compositions as wholes, and who form judgments "of modes and rhythms, of the classes of melodies and their combinations, of all those things about which there is to be discussion later on, and of the songs of the poets" (SR 14:142–43; 2/6:32–33).

These three kinds of people still inhabit schools and departments of music today: instrumentalists; composers and those who perform the music they create (Boethius would put singers here); and musicologists and theorists, the ones trained to judge and explain what others are performing or have composed. Modern thinkers leave the connections between music and ethics to the philosophers and theologians and the study of the sounding cosmos to astronomers. Boethius would not have approved.

RATIOS AND INTERVALS

Boethius himself may have established the practice of adding diagrams to *De institutione musica*, and medieval copies of his work are filled with a variety of visualizations of tones, scales, and intervals. Today it is common to teach the relationships between tones as represented by the keys of a piano, and translated to a staff with one or more clefs. But try to imagine that you did not have these things to help you, and that your task was to explain intervals (that is, the distances between pitches) and the patterns of scales without a keyboard or any knowledge of a keyboard, and sometimes by references to measurements made on a single string. If you can do this without resorting to pianos and clefs or notation, you have entered the world of Boethius and of early medieval music theory.

The simplest of diagrams can represent the octave, or diapason. Boethius says that "the consonance of the diapason is that which is made in the duple ratio." According to principles of harmonics, a single string vibrates down its whole length, creating the fundamental note we hear. But it also vibrates in various sections of its length, with each half, third, or quarter operating like a separate string. This generates a series of overtones, called "harmonics." The first few overtones also define the intervals known as "perfect" in classical Greek theory and in the Middle Ages: the unison, octave, fourth, and fifth.

These perfect intervals can be expressed in simple numerical ratios. The octave, for example, is created by a ratio of 2 to 1. To demonstrate this on a monochord (or a string on a piano, guitar, or violin), put a finger down in the middle of the string. The interval between the full string and the sound of the string divided in half (either half) is an octave. The same process can be followed for other perfect intervals expressed by numerical proportion.

The Pythagorean figure known as the *tetraktys* (Fig. 2.2) recalls the first four natural numbers, whose sum is 10: 1 + 2 + 3 + 4 = 10. The *tetraktys* (*tetra* means four in Greek), as expressed visually in triangular form, is a useful guide now as in ancient times for remembering the ratios of the most important intervals: the unison (1:1), octave (1:2), fifth (2:3), and fourth (3:4). The numbers generated by the *tetraktys* offered the building blocks for scales and melodies throughout the Middle Ages.

Like all the people encountered in this chapter, Pythagoras represents particular kinds of skills and knowledge. Much has been attributed to him that he either did not or could not have produced. With Pythagoras and with all great archetypes, we inhabit an area between myth and reality: all facts have mythic spins; all myths were created by people in particular cultures and so are real. The west facade of Chartres Cathedral displays a twelfth-century personification of music (Fig. 2.3). Pythagoras, who sits below Lady Music, is a thinker about music known, however shadily, from Greek antiquity. Music's monochord

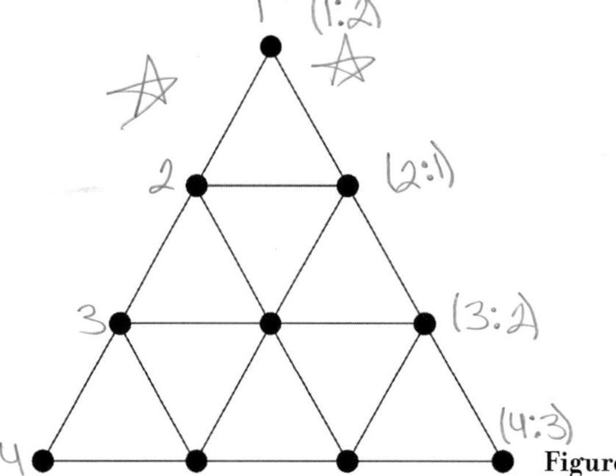

Figure 2.2: *Diagram of the* tetraktys

Figure 2.3: *Left, Lady Music seated above Pythagoras; right, Grammar above the Roman grammarian Donatus; from the twelfth-century south portal, west facade of Chartres Cathedral. Credit Henri de Feraudy.*

(at her right) has the bridge in the middle of the string, producing the interval of the octave between the open string and the sound of the string plucked above or below the bridge.

Boethius relates a story about Pythagoras and the ratios of intervals that had been in circulation for centuries. "By a kind of divine will, while passing the workshop of blacksmiths, he overheard the beating of hammers somehow emit a single consonance from differing sounds." Charmed, Pythagoras began to study how the consonance was made. Was it the force by which the men struck the anvils? No. Rather, it seemed the sounds were in proportion to the weights of the hammers themselves. So home Pythagoras went to conduct an experiment—and it is fortunate that he did, for the hammers-on-anvils trick really won't work (it is the sizes of the anvils and not the hammers that determine the pitches).

It was typical of Pythagoras and his disciples to prove their ideas through practical demonstration. Pythagoras assembled strings, pipes, and glasses filled with liquids, and all with the same results: sounding materials varied in specific proportions produced precise musical intervals. Boethius continued to use the hammer myth to demonstrate this idea, however faulty it might be: the consonance-producing hammers, Boethius says, weighed 12:9:8:6 pounds. So, the 12 and the 6 together made the octave (or diapason, 1:2); the 12-pounder and the 8-pounder made a fifth (diapente, 2:3); the 12-pounder and the 9-pounder made a fourth (diatesseron, 3:4). These are the perfect consonances of all medieval music; so says Pythagoras, and so proclaims Boethius.

SCALES AND TETRACHORDS

Boethius's understanding of intervals and their perfections also related to his development of a scale system. (See Primer III.1 for a discussion of the Greater Perfect System as Boethius explained it; Example P4 illustrates the tetrachords within the scale.) Key to understanding these proportions are the transposable four-note units, or tetrachords, that are the building blocks of the system Boethius promotes.

Greeks theorists thought in tetrachords as well, but they divided the pitches within each of them in three ways: enharmonically, chromatically, or diatonically. The outer pitches of each tetrachord remained constant, but the inner two notes moved according to the "genus" of the tetrachord and the scalar patterns that result from its transposition. For example, in a descending tetrachord whose outer pitches are A and E, the genera are as follows:

enharmonic: A–G♭♭–F♭–E (a major third and two quarter tones)
chromatic: A–G♭–F–E (a minor third and two semitones)
diatonic: A–G–F–E (two whole tones and a semitone)

The relationships of the movable inner pitches to the fixed outer pitches of the tetrachord were nuanced by the players, depending on the direction of the melodic line. We can only imagine these relationships imprecisely, because the mathematics is quite complex.

The system became less complicated as it moved to the West via the writings of Boethius and others. In the music of the Middle Ages and later periods, the Western tetrachord is fundamentally diatonic; that is, each tetrachord is made up of consistent relationships of half tones and whole tones.

RECONSTRUCTING AN EARLY MEDIEVAL HARP

The intervals and scalar patterns found in the writings of the ancient Greeks and in Boethius's adaptation of classical Greek theory were reflected in the design of musical instruments, both wind and stringed. The idea that instruments could mirror musical proportion and perfection played a role in medieval musical understanding, especially given that the master musician of the Western world, David the Psalmist, was known as a harpist in the Middle Ages. An Anglo-Saxon Book of Psalms found in the British Library, dating from the second quarter of the eighth century, contains a depiction of King David seated on his throne and playing a harp (Fig. 2.4). To the viewer's left is a scribe writing down the texts he sings, while another, on the right, stirs the inkpot. Musicians blow horns as dancers leap and clap for joy. If we zero in on the harp, we can count the strings: six.

Figure 2.4: *David composing the psalms, from the Vespasian Psalter, second quarter of the eighth century (Anglo-Saxon, London, BL Cotton Vespasian AI)*

Present-day singer and harpist Benjamin Bagby has used early iconography and surviving fragments of medieval harps to create an instrument resembling the one depicted in the so-called Vespasian Psalter. Its tuning is based on the principles described above relating to the most important intervals in early Western music. In this work, Bagby's interest is not in ecclesiastical chant, but rather in the poetry that was sung in the courts of abbots, bishops, and secular princes. He has used his harp to reconstruct the vocal and instrumental sounds of *Beowulf* and other Old English and Old Norse epic poems, with results that are both engaging and controversial. Like many performers who re-create medieval music in the twenty-first century, Bagby is interested in studying history, but also in interpreting it in his own way as an artist. He uses his imagination, musical skills, and long immersion in medieval music to become an improvising singer himself. And when he reconstructs epic poetry, the sound of the reconstructed harp becomes foundational.

We have uncovered several ways of putting musical sounds back into late antiquity, from the reimagined processions in early Christian Jerusalem; to a transcribable early hymn; to ideas about singing psalms, hymns, and spiritual songs; to the mathematical proportions inherited from classical Greece and translated by Boethius; to Benjamin Bagby's reconstructed harp. It is well to remember, before entering the world of ninth-century western Europe, that early repertories require painstaking study to be recovered. Some modern performers of early music take notation for granted, but historically it is the exception rather than the rule. Most early musical repertories from around the world were created within an oral tradition and were never written down. But many repertories of western European music *were* written down in the medieval period, and that is why we have more chapters to our book.

FOR FURTHER READING

Aillagon, Jean-Jacques, ed., *Rome and the Barbarians: The Birth of a New World* (Milan: Skira, 2008)

Boethius, Anicius Manlius Severinus, *Fundamentals of Music*, trans. Calvin Bower, ed. Claude V. Palisca (New Haven: Yale University Press, 1989)

Bradshaw, Paul F., *The Search for the Origins of Christian Worship: Sources and Methods for the Study of the Early Liturgy*, 2nd ed. (New York: Oxford University Press, 2002)

Den Boeft, Jan, "'Aeterne rerum conditor': Ambrose's Poem about Time," in F. G. Martínez and G. P. Luttikhuizen, eds., *Jerusalem, Alexandria, Rome: Studies in Ancient Cultural Interaction in Honour of A. Hilhorst* (Leiden: Brill, 2003), 27–40

Egeria, *Egeria's Travels,* ed. and trans. John Wilkinson, 3rd ed. (Warminster: Aris and Phillips, 1999)

Frank, Georgia, "'Taste and See': The Eucharist and the Eyes of Faith in the Fourth Century," *Church History* 70 (2001): 619–43

Hagel, Stefan, and Christine Harrauer, eds., *Ancient Greek Music in Performance* (book and CD; Vienna: Verlag der Österreichischen Akademie der Wissenschaften, 2005)

Mathiesen, Thomas, *Apollo's Lyre: Greek Music and Music Theory in Antiquity and the Middle Ages* (Lincoln: University of Nebraska Press, 1999)

Ousterhout, Robert, "Architecture as Relic and the Construction of Sanctity: The Stones of the Holy Sepulchre," *Journal of the Society of Architectural Historians* 62 (2003): 4–23

CHAPTER THREE

Chant and the Carolingians

The great empires of the East and West had either crumbled or declined between the sixth and eighth centuries, leaving new and more circumscribed political entities in their shadows to wax and wane. It was in this period that European Christianity became regionally defined, a trend that also undermined the universality of the Latin language. By the ninth century early forms of Romance languages were spoken alongside Latin, and the linguistically distinct Germanic, Slavic, Ugric (Hungarian and Finnish), and Celtic tongues had become established as well. Latin continued, however, as the lingua franca of instruction, learning, and the Church, which explains why the earliest surviving repertories of medieval Western music are set to Latin texts.

By the late seventh century, several major centers of chant and liturgy had evolved in western Europe. Each had its own practices and traditions, although Latin was the liturgical language in all of them: Rome, Milan, Ravenna, Benevento, and Aquilea; Mozarabic Spain, with its religious capital in Toledo; Braga in northern Portugal; Gaul (an area roughly corresponding to modern France, Germany, and parts of northern Italy), where there were many interrelated but independent liturgical and musical practices; Anglo-Saxon England; and medieval Ireland. (Most of Scandinavia and eastern Europe was not yet converted to Christianity.) Although the earliest musical repertories of many of these regions do not survive, these ancient lines of demarcation still explain some political and religious divisions in the twenty-first century.

FRANKISH CHANT: MYTHS AND MEMORY

Among the various Western cultures, that of the Franks in Gaul was ultimately triumphant. By the early eighth century, the region had been Christianized, giving rise to a variety of liturgical and musical traditions loosely subsumed under the label Gallican (SR 18:164–71; 2/10:54–61). In the mid-700s, a new line of kings was established with the blessing of the popes in Rome. It was there that the Frankish king Charlemagne was crowned Holy Roman Emperor on Christmas Day 800, sealing his connection with the city and with the regions that looked to it as a metaphorical capital.

Along with political change and territorial conquest came a desire to Romanize the chant and liturgy. The revised chant of the Franks, traditionally known as Gregorian chant, is the foundation of Western music. Frankish chant tended to follow the Frankish army wherever it went, supplanting the musical cultures of those who were conquered. The Beneventan tradition was the first to go, replaced in the eighth and ninth centuries, although substantial fragments remain. The chant and liturgy of Mozarabic Spain were not replaced until the late eleventh century (see Chapter 6). Frankish chant, like all of the world's great chant traditions, is vast and complex, and its development constitutes one of music history's most profound mysteries. The Church controlled the production and dissemination of chant, however political and secular the impetus for its development may have been. As a result, the first complete repertory of notated Western music is religious and was developed within the context of Christian ritual. The study of chant begins with a great creation myth promulgated by the Franks themselves over the two centuries starting around 750.

THE GREGORIAN MYTH

The Carolingian Renaissance takes its name from Charlemagne (Carolus Magnus), king of the Franks from 768 to his death in 814. In addition to consolidating a vast realm, he and members of his family were the first great patrons of music in the Latin Middle Ages (see SR 22; 2/14). They were deeply interested in using music to enhance their stature as rulers and unify the Frankish church under the auspices of what they believed was a correct and authentic practice. Like his father, King Pepin III ("the Short," c. 715–768), who desired to replace earlier Gallican liturgies (and the chants associated with them) with Roman texts and music, Charlemagne looked to Rome for musical and liturgical source materials, just as he endorsed the political idea of a Holy Roman Empire headed by himself. His attitudes translated directly into the Carolingian agenda for music: in 789, Charlemagne proclaimed that a uniformly ordered Roman chant and liturgy should be implemented throughout his realm. A letter by Helisachar, a major figure at the Carolingian court in the early decades of the ninth century, speaks of the importance of correctness and uniformity (SR 20:175–78; 2/12:65–68) (however long it was in coming).

Charlemagne's son, Louis the Pious (778–840), and grandson, Charles the Bald (823–877), continued to promote liturgical music and splendid ritual in their courts. This period of four generations saw the development of the chant tradition known as Frankish, Frankish-Romano, or Gregorian. In order to help establish this chant and its authority, the Carolingians created a legend that endured until the twentieth century. What is perhaps the first recorded version of this legend is given in a late-eighth-century account of the life of Pope Gregory the Great (c. 540–604) by Paul the Deacon, a liturgist at the court of Charlemagne. In this work a scribe, taking down Gregory's sermons on the Book of Ezekiel, is seen poking his stylus through the curtain to see why the pope keeps pausing. The scribe observes that Gregory is listening to a dove—a visual representation of the Holy Spirit in the Christian tradition—who is telling him the words of his sermons.

Later this story was adapted to include the writing down of chant, as shown in several portraits of Gregory from the late Carolingian period. The most famous of these is contained in a chant manuscript copied in the early eleventh century by a monk named Hartker at the Abbey of St. Gall (in what is now Switzerland), a major center for the production of musical manuscripts (Fig. 3.1). The illumination shows Pope Gregory dictating melodies with a dove on his shoulder, as a scribe notates (in this case with a stylus on wax tablets). The portrait demonstrates the canonical stature of the chant (straight from the Holy Spirit), the role of Gregory and the Roman Church as its source, and the act of notating music as essential to historical transmission. The notes the scribe is making are known as neumes—the dots, slashes, and other markings adapted from accents found in Latin prose and poetry. The Latin word *neuma* is a loan word from Greek meaning sign or gesture; *neume* is the French translation of *neuma*. As we will see below, learning to capture sound through signs was one of the great achievements of the Carolingian Renaissance.

TWO TRADITIONS OF "ROMAN" CHANT

The Gregorian myth encouraged people throughout the centuries to believe three things we now know are not true: that Frankish chant came straight from Rome, that it originated during the time of Pope Gregory the Great, and that Gregory had a role in composing and notating it. These ideas were challenged in the nineteenth and twentieth centuries, when a small group of forgotten manuscripts, containing what is commonly known as "Old Roman" chant, resurfaced. Old Roman chant was different from, though related to, Frankish chant. So the two "Roman" chant repertories, one from north of the Alps and one from Rome, were clearly not the same. What might this mean?

Figure 3.1: *Gregory the Great* (left) *as depicted in the Hartker Antiphoner, early eleventh century (St. Gall 390/391)*

Many explanations have been offered to account for the Frankish and the Old Roman traditions and their interrelationships. It seems most likely that an early repertory of Roman chant and liturgical practices spread north in several stages during the eighth century, supplanting and merging with various Gallican traditions. This hybrid repertory developed into what is commonly called Frankish or Gregorian chant, and writing came to play a role in how it was taught, memorized, and performed. Meanwhile, back in Rome, an early musical practice continued to evolve, but primarily in an oral tradition, and surely with influence from the Gregorian hybrid as well. By the time this other Roman practice was written down, it was distinct from the musical tradition that had developed north of the Alps and had been notated at least by the early tenth century and, in some form, well before this. A few written fragments of the Old Roman tradition survive from the earlier period, but the first fully neumed Old Roman Mass book dates from the late eleventh century, over 200 years after the earliest sources containing Frankish neumes.

Only comparative study of many sources, texts, and chants will eventually determine the relationships between these two chant traditions. Examining the two surviving Roman repertories side by side is like looking at the musical DNA of the Western world. Also buried within the surviving sources of these repertories are vestiges of older musical traditions, captured like flies in amber and waiting to be probed more deeply as the various layers of text and music are peeled away. Any early chant must be compared with other survivals, a few of which, like the Ambrosian chant of Milan, can be found only in written sources dating from the twelfth century forward, that is, even later than the Old Roman books. Each chant or group of chants constitutes a fragment of the skeletons of these intricate musical creatures who are our immediate ancestors.

THE FRANKISH MASS AND ITS MUSIC

The primary purpose of the earliest recorded Western music was for the singing of the psalms. But no medieval liturgical chant stood alone, as the concert pieces of later eras do. It is futile to study chants as individual works because they were not remembered, improvised, or sung out of context. Each was known as part of a group or genre, and each was rendered within the larger structures unfolding within a particular feast or season. As a result, every piece existed in relationship with many others each day and throughout a week, season, or year. Sometimes a piece or part of a piece even had multiple uses within a given day.

When it comes to Frankish chant, its afterlife throughout the Middle Ages and the Italian Renaissance, and its restoration in the nineteenth century (see the guide to the *Liber Usualis* in Primer I.3), the basic large-scale structures were two: the Mass and the Divine Office. As the earliest layers of recorded music belong to the Mass, we begin with it, but that is not to say that the Mass itself is older than the Office (that is, the Christian hours of prayer, to be discussed in Chapter 4). Both have their origins in the first century and grew out of Jewish practices that do not survive for study, perhaps with influence from other early worship practices as well.

The first Christians were Jews who lived in the Roman Empire, which was hostile to both religions. Early Christian musical and liturgical practices were often kept secret out of fear of persecution, and many of the first Christian places of worship were house churches, where traditional domestic rituals were gradually Christianized. The Mass, the most important Christian ritual, is usually interpreted as commemorating the Last Supper Jesus hosted with his 12 followers the night before his death. Thus it probably grew out of festive Jewish banquets like the Sabbath supper and the Passover seder, which included blessings of bread and wine along with religious teaching and songs. In its classic form, the Christian Mass is made up of two parts: first a series of readings from the Bible, then the blessing of bread and wine, with a prayer remembering how Jesus blessed bread and wine at his Last Supper.

All the Mass music composed in the Middle Ages related to understandings of this history and, as a result, had deeply symbolic levels of meaning, as can be seen in Table P3 in the Primer. By the Carolingian era, this ritualized meal had developed greatly in complexity. Although its components remained fixed, their specific texts and melodies changed day by day and season by season to reflect the passage of time in the liturgy. The Mass outlined in Table 3.1 is one that would have been familiar throughout Charlemagne's empire by the mid-

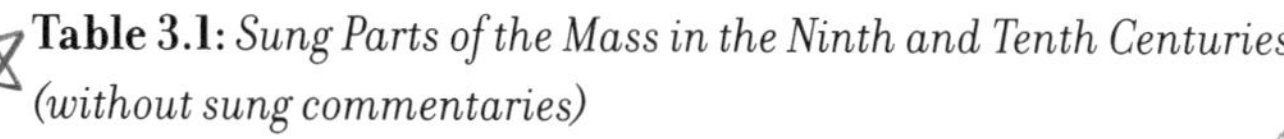

Table 3.1: *Sung Parts of the Mass in the Ninth and Tenth Centuries (without sung commentaries)*

PROPER CHANTS (*TYPE OF PSALMODY*)	ORDINARY CHANTS	READINGS	PRAYERS
	LITURGY OF THE WORD		
Introit (*antiphonal*)			Prayers of preparation
	Kyrie Gloria		
			Collect
		Epistle	
Gradual (*responsorial*) Alleluia (*responsorial*) Sequence[1] Tract[2] (*in directum*)			
		Gospel	
	Credo		
	LITURGY OF THE FAITHFUL		
Offertory (*responsorial*)			
			Preface
	Sanctus		Canon
			Pater noster
			Peace
	Agnus Dei		
Communion (*Antiphonal*)			
			Post-Communion
	Ite missa est		

[1] Gradually coming into use
[2] In solemn times, replacing Alleluia and Sequence

ninth century. Each part of it—chants, readings, prayers, and actions—has its own history and function. The divisions between these parts were underscored by the early practice of collecting chants, prayers, and readings in separate books.

Musicians in the ninth and tenth centuries had to master great amounts of material, some of which they copied themselves, in order to piece together the music for their liturgies into a composite whole. By the late Carolingian period, the monastic cantor held an office of major importance: he was in charge of book production and the scriptorium, or place of copying; he planned the liturgy; he composed new music; and he was often the historian, because he knew so much about time, feasts, and seasons, and when events occurred. Over time the numbers of books he had to use were reduced, as the tendency to combine functions increased, but his work was always complex. The cantor in monasteries and cathedrals had an assistant (the subcantor or succentor) and in some larger establishments, especially cathedrals, most of the purely musical work fell to him. In a cathedral chapter, the cantor was the second administrator in charge, after the dean.

THE MASS AS DRAMA

The story the Mass tells was interpreted allegorically by Carolingian authors, notably Amalar of Metz (c. 780–c. 850), whose writings about the liturgy and its music were copied throughout the Middle Ages (see Table P3 in the Primer). This narrative was constant, but inflected by the feast or festival for which the Mass was composed, the texts forming a libretto for the story of redemption. In this sense, the Mass was the first oratorio, or large-scale sung dramatic work, with a cast of main characters garbed in vestments that represented their offices, and soloists, a chorus, and a congregation that responded to and commented on the action and its progression through ritual time.

All the music we will study in Chapters 3, 4, and 5, and much of the music we will encounter in later chapters as well, was written for a particular time of the year. The church calendar consisted of two huge interlocking circles of time that cycled through once per year. One was called the *temporale* ("of the time"), commemorating events relating to the life of Jesus, including feasts related to Easter. (Easter is a movable feast in the Christian West, being celebrated on the first Sunday after the first full moon falling on or after March 21.) The other cycle, the *sanctorale* ("of the saints"), commemorated the days on which saints died and are assumed to have gone to glory.

The Mass was thus a double drama. It told the same story in a particular way every time it was enacted, through parts that were always present. But because some of these parts were varied, or were "proper" to feasts and seasons, they took on significant local variety; this was especially so in regard to feasts of the saints. For example, the Mass liturgy on the feast of St. Nicholas (December 6) would have Proper elements that related to the veneration of this early bishop; but all the parts would be present, and the basic narrative arc of the Mass would remain in place. Ordinary parts of the Mass, on the other hand, had texts that did not usually change, regardless of the feast or season, although various kinds of additions might be made to them, and their melodies did change according to festive time.

The drama of the Mass falls into two "acts." Act 1, the Liturgy of the Word, asks for forgiveness and then praises God for the gifts of creation. It teaches the miracles of the Christian Scriptures, intoning key texts from Scripture as related to the feast and season of the day and commenting on them with music. After thanksgiving and instruction, the participant is ready to encounter the deeper mysteries of the narrative.

Act 2, the Liturgy of the Faithful, is a ritual reenactment of the Last Supper, when Jesus proclaimed his forthcoming death and resurrection. According to the texts, Jesus asked that his followers commemorate his sacrifice through this meal: "Do this in memory of me" (1 Corinthians 11:23–26). At the close of this part of the Mass, each participant, or the person celebrating the ritual in his or her stead, partakes of the consecrated food and drink.

Each chant, according to Amalar of Metz, has a part in this dramatic scenario. These works shaped the imaginations of musicians for centuries as they sang, copied, and commented on the repertory for this commemorative extravaganza. As can be seen in Table P3, Amalar's overview of the Mass uses a variety of approaches, especially referencing historical events in the Bible to contextualize the chants. Amalar often speaks of individual chants as well, including the Gradual (sung on the steps, or *gradus*, leading to the altar) for Easter, *Haec dies*, which has symbolic meanings of special joy because it is sung throughout the week following the feast (see below).

PSALMODY IN THE MASS PROPERS

Proper chants in the Frankish liturgy, as they were written down before any others, constitute the earliest sources we have of medieval repertory. (The chants for the Mass Ordinary listed in Table 3.1 above do not appear in manuscripts until over 100 years later; they will be discussed in Chapter 4.) Every individual Proper chant not only belonged to a particular genre that had its own history and allegorical meaning, but also was sung during a particular season, for a feast, or for a category of feasts. The force propelling every Mass liturgy is the Gospel of the day, a reading from Scripture that centers worship on events in the life of Jesus, or of his disciples and other holy people. A cycle of Gospel readings was already established in Rome in the mid-seventh century, and this ordering of biblical texts forms the backbone for the entire church year. The Gospel for Easter Day, for example, tells the story of three women approaching the tomb of Jesus to anoint his body, only to be greeted by an angel (or angels) who announce to them that he has risen from the dead—the story that Egeria believed actually unfolded at the Anastasis in Jerusalem (see Chapter 2).

The Propers usually have psalmodic texts, and these change in accordance with feasts or seasons. Two Proper chants are antiphonal and may have included the recitation of an entire psalm early in their histories. These are (or once were) action chants, places in the liturgy where there was a need for procession to or from one or another place in the church. The Introit, for example, is the opening chant, a time for greeting the presider and his entourage as he comes forth to celebrate the mysteries of the Mass; it usually includes only one psalm verse and the Doxology (see Primer I.4). The other antiphonal chant is that of Communion, which was also losing its verses in the Carolingian period. Communion became less and less of a communal affair as the Middle Ages wore on because people were increasingly less likely to partake of the elements (bread and wine), and the priest received them in their stead. There was no need, then, for a full Communion psalm to support the action of many people eating the ritual meal.

Responsorial chants are of a completely different musical style from antiphonal chants. In the Mass liturgy, they are three in number: the Gradual, the Alleluia, and the Offertory. Most responsorial chants are made up of a psalm verse (the respond) that serves as a refrain (and so may be repeated in full or in part) and a second verse, this one usually sung to a tone, or melodic formula for the recitation of a text. This style of psalmody involves the singing of a soloist on the "verse" (so-called to distinguish it from the respond, and often designated by a V in the sources). The most highly melismatic chants in the repertory are those associated with responsorial psalmody, and of those the wildest were the verses of the Offertory chants.

The various genres of responsorial chants often follow the intonation of a significant passage of reading, providing a time for contemplation. Musical formulas are especially important in the structures of responsorial chants, as they are crucial for memorizing long, elaborate melismas and relate to the various characters of the modes (see Primer III.2 and below). Tracts are Proper chants that were sung in place of the Alleluia on especially solemn feast days, and throughout the season of Lent before Easter. Soloistic in character and highly formulaic, Tracts are the only pieces in the repertory that are chanted *in directum*, that is, with one verse following another all the way through, with no intervening responses or antiphons (see *Qui habitat* below).

Each Proper Mass chant reflects the themes of the day or season, while at the same time relating to its position within the liturgy and to other chants of the same genre or mode. The discussion below (and in Primer I.4 and II.2) of the antiphonal Introit for Easter and the responsorial Gradual for the same feast offers a more detailed introduction to the multidimensional thought processes needed to understand this ancient liturgical repertory, and demonstrates the differences between these two genres and the performance practices they embody.

THE DEVELOPMENT OF CHANT NOTATION

The chant in all its many guises raises numerous questions about the ways in which it was stored within memories both before and after musicians developed various systems of neumatic notation to help them remember the repertory (see Primer II.2). Comparison of a single verse from the Frankish and the Old Roman traditions demonstrates that singers of at least some genres of chant were virtuosos who had memorized many musical formulas and artfully linked them to create pieces. Because the music served to proclaim and ornament Latin texts, we must always be attentive to how the words shaped such musical processes.

Tracts originally developed as the work of highly skilled singers. Angilram, bishop of Metz (768–791), listed several Tracts as examples of pieces for which singers were well paid. One of them, *Qui habitat*, is a setting of many verses of Psalm 91 (90) that lasts 15 to 20 minutes, making it the longest piece of chant in the entire repertory. As such, it is an excellent illustration of how music was remembered. Each verse unfolds with four musical formulas, each of which is used, with some variation, for a part of the verse throughout much of the setting. Example 3.1 shows two opening formulas, one from the Old Roman and one from the Frankish version of the chant. Their purpose is to allow the singer to establish the fundamental pitch of D, which is also the final (or last pitch) of the entire chant, and of many sections and phrases. The first verses of Tracts allowed the singer to "tune up" and prepare his mind and voice for the arduous work ahead.

Once Charlemagne decreed musical and liturgical uniformity within his kingdom, older modes of teaching and transmission may have seemed deficient. He tried to procure presumably "authentic" and "correct" liturgical books from Rome, but the prayer book that Pope Hadrian sent him was not sufficient for the purpose of churches in his realm. As a result, the monk Benedict of Aniane, who become the chief liturgical advisor to Charlemagne and then to Louis the Pious, wrote a supplement in which he adapted the prayer book to the needs of Frankish churches. Similar adaptations must have been widespread in the late eighth and early ninth centuries. Cantors grappled with various systems of writing music down, probably to aid in achieving correctness, their first neumed copies dating from the second half of the ninth century.

During this time the improvisatory practices fundamental to the development of a Tract like *Qui habitat* must have slowly diminished as notation came to

Example 3.1: *Opening of the Tract* Qui habitat

(a) Old Roman

Qui ha-bi - tat___ in___ ad-iu-to - ri - o___

(b) Frankish chant

Qui ha - bi - tat___ in ad - iu - to - ri - o

He who dwells in the help [of the Most High]

play an ever more important role. Neumes appearing across various Gregorian manuscript traditions and systems of writing demonstrate the basic similarity between certain melodies set to a given text in the earliest layers of chant. Yet a more detailed look would reveal a good deal of minor variation between the various versions of a melody. Some variants are of the kind that would have arisen if the music were transmitted through notated copies, while some suggest that oral transmission was in effect just as the copies were being inked.

Two things are clear about the earliest surviving notated manuscripts: that notation worked alongside memorization, supplementing the oral tradition rather than replacing it; and that it is difficult to pinpoint either when the experiments that produced notation began or when the practice was standardized. Many regions developed notation in this period and the systems of writing were often related, using neumes that expressed the rise and fall of pitches within a melodic line. As we will see in Chapter 5, however, pitch specificity did not become a standard feature of notation until the early eleventh century. Early neumes were not precisely heightened so precise pitches could be read. Instead, these neumes were meant to trigger the memory, working with the system of tonal organization that was also part of teaching children to sing. Such neumes are also called adiastematic, that is, "without (precise) intervals" between the notes. (See Primer II.1 and II.2 for a discussion of neumes, and Primer II.2 for a lesson in transcribing part of the Gradual *Haec dies*.)

There were many different ways of expressing ideas about musical sound and the rising and falling of pitches. Notational dialects include neume shapes indicating the basic directions of pitch, acute for rising and *gravis* for falling. From these signs the *virga* (rod) developed for rising motion and, in addition to the *gravis*, the *punctum* (point) or *tractulus* (dash) for the same or lower pitch. Two-note shapes incorporate the *virga* and *gravis* to make new neumes, and these neumes in turn can be compounded themselves. The *pes* (or *podatus*) indicates two notes, the second of which is higher; the *clivis* (or *flexa*) indicates two notes, the second of which is lower.

EARLY CHANT BOOKS AND DATABASES: MODE AND MEMORY IN THE NINTH CENTURY

Some of the oldest and most important complete chant manuscripts in the world are at the Benedictine Abbey of St. Gall in Switzerland. The manuscript known as St. Gall 359 was copied in the early tenth century (Fig. 3.2). Its anonymous scribe was doubtless a highly skilled musician who made the collection for his own use as a leader of song and a teacher: the book, called a *cantatorium*, contains the solo chants sung by the cantor himself. By studying his neumes, you can enter his world and share in his achievements. He couldn't discern precise pitches from his notation, but that was irrelevant, because he knew the melodies by heart. The notation triggered his memory, and he wanted to remind himself

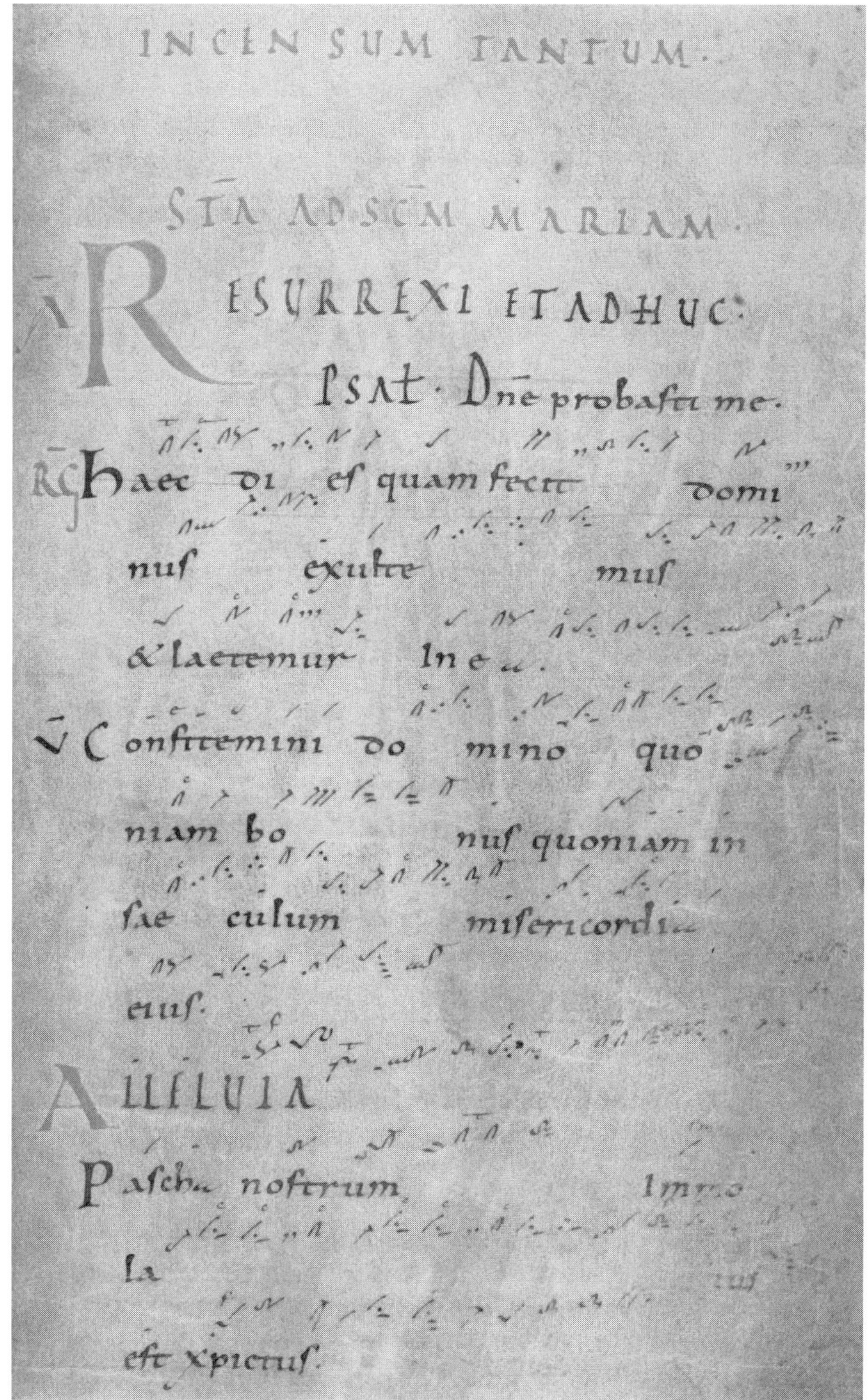

Figure 3.2: *Neumation for the opening section of the Easter Gradual* Haec dies, *a chant sung on Easter and every day of the week following (St. Gall, Stiftsbibliothek, Cod. Sang. 359, p. 107)*

how to interpret the chant. In short, he was encoding a performance practice in which he had been trained to sing, probably from childhood.

This book contains only two genres of Mass chants, both of which featured the work of a soloist and are responsorial: Graduals and Alleluias. Offertories, with their elaborate verses, are not found here, nor are antiphonal Mass chants. These latter are simpler and belonged to the choir: Introits and Communions are only indicated by textual incipits in St. Gall 359. The late-eighth-century Introit, Gradual, and Alleluia discussed below and in Anthology 3 exemplify the range of Proper chant genres used in the Frankish Mass liturgy (see Primer IV.1).

The notation used by the scribe of St. Gall 359 evolved within a framework of theoretical understanding. The medieval modes (early theorists often call them "tones" as well) are a system of scales that worked in pairs, each of which had the same final note; thus the eight modes were divided into four pairs that came to be called *maneriae* (see Primer III.2 and Example P5). The higher of the two modes in each pair was called authentic; the lower, plagal. Like our major and minor scales, each mode has its own character, which is determined by a unique relationship between whole and half steps above and below the final pitch. But in addition, every mode has a unique musical grammar, with characteristic beginning and ending points, leaps, and formulaic gestures. The opening of *Qui habitat* (see Ex. 3.1 above) establishes the pitch D, the final of mode 2. The Gradual *Haec dies* (discussed below) is also assigned to mode 2, but it fits uneasily into this category, perhaps as a result of its great age. Its final pitch is A rather than D. This chant, and the family to which is belongs, are now viewed as having been transposed up a fifth from their original mode.

Modal theory was superimposed on Frankish chant at some point after the repertory was in formation, making it necessary to adapt theory to practice. The chant came first; then came early tonaries (chant books arranged by mode) to help with the belated superimposition of the modes and the generation of new pieces; and then came the beginnings of music notation itself. But even as the practice of notating chant become more important, tonaries continued to be copied and memory still mattered.

EARLY TONARIES

Tonaries initially listed the opening words of small numbers of pieces, classified according to the eight modes; they were later expanded to include many genres of chant. Thus they both recorded memorized repertories and served as a kind of user's manual for the new technology of notation. Tonaries were crucial to cantors who functioned within an oral tradition; they were important, too, for those who used written music along with their well-stocked musical memories as they sang their solos, led choirs in the practice of chanting the psalms, and taught children how to sing.

The first surviving primitive tonary is appended to the so-called Psalter of Charlemagne that dates from around 795. It lays out the modes and lists a handful of chants sung to each of them. A tonary copied in Metz and dated to around 875 (although believed to be a copy of a far earlier manuscript) is usually cited as the first full tonary, a book in which all the opening words of several genres of chants from the Mass and Office are categorized by mode. The Metz Tonary actually is three tonaries, one for Introit and communion antiphons; one for Office antiphons; and a very sparse one for Office responsories. Sandwiched in between are two short theoretical treatises. The page reproduced as Figure 3.3 demonstrates what a useful tool such a book would have been for anyone singing or leading the singing, and needing to pick his way through thousands of memorized melodic formulas and texts, as he set the tone for the music of a given piece.

The cantor who created this book wanted to organize the music sung and taught in two ways: by genre within the liturgy, and by mode and theoretical understanding. The treatise *De octo tonis* (On the Eight Tones [or Modes]) was probably written in the early ninth century and is often appended to tonaries. The modes, the anonymous author says, hold melodies together like "a kind of glue." In this period, Frankish cantors were studying theoretical principles learned from and about Byzantine liturgical music and adapting them to their own use. Theoretical ideas that first developed in Jerusalem, and spread from there all over the Byzantine Empire, were transmitted to the Roman world through the Franks in the late eighth century and received in a variety of ways throughout the ninth century.

ANTIPHONAL AND RESPONSORIAL PSALMODY

Resurrexi, for Easter Sunday, is a mode 4 Introit and so belongs to a class of pieces with a final pitch of E (see Anthology 3.1). Its psalm verse, sung to a special tone developed for Mass Introits, is recited on A. However, the Introit antiphon places a great deal of emphasis on F. As this melody illustrates, the E modes (numbers 3 and 4) often shy away from the final. The two parts of the chant are clear to the ear, making its form apparent. The first section is the antiphon, which is neumatic in style—often with two to three notes per syllable of text—as is typical of this genre. The psalm verse, however, is syllabic, and the music proclaims the text directly and simply. When the antiphon returns, the contrast is clear.

Haec dies is a responsorial chant, a Gradual, for the Mass liturgy (see Primer II.2). The first part of this chant text is verse 24 from Psalm 118 (117): "This is the day the Lord has made; let us rejoice and be glad in it." Unlike English, Latin syntax does not depend on word order but rather on inflected endings of words; the Latin version arranges the words somewhat differently: "This day that made the Lord: let us rejoice and be glad in it." The ends of the two phrases get the most

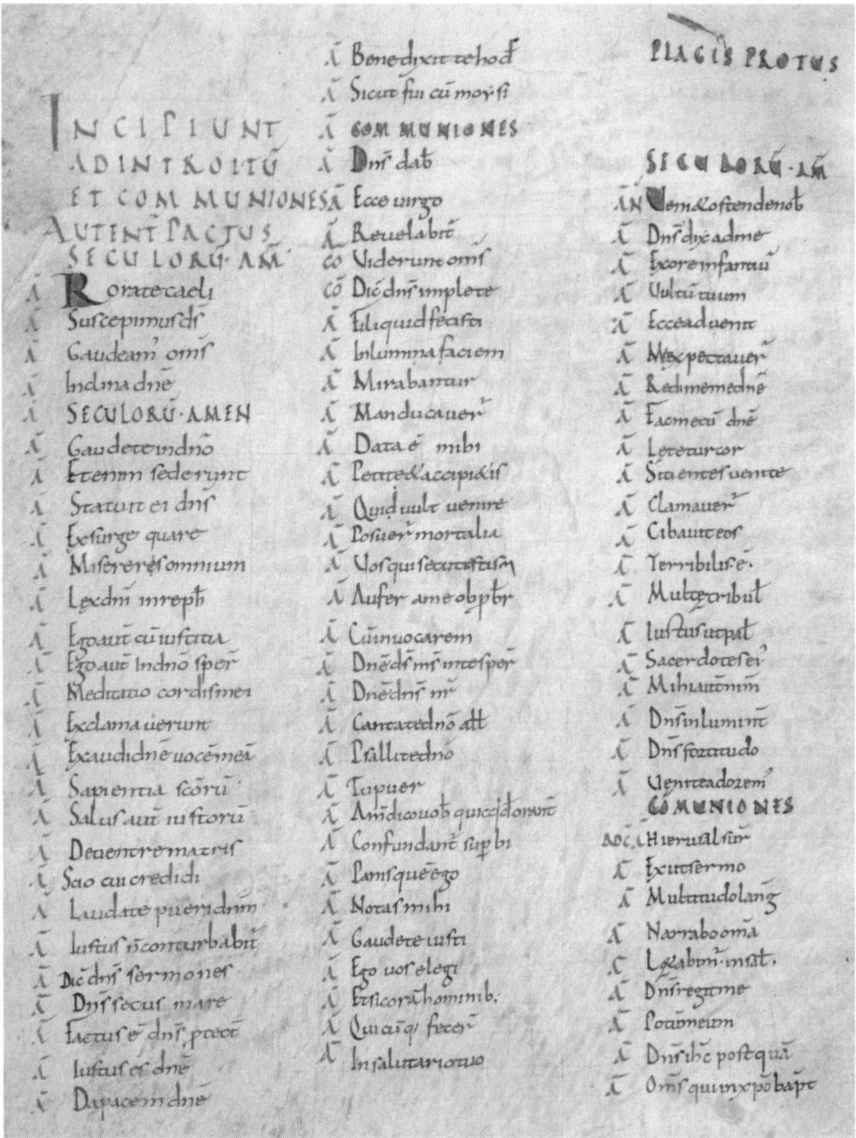

Figure 3.3: *Page from the ninth-century Metz Tonary, showing groupings of Introits and Communion chant text incipits arranged by mode (Metz, BM, MS 351, fol. 66v)*

notes, emphasizing the word for "Lord" and "it." This strategy highlights the first break in the sentence as well as its close, demonstrating the close relationship between the text and the articulation supplied by the music.

The music of this Gradual for Easter Sunday contrasts powerfully with *Resurrexi*, as can been seen from the openings of the two chants (Ex. 3.2). Like all responsorial psalmody, *Haec dies* is ornate and highly melismatic, a musical tour

Example 3.2:

(a) *Opening of the Introit* Resurrexi, *pitches from the* Liber Usualis *(antiphonal chant)*

I have risen, and am still with you. Alleluia.

(b) *Opening of the Gradual* Haec dies, *pitches from the* Liber Usualis *(responsorial chant)*

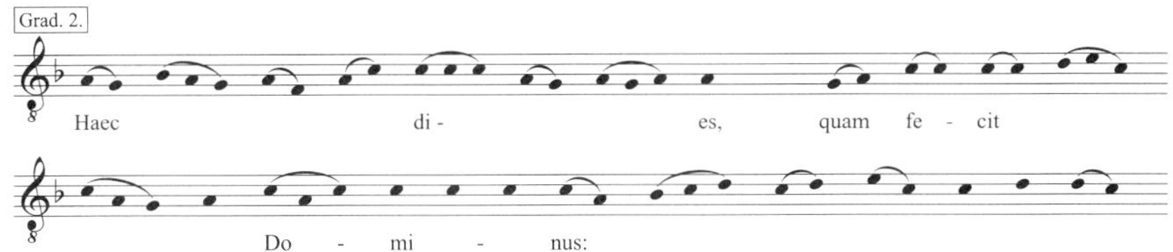

This is the day which the Lord has made.

de force for the cantor who rendered its verse and the small group who joined to sing the response. There was a traditional way of connecting the melodic formulas that make up *Haec dies* into a longer piece, but for the Carolingians this was no longer enough; oral practice demanded written cues to ensure some kind of correctness. These early responsorial chants enable us to imagine the wonderfully flexible voices, musicality, and improvisational skills of the Carolingian cantors, the greatest of whom were surely the equals of singers in any age. Speeding up or slowing down in accordance with meanings of the words, they interpreted the chants in a lively and boldly dramatic manner. (For an example of a Gradual in a different mode, *Viderunt omnes* for Christmas, see Anthology 3.2. Another ornate responsorial Mass chant is the Alleluia, studied in Anthology 3.3 and Chapter 4.)

MODES AND EARLY THEORETICAL UNDERSTANDING

Musica disciplina (The Discipline of Music) by the Frankish writer Aurelian of Réôme (fl. c. 840–850) is now thought to be the earliest theoretical compilation of its kind. Its opening chapters combine the treatise *De octo tonis* with other early sources. Aurelian describes each of the modes, explains how each type of chant uses particular modes, and discusses how antiphons are connected to psalm verses. By Aurelian's time theoretical understandings regarding the modes had been applied to a practice of singing the psalms. In Chapter 19 of his treatise, Aurelian demonstrates that he is living in a world somewhat different from that of the early tonaries, dependent as they were on an art that could "operate with a notationless music culture." He refers to *notae*, signs used for writing down melodies, but none of the early treatises contain the notation he specifies. Aurelian's work also suggests that the medieval theorist was usually a learned compiler of various materials he knew in either written or oral forms (see the discussion of Franco of Cologne in Chapter 10 and Primer II.4).

MUSICA ENCHIRIADIS AND *SCOLICA ENCHIRIADIS*

Slightly later than Aurelian are two works that take us more deeply into the musical sensibilities of the later ninth century: *Musica Enchiriadis* and *Scolica Enchiriadis*. The titles literally translated from the botched Greek would say *Music by Handbook* and *Lecture Notes by Handbook*, the word for handbook being treated as if it were a proper name. Since this would be nonsensical, they are usually called *Music Handbook* and *Notes on the Handbook*. These works are driven by the reception of Boethius's teachings into monastic and cathedral schools, and the desire to continue to teach practical knowledge of the chant, while offering theoretical understanding consonant with some version of Greek music theory.

The *Enchiriadis* treatises emphasize the tetrachords built on the finals of the four pairs of modes as building blocks for musical understanding. The finals are D, E, F, and G; chants in every one of the eight modes should end on one of these pitches. Pairs of scales were numbered: "protus" (on first) was assigned to modes 1 and 2, authentic for the higher scale and plagal for the lower (see example P5 in the primer). The tetrachords of the finals consist of a whole tone, a semitone, and a whole tone—what sounds to our ears like the opening four pitches of a minor scale. This tetrachord forms a unit that was helpful to medieval musicians in understanding the workings of the gamut, or two-octave scale. The nature of the gamut derived from the tetrachords of the finals depends on whether the tetrachords are disjunct (that is, not overlapping) or conjunct (with the same pitch ending one tetrachord and beginning another).

The gamut found in *Musica Enchiriadis* (see SR 24:190; 2/16:80) follows the TST (tone-semitone-tone) pattern in every tetrachord, and the tetrachords are all disjunct. "The 'system' is in essence a multiplication of a single tetrachord." The beauty of the system from the theorist's point of view is that the new tetrachord that starts on every interval of a fifth has the same name and quality as that a fifth below. The system is quite different from the modified Greater Perfect System (discussed in Chapter 2 and Primer III.1), and from Hucbald's system (discussed in Primer III.4). However, every eighth note has a different name and quality from the starting note, so some octaves are not perfect.

Although their major purpose relates to plainchant, the *Enchiriadis* treatises also include sections on the polyphonic ornamentation of chant, demonstrating the practices of doubling pitches at the octave, fifth, and fourth. Three kinds of motion are possible for the organal voice, the voice that decorates the plainsong through singing along with it: parallel motion (moving in the same direction at the same intervals), oblique motion (staying on a single pitch while the plainsong moves), and contrary motion (moving in the opposite direction from the plainsong). *Rex caeli* is a chant that exists in full in only one manuscript, where it is also copied in conjunction with rules relating to organum. In the polyphonic example (Ex. 3.3), the lower or organal voice begins on the same pitch as the chant, and then remains on that pitch until the chant is a fourth above it (oblique motion). At this point the organal voice moves in parallel fourths until the cadence, when it proceeds in contrary motion to catch up with the chant on the penultimate pitch, and then moves with it to a unison final pitch. In this way, the fourth below the pitch E, B♭ in this system (because the first tetrachord is G–A–B♭–C, or T–S–T), which would produce a tritone, is avoided throughout. Carolingian musicians exercised their art of memory by practicing the rules of improvising polyphonic works such as these, using combinations of parallel, oblique, and contrary motion, and avoiding the forbidden interval of the tritone, while keeping the organal voice closely wedded to the plainchant it decorated.

Because the obscure form of letter notation employed in the *Enchiriadis* treatises allows for precise rendering of pitches, the music can be sung today, and even put into practice as a way to improvise a second voice in the singing of chant. What we understand to be polyphony the treatises call *symphonia* (symphony, from the Greek meaning "sounding together"). The practice is not treated as something new or special, suggesting that ornamenting festive chants with polyphonic voices was well accepted by the late ninth century, and demonstrating that the practice was taught as part of a singer's training. The Carolingians were skilled polyphonists, but their art was one of improvisation. Other than in these two treatises, they did not write down their polyphonic works; there was no need to do so, and the ornamented chants were not understood to be fixed pieces, or what we would call "compositions."

Scolica Enchiriadis provides lessons in dialogue form for the skilled singer, and the importance of interpretation shines through: "I say that the rule of distinctions must be observed, that is, that you know what is appropriate to unite and what is appropriate to separate. What tempo is suitable for this or that melody must also be understood. Whereas one melody is better sung more quickly, another is sweeter when sung more slowly. For one can know by the

Example 3.3: *Organum from* Musica Enchiriadis *(mid-ninth century)*

Rex coe - li Do - mi - ne ma - ris un - di - so - ni
Ti - ta - nis ni - ti - di squa - li - di - que so - li,

King of heaven, Lord of the resounding waves, of the bright Titan [sun], and of the artful earth

very formation of a melody whether it is composed of fast or slow phrases." Would that the unknown author had provided clearer examples of his understandings, which modern editors can only attempt to re-create from this and other surviving texts. In any case, these works provide encouragement for today's performing musicians to be creative, within a framework of knowledge about the period, just as ninth-century musicians were expected to interpret the music they sang and played.

The system for writing music down that developed in the ninth century depended on emerging ideas about music theory. The longer chant was written down, the more standardized it became. The chants for the Propers of the Mass, because they were written first, are the most standardized of all. Earlier manuscripts and layers of the repertory demonstrate that written and oral ways of remembering and learning coexisted for long periods. This is not to deny that some early systems of notation that do not survive may have existed or that some places continued to transmit the chant only orally for some time before writing emerged to exert a major influence. Other factors need to be considered as well: chronology, region, center, and even the skills and proclivities of particular individuals. What we do know is that a well-organized theoretical system was in place by the end of the ninth century, and that this system accounted for both melodic and harmonic practices within an enormous repertory of chants that was being copied in notation throughout a vast geographical area, one that included the heartland of the Carolingian Empire.

FOR FURTHER READING

Boynton, Susan, "Plainsong," in Mark Everist, ed., *The Cambridge Companion to Medieval Music* (Cambridge: Cambridge University Press, 2011), 9–25

Crocker, Richard, *An Introduction to Gregorian Chant* (New Haven: Yale University Press, 1999)

Fassler, Margot, "The Office of the Cantor in Early Western Monastic Rules and Customaries: A Preliminary Investigation," *Early Music History* 5 (1985): 29–51

Hiley, David, *Western Plainchant: A Handbook* (Oxford: Oxford University Press, 1995)

Jeffery, Peter, *Re-Envisioning Past Musical Cultures: Ethnomusicology in the Study of Gregorian Chant* (Chicago: University of Chicago Press, 1992)

Levy, Kenneth, *Gregorian Chant and the Carolingians* (Princeton: Princeton University Press, 1998)

Page, Christopher, *The Christian West and Its Singers: The First Thousand Years* (New Haven: Yale University Press, 2010)

Rankin, Susan, "Carolingian Music," in Rosamund McKitterick, ed., *Carolingian Culture* (Cambridge: Cambridge University Press, 1994), 274–316

Treitler, Leo, *With Voice and Pen: Coming to Know Medieval Song and How It Was Made* (Oxford: Oxford University Press, 2003)

CHAPTER FOUR

The Office, the Mass Ordinary, and Practices of Troping

It is difficult to say when the Carolingian Era came to a close. Charlemagne's kingdom was partitioned in the mid-ninth century. The central portion, Lotharingia, was always unstable, its leadership contested by more-powerful neighbors to the east and west. The last Carolingian king of the West Franks (modern-day France) died in 987 and was replaced by the Capetian line; the Ottonians, Saxon kings, ruled in East Francia (modern-day Germany) throughout most of the tenth century and into the eleventh.

Beset by invasions—Vikings from the north, Magyars from the east, and Arabs from the Mediterranean—European kings in this period relied on counts, dukes, and other "strongmen" who would give them military allegiance in exchange for land and power. This system, the basis of the familial territories of the medieval European nobility, is known as feudalism. The large landholders of feudal fiefdoms were Christians who built churches and welcomed monastic orders to provide stability, just as they constructed fortresses in strategic locations to anchor their garrisons. The complex affiliations between secular lords and monastic churches and cathedrals (churches where the bishops had their thrones or *cathedrae*) were motivated by political exigencies as well as piety. Monasteries and cathedral chapters managed huge tracts of property that offered suitable administrative work for the sons and daughters of local nobility. The political situation might well call to mind a game of chess; it's no coincidence that chess was beginning to achieve popularity in northern Europe at this time. The concerned expression of the twelfth-century queen from the Lewis Chessmen (Fig. 4.1) demonstrates that she is a proper consort. Women played major roles in plotting strategies, especially through arranging marriages to consolidate blocks of territory to help their lords, and suffered egregiously along with them when their plans were foiled.

Just as lords, ladies, and their large networked families frequently clashed over territory and governance, so too was there tension between monastic and cathedral churches over control of land, influence, and liturgical and musical practices. As we have seen in previous chapters, to sing chant was to re-create history. Those who wished history to reflect their institutions in particular ways had vested interests in how such communal memory was created, especially in regard to the veneration of local saints (see Chapter 5). Much new music of the tenth and eleventh centuries has political subtexts of one sort or another.

Figure 4.1: *Concerned queen from the Lewis Chessmen, a collection of twelfth-century chess pieces discovered in the Outer Hebrides of Scotland in 1831*

MUSIC IN MONASTIC AND SECULAR CHURCHES

Monastic institutions and their dependencies, cathedrals, and parish churches all relied on the cantors we met in Chapter 3 to instruct in the singing of psalms in the daily hours of prayer. Monks and nuns living in monastic communities headed by abbots and abbesses followed a "rule," a book setting out how the way life was to be lived. The *Rule of St. Benedict* (SR 17:159–64; 2/9:49–54), written around 530 and favored by Charlemagne and his court, is crucial to understanding medieval music and its practice. It provides for the singing of all 150 psalms in weeklong cycles throughout the year. This order was followed throughout much of Europe until the monastic reforms of the twelfth century brought modifications to some institutions.

While control of monastic churches was in the hands of their abbots and abbesses, secular churches were regulated by a bishop and an entourage of administrators, and served by a chapter or group of canons, the clerics who received their livelihoods from some part of the wealth of the cathedral's properties and endowments. Some canons were in residence at the cathedral, while others had responsibilities that took them to other parts of the diocese (the region governed by a bishop). The bishop, his staff, and the cathedral canons oversaw hundreds of dependent parish churches. Like feudal lords, bishops managed extensive properties from which they received income. They saw to it that every church in the diocese had suitable music for religious services. Hours of prayer were also observed in every cathedral. The psalms were sung there according to an ordering that differed somewhat from that found in monastic churches, although the essential structure was the same (see Primer IV.3). The music of a cathedral and the particularities of its liturgical practices pumped like blood from a heart into all the churches of the diocese; this is one of the major reasons that every region had unique ways of making liturgical music. Indeed, when the manuscripts preserving the works of music theorists are studied, it can sometimes be told where they did their work from the nature of the chant variants, as with the theorist John (see Chapter 5).

HUCBALD OF ST. AMAND

In spite of these local variations, some musical practices in the old Carolingian heartland were more uniform in the early tenth century than in the mid-800s, when Aurelian of Réôme noted the variety of ways of singing (see Chapter 3). This uniformity made it possible to lay out the tones of psalm singing in ways that were regulated by the modes (see Primer III.2 and III.3).

Hucbald of St. Amand (c. 850–930) was one of the most significant music theorists of his age. A skillful poet who wrote new music for the Mass and Office, he also wrote about music and how it worked; his treatise *De musica* (On Music) was a handbook to help teachers and singers align their own musical practices with Boethius's teachings about Greek music theory, as discussed in Chapter 2. (See Primer III.4 for a "lesson" with Hucbald.)

Hucbald was somewhat different from ninth-century thinkers who made various principles of Greek theory foundational to their work or who, like the Enchiriadis theorists, were somewhat removed from the Greeks. In Hucbald's theoretical realm of understanding, chant and the modal system that governed it became the bases for the medieval understanding of Greek music theory as received through Boethius (rather than the other way around). A new synthesis was in the making. By the beginning of the tenth century, at least in some places, modes and the theoretical teachings necessary for using new notation and organizing the chants into various musical categories provided much more information than had been found in early tonaries. The formulas crucial to the early art of memory had been enhanced by development within the modes, and this expanded system was especially important for the antiphonal and responsorial psalm singing of the Divine Office. From knowledge of the modes and of theory, medieval musicians could improvise and compose more readily as well; these tools were not only about memory, but also about creating new works. The ways in which the modes came to dominate musical practice is seen in the psalmody of the Divine Office.

MUSIC FOR THE OFFICE

The brief plan of hours of prayer found in Table 4.1 reveals what a grand musical production took place day in, day out in monasteries and cathedrals throughout the Latin West. On major feast days, the music was even more ornate and the individual hours even longer (for a detailed description, see Primer IV.3). Like the Mass, the Office unfolded in accordance with a particular order for singing and intoned readings, and for Ordinary and Proper elements. The structure was fixed, as were the kinds of pieces within it, but the variable elements transformed each Office in accordance with the rhythms and themes of the church calendar, and with regionality.

In the Carolingian period, most learned Christians were clerics, monks, or nuns; as such, they would have sung for four to six hours per day, and on some days even longer. It was from singing the Office that a great amount of text could be fixed in the memory: the psalms and hymns, the readings of Scripture, commentaries on these readings by early church fathers, and innumerable prayer texts (see also Primer IV.3). Although there was an underlying ordering of psalmody, every feast and season had its own special psalms and antiphons to define themes and to make the passing of time more tangible and thus more dramatic. On special feasts, Proper psalms, such as the Advent antiphon and

Table 4.1: *Overview of the Office as Outlined in the* Rule of St. Benedict (RB)

TIME	COMMON MEDIEVAL DESIGNATION	RELATIVE DURATION ON MAJOR FEASTS
2 a.m.	Matins (RB: Vigils)	two hours
Dawn	Lauds	Under an hour
6 a.m.	Prime	Under half an hour
9 a.m.	Terce	Under half an hour
	(The major Mass of the day commonly was sung after Terce)	
12 p.m.	Sext	Under half an hour
3 p.m.	None	Under half an hour
Sunset	Vespers	Under an hour
Before bed	Compline	Under half an hour

Although the Office was sung in all medieval monasteries and cathedrals, and in many other churches, there were many variables. In the later Middle Ages, for example, Matins was often sung the night before. For a full table, see Primer IV.3.

the responsory for the Virgin Mary discussed below, would replace the so-called ferial (nonfestive) psalms and their antiphons. Learning took place for most people within a community of song whose repertory changed constantly in accordance with the calendar. Musical events, in spite of formal uniformity, were ever inflected by the passing of time.

The singing of the Office took place in the area of the church behind the main altar, known as the choir, named for the group that sang within this architectural space. Choirs were divided in half, as antiphonal singing required that the verses of the psalms be chanted in alternation. Antiphonal, or back-and-forth, singing promotes the idea that the members of the community are in a relationship, mutually supportive of each other. Each singer rendering a psalm verse could look at a familiar group of faces across the choir, and hear the voices of people who had been singing throughout their entire lives. Children in monastic and cathedral schools had to memorize the psalms and learn to sing hymns. As they were taught to sing, they gained a well-developed sense of the past as proclaimed in the texts—the majority of which were from the Bible and the Church fathers. These texts, in turn, were all related to the particular feasts and seasons of the unfolding of church year, allowing for multiple senses of time and history, all created through song. The presence of young people in these institutions inspired the use of their high and clear voices (in both monophonic and polyphonic singing), as well as the production of various kinds of sung liturgical plays, which they apparently took great delight in performing.

Although members of monastic communities were seated according to seniority, that is, by the order in which they had entered the monastery, the abbess or abbot and other high officials sat apart from the rest. In cathedrals, the bishop had a special throne-like chair called a *sedes*. The two sides of a cathedral choir were officially ruled by the dean (often the south side) and precentor or cantor (often the north side), the two highest-ranking officials in the chapter. Yet another figure, the succentor (subcantor), bore many of the responsibilities for the music. Choirs in cathedrals were all male, but in monasteries the choirs were members of their respective male or female communities. Child choristers were employed in most cathedral liturgies, whereas monastic practice varied, some having schools and child singers, and others not; but when they were present, they had a special place to sit, usually in the front. While the space for the choir can still be seen in many medieval churches, very few complete choir stalls survive; those of Cologne Cathedral in Germany, carved in oak in the early fourteenth century, are among the finest (Fig. 4.2).

Medieval memories were filled to the brim with the sounds of psalms, canticles, and the antiphons proper to them; most monks and cathedral canons, at least until the eleventh century, were trained first in the church as children through singing the psalms. Whenever a psalm text or a scriptural antiphon text was read outside the choir, in a book or treatise, that text would "sing" in the memory. Monks and nuns often read or intoned aloud, in the cloister or

Figure 4.2: *Fourteenth-century choir stalls in Cologne Cathedral*

refectory (the eating place), an experience that must have been very different from modern silent reading. Both monks and nuns produced monastic books; until the twelfth century they were the major book producers of medieval Europe. Thus, the monastic cloister was set up for work as well as reflection, and time in the cloister was built into every day's regime. The hours of prayer required not only constant singing, but also an industry of copying, correcting, and composition (Fig. 4.3). Rules of silence imposed in many monasteries privileged music and the act of singing as the only acceptable form of communication.

THE MODES AND TONES OF THE OFFICE

As discussed in Chapter 3, the Mass liturgy always tells the same story, flavored with Proper texts reflecting feasts and seasons. The Office, on the other hand, always tells a particular story, usually of one event in the life of Jesus and his followers or of the life and miracles of a saint. Advent, the four-week season leading up to Christmas on December 25, provides an example of how the Office worked in the celebration of a time of year. Although much of the music sung in the Office was dependent on the memorization of tones for the psalmody, the music, like that of the Mass, was written down, with examples surviving from the tenth century. *Antiphoners* (or *antiphonales*), books con-

Figure 4.3: *Twelfth-century cloister, St. Sophia, Benevento. Credit Peter Jeffery.*

taining the music for the Office, are usually organized by the church year. Early antiphoners mixed feasts of the *temporale* (relating to Jesus) and *sanctorale* (relating to the saints), but by the eleventh century they were often divided into two sections, feasts of the *temporale* and the *sanctorale*. By this time as well, the cycle usually began with Advent—for medieval Christians, a time of penance and expectation.

As in the medieval Mass, psalms in the Office were sung both antiphonally and responsorially. Both ways of singing used melodic formulas to aid singers in the arduous work of memorization. But there are far fewer genres of chant associated with the Office liturgy than with the Mass, as there are not so many particular liturgical actions. Instead, in addition to hymns (see Chapter 2), the music is primarily antiphons, sung with intoned psalms or canticles, and great responsories (long chants following readings). We will study these two styles of chant in turn.

Office antiphons are short melodies used to frame the singing of a psalm or canticle to one of the tones. Each psalm to be sung was paired with an antiphon, which framed it by being sung both before and after. The psalm was intoned to a formula verse by verse, although the inflections of the tones varied from mode to mode and region to region. Example 4.1 below shows the ending of an antiphon from the Advent season and the setting of the first verse of the psalm sung with it; in practice, the entire psalm text was sung, followed by the *Gloria Patri*, the Doxology (see the Primer, III.3 for discussion of the psalm tones and examples, and Anthology 4 for the entire psalm with antiphon). The antiphons and the psalm tones formed the backbone of medieval chant. They not only allowed for the memorization and proclamation of the most important texts for singing from the Bible, but also promoted through the tones a very successful way of learning music. By emphasizing the constant repetition of basic intervals, the psalm tones embodied a system that assured musical competence for large numbers of people. The psalm tones for the medieval Office are slightly less complex than those used for the antiphonal singing of the Introit of the Mass liturgy studied in Chapter 3, or for canticles of the Office, such as the *Magnificat* (see below), but the principles are the same.

Example 4.1 demonstrates the intimate connection between mode and psalm tone in the practice of antiphonal Office psalmody, using the example of the seventh tone. The psalm tones are numbered 1–8, and each corresponds to one of the modes, also numbered 1–8. (Yet another tone, the *tonus peregrinus* or wandering tone, is used more rarely and has two reciting pitches, one for the first and the other for the second half of the verse.) Each of the eight psalm tones has a reciting pitch, which for authentic modes is usually a fifth above the final, and for plagal modes a third above the final. This pitch is used continuously through the rendering of the tone and carries the text, which is inflected at the ends of phrases and lines. Tones that would have B as a reciting pitch came to

Example 4.1:

(a) *Mode 7 antiphon (ending) and cue for its* differentia, *or termination formula*

For He will come and not tarry, alleluia. [Seculorum Amen]

(b) *First verse of Psalm 147 (146),* Laudate Dominum, *and its* differentia

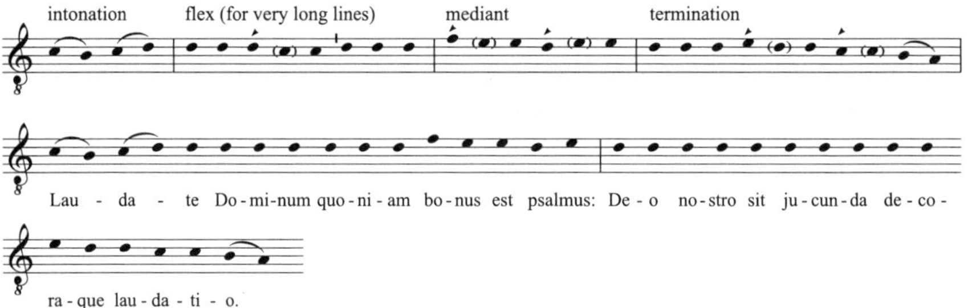

Praise the Lord, because a psalm is good: to our God be joyful and comely praise.

be changed early in the Carolingian period; thus the reciting pitches for modes 3 and 4 are C and A, respectively, and for modes 7 and 8, D and C.

Each psalm verse has an opening formula (used for the first verse only in Office psalms, but for every verse in the *Magnificat*), a middle phrase (mediant), and a termination formula (*differentia*; plural, *differentiae*), all three serving as musical punctuation marks (see Ex. P7 in the Primer). A short line, or *flex*, is also provided for long texts. One can think of the *flex* as a kind of comma, whereas the mediant is a semicolon, and the *differentia*, a period. The several ending formulas for mode 7 shown in Anthology 4 are among the possible *differentiae* for that tone; which one the singer chose depended on the antiphon to be sung with that particular psalm. The *differentiae* are inflected endings for the tone, chosen to create a smooth musical transition between the intoned psalm and the antiphon repeated at its close. Each region and even each religious house had its favored *differentiae*, and the ones found in the *Liber Usualis* are a representative compendium. As can be seen in Example 4.1, the *differentia* is labelled by letters representing the end of the doxology.

Canticles, drawn from biblical passages in which characters burst into song, were also sung antiphonally to tones throughout the week; many of those from the Hebrew Bible were assigned to the hour of Lauds. The three most important canticles were each assigned to a particular hour of prayer: the *Benedictus*, the song of the priest Zechariah, father of the Christian prophet John the Baptist (Luke 1:68–79), was sung at Lauds; the *Magnificat*, the song of the Virgin Mary (Luke 1:46–55), was sung at Vespers; and the *Nunc dimittis*, the song of the prophet

Simeon (Luke 2:29–32), was sung at Compline. The tone for the *Magnificat* is slightly more complex than that used for the psalms, just as the antiphon itself is usually longer and more ornate than that used for the psalms. The text of the *Magnificat* antiphon often summarizes the meanings of the feast as a whole.

A RESPONSORY FOR THE VIRGIN MARY

Antiphons with psalms were sung in the Office alongside great responsories. As we saw in Chapter 3 and Anthology 3.2, responsorial chants for the Mass liturgy are made up of two components, a respond and a verse. Great responsories in the Office, by contrast, often have an additional component, a portion of the Doxology (a formula of praise to the Trinity). In addition, the verses and Doxology of Office responsories were often sung to elaborate tones that were specific to each mode (see Primer IV.3). We will study two great responsories: *Stirps Jesse* for the Virgin Mary (see below) and *Ex eius tumba* for St. Nicholas (see Chapter 5). Together they represent the range of musical processes explored in the great responsory repertory of the Office in the eleventh century.

Even a famous saint like the Virgin Mary needed a way to be particularized. At Chartres Cathedral in northern France, centuries of legends, music, and artworks transformed her into "the Virgin of Chartres," exemplifying the localization of saints in music and the other arts throughout Europe in the eleventh century, a process that we will examine further in Chapter 5. The main relic at Chartres was a bolt of ancient cloth from the East, believed to be the robe Mary wore at the birth of Christ. By the eleventh century it was seen as responsible for the French defeat of the fierce Viking Rollo in 911. By the twelfth century, an early bishop of Chartres was depicted waving the garment from the city walls, causing attackers to flee. Soldiers wanted bits of it to take to battle; women clutched pieces of the cloth in the agonies of childbirth.

Fulbert, bishop of Chartres in the early eleventh century, was mythologized as the author and composer of new texts and music for the Feast of the Virgin's Nativity on September 8. As this feast celebrated Mary's birth, it was strongly related to the relic, also emblematic of her flesh. The most popular of the compositions attributed to Fulbert is the responsory *Stirps Jesse* (see Anthology 5). Unlike *Ex eius tumba*, *Stirps Jesse* is a fairly free composition that does not employ formulas for its verse. The melody is unique, unlike a significant percentage of responsory melodies composed in the Carolingian period that were highly formulaic, but like many melodies of the tenth and eleventh centuries. The text offers a fine example of image-laden Christian commentary on two Old Testament themes, one from Isaiah 11, the shoot of the house of David, and the other from Numbers 17, the flowering rod of Aaron. The beautiful melismatic setting of the words "flos Filius eius" (the flower, her Son) was one of the most beloved melodies of the entire medieval period, and was used in a variety of settings (Ex. 4.2; see Chapters 6 and 9).

Example 4.2: *Melisma from the great responsory* Stirps Jesse

The flower, her son

At Chartres, *Stirps Jesse* was a theme song, built into the musical and liturgical fabric of that place in several ways. Both singer and listener are encouraged through this music to enter into a world of biblical exegesis where the words of one text were redefined by those of another, and meaning was created as the mind moved between the two. *Stirps Jesse* became known throughout Europe as a composition originating in Chartres and proclaiming the power of the Virgin and her relic—another example of music creating history in communal memories and of using music to define a region.

THE MASS ORDINARY AND ITS TROPES

The Mass chants studied in Chapter 3 are Propers; that is, their entire texts changed in accordance with the feasts and seasons. But there is another category of chants whose texts (or at least parts of them) did not change to reflect the time of the year. These are the so-called Ordinary chants, as shown in Primer IV.2 and Table P3: Kyrie, Gloria, Credo, Sanctus, Agnus Dei, and *Ite missa est*. In common with Proper chants of the Mass, each category of Ordinary chant forms a genre with its own musical character, depending on its liturgical function and historical understanding: how it conveys the stories connected with Scripture.

Most of the Mass Ordinary texts are very old, but they are not psalmodic. Rather, each is an ancient prayer and functions in places within the liturgy where the congregation or entire monastic community was expected to emote, pray, or perhaps even sing along with those leading the service. Most Ordinary chants are musically simpler than Proper chants, and none feature the singing of soloists. It was these chants and their texts, rather than the Proper chants, that developed into the polyphonic Masses of the later Middle Ages, Renaissance, and later periods, which are frequently heard in concert halls today.

GLOSSING TEXTS AND MUSIC

Additions to Ordinary chants are glosses on liturgical action as well as on the texts themselves. Identifying the relative dates of these added texts is complicated. When Ordinary chants were first being written down in the tenth century, the texts were often supplemented by commentaries on their meanings. The terminology for the three basic types of additions was inconsistent in the Middle Ages, as it is in modern times. For ease of understanding, we will distinguish the three types as follows: a trope is an addition of both text and music; a prosula is the addition of a text to a preexisting melisma; and a neuma is a melismatic phrase of music. Because tropes or prosulae for Ordinary chants may have been created at the same time the entire piece was composed, the chant repertories of northern and southern Europe, which were no longer parts of a unified Carolingian Empire, varied substantially.

Many commentaries on the Bible were written in the late antique period by Church fathers, including Jerome, Augustine, and Gregory the Great (see Chapter 3). The Carolingians copied these to provide texts for the Office readings, filling in gaps with sermons by the Anglo-Saxon Bede (672/673–735). Medieval scholars carried on older exegetical traditions, writing new commentaries, but they also created glossed versions of the books of the Bible, particularly the Psalms. A gloss is a different kind of commentary from the longer ones described above and is crucial to understanding the idea of troping. Glosses were comments inserted next to the biblical text, either between lines or in the margins, and they served a variety of purposes, all the way from simply defining words or grammatical structures to more complicated glosses that expanded upon the meanings of scriptural texts.

Ekkehard IV (c. 980–1056), a monk at the Abbey of St. Gall, was involved in music and manuscript production. The tenth-century manuscript known as St. Gall 159 is a collection of letters and sermons from famous fathers of the Church, probably compiled for reading in the abbey during meals. Ekkehard glossed the manuscript from his eleventh-century vantage point, writing in the margins and between the lines, making corrections, and adding punctuation for greater clarity (Fig. 4.4). This kind of work was very much like that of the troping musician who wished to further expound upon Mass chants, and perhaps clarify or add meanings. We'll have more to say about such musical glossing below.

Commentaries were not only written and recited, but also sung within the liturgy itself. Indeed, much new music composed for the Mass from the late ninth through the eleventh centuries was—or appeared to be—some kind of gloss on earlier music, its text, and its liturgical function. Glossing became a favored musical concept, and musicians were eager to show how new compositions related to the traditional pieces they were sung with, even if the older pieces were engulfed or subsumed in the process. As discussed in Chapter 1, meanings depended on many kinds of intertextual relationships between older and newer pieces of music that combined to form a whole.

THE KYRIE AND GLORIA

The Ordinary Mass chant *Kyrie eleison* was frequently glossed in the tenth and eleventh centuries. Its brief text and three-part structure provide ample opportunity for expansion. Also, the chant is highly melismatic, and so was ideally suited to commentary in the form of a prosula.

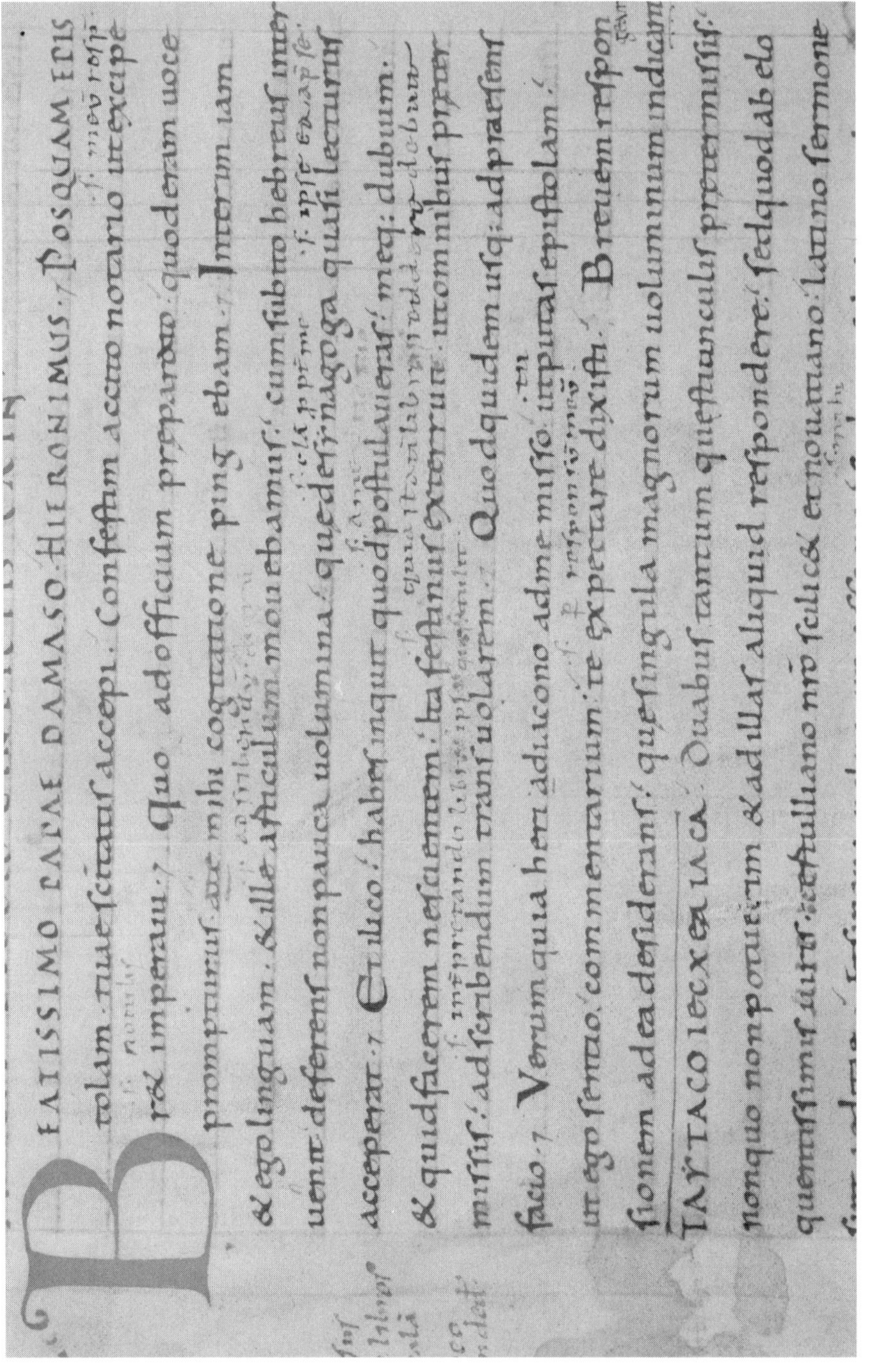

Figure 4.4: *Page from St. Gall 159 showing interlinear glosses in the hand of Ekkehard IV (980–c. 1060), who wrote a history of the monastery, including descriptions of Notker and his companions (St. Gall, Stiftsbibliothek, MS 159, p. 6)*

As a genre, the Mass Kyrie has many features that are traditionally part of penitential rites, including the repetitions of words or phrases that often accompany requests for help. The three-part Greek text signals the age and seriousness of an ancient plea found in all early Christian liturgies, both eastern and western: "Kyrie eleison, Christe eleison, Kyrie eleison" (Lord, have mercy; Christ, have mercy; Lord, have mercy). Since Carolingian times the pleas have had a ninefold structure, as reflected in the musical form **AAABBBCCC'** (or **CCD**). *Cunctipotens genitor* (see Anthology 6) is an example of a Kyrie that is glossed with a prosula. In Example 4.3, two versions of line 1 are presented: a melismatic setting of the text *Kyrie eleison*, and a statement of that same line with syllables for every note. The addition of text to a melismatic line transforms it completely, yet keeps it alive as well. Through such glossing, musicians joined several layers of understanding in their works. With Ordinary chants, it is often difficult to say if the prosula was composed at the time the melody came into being, or was added later to a preexisting melismatic version of the chant.

Treatises written in the Middle Ages concerning relationships between humans and divinity emphasize the importance of humility and the request for forgiveness, the "fear of the Lord" that was believed to be the beginning of the spiritual journey as reflected in the Kyrie. After forgiveness comes joy and praise, just as the Gloria, another Ordinary text, follows immediately after the Kyrie in the Mass liturgy, with no break. *Gloria in excelsis*, one of the longest chants in the entire repertory, is a jubilant prayer, and is not sung in the penitential seasons of Advent and Lent. Some 50 medieval melodies for this text survive, and 15 of them can be found in the *Liber Usualis*. The idea of congregational song is also embodied in early layers of the Ordinary chant repertory, as suggested by the Gloria, which is syllabic and easy to sing. In Example 4.4, depicting the opening of Gloria III (numbers assigned in the modern chant books have become standard), the musical phrase fits the Latin like a glove, as can be seen

Example 4.3: *First line of the Kyrie* Cunctipotens genitor

(a) *Without prosula*

Lord, have mercy

(b) *With prosula*

All-powerful Father, O God, Creator of all things, have mercy.

Example 4.4: *Opening of Gloria III as found in the* Liber Usualis

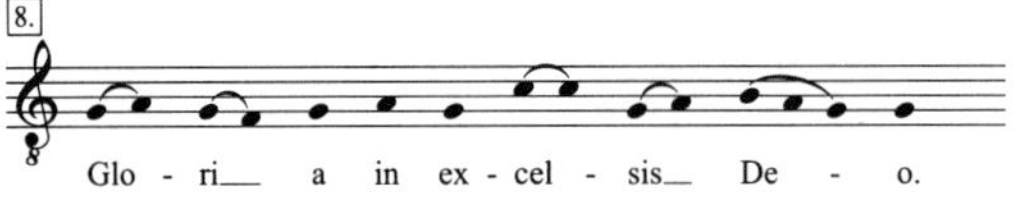

Glory to God in the highest

in the way the high point of the line falls on the syllable "-cel-" of "excelsis" ("highest"). Gloria melodies are often exceptional in their ways of declamation, and sometimes contain interrelated or repeating phrases of music.

Like the Kyrie, the Gloria had its own ways of being glossed. There were prefatory tropes, interlinear tropes (which might migrate from one piece to another), and prosulae, or sets of words written for melismas. One of the most famous is the trope verse with music *Regnum tuum solidum permanebit in eternam* (Your reign will last forever). In many versions the melisma or neuma on the syllable "per-" was itself glossed with a prosula, making this chant an expansion of an expansion. Like the "flos Filius" melisma discussed above, the *Regnum* melody demonstrates how important some melismas were: they became popular tunes that appeared in a variety of guises and nurtured many genres of chant. In fact, the *Ite missa est* that closes the Mass and the *Benedicamus Domino* that ends hours of prayer in the Office (and sometimes the Mass as well, in very solemn times) often featured beloved melismas, many of which might be borrowed from the Kyrie. Example 4.5 shows how the melisma of the Kyrie *Cunctipotens genitor* (see Ex. 4.3) was adapted for the *Ite missa est* to form a powerful kind of intertextuality, so that a chant that falls early in the liturgy is musically joined to the closing piece of the Mass. The same melisma might also be used for the *Benedicamus Domino*, the last chant for most Office hours.

THE CREDO, SANCTUS, AND AGNUS DEI

The Nicene Creed—the textual source of the Credo in the Ordinary—is a fourth-century statement of faith. It is thought to have been brought into the Roman rite by Charlemagne, and in the Frankish liturgy it opens the second section of the Mass. Only a small number of settings survive from the Middle Ages; these as well as later chant settings of the Credo are invariably syllabic. Because it outlines essential tenets of the faith, the Creed was rarely expanded with tropes or other additions.

The Sanctus and Agnus Dei, on the other hand, were frequently troped, and the additions help explain the meanings of the Liturgy of the Faithful, the second half of the Mass. The Sanctus chant has two parts, the Sanctus and the Benedictus. The former refers to the singing of the seraphim as found in Isaiah 6:3; this text is also sung in the Jewish liturgy (*Kadosh kadosh kadosh Adonai tz'vaot m'lo khol ha-aretz k'vodo*), forming part of the Amidah, a central prayer of blessing said

Example 4.5: *Chant texts set to a phrase from the Kyrie* Cunctipotens genitor

(a) *For the ending of the Mass*

Go forth, it is finished. Thanks be to God.

(b) *For the ending of the Office hours*

Let us praise the Lord.

while standing and facing the Ark that houses the Torah scrolls. In the Christian Mass liturgy, the prayer is sung at the very close of the variable prefatory prayer and just before the beginning of the *canon*, the eucharistic prayer of consecration, which was spoken rather than sung.

To the Sanctus was added the Benedictus verse: "Blessed is he who comes in the name of the Lord, Hosanna in the highest," a reference to Jesus's entrance into Jerusalem on Palm Sunday. In the context of the Mass liturgy, the Benedictus proclaims that Jesus is about to "enter" into the elements of bread and wine. As with so many aspects of the chants of the medieval Latin liturgy, a text originating in Jewish Scripture is transformed through translation and a new context. Tropes to the Sanctus are most often introductory and interlinear, with occasional prosulae for some melismatic portions.

COMMENTARIES ON THE ALLELUIA

The Alleluia is a responsorial Proper genre, constituting a layer of medieval chant that is somewhat later than the Graduals, Tracts, and Offertories discussed in Chapter 3. Coming just before the intoning of the Gospel, the major scriptural text of any feast, the Alleluias are, along with the Graduals, the musical high point of the first half of the Mass. Because the singing of the Gospel was prefaced by an elaborate procession with the Book (often the most magnificent object in the church), it was an ideal moment for singers to ornament the service. In addition, the Alleluia was the point in the Mass when the heavens opened: just before the Word was present in the reading of the Gospel, worshippers were encouraged to hear a flutter of wings and remember that they sang their liturgy along with a parallel worship service in heaven. The long, wordless melismas reminded listeners of the unheard "otherness" expected of angelic music.

Compared to many Proper Mass chants, Alleluias were fairly flexible, not only in their tripartite musical form, opening and closing with a long melisma called a *jubilus* (see the commentary on *Pascha nostrum* in Anthology 3.3), but also in their performance practice. Alleluias were particularly beloved by medieval musicians; they created a place in the liturgy for singers and composers to shine, as well as a place to add new commentaries. On the other hand, the melodic lushness of the Alleluia may have caused anxiety for child soloists and choristers: there were so many notes to remember, notes that often had to be rendered without texts as guides; the small, repeating melodic phrases built into the musical fabric would have helped.

Many Alleluia melodies were set repeatedly to different texts—it was one of the few chants in the Frankish repertory to be reset in this way. The Old Roman repertory contained just four basic Alleluia melodies, each of them very ornate, that could be adapted for numerous occasions and texts. This sparseness in the Old Roman repertory contrasts with the hundreds of Alleluias that survive from north of the Alps, such as *Pascha nostrum.*

NOTKER AND THE SEQUENCE

The history of commentaries on the Mass Alleluia usually begins with Notker Balbulus (Notker the Stammerer) of St. Gall (c. 840–912). A poet, scribe, historian, singer, and composer, he was described by Ekkehard IV as "frail in body, though not in mind, a stammerer in voice but not in spirit" and "most assiduous in illuminating, reading, and composing."

It was Notker himself who recorded one of music history's favored legends in the preface to his *Liber hymnorum* ("Book of Hymns," but actually a collection of sequence texts). Apparently, by Notker's time there was a repertory of long melismas that took the place of the repeat of the Alleluia with its jubilus for some feasts. On major feasts in the Carolingian period, the shape of the Alleluia was as follows:

Alleluia
Verse (often from a psalm)
a repeat of the Alleluia, or
a very long melody (sometimes called a sequence),
which took the place of the repeat of the Alleluia

Notker says that he found it difficult to remember the "very long melodies" of the Alleluias, these being works that grew out of the jubilus, the long melisma on the final vowel of the word "alleluia."

Notker reports that a monk fleeing from the Viking raids on Jumièges in northern France arrived at St. Gall with a book containing texts he had composed for these long melodies. Admiring the monk's efforts but thinking he could do better, Notker began to compose texts for the melodies himself. Eventually, he collected these sequences (or "proses") in the *Liber hymnorum*. If Notker's account is true, sequences were originally prosulae. But there is disagreement over the degree to which the Notkerian sequences are really based on melodies that were once associated with Alleluias. Whatever the case, the melodies are not like early Frankish chants in style, but more like the melodies composed later for the Ordinary. Their texts make them even more removed from any other genre: unlike hymns, they are through-composed, and they are longer than any other chant written as a commentary within the liturgy. Some early sequences are clearly related to particular Alleluias, and to very long melodies sometimes called by the modern term *sequelae*, and the new sequence text may reflect the liturgical position of the parent Alleluia as well.

A Notkerian sequence is a magnificent liturgical song by one of the greatest poets of the Middle Ages, rich with biblical illusions and festive resonance. The poetry is expressed in a kind of heightened prose and unfolds with a single line of text followed by couplets of varying lengths, and sometimes ending with a single line. The two lines of each couplet are set to the same melody, yielding the musical form **ABBCCDD** and so on. This fluid form, which contained as many couplets as desired by the composer, also creatively mimics the repetitive cries of the Alleluia melodies. Early sequence melodies are often powerful but lack the ornamentation of other Gregorian genres.

Notker, by his own account, set new words to melodies he learned from west of the Rhine, so the sequence repertory contains many works whose melodies are known from other traditions, such as his *Sancti Spiritus assit nobis gratia*. Notker adapted his text to the very long melody *Occidentana*, which was also used in the West Frankish sequence repertory for the sequence *Rex omnipotens die hodierna*, for the Feast of the Ascension. Both these sequences are related to an Alleluia that was sung on the Feast of Pentecost (see Anthology 7). The way in which the two sequences from two different regions are intertextually related is apparent from their opening lines, as shown in Example 4.6, which also includes the opening of the very long melody *Occidentana*.

Notker's text *Sancti Spiritus* is about the bodily ascension of Jesus into heaven 40 days after Easter. At that time, he promised his disciples that a "comforter" would come to them, and this is interpreted as the Holy Spirit, who then descended in fiery tongues on the Feast of Pentecost. In adapting his text for the Ascension to a melodic tradition associated with Pentecost and the Holy Spirit, Notker used music to underscore the meanings of his words, creating a kind of foreshadowing in his work. His texts were closely wedded to the Bible and to standard commentaries on it, but his powers as a versifier come through loud and clear. He was creating settings that would underscore both small melodic cells of music to relate to individual words and the larger forms of complete phrases to express sentences, an art of adaptation that is central to the work of medieval composers.

Example 4.6: *Openings of related sequences*

(a) *West Frankish:* Rex omnipotens die hodierna

On this day the all-powerful king

(b) *East Frankish: Alleluia and* Sancti Spiritus assit nobis gratia

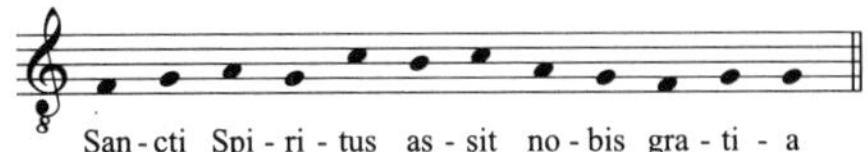

Alleluia / May the grace of the Holy Spirit be with us

(c) *Opening of* Occidentana

In Notker's *Sancti Spiritus*, Ascension is related to Pentecost, as was the case in the liturgical cycle of feasts, in that Jesus predicts that the Holy Spirit will descend after he ascends. Medieval listeners would have been mindful of Ascension on Pentecost, and the setting would have reinforced the association. Music is powerfully symbolic when used in the liturgy through the power of memory. Through their tropes and sequences, medieval musicians were able to outdo the commentator Amalar of Metz himself in the scope and allegorical power of their creations. The East and West Frankish sequence repertories were separated by a kind of geographical barrier. Tropes passed through this barrier and mingled, but many sequences did not, at least until the barrier began to break down in the later eleventh century. Thus sequences were "regional"—yet another way this later layer of chant is distinguished from the Proper Mass chants studied in Chapter 3. Sequences thus constitute evidence of the highest order for understanding the religiosity of particular areas and even of individual churches.

TROPES FROM THE WORKSHOP OF ADÉMAR OF CHABANNES

The Alleluia and its many musical commentaries illustrate the range of newer chants and texts associated with just one genre of chant. But hundreds of other musical commentaries were being written in the tenth and eleventh centuries. The eleventh-century manuscript Paris, BN lat. 1121 is a compilation including a variety of these kinds of chant. Measuring roughly 10.5 by 6.5 inches, it was clearly intended for a single person to use—a utilitarian book that singers could consult in conjunction with other sources and with their musical memories. All the chants copied in lat. 1121—including tropes, prosulae, Offertories (with their verses), Tracts, Alleluias, a kind of antiphon sometimes sung before the Gospel, a few Office pieces, and a short tonary—call for a soloist.

We know who wrote the neumes in this book: it was Adémar of Chabannes (c. 988–c. 1034), a monk in residence, at least some of the time, at the Abbey of St. Martial in Limoges. Adémar's anthology provided repertory from which to choose pieces to sing in conjunction with the chants in the Mass that the singer wished to decorate. Lat. 1121 also contains sequences of various types, some of which have been attributed to Adémar.

All the Proper tropes copied by Adémar are for particular feasts of the temporale and sanctorale; other tropers from this period contain tropes for common categories of saints (apostles, bishops, martyrs, virgins, and others). Any saint not important enough to have a Mass or Office proper to him or her would be given an appropriate set of chants from common Masses or Offices (organized according to these categories); some of these chants were troped as well. Lat. 1121 reinforces the idea that cantors had to put services together from a variety of books, taking one kind of piece from one, another from another.

The chants we have been studying from the tenth century were not written down in precisely heightened notation. It was in the eleventh century that notators began to write precise pitches in liturgical books, so that, as with the particular style of notation in the *Enchiriadis* treatises from a century before (see Chapter 3), which never caught on in a major way, specific intervals can be read and transcribed. In lat. 1121, Adémar was notating music in a new way. He had mastered the ability to map the intervallic spaces between notes onto his manuscript page, a technological advance of great magnitude. Thus the chant in lat. 1121 can be securely transcribed (once one determines the pitch of the opening notes of a given chant).

Adémar wished to give the monastic patron saint Martial the stature of an apostle of Jesus. To further this agenda, he wrote special chants and changed others, demonstrating how closely tied musicians of the times were to the saints; they shaped the saints' characters through their compositions and control of liturgical books, populating the dramatic stories of Mass and Office and creating historical understanding through song and ritual action, as we will see in our study of St. Nicholas in Chapter 5. Keys to all this were Adémar's liturgical glosses, two different types of which are discussed below.

THE *QUEM QUAERITIS* TROPE

The Gregorian Introit *Resurrexi* for Easter Sunday (see Primer I.3 and II.1 and Anthology 3.1) is one of many Proper chants that were transformed through the additions of tropes in the late ninth, tenth, and early eleventh centuries.

Adémar copied a number of trope sets for *Resurrexi*, and all but one of the tropes work interlinearly, like glosses on biblical texts. Line by line, the texts of the Introits were explained by their tropes. Every Introit for a major feast had standard ways of being divided up for troping, but the actual elements of the tropes chosen for use are often regional. Each trope manuscript contains its own set of musical and textual phrases, fingerprints that can reveal fascinating details about music and culture, and many cantors had more choices than they could use on major feasts.

One trope in Adémar's book, the first one he copied out for *Resurrexi*, is not interlinear but stands alone at the very opening of the textual cue to sing the Introit. *Quem quaeritis* is the earliest type of trope, an introductory trope of special importance (see Anthology 8). In Paris, BN lat. 1121, it conforms to the way it was sung in southern French sources: first as a three-line dialogue (Ex. 4.7), then followed by two verses (beginning "The angel encamped") that sum up its meaning, just before the Introit cue:

> "Whom do you seek in the tomb, O Christian women?"
> "Jesus the Nazarean, who was crucified, O heavenly beings."
> "He is not here, but He has risen, just as He foretold. Go! Say that He is risen! Alleluia."
> The angel encamped at the tomb reports that Christ has risen.
> And behold that is fulfilled which He himself had said before to the Father through the prophet, singing, "Resurrexi . . . "

Example 4.7: *First four lines of the* Quem quaeritis *trope, as found in Paris, BN lat. 1121*

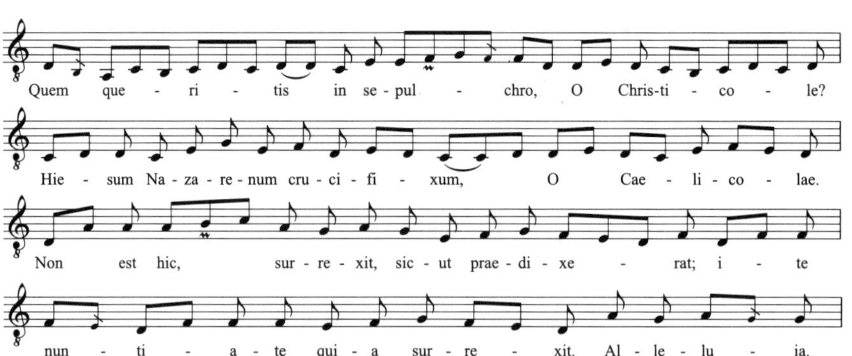

"Whom do you seek in the tomb, O Christian women?" "Jesus the Nazarean, who was crucified, O heavenly beings." "He is not here, but He has risen, just as He foretold. Go! Say that He is risen! Alleluia."

The opening three lines constitute an example of the *Quem quaeritis* trope, a short dramatic dialogue that came to be sung throughout Europe after the late ninth century, the time of its probable origin. Depending on geographical location, the dialogue was sung as a trope to the Mass Introit, or functioned in the Easter Office, or as part of a gathering ceremony or processional before Easter Mass. The melodies vary from region to region, but most share the same basic contour. The action represents the central mystery of the Christian faith and would have transported worshippers to where medieval Christians most wanted to be: the tomb of Jesus in Jerusalem, the symbolic source of every altar in every church. Adémar was writing down a musical play, a forerunner of the liturgical and religious dramas that we will study in Chapters 5 and 7. It is fitting that when he died in around 1034, it was as a pilgrim in Jerusalem.

HROSWITHA'S NARRATIVE OF THE ASCENSION

The nun Hroswitha (Hrotsvit) of Gandersheim (c. 935–c. 975) is another creative giant who flourished in this period. Like Adémar, the Saxon Hroswitha fits the profile of a cantor-historian: in addition to music, she wrote saints' lives, six dramatic works, and three histories. Unfortunately, none of her music survives, but her extremely learned corpus is rich with allusions to the art of music as well as to liturgical texts. In her narrative describing the Ascension, Christ's dramatic journey from earth to heaven in the presence of his disciples and mother, music joins heaven and earth, ancient times and the present, like a mighty trope:

> There came also in troops the ancient prophets, in whose midst was King David, skilled in song, amid the joyful strains of the lyre chanting these words, as he exhorted the Son of the Most High to seek His heavenly throne: "Lift Thyself . . . " Encouraging the angelic hosts, the prophet continued, "Exalt our God with a sweet song, glorifying Him with frequent prayer on His sacred mountain."

The tenth and early eleventh centuries were extraordinarily creative times for music: musicians wrote new Offices, melodies for the Mass Ordinary, tropes, sequences, and liturgical dramas. Perhaps it was the existence of so much new music that inspired new ways of notating: how else could music be transmitted and learned, when it did not exist in the collective memory? Whatever the reason, it was in the first half of the eleventh century that musicians began to use ways of expressing pitch by precisely arraying the neumes. As far as we know, they first did this with consistency in the Aquitaine, the region in which the Abbey of St. Martial was located. This is not to say that music ceased being an art of memory in such places. But from this time on, regional musical practices would diverge as a result of increasing dependency on notational advances. Much music of the European West, both sacred and secular, would evolve as part of a written practice, the legacy of the Carolingians and their immediate successors.

FOR FURTHER READING

Bjork, David A., *The Aquitanian Kyrie Repertory of the Tenth and Eleventh Centuries*, ed. Richard L. Crocker (Aldershot, Hampshire, and Burlington, VT: Ashgate, 2003)

Cochelin, Isabelle, "When the Monks Were the Book: The Bible and Monasticism (6th–11th Centuries)," in Susan Boynton and Diane Reilly, eds., *The Practice of the Bible in the Middle Ages: Production, Reception, and Performance in Western Christianity* (New York: Columbia University Press, 2011), 61–83

Crocker, Richard L., *The Early Medieval Sequence* (Berkeley: University of California Press, 1977)

Fassler, Margot E., and Rebecca A. Baltzer, eds., *The Divine Office in the Latin Middle Ages: Methodology and Source Studies, Regional Developments, Hagiography* (New York: Oxford University Press, 2000)

Grotans, Anna A., *Reading in Medieval St. Gall.* (Cambridge: Cambridge University Press, 2006)

Harper, John, *The Forms and Orders of Western Liturgy: From the Tenth to the Eighteenth Century* (Oxford: Oxford University Press, 1991)

Haug, Andreas, "Re-Reading Notker's Preface," in David Cannata et al., eds., *Quomodo cantabimus canticum? Studies in Honor of Edward H. Roesner* (Middleton, WI: American Institute of Musicology, 2008), 65–80

Planchart, Alejandro, "On the Nature of Transmission and Change in Trope Repertories," *Journal of the American Musicological Society* 41 (1988): 215–49

Rankin, Susan, "The Earliest Sources of Notker's Sequences: St Gallen, Vadiana 317, and Paris, Bibliothèque Nationale Lat. 10587," *Early Music History* 10 (1991): 201–33

PART II

Conquest and Devotion in the Eleventh and Twelfth Centuries

The period from the late eleventh through the twelfth century was a time of conquest, crusade, and pilgrimage. The old order of things was challenged as political entities waxed and waned. Theological and artistic modes of understanding shifted as well. One of the most important areas of transformation had to do with the development of what has been called the symbolist mentality, a way of interpreting biblical texts and the natural world. This way of thinking depended upon traditional ideas about how to interpret Scripture. There were four levels: historical, allegorical, tropological, and anagogical, and so, for example, the historical Mary was discussed as the mother of Christ. The allegorical Mary was represented by a large number of architectural images in Scripture, for she was an allegory, or type, of the Church. She speaks tropologically, or morally, about how a person should relate to God. Last, the anagogical Mary portends future events, the Second Coming of Christ, the Last Judgment, and the end of time.

If the Virgin Mary, or any character or event found in Scripture, could be read on many levels, however, so too could other complex manifestations of God. The natural world, for example, could be interpreted as a kind of language for human beings, as it was believed to have been created by God. The sacraments of the Church—its liturgical actions—were also seen as powerfully symbolic. Master thinkers of this period used symbolism to find various levels of meaning in Scripture, nature, and the liturgy; these meanings extended to such epic sagas as the quest for the Holy Grail, and, in the world of secular literature, to allegories of Ovid and Virgil as well. The symbols behind the meanings gleamed brightly with inner realities, as they often were seen to contain the essentials of the larger truths they represented.

Likewise, the art of music was transformed in the later eleventh and twelfth centuries into a vehicle capable of expressing multiple layers of meaning. This new expressivity was different from, although surely related to, the ways that music had been symbolic in earlier periods. Throughout the Carolingian Era, chants and genres of chant belonged to particular parts of the Mass and Office liturgy and functioned symbolically within those contexts. The singing of an Office psalm, for example, related to views about community and the power of music to sustain communication around the singing of these central texts. The clear, high sound of voices in a piece such as an Alleluia (sometimes performed by children) suggested the singing of the angels.

Although earlier symbolic ideals continued to operate, music gained new powers of representation in the eleventh and twelfth centuries. This was true in both polyphonic and monophonic repertories. As a result, several kinds of musical works were created that contained multiple levels of meaning on an even grander scale. The intense desire to represent the saints through art and music led to multimedia displays in eleventh-century churches built of stone in the Romanesque style, whose thick walls provided extraordinary resonance

Europe in the Twelfth Century

for music. The display of relics in processions with many genres of music, as described in Chapter 5, depended on the visual and musical, as well as on motion.

New developments in notation would speed the ways this multiplicity of meanings operated in music. We have already seen in Chapter 4 that musicians in the area around the monastery of St. Martial in Limoges were learning how to notate music with specific pitches. Later in the eleventh century, as will be shown in Chapter 6, singers created polyphonic lines that unfolded with their own musical integrity above slowly moving plainchant melodies. Scribes began to notate this texture of music, sometimes called florid organum, for the first time around 1100 and in the region around St. Martial. In such pieces, the plainchant formed both a musical and a symbolic foundation for the exegesis delivered by the polyphonic voice. The ways that one voice could sustain an idea or theme while another elaborated upon it developed further in the twelfth century in many polyphonic textures.

Yet another way to create musical symbols emerged during the twelfth century in the Parisian sequence repertory (which we will explore in Chapter 7), drawing upon earlier ways of using contrafacta. Composers like Adam of St. Victor discovered that a sequence could be fashioned from a single symbolic melody, which then permeated the fabric of the new work with the theme of the older one. *Laudes crucis*, a sequence for feasts of the Cross, begins with a melody taken from an Alleluia sung on similar feast days. In the hands of the anonymous northern French composer who wrote this mighty work, the melody of the Cross Alleluia is referenced throughout, playing in the memories of the singers as they rendered the sequence, but then contrafacta were created for this sequence, building enormous sonic structures with symbolic meanings. Similarly, the nun Hildegard of Bingen used an existing Marian antiphon to convey symbolic meanings both in a newly composed responsory for the Office and in her play *Ordo virtutum* (The Order of Virtues).

Rhyme permeated several newly created genres of music in the twelfth century to a greater degree than ever before. Rhyming song texts, in both Latin and vernacular languages, allowed words and music to interact in new ways; often verbal and musical "rhymes" played against one another. The new style of song that arose in the later eleventh century, as discussed in Chapter 5, continued to develop through the twelfth century, yielding more-intricate rhythmic-textual units as well as shapely melodic cells that could be readily transposed from one pitch level to another.

Another major feature of musical aesthetics in the twelfth century relates to the development of Gothic art and architecture, which arose in the mid-twelfth century around Paris, where types of limestone good for intricate carving were found in abundance. The Gothic style uses many individual elements in repeated patterns that have powerful exegetical meanings. A large structure in which many elements cohere to form a whole can be found in many musical works of this period as well, from the hymn collection of the renowned scholar Peter Abelard, to the huge families of sequences composed at the Abbey of St. Victor in Paris, to elaborate dramatic works such as the early-thirteenth-century *Play of Daniel*. The idea that enormous formal structures could work through the combination of individual symbolic elements would inform much of the music and art of the later Middle Ages as well. We observe the beginnings of this kind of complexity in the period studied in Part 2.

CHAPTER FIVE

Teaching and Learning in the Late Romanesque

The Mass and the Office were highly dramatic ritual events in the Middle Ages; in major liturgical centers, they were exquisitely choreographed as well. Both unfolded around altars and in buildings that recalled the Church of the Holy Sepulchre in Jerusalem, built on the site believed to be where Christ was crucified, was laid in the tomb, and arose on Easter night. The dramatic scenes at the empty tomb formed the basis of hundreds of Easter plays, the kernel of which was the *Quem quaeritis* dialogue that we studied in Chapter 4.

In the eleventh century the size and materials of many church buildings in northern Europe changed. In some cases what had been various smaller buildings, including places for baptism, were drawn together and housed under one roof. As a result of new building styles and changing functions, interiors became grander and more resonant and better adapted for dramatic displays of many types. In these urban and monastic spaces, events in the life of Christ were depicted not only through the celebration of the Mass and Office, but also through vivid processions, elaborate ceremonies, and plays. One of the most highly developed and widespread dramatic rituals was associated with Palm Sunday, a week before Easter, and featured a reenactment of Christ's entrance into Jerusalem on a donkey for the Passover feast. As described in the Gospels, he was hailed by crowds that would turn on him and demand his death only a few days later.

On Palm Sunday in the Middle Ages, many European landscapes were transformed into stylized replicas of Jerusalem, often using the local topography to re-create what was known about the Holy City. By the twelfth century, many places had artworks that could be brought out for the occasion, such as a statue of Jesus riding a wooden donkey, sometimes mounted on wheels (Fig. 5.1). Special music was adapted for the processions, which often lasted for many hours. Townspeople joined in the fray along with local monks and clergy, waving greenery that represented palm fronds and shouting "hosanna." (The word is a Latin translation through Greek of the Hebrew word *hoshi'ah-nna*, which literally means "save, I pray," but also is used as a praiseful greeting because it was once shouted at kings.) Child choristers had special music to sing during the elaborate reenactment. In many cathedral towns, the bishop played the ceremonial role of Christ throughout the day, and the festivities ended up in the cathedral or other main church after stations (specific ceremonies of prayer) had been offered at other places.

Figure 5.1: *Twelfth-century wooden replica of Christ on a donkey, for processional use*

ADÉMAR'S DESCRIPTION OF A RELIC IN ACTION

Dramatic depictions of events in the life of Christ were expanded in the eleventh century to include events from lives of the saints, whose presence was evoked through relics and reliquaries (ornate vessels in which sacred relics were preserved). There is nothing today quite like the widespread veneration of relics practiced in the Middle Ages, although the way people idolize rock stars and sports figures, longing to touch their clothing or possess bits of their hair, comes close. The community of saints was believed to support people, to pray for them in heaven, and to intercede for them in times of trouble, including the devastations of war, famine, childbirth, and disease. Veneration often took the form of fairs held on major feast days, at which the saints' relics were paraded through the streets to the accompaniment of elaborate musical settings.

What if a film clip of such a musical extravaganza existed, written and produced by one of the most skilled musicians of his age? The next best thing is found in the chronicles of Adémar of Chabannes, whom we met in Chapter 4. In his account of an event that took place in 1016, he describes a display of ritual pomp surrounding the reception of a new relic, the head of the Christian martyr John the Baptist, in the monastic Church of St. Savior in Charroux, located in western France. According to Adémar, who may have been an eyewitness, people from all over France, Italy, and Spain flocked to Charroux, including the king of France, Robert the Pious, who brought a bowl of pure gold weighing 30 pounds and brilliantly colored silks to decorate the church. The idea that a new relic had been stolen or otherwise procured from the Holy Land, and thus was "authentic," had great prominence in the central Middle Ages.

Monks and secular clergy (clerics not attached to monasteries) from the surrounding area brought their own relics, forming an enormous procession of saints to whom the marching crowd sang hymns of veneration. When the procession arrived at its first station, the monks of Charroux came out to greet it. They then escorted the people back to the Church of St. Savior and up to the altar, all the while singing hymns "in a loud voice." After a religious service, there was another procession to a nearby church dedicated to John the Baptist. Although it was October, the Mass celebrating the Birth of John the Baptist, normally sung in June, was celebrated to give special honor to the saint and the newly acquired testimony to his presence. Tropes and the Gloria were sung antiphonally by monks from one church and canons from another, thus creating a sonic emblem of communal praise. At the end, the head of John the Baptist was brought forward and blessed the crowd (Fig. 5.2). One can imagine the relic moving up and down in ritual benediction, encased in a head-shaped reliquary that doubtless gleamed with gold and jewels. Adémar says that all along the road leading back to individual churches, there were reports of miracles.

All the kinds of music studied in this chapter and in Chapters 3 and 4, from the simplest hymns to sophisticated tropes, would have been heard on this

Figure 5.2: *Twelfth-century head reliquary, thought to have contained relics of John the Baptist*

festive day. As much as a religious ceremony, the procession was a vibrant concert combining many genres and performing styles in a multimedia display that involved many groups of people. The singing may have included improvised polyphonic versions of selected chants as well, for, as we will see in Chapter 6, there was a regional tradition of decorating the chant in this way. Moreover, such polyphonic elaborations were being notated in this very area in the late eleventh century.

MUSIC AND ROMANESQUE ARCHITECTURE

In the center of Charroux, where the ceremony described above took place, a single striking feature of the eleventh-century abbey church still remains: a tower built in an architectural style of the tenth through twelfth centuries (and continuing later in some places) commonly known as Romanesque (Fig. 5.3). The name refers to Rome, where many architectural features found in the style prevailed in buildings from antiquity. Typical of the style are buildings made from large blocks of stone and incorporating rounded arches, thick walls, and windows that are proportionately small. Massive towers like that of St. Savior made a statement about the Church's power. As places of singing and proclamation, they

Figure 5.3: *The Romanesque tower of the Church of St. Savior in Charroux, France (mid-eleventh century)*

also created an appropriate acoustical environment for the magnification of the sounds Adémar describes.

The tower of Charroux is built in an octagonal shape in imitation of the Church of the Holy Sepulchre, reflecting a tradition observed in numerous other buildings constructed throughout Europe to create a "New Jerusalem." The tower was located in the east end of the Church of St. Savior, surrounded by circular walls, an arrangement reflective of the Anastasis in Jerusalem (see Chapter 2). As centers for the cults of the saints that proliferated in the eleventh century, these medieval buildings were crowded with congregants and visitors eager to be among saints' relics.

Romanesque churches in general were larger and higher and had more stone surfaces than wooden churches built in earlier centuries. Stone churches were extraordinarily resonant, and thus good for the projection of intoned readings, monophonic chant, certain kinds of polyphonic improvisation, and the music of organs (which began to appear regularly in this period). For example, the vast crypt of Chartres Cathedral, built in the 1020s, amplifies singing over long spaces, making it possible for a huge crowd to be connected by music to liturgical action that is taking place over a football field away. By the same token, the resonant spaces of Romanesque churches blurred the spoken word, and it is no wonder that texts had to be sung, or at least intoned, to be heard in these buildings. The new chapels and side aisles with which Romanesque churches were equipped also offered more-intimate spaces for singing, and here too, modest musical means could make a substantial sound. Medieval musicians could sing for the requisite hours upon hours because they never had to push their voices to be heard.

CREATING CHARACTERS THROUGH MUSIC: THE SOUNDS OF THE SAINTS

In medieval Christian society, it was the saints who stood closest to individuals and communities, and helped them be strong or work out their innermost conflicts. Saints are holy people who died in a state of sanctity and are believed to live on in heaven. Some were officially recognized by the Church, but the bureaucratic processes necessary to do so were not in place until the later Middle Ages, and most saints from the eleventh century and earlier were local products. Medieval Christians talked to their saints, sang with them, and found in their miraculous lives instructions about how to live and how to understand the faith tradition and its sacraments. Yet saints were not only promoters of peace. Wars over saints' relics could be violent, and some saints' cults were used to foment hatred for marginalized groups, especially later in the Middle Ages. (The word *cult* at this time did not indicate a group of religious extremists; it comes from the Latin *cultus*, meaning "devotion" or "observance.")

To understand the saints is to know the Latin Middle Ages. Saints were not only inspired monks and local bishops; they were also men and women who exemplified calls to action and bravery: Agnes endured getting her breasts sliced off, Laurence was roasted on a grill, Sebastian was used as a target for archery practice. They were the men who slayed dragons (St. George) and the women who gave up potential husbands and riches to serve as medieval abbesses (Bridget of Kildare). The lives, or *vitae*, of the saints were often written to be intoned as readings in the Office, and chants and antiphons composed to accompany the stories restated or advanced the narrative in a variety of ways.

When a wealthy donor established a shrine for a saint's cult, he or she was not just creating a physical space for the performance of public and private devotions, but also paying for the work of singers and, if they were young, for their educations as well. The prospect of founding a chapel in the Middle Ages often inspired donors to give, just as endowing a building at a college or university does today. To endow a chapel meant that music, books, singers, services, artworks, furnishings, and clergy would all be supported for the work of liturgical prayer, a commodity that was a highly valued form of knowledge and that required refined training.

THE CULT OF ST. NICHOLAS

Nicholas was a saint of great importance to young singers and students in the Middle Ages, and several musical genres were associated with his cult. Nicholas was a fourth-century bishop whose relics, preserved in the Turkish city of Myra, were stolen in the eleventh century and moved to Bari in southern Italy. The church that was built there to house them, with its subterranean tomb, became s for its miracles and as a popular pilgrims' shrine. On December 6, as's feast day, choristers would often elect one of their number to be "boy bishop" for the season, allowing for the temporary inversion of rightful rule.

The great responsory for Matins *Ex eius tumba* tells the story of the miraculous oil emanating from Nicholas's marble tomb, which had the power to make the blind see and the deaf hear. Later, a version of a melisma in the chant was provided with syllables of text, constituting the prosula *Sospitati. Sospitati*, which became exceedingly popular in its own right, was written in a musical and poetic style that was coming increasingly into fashion in the eleventh century. The tuneful prosula, the opening of which is found in Example 5.1, called to mind the saint's miraculous powers, even as the oil from Nicholas's tomb was kept in reliquaries and displayed.

The sharp contrast between the flowing melismas of the responsory *Ex eius tumba* and the sharply marked and rhyming prosula is typical of the clash of musical styles found in the Mass and Office of the eleventh century, as newer texts in rhyming accentual verse were juxtaposed with earlier layers of chant. *Ex eius tumba*, a mode 1 chant, was part of a modally ordered set of responsories, generally placed last in the group of nine Matins responsories, providing a return to mode 1 after all eight modes had been sung through. Such a set of pieces was a mighty tour de force, for both performers and listeners, and demonstrates the systematic display of the modes within a particular genre of liturgical music. Example 5.2 depicts the verse of *Ex eius tumba*, sung to the formulaic tone for mode 1 used for responsory verses in mode 1. It can be seen that there is great emphasis on the reciting tone of A. In this case, as in countless other Office responsories, the formulaic tone for the mode has been adapted to fit the needs of the text. The responsory verses embody a method of improvising music for a text according to well-known formulas established for a particular chant genre (see also Primer IV.3).

The widely popular sequence *Congaudentes exsultemus* for St. Nicholas (see Anthology 9), written in the later eleventh century, was created in a style that would only intensify in the twelfth century. The so-called new song, features rhyming, syllable-counting poetry (known as accentual or rhythmic), with crisply marked musical phrases to match. Even the first musically paired lines

Example 5.1: *The Office prosula* Sospitati, *for St. Nicholas*

An abundance of oil delivers the sick to health; Nicholas was present for the protection of the shipwrecked.

Example 5.2: *The verse for the great responsory* Ex eius tumba, *for St. Nicholas, followed by the first half of the Doxology, sung to the same tone. In between, part of the respond would be sung.*

People rush on in swarms, wishing to see the miraculous things that are done by him. . . . Glory be to the Father and to the Son and to the Holy Spirit.

Example 5.3: *First two lines of the eleventh-century sequence* Congaudentes exsultemus, *a "new song" for St. Nicholas*

Rejoicing together, let us exult with tuneful harmony on the sacred Feast of St. Nicholas.

of *Congaudentes* (Ex. 5.3) announce that we are in a different world from that of the Notkerian sequence (see Anthology 7), although we can see the beginnings of such a style in Notker's poetry and its musical settings. In both styles, constantly repeating cadential phrases serve as anchors for individual pairs of lines. Yet it is the combined power of accent, syllable-counting lines, and rhyme that sets *Congaudentes exsultemus* apart from its ancestor.

Congaudentes exsultemus offers a narrative of St. Nicholas's life, beginning with miracles from his childhood and then moving to those he performed for others, including the saving of three virgins from poverty and depredation, and the rescuing of storm-tossed sailors. The hope is that Nicholas will hear the singers' petitions and offer aid to them in the tumultuous sea of life. Like the responsory *Ex eius tumba*, the end of the sequence refers to the miraculous oil said to exude from the saint's tomb and pleads for its healing power. Many sequences from the period similarly bring the action of a saint's life or of a scriptural event into the eucharistic celebration. By inserting popular saints' legends within the larger drama of the Mass, such pieces helped singers and listeners feel close to relics and their powers.

THE FLEURY PLAYBOOK

In addition to such purely musical narratives, Nicholas's stories were sometimes turned into short plays starring the saint himself. The so-called Fleury Playbook, one of the most significant collections of twelfth-century dramas, contains four plays for St. Nicholas. In these works some of the miracles featured in the Office chants and in *Congaudentes exsultemus* come to life, portrayed by flesh-and-blood characters who sing their sorrows and rejoice in the saint's generosity. One play involves a Jewish merchant whose wealth is restored by Nicholas and who comes to honor the saint. In another, a Muslim king steals the child of a Christian couple and enslaves it; on St. Nicholas Day a year later, the saint miraculously restores the child to its parents.

Yet another play is based on the legend of three scholars traveling to school who are robbed, slaughtered, and put into brine by an evil innkeeper and his wife. One can imagine how deeply this work would have resonated with students of the times, who were often mistreated when on the road. Nicholas invokes God's powers to raise the three scholars from their watery "graves," and as a result the saint is often associated with baptism. The story was often depicted in the carvings and decorations on fonts, large standing basins in which infants were bathed with water during administration of the sacrament.

The play *The Three Daughters* is also built around a famous Nicholas legend. It features a once-rich man who has fallen upon hard times. He has three daughters whom he can neither support nor provide with dowries so they might marry. Prostitution seems to be the only option. Yet, one by one, they are saved by bags of gold heaved through the window of their house, and in each case a suitor immediately appears to marry the newly endowed daughter. After the third miracle, the father waits to see who his benefactor is: he discovers St. Nicholas, only to be told that the glory belongs to God. (Moderns, of course, would recognize the saint as Santa Claus, "Claus" being an abbreviated form of Nicholas.)

An eleventh-century version of *The Three Daughters* (unfortunately without music) provides the foundation for the text of the late-twelfth-century play in the Fleury Playbook that does have music (see Anthology 10). This twelfth-century version has many of the features characteristic of later sequences and their poetry (see Chapter 7). As with all the Nicholas plays mentioned here, music is the sustaining force that underlies the narrative and aids in character development. We can assume too that this was the way epics and other kinds of poetry were declaimed to music. The *chansons de geste* are narrative works of many strophes, set to repeating melodies that could be reshaped by the performers for dramatic intent. The music generally cannot be reconstructed, although attempts to do so have been numerous.

There is no spoken text in the Fleury Nicholas plays; rather, they are sung throughout. Musically, *The Three Daughters* is one of the simplest, set to a small

Figure 5.4: *St. Nicholas (*left*) handing a purse to the three lamenting daughters and their father, on the thirteenth-century south portal of Chartres Cathedral*

group of repeating melodies that are tuneful and easy to sing. Yet it serves both to foreshadow the action and to delineate characters or groups of characters. It was music that could unfold with little effort as the energetic boy actors moved through the action of the play, sometimes, we might imagine, with comic effects. A thirteenth-century sculpture from Chartres Cathedral depicts the suffering father, with his daughters surrounding his bed. To our left, Nicholas hands a purse through a window (Fig. 5.4). Office and Mass chants, special prosulae and sequences, art works, dramatic scenes and plays—all combined to give life to characters from the Bible and hagiography (writings about the saints).

TEACHING AND LEARNING IN THE ELEVENTH CENTURY

The new churches built throughout Europe, and decorated and filled with wall paintings, were parts of monasteries or served as hosts for cathedral schools. As such, they were places of learning as well as prayer. There were generally not yet colleges and universities in Europe in the eleventh century (the University of Bologna, which claimed to be the oldest, was not founded until 1088). Young people who wished to be trained academically attended schools sponsored by the Church. We have seen that music was central to the ways children were taught from early childhood (see Chapter 4). The trained child singers in cathedral schools were all boys. Less is known about how girls were taught by nuns in monastic schools, although many of them were carefully instructed. In any case, ways of learning were in transition in the eleventh century, as we will see below.

The first things children were taught were the psalms, which they would have memorized and sung to tones (see Chapter 4). Psalters used for teaching were often glossed with words and phrases; children thus learned grammar and vocabulary as they engaged with the psalms. Many children had responsibility for performing tasks in the liturgy and for singing some of the more ornate categories of chants. All this teaching and learning is reflected in the work of music theorists from the first half of the eleventh century, who sought new and better ways to instruct the children in their care.

In southern Germany, the monastic reformer and builder Berno of Reichenau and his student Hermann of Reichenau (Hermanus Contractus, or Hermann the Lame) were responsible for new Offices suited to Romanesque churches, for treatises on music, for writings on astronomy and mathematics, and for history-writing as well. A similar versatility characterized their contemporary Odorannus of Sens, a musician, historian, and artist from northern France. Both Hermann and Odorannus compiled tonaries, and Hermann wrote a theoretical treatise, reflecting his interest both in musical speculation and in relating theory to practice. In two of his compositions, Hermann experimented with interval notation that used Greek and Latin letters, and wrote series of chants that rose systematically through the modes. One of the most beloved chants of the entire Middle Ages, *Alma redemptoris Mater*, for the Virgin, has often been attributed to him. The piece belongs to a group of four Marian antiphons that also includes *Ave Regina caelorum*, *Regina caeli*, and *Salve Regina*, all of which will be studied later in this book. So popular were these eleventh-century creations that they eventually became featured at Compline, the last Office of the day, as freestanding works, one eventually assigned to each of the four seasons of the year.

At the same time that Hermann and Oderannus were doing their work, and that Adémar of Chabannes was transcribing music in heightened neumes, a sophisticated group of musicians in northern Italy were experimenting with technical innovations in their teaching. Among them were Odo of Arezzo, who produced a tonary including a discussion of the modes, and an unnamed contemporary who wrote the *Enchiridion musices* (Musical Handbook, also known as the *Dialogue on Music*). The preface to this work, once part of a now-lost antiphoner, makes some fairly extraordinary claims: "Indeed, when I lived among you, I instructed, with no help other than that of God, certain of your boys and young men in this art. Some of them after three days of training in it, others after four days, and others after a single week, were able to learn several antiphons and in a short time to sing them without hesitation, although they had not heard them sung by anyone." How could these boys do "something which until now ordinary singers had never been able to do, with many of them continuing in vain to practice and study singing for fifty years" (SR 26:199; 2/18:89)?

The alphabetical notation advocated in the preface is utilized in the anonymous treatise; with it, students could sing at sight by associating particular letters with specific pitches. This was not a brand-new idea, but it was becoming part of a pedagogy that would change the teaching of music in Europe. Now, it was claimed, music did not have to be learned by rote or retained exclusively in the memory, but could be "read" from the page. Music was still an art of memory (see Chapter 3), but written sources would increasingly have a role to play in the way it was stored in the mind.

GUIDO OF AREZZO

The greatest and most innovative music teacher in the eleventh century, Guido of Arezzo (c. 991–after 1033), was heavily influenced by the figures from his region mentioned above and the ideas in circulation there. The antiphoner he prepared does not survive, but its prologue does. In this work he speaks about how foolish singers are because they have to learn everything by rote; even farmers know more! The time they waste on memorization would be put to better use learning all the sacred and secular musical literature. Guido describes what would make singing at sight from his antiphoner possible: "The notes are so arranged, then, that each sound, however often it may be repeated in a melody, is found always in its own row. And in order that you may better distinguish these rows, lines are drawn close together, and some rows of sounds occur on the lines themselves, others in the intervening intervals or spaces" (SR 27:212; 2/19:102). This is thought to be a description of something resembling the musical staff. Guido also used colors (yellow and red) to help identify the "rows" or lines in the staff.

In another work, the *Epistola de ignoto cantu* (Epistle Concerning an Unknown Chant; SR 28:214–18; 2/20:104–108), Guido says that he has long been misunderstood and abused by those who are either ignorant or envious. He compares his own situation to that of the early Roman artisan who discovered how to make molten glass strong and who was killed so that his innovations would not make royal gems worthless. How many singing teachers would be put out of business by Guido's teaching system? To hear him tell it, almost all of them.

How did Guido teach? In addition to his work with precisely heightened notes on lines and spaces, he developed a system of teaching sightsinging using what we call today solfeggio, sol-fa, or solfège. Drawing on ideas concerning monastic education already in place, he made the hymn *Ut queant laxis* for John the Baptist—who was held up as a model for monastic life—into a kind of medieval "Doe, a deer" (from the song "Do-Re-Mi" by Richard Rodgers and Oscar Hammerstein II in *The Sound of Music*, through which children are instructed in the solfège syllables). Each phrase of the hymn begins with one of the first six notes of what we would call the major scale, but set to particular syllables. Underlining the first syllable of each phrase, one has *ut* (C), *re* (D), *mi* (E), *fa* (F), *sol* (G), and *la* (A), making a hexachord, a series of six pitches (Ex. 5.4).

If a student learns the pitches with these syllables, and then superimposes this understanding of the relationships between whole and half steps on actual phrases and melodies, he will be able to sing at sight. What to do when the melody exceeds these six notes? For that we need to wait a generation or two, but eventually musicians would begin to modulate from one hexachord to another, in an action called mutation. People who can sing at sight have a row of relationships between half and whole steps memorized and move it like a grid over any piece of notated music. Memory still matters in such a system, but not as absolutely as when music was learned exclusively in an oral tradition. If one learned the system, notation could be used to store sets of pitches that could be retrieved, even if they were not memorized. In Guido's system, singing became more like reading words from a book. Yet musicians still needed to memorize other aspects of the melody—its rhythm, ornamentation, and style—and they got increasingly less help with these dimensions of music from notation as the eleventh century wore on. They also needed to learn the rules for improvising polyphonic voices to decorate the chant, a practice already well established in the ninth century (see Chapter 3).

In Chapters 18 and 19 of his treatise *Micrologus*, Guido provides lessons for improvising a polyphonic voice to a piece of chant to create organum "in which

Example 5.4: *The hymn* Ut queant laxis, *for John the Baptist*

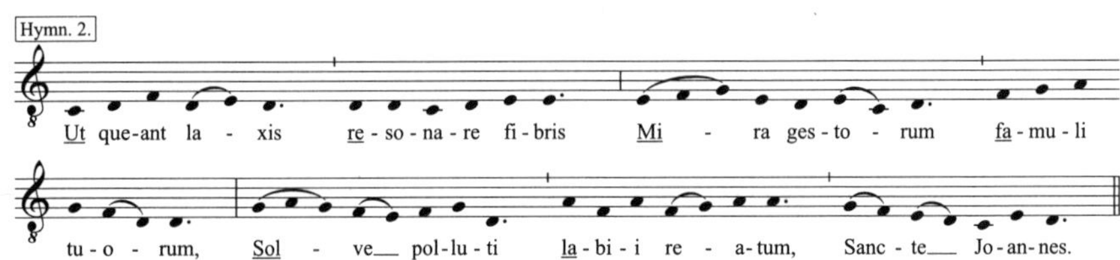

So that your servants may, with loosened voices, resound the wonders of your deeds, cleanse the guilt from our stained lips, O St. John.

notes distinct from each other make dissonance harmoniously and harmonize in their dissonance." He is very interested in how to arrive at cadences, and offers several examples of how to harmonize dissonance properly by means of voice-leading. He accepts both motion ascending stepwise to a final pitch and motion resting on the final until the principal voice arrives. He also offers an example in which the organal voice stays on a pitch while the principal voice moves both below it and above it, arriving at a unison cadence from above. (See below for a discussion of organum.)

The hexachord system and the so-called Guidonian hand are not described in the writings of Guido that survive, although later theorists attributed them to him. The "hand" used the knuckles and joints of the fingers to represent pitches as an aid in memorizing both music and theoretical concepts (see Fig. 5.5 below). It was one of many mnemonic devices in the Middle Ages that used the readily available visual aid of the human hand.

ORGANS AND ORGANUM

To increase magnificence and add splendor to their liturgies, many churches in the late tenth and eleventh centuries installed organs. The most vivid description of one of these early instruments was offered by Wulfstan, cantor of Winchester Cathedral in England in the 990s, who says (undoubtedly with some exaggeration) that its gargantuan instrument made 70 strong men "drip with sweat" to operate its bellows, and sounded so loud that "the music of the pipes is heard everywhere throughout the town." Two monks played the organ by pulling on sliders (strips of wood used to control the feed of wind to the pipes), of which there were twenty. Two players were required, apparently because the action was very slow.

Organs (from the Latin *organum*) allowed the proportions of musical intervals to be simultaneously seen (from the lengths of the pipes) and heard. One of the great mysteries of Western music history is how the organ, a squalling, loud instrument originally used for entertainment at court in the late antique world, became the only instrument welcomed into medieval churches. The evidence for the acceptance of organs in churches by this time is abundant, although no actual music for the instrument survives until the late fourteenth century. Other instruments, associated as they were with secular entertainment, were forbidden in churches. In general, music for instruments (including organ) was improvised, so there was no need to write it down. As a result very little instrumental music survives from the Middle Ages (see the introduction to Part III). Organs must first have been used for the most festive sacred pieces, perhaps located in lofts or galleries above the doors of churches to call people in during processions and welcome them with the kinds of elaborate musical displays that were favored for honoring the saints. The German theorist Aribo described the ways of measuring the shapes of bells to produce accurate pitches, the dimensions of organ pipes, and the intervals of the monochord, linking these to the numerical proportions of musical intervals, and thereby providing a strong rationale for understanding the organ in a religious context. His treatise *De musica* (On Music), written sometime between 1068 and 1078, demonstrated that the structure and sounds of the organ reflect the divine principles of number, proportion, and weight according to which the world was created.

The splendid character of the music and liturgy in eleventh-century Winchester is further demonstrated by the troper of Winchester Cathedral, Cambridge, Corpus Christi College Ms 473, the first surviving liturgically organized collection of polyphonic music. This volume, now dated to the 1020s and 1030s, contains many of the kinds of musical glosses described in Chapter 4, as well as a repertory of music for an organal voice, which, when sung with its intended parent chants, produced a significant body of polyphonic works. The Winchester Troper also includes other works intended mostly for soloists: Introit tropes, Kyries and Kyrie tropes, Glorias and Gloria tropes, Alleluias, sequences, Tracts, and Office responsories. The careful habits of the musical scribes, who tried to make it possible for singers to read from this tiny book, demonstrate yet again how vital increasingly sophisticated ways of writing were to the expansion of, and troping on, earlier practices that had developed in the eleventh century. The polyphonic repertories of the Winchester Troper show how far musicians were advancing through experiments with recording pitch, just by using the neumes themselves (see Anthology 11).

Musicians from the ninth century forward used the word *organum* when applied to singing to designate music expressed in a multi-voiced or polyphonic texture. Organum was exclusively created extempore until the eleventh century, when some scribes began to notate polyphonic works. In addition, as we have seen, *organum* could denote a musical instrument. It was also used to mean a song or psalm, as well as the great symphony of sound that characterizes the universe. It is hard to tell in some medieval writings, then, which sense is meant when the word is used. Central to all the music featured at Winchester in the eleventh century was a sense of proportion—in the resounding universe, on the organ, and in the well-made piece of music.

In Example 5.5 from the Winchester Troper, the chant or principal voice (*vox principalis*, abbreviated CV) is on the upper staff, which contains the opening of the Easter Alleluia *Confitemini*, and the organal voice (*vox organalis*, OV) is on the lower staff. The words provide the "bar lines," keeping the voices together. The scribe-musician of the organal voice probably worked with a copy of a chant manuscript at his elbow and wrote the voice out from the practice he knew, notating the organum in close relationship to the character of the chant—its phrasing, text setting, and especially, melodic contours. The modern editor must supply the chant for the principal voice from an appropriate contemporary manuscript, and in many cases these chants are in other fascicles (sections) of the same book, as here.

Example 5.5: *Opening of the Easter Alleluia verse* Confitemini, *as found in the Winchester Troper*

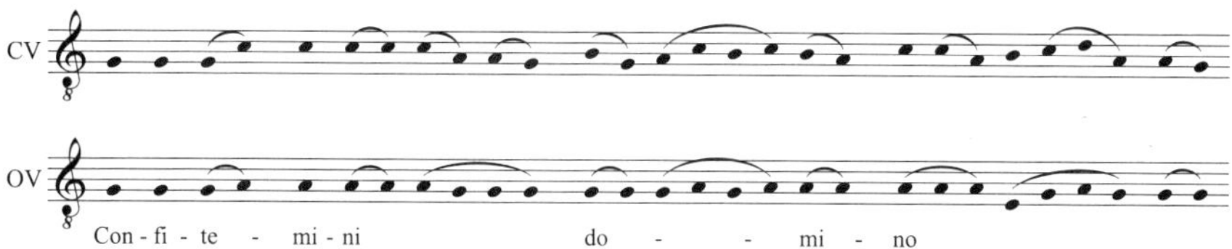

Alleluia, confess to the Lord

In this practice the organista (the singer of the organal voice) aimed to sing in unison with the chant at the ends of words or phrases, but could anticipate the pitch upon which a phrase would close, as in the final syllable of "confitemini," where the organista sings G while the singer of the chant descends to G through A. The organist might delay this moment of union (called, following Guido, an *occursus*) until after the principal voice has arrived on the final note. The organal voice stands out in character from the principal voice, with many phrases that consist of a series of *puncta*, or musical "sentences," giving the singer's work a kind of measured freedom not seen in the ninth-century examples found in the *Enchiriadis* treatises (see Chapter 3).

The dissonances that these practices generate make for a lively texture of push and pull, and allow the organista to experiment with ways to make his own line musically satisfying while operating within carefully fixed rules about range, intervals, and approaches to the unison pitch at the ends of words and phrases. The dissonances thus seem on some occasions to articulate syntax or to emphasize particular words.

On the Continent too, at Chartres and other major centers for chant, musicians were beginning to write down their polyphonic practices rather than being content only to create extempore. The new ways of notating music inspired them to record what had been solely an art of memory and to preserve written records of their achievements. The teaching of music in the early 1000s would develop further in the course of the century, as can be seen in the writings of an elusive music theorist whose name was John.

TEACHING MUSIC AT THE TURN OF THE TWELFTH CENTURY

John wrote *De musica* (On Music), one of the most widely copied theoretical works of the later Middle Ages, around the year 1100. He was once thought to be an Englishman named Cotto, from an inscription in his treatise, but now the designation "cotto" is thought to refer to his cantor's garment. The nature of his theoretical knowledge and the local variants in the chants he cites locate him both in Belgium and in Switzerland and southern Germany; there was constant exchange between monastic reformers in these two regions during this period. *De musica* is an intensely practical volume, written by a learned monk or cleric who knew Guido of Arezzo's theoretical writings and who wished, as theorists often do, to tame a large body of often-conflicting opinions into comprehensible clarity.

John's treatise is filled with charming asides that take us into the workaday world of the late eleventh century. At the beginning he mentions the use of solfège syllables and the Guidonian hand:

> So let him who strives for knowledge of music learn to sing a few songs with these syllables (ut, re, mi, fa, sol, and la) until he knows fully and clearly their ascents and descents and their many varieties of intervals. Also, let him diligently accustom himself to measuring off his melody on the joints of his hand, so that presently he can use his hand instead of the monochord whenever he likes, and by it test, correct, or compose a song.

The "hand" that John describes demonstrates that he was thinking not in terms of the tetrachords that were central to music theory in the ninth and tenth centuries, but rather in terms of hexachords, the six-note rows of pitches described above, in which a half step falls between *mi* and *fa*. Over the course of the twelfth century, John's views would be standardized into a three-hexachord system, one that would allow for mutation, or modulation, from one hexachord to another in order to move throughout a wider vocal range.

Figure 5.5 is a modern adaptation of medieval depictions of the Guidonian hand. If one follows from the tip of the thumb, where the first pitch, "ut" (do), is located, it is not hard to sing the first hexachord, which ends on the lowest joint of the ring finger, and then repeats beginning with ut again on the lowest joint of the little finger and ending on the top of the middle finger. Every ut begins a hexachord; another hexachord begins, for example, on the lowest joint of the index finger. Hexachords can begin on G, C, and F, as can be seen on the hand.

John gives names to the three hexachords. The one beginning on G is the "hard" hexachord, as it contains B♮, sometimes written with a square shape; C begins the "natural" hexachord, and F the "soft" hexachord, because B must be flatted, sometimes written with a round shape, or with a flat sign with a round shape:

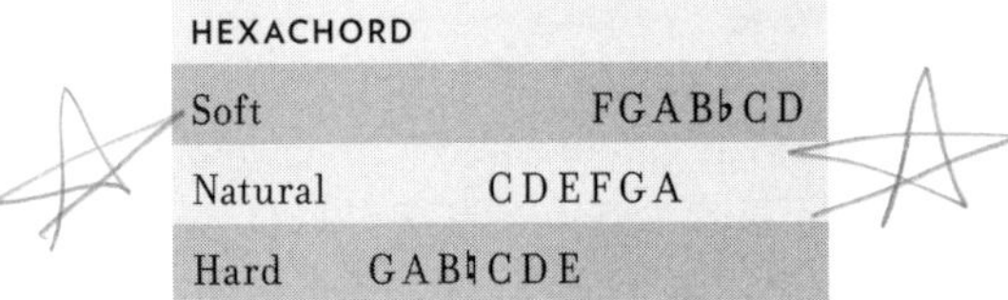

HEXACHORD	
Soft	F G A B♭ C D
Natural	C D E F G A
Hard	G A B♮ C D E

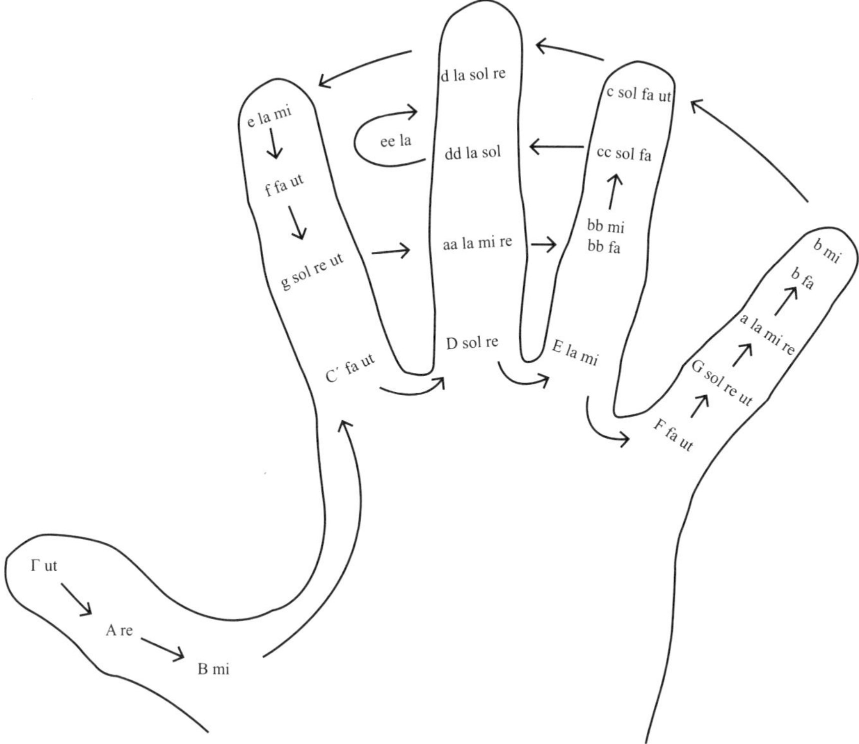

Figure 5.5: *Modern adaptation of the most common medieval version of the Guidonian hand*

Relationships between whole and half steps in each hexachord are the same, meaning that it is possible to modulate or transpose a melody from one to the other and re-create the same sounds at a different pitch level. The system of hexachords allowed musicians to increase the range of rationally controlled pitches, while remaining grounded in a well-understood group of pitch relationships.

The hand and the hexachord system provide a pitch name for each note on the gamut, from low G to the E nearly three octaves above it, allowing musicians to see and hear where they are in one or more hexachords with each particular pitch. (Gamut is short for *gamma-ut*, gamma being the Greek letter used for the pitch G, the first pitch of the system.) The distinctive names for each pitch are derived from their places in the system. For example, the C that falls on the first knuckle is fa in the hard hexachord and ut in the natural hexachord, and so known as C fa-ut. It is the first point of mutation, where a singer could move from the hard to the natural hexachord.

John goes more deeply into ideas about the power of music and its aesthetics than his model, Guido of Arezzo, but both thought of music in terms of phrases that were constructed and ordered in ways similar to the verses of poetry. John, like Guido, shows how to compose music using the vowels of the words to select pitches, the simplest manner of which is demonstrated in Example 5.6. The reader, called "you" by John, is instructed that to make this composition, using the text "Maria veri solis Mater libera" (Maria, free mother of the true son), you make two parallel columns, one with the vowels a–e–i–o–u, and the other with the "tetrachord of the finals" (D–E–F–G; see Primer III.4), plus one pitch. The result works quite well. After discussing other examples, John says: "See to it that the arrangement of vowels that we have presented does not lead you to suppose that they must always be arranged thus. Just as painters and poets are free to undertake whatever they wish, so, of course, is anyone composing thus." The idea of carving music to fit vowels would become an important device, especially in Renaissance motets and Masses. To make musical motives out of the sounds inspired by letters is yet another different but related concept, used most famously by J. S. Bach in his "B–A–C–H" musical signature created by assigning a pitch to each letter of his last name (H is B♮ in German notation).

The eleventh century's bold innovations in the dramatic arts, composition, musical form, theory, and teaching provided the groundwork for the individualism of the twelfth century, which we will explore in Chapters 6 and 7. Through their notational advancements and new theoretical constructs, eleventh-century musicians also ensured the preservation and survival of the music composed by the Carolingians in the ninth century.

Among their most lavish productions were the Offices they composed for especially favored saints. Such elaborate compositions summarize the theoretical and compositional innovations of this dynamic century, one that advanced the art of music and its structural principles in ways that are as historically important as the great strides made in art, architecture, and drama. All these arts went forward hand in hand, and it must have been thrilling to sit at the table with the cantors, builders, and patrons who planned new buildings and new musical endeavors to inspire people to pray with their saints.

Example 5.6: *Opening of a composition, following the method for generating new works suggested by music theorist John*

u	a													tu	a	u
o	G						so								G	o
i	F		ri			ri		lis			li				F	i
e	E				ve					ter		be			E	e
a	D	Ma		a					Ma				ra		D	a

FOR FURTHER READING

Fassler, Margot, "Adventus in Chartres: Ritual Models for Major Processions," in Nicholas Howe, ed. *Ceremonial Culture in the Pre-Modern World* (Notre Dame, IN: University of Notre Dame Press, 2007), 13–62

Forsyth, Ilene, "Magi and Majesty: A Study of Romanesque Sculpture and Liturgical Drama," *Art Bulletin* 50 (1968): 215–22

Hahn, Cynthia, "The Voices of the Saints: Speaking Reliquaries," *Gesta* 36 (1997): 20–31

Haines, John, "The Origins of the Musical Staff," *Musical Quarterly* 91 (2008): 327–78

Jones, Charles W., *The Saint Nicholas Liturgy and Its Literary Relationships (Ninth to Twelfth Centuries)*, with an essay on the music by Gilbert Reaney (Berkeley: University of California Press, 1963)

Kruckenberg, Lori, "Neumatizing the Sequence: Special Performances of Sequences in the Central Middle Ages," *Journal of the American Musicological Society* 59 (2006): 243–317

Rankin, Susan, ed., *The Winchester Troper* (London: Stainer and Bell, 2007)

Remensnyder, Amy G., "Legendary Treasure at Conques: Reliquaries and Imaginative Memory," *Speculum* 71 (1996): 884–906

Wright, Craig, "The Palm Sunday Procession in Medieval Chartres," in Margot Fassler and Rebecca A. Baltzer, eds., *The Divine Office in the Latin Middle Ages* (Oxford: Oxford University Press, 2000), 344-71

Young, Karl, ed., *The Drama of the Medieval Church*, 2 vols. (Oxford: Oxford University Press, 1933)

CHAPTER SIX

Conquest, Changing Tastes, and Pilgrimage in the Twelfth Century

Flete viri, lugete proceres,
Resolutus est rex in cineres;
Rex editus de magnis regibus,
Rex Guillelmus bello fortissimus,
Rex Anglorum et Dux Normaniae,
Cenomannis Dominus patriae.

Weep, you men; grieve, you, princes: the king has dissolved into ashes;
The king, chosen from the great kings, King William, most powerful in battle,
King of the English, Duke of the Normans, Lord of his fatherland, Le Mans!

These verses are from a lament for William the Conqueror, who came from Normandy, an area in northwestern France that was politically independent from the French king. William became king of England after he crossed the English Channel and triumphed over the Anglo-Saxon army in the battle of Hastings on October 14, 1066. The story of the battle is told in the famed Bayeux Tapestry, an elaborate and colorful embroidery some 230 feet long, created in

Figure 6.1: *William the Conqueror's warships as depicted in the Bayeux Tapestry, probably made in England in the 1070s*

the late eleventh century. In Figure 6.1, William's well-stocked fleet is depicted arriving at Pevensey Bay, about 11 miles from Hastings, on the southern coast of England. The equipment of war can be seen on the ships, including shields and horses; the postures of the zoomorphic figures in the margins of the embroidery portend the future outcomes of depicted events.

The song quoted above is of a type that would have been featured at court in the twelfth century; it is, however, a rare example of secular Latin poetry that survives with music actually notated at that time (Ex. 6.1). It is written in rhyming, accentual Latin verse, the poetic style that dominated in the late eleventh and twelfth centuries in liturgical song throughout Europe, the new song of a new age. It is a lament, written for a great king who conquered a neighboring region and was able to replace its existing culture—legal and administrative, linguistic, architectural, liturgical, and musical—with his own.

Example 6.1: *Lament for William the Conqueror, first line*

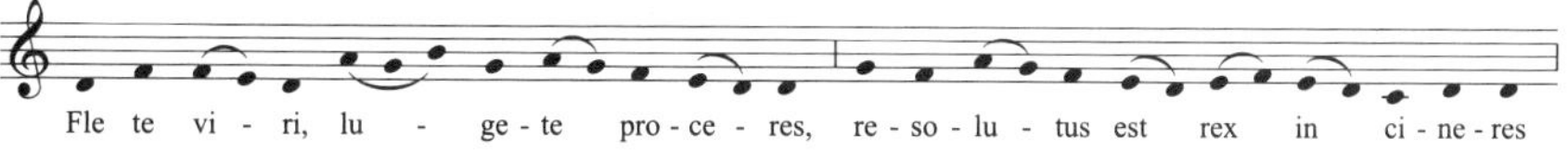

Weep you men, grieve you princes, the king has dissolved into ashes.

MUSIC AND CONQUEST

The conquest of England by the Normans was only one of many dramatic political and military shifts of power in the twelfth century. In all of them, music played a role. Musical practices in some areas, like England, were little affected by changes taking place in the twelfth century; the English already celebrated a form of the Roman rite, although their practices were altered. More-significant shifts occurred in Sicily, another area conquered by the Normans. Meanwhile, in the liturgical music of Spain, centuries of musical tradition were replaced by Frankish chant; this development left in its wake hundreds of notated Old Spanish melodies, seemingly of the finest quality, that cannot be accurately transcribed today.

The first age of crusading began at the end of the eleventh century: Normans and their allies marched to the Holy Land, bringing their liturgical and musical practices with them, and retook Jerusalem from the Muslims. Meanwhile, new religious orders sprang up, challenging older monastic traditions and bringing new ideas about the workings of liturgical chant to the fore. This was also an age of pilgrimage. Most pilgrims visited local shrines, but many longed for more-famous places, traveling from all areas of northern Europe to the shrine of the apostle James at Compostela, in far northwestern Spain.

Northern Europe was predominantly Christian in the twelfth century, as it had been for generations. But that faith became more militant as distant travel produced new encounters with Muslims in Spain and the Holy Land, and with Orthodox Greeks in Byzantium. Challenges from non-Christian faith traditions, along with those posed by new popular leaders and groups of people branded as heretics, demanded study and learning to defend cherished positions, and ushered in an increasingly virulent anti-Jewish strain in European life and thought.

Monasteries still maintained the most important scriptoria and so continued to be in charge of book production, including notational systems. The musicians who sang, played, and notated twelfth-century song were still by and large men of the Church, but the earlier monastic view of urban life as something to be avoided, or at least ignored, could not endure at a time of increasing travel, exchange, and economic development. Augustinian canons, for example, lived according to a rule composed by St. Augustine and so were monks of a sort, but they established their houses in or near major urban centers, where they could influence large numbers of people. The most important twelfth-century Augustinian houses were located in Austria and in Paris. The Abbey of St. Victor was established on the west bank of the river Seine, and an important school flourished there in the early 1100s. While local cathedral and monastic schools were still of major importance, many students and teachers gravitated toward Paris as a center of learning, in part because of the fame of the Augustinian Hugh of St. Victor and his contemporaries at the cathedral school of Notre Dame, which included Peter Abelard (see Chapter 7). The climate was warming, the population of Europe was growing, and more people were beginning to move from rural hamlets to the cathedral towns that would become the cities of later medieval Europe.

Thanks to the growth of secular learning, especially the increased interest in the literature and art of classical Greece and Rome, the twelfth century is known as a time of "renaissance" or rebirth. Henry of Blois, bishop of Winchester, perhaps the century's greatest patron of the arts, brought back statues from Rome to decorate his palace and other buildings. He also encouraged the production of lavishly illuminated Bibles and other books, supported artists influenced by the Byzantine style, and kept a menagerie of exotic animals. Henry's wide-ranging interests and penchant for travel made him part of a new learned elite that developed in the twelfth century, men and women who cultivated and appreciated music and art from many realms, sacred and secular, antique and new.

NORMANS ON THE MOVE IN ENGLAND, SICILY, AND JERUSALEM

The Norman Conquest brought significant change to several parts of Europe. French became the language of court in England, displacing Anglo-Saxon. New bishops and abbots came to rule over groups of Anglo-Saxon monks and clergy, bringing in Norman cantors to reorganize the repertory. The musical and liturgical traditions of the Anglo-Saxon kingdom were already essentially Frankish as a result of cultural exchange in the tenth and eleventh centuries. But English people had their own local saints, their own variants of Frankish chant, and distinctive repertories of tropes and sequences. In Glastonbury, some monks were purportedly killed while resisting the liturgical and musical changes imposed by the Normans.

In a long series of battles, the Normans also slowly took over blocks of territory in southern Italy. By the mid-twelfth century, their kingdom included almost one-third of the Italian peninsula, as well as Sicily, Malta, and territories in northern Africa. The splendid music imported into the Kingdom of Sicily at this time was completely French. It might seem unusual to have a Norman king in Sicily, surrounded by musicians producing northern repertories of sequences, Ordinary tropes, *Benedicamus Domino* melodies, Offices, and liturgical dramas. But such was the realm of King Roger II, who united all Norman territories in southern Italy under his well-managed administration, and defended the legal needs of his Muslim and Byzantine subjects as well.

Beginning in the late eleventh century, the Normans and their allies from northern Europe set their sights on Jerusalem, a city that had long fired the imaginations of western European Christians such as the nun Egeria, whom we met in Chapter 2. The reconquest of Sicily and areas of Spain from the Muslims made Christians hungry for further gains. The First Crusade was preached by Pope Urban II in the French city of Clermont in 1095 as a war to retake Jerusalem and contingent territories from the Muslims. Christians who fought and died would be honored by the Church as martyrs. A song designed to rev people up for conquest, *Jerusalem mirabilis*, begins with the exhortation "Marvelous Jerusalem, city more blessed than the others, there we must go!" (Ex. 6.2).

Some people embarked early, inflamed by the sermons of Peter the Hermit in Amiens, who organized children and peasants as well as knights into cadres. This movement inspired splinter groups, the most notorious of which marched through the Rhineland, sometimes killing Jews as they went. The climax of the First Crusade was the taking of Jerusalem in 1099, the culmination of a siege and battle that were proclaimed gloriously throughout Christian Europe and occasioned the institution of a feast commemorating the day.

Example 6.2: *Opening of the crusaders' song* Jerusalem mirabilis

Marvelous Jerusalem, city more blessed than the others

CRUSADERS' SONGS

Music played a fundamental role in the First Crusade, both at the beginning and in the settling of territory. According to one chronicler, Raymond of Aguilers, the Christians were about to concede defeat when a council of leaders commanded that they come together in common action. As a result, crusaders gathered outside the walls of Jerusalem, chanting with their relics and crosses, "blowing trumpets, brandishing arms, and marching barefooted." The power of relics and ritual action seems to have united the forces, for the next day, July 15, Jerusalem was entered and taken. The many tales surrounding the event spread throughout Europe and were retold throughout the twelfth century, empowering and redefining other services and inspiring many songs. The establishment of Latin kingdoms in the Holy Land in the wake of the conquest of Jerusalem meant that chant and liturgy were sung throughout the entire region. For three generations, Egeria's ideals lived again in Jerusalem and inspired countless other pilgrims to follow in her footsteps. If a trip to Jerusalem was not possible, there were other routes of pilgrimage through France, to Compostela in northern Spain.

One of the earliest crusaders' songs that survives with music was written by the troubadour Marcabru (fl. c. 1129–c. 1150).Troubadours were poet-musicians who lived in the south of France in the twelfth and thirteenth centuries. *Pax in*

Example 6.3: *Opening of* Pax in nomine, *by the troubadour Marcabru*

Peace in the name of the Lord! Marcabru made the words and the song.

nomine is thought to have been composed in the 1130s or 1140s, though it was written down much later (Ex. 6.3). Although it begins with a Latin phrase, the poem is in Old Occitan, the language of southern France, thus providing an early example of a religious song written in the vernacular. The song describes two bowls, one in Compostela and one in Jerusalem; listeners are called upon to wash themselves in one or the other. "Those who keep themselves at home will meet a powerful foe [the Devil]. They deserve to come to such an end." Marcabru is known for his moralizing tone, and the song demonstrates the pressure his contemporaries felt to make a pilgrimage of some sort during their lifetimes. (We'll have more to say about Marcabru in Chapter 7.)

Inspired by the crusaders' exploits and tales, Christians who stayed in Europe found many ways to represent the Holy Land in music, sculpture, and stained glass. By the time Jerusalem fell again, this time to the Muslim ruler Saladin in 1187, a sense of longing was reestablished in Western culture. The city would stay rooted within the artistic imagination, a sacred place that Christians believed to be their own, long after the Seventh Crusade had failed and Acre, the last Christian city in the Holy Land, had fallen in 1271.

MUSIC AND MONASTICISM: CLUNY IN CONTEXT

Many pilgrims who joined the route to Compostela from northern France and elsewhere would have begged hospitality from monasteries along the way, and many of these monasteries were shaped by the spirit of religious reform that spread throughout Europe in the twelfth century. Reformers took over weaker churches and monasteries, making accusations—false or true—of lax moral or liturgical practices, and then imposing their own customs, liturgies, and music in the process of reform.

Each monastic movement had its own approach to music and liturgy. Cistercians sought to simplify liturgical and musical practices, and built churches that avoided figurative decoration. Augustinian canons lived in towns and cities, and, hoping to reform the secular clergy of cathedrals, championed sequences in the new rhythmic style and their communal messages. Carthusians stayed in their individual cells, worshipped without tropes and sequences, and sang communally only twice per day. All three of these religious orders distinguished themselves from the most powerful and famous monastic foundation of the twelfth century, the Benedictines of Cluny.

Cluny (in modern-day Burgundy), founded in 910, was of major importance in the original formation and transmission of the Gregorian repertory. By the mid-twelfth century, it was one of the largest and most important monasteries in Europe. Attacked by reformers as being bloated with lavish liturgical practices and warehouses stocked with luxurious food and drink, Cluny was actually under a great deal of financial stress at this time, and, keen not to lose ground to the newer orders, strove to retain its share of the reforming pie. Its location and that of many of its daughter houses on the major routes of travel for pilgrims and crusaders proved essential to the goal of maintaining its influence.

Peter the Venerable was abbot of Cluny in the mid-twelfth century, the time of the Second Crusade (c. 1145–49). Like all Benedictine abbots, Peter was expected to conform to the model of Christ, but because Cluny was exempt from the oversight of local bishops, he had greater power than most. And he had charge of an enormous monastic complex. A modern plan of so-called Cluny III (the church into which the monks moved in 1122) and the buildings surrounding it suggests the various activities of the some 300 monks in residence during Peter's tenure and the splendor of their processions and liturgical activities (Fig. 6.2). The complex included a dormitory, a refectory, an infirmary, a guesthouse, an enormous church, gardens, a cloister for study, a scriptorium, and a library.

By virtue of the dispensations given to Cluny at its founding, it managed to retain a significant degree of freedom from secular and sacred authorities alike, creating independence in its own territories and wherever daughter houses were established. Many abbeys and priories in the far-reaching network affiliated with Cluny, eventually comprising some 2,000 institutions, attempted to follow the liturgical and musical practices of the mother house, at least to a degree. Cluniac monks, with so many churches to reform, were early masters at codifying liturgical practices through the production of customaries, books that filled out the *Rule of St. Benedict* with more detailed discussions, often with an emphasis on liturgical and musical practices.

Abbot Peter's views of music reveal a good deal about his times. He believed that music should be closely tailored to the season and hours of the day and the liturgical occasion, and he was willing to remove or alter pieces that didn't fit this prescription. Like many reformers of his age, Peter wanted the spiritual reality, or inner state, of a worshipper to be matched by what happened outside—by the words, the action, and the music. Ideas like these reflect the burgeoning interest in the individual in the twelfth century (as shown by the composers to be studied in Chapter 7).

The musical practices of Cluny demonstrate a great emphasis on the Divine Office. The Office for the Transfiguration of Christ, for example, featured strong

Figure 6.2: *Artist's reconstruction of the complex of buildings at the Abbey of Cluny, France, after the major building campaign of 1088–1121 (Cluny III)*

visual images, appropriate for an age when the powers of sight were appealed to in works of art, dramatic productions, and ceremonial re-creations of events in the Holy Land. A responsory from the Office reads: "Jesus took with him Peter, James, and his brother John, and brought them away to the top of the mountain. There he was transfigured and gave them to contemplate the brilliance of his glory. So that the sight of His Passion, far from troubling them, strengthened them still more."

The saints witnessing this miracle are Peter, whose head was kept in a reliquary at Cluny, and James, some of whose body parts were also enshrined at Cluny. St. James was the patron of the Cathedral of Compostela in Spain, the destination for so many pilgrims. Chants such as this responsory, sung near the relics of the figures involved, put Christian pilgrims in touch with St. James and helped them prepare psychologically for the long journey ahead. They might not make it all the way to Jerusalem, but they could "travel" there through the power of music and sense the miraculous presence of biblical figures. Brilliant capitals (sculptures at the top of columns) at Cluny prominently displayed the modes, as one of the remaining fragments shows (Fig. 6.3). The many ways in which music sustained the work of the Church and its liturgy were proclaimed in such architectural decorations.

Figure 6.3: *From a twelfth-century capital at Cluny representing the third mode; the figure plays a lyre*

POLYPHONIC REPERTORIES IN SOUTHERN FRANCE

The many liturgical manuscripts collected and preserved by the early-thirteenth-century cantor and librarian Bernard Ithier of St. Martial, located in the region of southern France known as Aquitania (or the Aquitaine), represent the most significant collection of twelfth-century music from all of Europe. The manuscripts contain everything from short monophonic works with rhyming accentual texts, to liturgical plays, to a variety of polyphonic pieces—works that were expressed in differing notational and musical styles, yet frequently maintaining intertextual relationships with preexisting repertories. In these manuscripts can be seen the kinds of music that cantors were collecting and writing down from the beginning of the twelfth century to the end.

As a result of changing tastes, some types of music were being replaced in the twelfth century to make room for new repertory. The music that was most vulnerable and open to change was usually that which had been added recently, comprising genres that were still in flux. There was dramatic change in the twelfth-century repertories of tropes, sequences, and newer music written to ornament parts of the services that required processions. Whereas the oldest layers of Frankish chant, the Mass Propers (studied in Chapter 3), remained in place and relatively unchanged, new Offices were always being written, increasingly in rhyming accentual poetry. As Proper tropes died out in many regions, newer repertories of sequences, Ordinary tropes, and various incidental works supplemented or replaced older repertories, and new relationships were formed with the older layers of chant. The Aquitanian sources feature many repertories of sequences and groupings of short pieces that allow for dramatic exploitation of rhyme and rhythm. These works, called *versus* in the Aquitanian repertory and *conductus* in northern repertories, existed in both monophonic and polyphonic forms, and represent the cutting edge of musical developments in the twelfth century.

The polyphonic repertories found in the twelfth-century books collected by Bernard Ithier were inscribed using a variety of notational strategies. Until the eleventh century, polyphonic works were ornamentations of plainsong, created on the spot and not written down. When they began to be transcribed, the practice slowly changed and the idea of a polyphonic "composition" emerged over several generations. We have encountered three ways of writing down polyphonic works so far in this book: using some sort of letter notation, as in the *Enchiriadis* treatises and other pedagogical works (see Chapter 3); writing out a polyphonic voice and expecting that knowledgeable musicians could supply the chant being ornamented, using the text as a guide, as in the Winchester Troper (see Chapter 5 and Anthology 11); and writing the music out with one line directly above the other, as was done in some early examples from Chartres (also mentioned in Chapter 5). However, newer ways to notate music were needed for polyphonic works that were increasingly elaborate and were no longer in note-against-note style.

Around the year 1100, musicians who copied early layers of Aquitanian polyphony wrote some parts successively, one voice following the other (Ex. 6.4a). Successive notation can cause problems for those who transcribe, especially given that some of the scribes were careless in making the copies. Soon after the triumph of successive notation, composers began to experiment with pieces written in what we would call score notation (Ex. 6.4b), see Anthology 12. This allowed them to depict one voice moving for significant numbers of notes, especially on a melisma, while another remained still, something that would have been difficult to express in successive notation or in other early ways of notating polyphonic repertories. But score notation, too, is problematic in many of the pieces that survive from the twelfth-century Aquitaine, especially when it comes to discerning precise relationships between the voices at cadences. This repertory, transcribed in

Example 6.4: Annus novus: *opening of polyphonic refrain*

(a) *written in successive notation*

(b) *written in score notation*

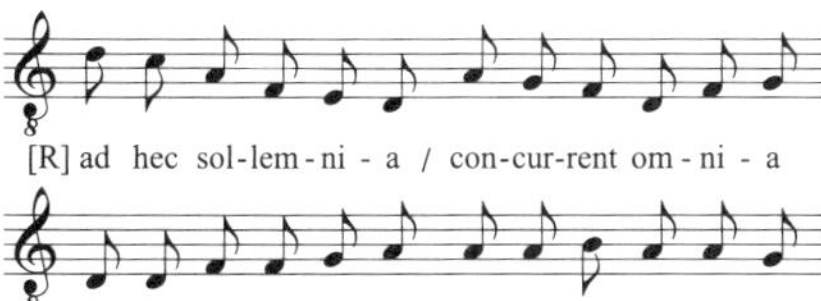

Let everything unite in this solemn festival

experimental kinds of notation, existed in a period of time of increasing dependency upon written and precisely heightened music manuscripts, and offers a host of challenges to performers today.

THE *BENEDICAMUS DOMINO*

A representative genre within the vast repertories of the Aquitaine is the *Benedicamus Domino*, a quintessentially intertextual piece. It was a versicle sung at the end of every hour of prayer (except Matins, where the *Te Deum* was sung), and also at the close of Mass during penitential seasons. The versicle in turn had two parts, *Benedicamus Domino* (Let us praise the Lord) and *Deo gratias* (Thanks be to God), both sung to the same music. Melodies for the genre were often melismas borrowed from well-known Office chants and so provided a musical summary, referencing works heard earlier in the day, much in the way of the *Ite missa est.* Because medieval composers abhorred an untexted melisma, *Benedicamus Domino* melodies were often served with prosulae, or were troped with additions of both texts and melodies (see Chapter 4). So popular was the form that the troped *Benedicamus* became a genre in its own right.

Sometimes the versified *Benedicamus Domino* shows a distinct playfulness. In *Annus novus* (see Anthology 12), the accentual, rhyming text mimics a Latin classroom exercise, the noun *annus* (year) appearing in a different case at the beginning of each strophe. This charming song for New Year's Day in praise of the cantor and his office may have been performed in celebration of the Feast of the Circumcision (January 1), also often a day of general revelry. On this day in many medieval cathedrals, one of the youth would be elected to serve as cantor, sometimes usurping the cantor's magnificent rod and cape. In *Annus novus,* the youthful singers may in fact be praising one of their own who is serving in a position of authority for a single day.

Different kinds of texture and notational styles are represented in *Stirps Jesse florigeram* (see Anthology 13). In this double-texted *Benedicamus Domino,* the lower voice sings *Benedicamus Domino* in slow, sustained notes borrowed from the famous Marian responsory *Stirps Jesse* (discussed in Chapter 4), specifically from the melisma *Flos Filius eius* ("the flower, her Son"). Above it, a second voice sings the text of a different melody that ends with the word "Domino." This texture is commonly known as florid organum. The entire piece is powerfully linked to the early-eleventh-century responsory *Stirps Jesse* (see Anthology 5) and expands upon the meaning of its text. The new styles of polyphonic music created on the pilgrims' road in southern France were often tied to music that all would have recognized, no matter from where in Europe they came.

MEDIEVAL IBERIA IN AN AGE OF RECONQUEST

No region in twelfth-century Europe was more contested than the Iberian peninsula (much of which is modern-day Spain). In the early eighth century the region had been conquered by Muslim invaders, who took it from its

Visigothic Christian rulers with striking rapidity. For almost two centuries, Jews and Christians lived under Muslim rule in Spain, and in the eighth and ninth centuries both groups paid taxes to be allowed to practice their religions. Things began to change in the ninth century. Slowly areas in the north were returned to Christian rule, and this reconquest continued until 1492, when all non-Christians were formally expelled from what was becoming modern-day Spain. But other kinds of conquest were taking place as well. The historiography is fraught with difficulty as each group—Muslims, Jews, and Christians—created their own sense of the past. As this is a music history book, most of our work will center on Christians who lived in Iberia and the period in which they became dominant once again (see Chapters 8 and 12). Here too monasteries were centers of manuscript production and Christian learning, just as they were elsewhere in Europe, but in the eleventh century they were about to be conquered too, and by other Christians.

For centuries the Christian Church in Spain, even under Muslim domination, had resisted the sway of Rome and the Roman rite, fostering its own liturgical traditions. It developed the cult of St. James as its own apostle, in opposition to St. Peter. During the eleventh and twelfth centuries, however, the old Spanish rite and its music was replaced by the Roman rite as promoted by the monks of Cluny, who were strong advocates for papal supremacy. The takeover began in 1028, when a monk from Cluny became abbot of San Juan de la Peña in Aragon and carried out reforms that made it the first church in the region to use the Mass of the Franco-Roman rite, and continued from there with greater intensity. Reformers who introduced the Frankish chant, as sung at Cluny, also brought Romanesque architecture to Spain. In León, for example, Queen Urraca of León-Castile built a church dedicated to St. Isidore that was Romanesque in style, with 200 carved capitals, a building perfectly suited to the newly imported chant and liturgy.

The chant of the Old Spanish rite is preserved in manuscripts dating from the ninth to the twelfth centuries. Those manuscripts that survive were produced almost exclusively in northern Spain and in southern France. Some sources from the twelfth century represent a repertory in transition, as one melodic and liturgical use supplanted another. The archival library of the monastery of San Domingo in Silos is especially rich in Mozarabic manuscripts. One of these books contains a small number of melodies written in Old Spanish notation, with heightened Aquitanian neumes in the margins.

There are a handful of other examples, but in general the Frankish and Cluniac musical conquest of the Old Spanish repertory was complete by the late eleventh century—and devastating, since we have so much direct evidence of the music that was replaced, but can only imagine its magnificence, given that the music was written in unheightened neumes and so cannot be transcribed. The Mozarabic chant and liturgy survived for two centuries, perhaps longer, in Toledo. But when it was finally written down in the sixteenth century, the practice seems to have been completely transformed by Frankish traditions.

THE CODEX CALIXTINUS

At the same time that the Old Spanish rite and its chant were being replaced in Spain, the shrine of St. James in the cathedral at Compostela was becoming the major pilgrims' site in all of Europe (see Fig. 6.4). The cult of St. James was celebrated through the music and texts found in a shrine book (a collection made specifically for the veneration of a saint's tomb) kept in the Cathedral Library of Compostela. It is a collection of varied materials: important Masses and Offices, miracle stories, a fascicle of polyphonic works, and a guide for pilgrims about how to get to their desired destination and what to look for upon arrival. Now called the Codex Calixtinus, after a pope to whom it was attributed, this collection provides an example of a mid-twelfth-century compilation created by composers from northern Europe for import into another region, and used by them to promote their own religious ideals (and economic agendas) in a place far from home. The ties to Cluny are strong, and the music has nothing to do with the Old Spanish chant. So at the heart of Spain's most revered shrine was yet another example of musical conquest. Although some Spanish scribes may have made contributions to the copying of the manuscript, its contents were clearly French.

The compilers of the Codex Calixtinus combined material usually found in lectionaries (books of readings), antiphoners (Office chants), graduals (Mass music), or troper-prosers (collections of tropes and sequences, which are often

Figure 6.4: *Musicians on the Portico de la Gloria of the Cathedral of Santiago de Compostela, Spain, third quarter of the twelfth century*

called proses in French-speaking regions). Apparently, a feast of St. James was ongoing throughout the year and then lavishly performed on the days actually dedicated to the saint. The book provides the best available example of the many ways that music worked within the cult of a particular saint in the twelfth century. Although the most important surviving copy served at the Compostela shrine, there are several other extant copies of the book, and the anthology might supply materials for the celebration of St. James in any church along the pilgrims' way.

We can imagine the throng singing the pilgrims' hymn *Dum Pater familias* at the end of the Codex Calixtinus. The musical instruments mentioned in Book 2 recall those shown on the Portico de la Gloria of Compostela Cathedral, which was under construction in the 1160s, making it nearly contemporaneous with the compilation of the Codex Calixtinus. The doors depict figures tuning their instruments and preparing to play at the imminent coming of Christ (Fig. 6.4). The description of the pilgrims provided in the Codex, even if idealized, is one of the few we have of twelfth-century pilgrims singing and praying at a shrine:

> Whoever sees these choruses of pilgrims keeping vigil around the venerable altar of Blessed James marvels with extreme delight. Germans remain in one area, French in another, Italians in a throng in another, holding burning candles in their hands, from which the whole church is lit up like the sun on the brightest of days. Each one sagaciously carries out his vigils by himself with his countrymen. Some sing with lutes, some with lyres, some with drums, some with flutes, some with pipes, some with trumpets, some with harps, some with viols, some with British or Gallic wheels [hurdy-gurdies], some with psalteries. Some keep vigil by singing to the various kinds of music; some lament their sins; some read psalms; and some give alms to the blind. Various languages are heard there: various barbarian calls, the speeches and cantilenas of the Germans, English, Greeks, and the other tribes and various peoples of all the regions of the world. . . . A solemn feast is always being celebrated there without cease; a feast is performed zealously; a great gathering is cultivated day and night; praise and jubilation, joy and exultation are sung together.

The Codex Calixtinus gave cantors a wealth of music from which to choose, claiming to offer the best that could be found in all of Europe for the glory of St. James (and some of it is attributed to Fulbert of Chartres!). There are Masses and Offices for the Vigil and Feast of St. James (July 25), a Mass for the Translation of the Relics Feast (December 30), a Mass for the Feast of Miracles of St. James (October 3), another Mass for any feast of St. James, verses to be sung with refrains in processions, and many instructions for what to do and when to do it, liturgically and musically. Of course there was no instrumental music; that would be left to the untutored pilgrims who may have been allowed to play in the nave of the church, at least in the twelfth century.

Many of the monophonic chants are contrafacta, preexistent melodies with new words chosen for St. James. We have seen that the creation of contrafacta was one of the most important ways that medieval musicians created intertextuality. The antiphon for the Gospel canticle of Compline, *Alma perpetui*, is a case in point (Ex. 6.5). Here the composer sets new words to the melody of the beloved eleventh-century Marian chant *Ave regina caelorum*. The stories of the two saints, Mary and James, have thus been drawn together through the power of music, using a melody that would have been recognized by all pilgrims gathered around the shrine and hoping for something miraculous in their lives. This chant, so familiar and yet with words so different, would have been the very last thing exhausted pilgrims heard before shuffling off to their modest sleeping arrangements.

Example 6.5:

(a) *Opening of the Marian antiphon* Ave regina caelorum

Hail, queen of heaven; hail, ruler of angels

(b) Alma perpetui, *a contrafactum for St. James from the Codex Calixtinus*

Nourishing light of the perpetual lamp, Apostle James

THE POLYPHONIC FASCICLE OF THE CODEX CALIXTINUS

The 20 polyphonic pieces contained in a separate section of the Codex Calixtinus suggest how multi-voiced music worked in the later twelfth century. Music in this special fascicle provides an early example of score notation. The pieces suggest great knowledge of the chant repertory: they may be the kind of music that composer-performers made as they improvised polyphonic lines for preexisting chants. The works were inscribed in northern French neumes, but because they are placed on staves, their pitches can be securely transcribed. The notator has also often drawn lines at the ends of phrases, ostensibly to keep the parts together at the cadences. This kind of clue is often missing in polyphonic works from the Aquitanian repertory.

The Mass for St. James from the Codex Calixtinus is filled with tropes of all kinds, and contains a sequence as well. The Gradual and Alleluia for this Mass are given in optional polyphonic settings. It appears that polyphony was used only for those sections of the chant normally sung by soloists: the opening intonation and the verse. These are notated with two voices; the remainder of the Alleluia is sung in plainchant. The plainchant Alleluia, not otherwise known outside this source, may have been designed for use in several contexts. It is wonderful to see what happens with the addition of a second voice. Jesus called James and John "sons of thunder" (using the Greek *boanerges*, as in Mark 3:17). The style of organum in the opening of the example is essentially florid, with longer-held notes in the lower voice (Ex. 6.6), as with *Stirps Jesse florigeram* from the Aquitanian repertory (see Anthology 13).

But the setting of some words shows another polyphonic texture not encountered before. In this style, which can be called "discant," the voices move at nearly the same speed, but in a prevailing contrary motion, for a startling effect. This can be seen in Example 6.6 on the final syllable "-ges." The upper voice in these discant sections unfolds in melodic sequences (or phrases) repeating the same motives on different pitch levels, artfully exploring particular melodic shapes. (As we will see in Chapter 9, this texture played a prominent role in Notre Dame polyphony of the thirteenth century.)

Of all works in the polyphonic fascicle of the Codex Calixtinus, the setting of the *Benedicamus* versus (conductus in northern parlance) *Congaudeant catholici* (see Anthology 14) has been the most discussed, edited, and performed. It is attributed to Albertus Parisiensis (Master Albert), assumed to be the cantor of Notre Dame in the mid-twelfth century, a figure at the heart of the Parisian musical establishment in that extraordinary time (see Chapter 9). Whether the voice added in a different-colored ink is meant to be sung with the two other parts, or is merely an alternative second voice, is a subject of controversy. The extreme dissonances produced by performing it as a three-voice setting have led some scholars to the latter conclusion. But if all the notated parts were intended to be sung together, *Congaudeant catholici* would be the earliest known three-voice polyphonic composition.

Even amid so much innovation in both the monophonic and polyphonic repertories in the twelfth century, *Congaudeant catholici* stands out as a sign of times to come, when polyphony would become the playing field for musicians' greatest creative endeavors.

Example 6.6: *Excerpt from the Alleluia for St. James in the Codex Calixtinus, showing passages in florid organum and "discant" style*

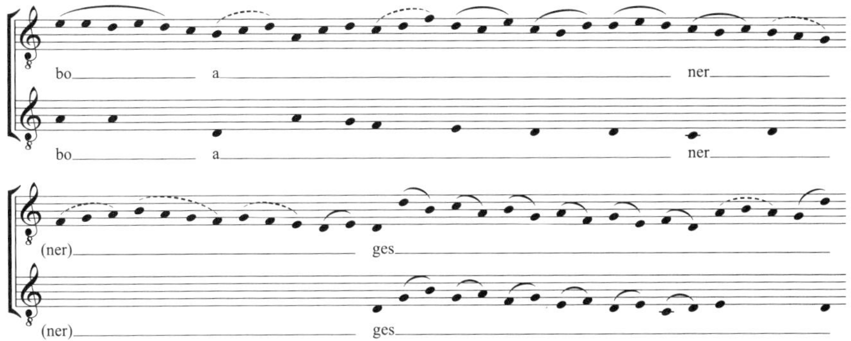

Sons of thunder

Many people in twelfth-century Europe made the journey from the northern reaches of the Continent, down pilgrims' roads past Cluny to Compostela, or through other routes by land or sea to Sicily, Constantinople, or Jerusalem. As well as feeding the desire for military conquest and for land and riches, this popular piety was important to the growth of trade and of the mercantile classes. Wherever people traveled, they brought their musical traditions with them. They also heard new styles of song and singing, and may even have witnessed new notational practices.

The regional differences that characterized the eleventh century continued throughout the twelfth century, but religious leaders increasingly sought to impose musical and liturgical uniformity in a Europe that was becoming more and more culturally diverse. At the same time, some religious orders manifested a desire for authenticity in the celebration of the liturgy. The Cistercians, for example, aspired to sing chant as it had been sung in the time of St. Benedict in the sixth century. Although such historical accuracy was a chimera, then as now, the twelfth century fostered a new respect for the music of the past just as people were looking to forge a new future through conquest, crusade, and pilgrimage.

FOR FURTHER READING

Abels, Richard P., and Bernard S. Bachrach, *The Normans and Their Adversaries at War* (Woodbridge, Suffolk: Boydell and Brewer, 2001)

Boynton, Susan, *Shaping a Monastic Identity: Liturgy and History at the Imperial Abbey of Farfa, 1000–1125* (Ithaca, NY: Cornell University Press, 2006)

Boynton, Susan, and Isabelle Cochelin, eds., *From Dead of Night to End of Day: The Medieval Customs of Cluny* (Turnhout, Belgium: Brepols, 2005)

Crocker, Richard, "Two Recent Editions of Aquitanian Polyphony," *Plainsong and Medieval Music* 3 (1994): 57–101

Fuller, Sarah, "Perspectives on Musical Notation in the *Codex Calixtinus*," in José López Caló et al., eds., *El Códice Calixtino y la música de su tiempo* (A Coruña, Spain: Fundación Pedro Barrié de la Maza, 2001), 182–234

Roesner, Edward, "The Codex Calixtinus and the Magnus Liber Organi: Some Preliminary Observations," in López Caló et al., *El Códice Calixtino*, 135–61

Shailor, Barbara, *The Medieval Book: Illustrated from the Beinecke Rare Book and Manuscript Library* (Toronto: University of Toronto Press, 1991)

Stones, Alison, Paula Gerson, et al., eds., *The Pilgrim's Guide: A Critical Edition* (London: H. Miller, 1998)

CHAPTER SEVEN

Poet-Composers in an Age of the Individual

The twelfth century, a time of increased self-awareness and self-expression, is sometimes called an "age of the individual." The new knowledge, especially concerning science and philosophy, that flowed into northern Europe from Spain and the Near East prompted a rethinking of the relationship between faith and reason. The traditional ways of defending Christianity were threatened not only by new methods of argumentation, but also by the rise of various heretical movements, especially the Albigensians in southern France and northern Spain. Just as theologians were pushing against the boundaries of orthodoxy, so musicians and poets were increasingly interested in how people related both to God and to each other across various cultural and social barriers. The troubadours, who flourished in what is today southern France and wrote in the region's distinct language, Old Occitan, were highly conscious of social rank, and often lamented unrequited love for aristocratic women who were beyond their reach.

The male and female poet-composers of the twelfth century were more willing than their predecessors to describe inner emotional states in their writings and music. As a result, we can for the first time place some of the music we study in the context of individual lives. By the same token, this is the first time that human love is explored in detail through music. All the poets we will meet in this chapter are concerned with the meanings of love that human beings have for one another and for God, both as individuals and in community. In some works human and divine love are explored simultaneously, touching on emotions that are deep, rich, and sometimes playful or ironic. At a time when many became passionate by identifying with the Virgin Mary at the foot of the Cross, the expression of emotion in music and the visual arts became more dramatically intense than in earlier periods. The scriptural *Song of Songs*, a book of the Old Testament, was increasingly interpreted as a contemporary love song, with Mary as its leading character, and poets and musicians found yet another framework for their new explorations within Scripture itself.

The new emphasis on individual psychology had further religious dimensions as well. In this period clergy became increasingly interested in learning to read people's confessions and probe their reasons for acting or feeling in certain ways. Manuals of penance for use in examining the consciences of people confessing their sins to a priest were compiled beginning in the later twelfth century by men at the Abbey of St. Victor in Paris. Members of this order of Augustianian canons were the confessors to the students who came to study in the city in ever-increasing numbers. Confession through examination of the conscience, necessary before taking communion at Mass, and the study of sin and its various motivations, provide the beginnings of the field of psychology. During this time, the confessor became increasingly like a doctor looking to the care of individual souls.

ABELARD AND HELOISE: LOVERS AND RELIGIOUS REFORMERS

Peter Abelard (1079–1142) and Heloise (c. 1090–1164), the century's most famous couple, drank from several fountains: first that of desire, then of theology, and finally of religious reform; but ultimately, the source was love. Their story, remembered continuously from the twelfth century to now, exists in many guises. These include two groups of letters (one accepted as authentic and the other not), in which Heloise's talents are on display; Abelard's autobiography, the *History of My Calamities* (written as a letter to a friend, but actually an attempt to achieve public rehabilitation); and some liturgical materials that relate to the Paraclete, the religious community for nuns the couple founded after their ill-starred marriage had come to an end. Abelard's work in philosophy and ethics included study of the inner motivations for external actions, a field related to new currents of twelfth-century understanding.

In 1114, Abelard, then a famous scholar in his late thirties who taught at the cathedral school in Paris, and Heloise, a brilliant student in her twenties, came together at Abelard's instigation. Although her uncle Fulbert, a canon at the Cathedral of Notre Dame in Paris (not to be confused with the early-eleventh-century figure of the same name whom we encountered in Chapter 4), trusted

Abelard's reputation for both learning and chastity, the woman was immediately seduced. At first Abelard seems to have hoped that Heloise would become his learned and elegant mistress, of the type that men of the secular clergy often enjoyed. When Heloise became pregnant, she was sent to have her child at the estate of his family in Brittany. Then, against her better judgment, the couple secretly married, for they had fallen deeply in love.

When Abelard asked Fulbert for his forgiveness, the canon pretended to give it and vowed to keep the marriage secret. Heloise, for her part, took the nun's veil to protect Abelard's position in ecclesiastical education. But Fulbert's men bribed Abelard's servant, gained entrance to Abelard's quarters as he slept, and castrated him. It seems that all of Europe knew of Abelard's shame. The rival philosopher Roscelin taunted him in a letter: "I am quite certain that names normally lose their proper meaning should the things they signify happen to lose their wholeness . . . you should be called not Peter but imperfect Peter." Abelard soon became a monk, joining Heloise in a life of celibacy.

Abelard's autobiography and Heloise's response offer a chance to examine a dialogue between them long after their intial encounter. Abelard's description of his tribulations is calculated to elicit sympathy. If you think *you* have a hard life, he seems to say, just look at mine and rejoice. A copy of this self-pitying document was passed to Heloise, who was pained by Abelard's misery and her role in it. Her reply is a noble defense of love in which she shoulders his troubles and blames herself for them. Both mention that Abelard wrote many love songs and that his works traveled far and wide. None of Abelard's love songs have been recovered, but the musical gifts that Heloise praised in one of her letters can be discerned in several chants attributed to him (some more securely than others): a hymn tune, three sequences, and seven laments—lengthy songs put into the mouths of biblical characters and perhaps composed to console Heloise.

ABELARD AS COMPOSER

The tune for Abelard's hymn text *O quanta, qualia* is one of the most beloved of the Middle Ages; it demonstrates how a simple modal melody can support a particular group of strophic texts (Ex. 7.1). Abelard composed an entire cycle of hymns—texts and melodies—for the Paraclete. Although the texts survive, the melodies, save this one, do not. Abelard created inventive texts that may have been challenging to sing, and so he produced the works in sets, each with its own melody and rhythmic scheme. The texts reveal Abelard's and Heloise's desires for dramatic hymns that were ideally suited to the liturgical occasion, by direct reference to the season, feast or day of the week to be celebrated. This can been seen in *O quanta, qualia*, composed for Vespers of Saturday. The text descibes longing for an "eternal sabbath," here placed in the circumstances of communal prayer in a particular place in the liturgy, "sabbatum." Saturday was often called Sabbatum in Christian liturgical books, and Sunday, Dominica (the Lord's day). It is

Example 7.1: *First strophe of Abelard's hymn* O quanta, qualia

Oh how many, how great are the Sabbaths which the celestial court celebrates eternally; which are the rest of the weary, the reward of the strong, when God will be all things in all things.

the kind of lexical and theological play that is found in many of Abelard's texts, always deeply rooted in knowledge of the liturgy as well.

First Vespers on Saturday was the beginning of the Sunday celebration. To make the connection, Abelard describes the endless Sabbaths of heaven's eternal liturgy in the first strophe of his hymn:

O quanta, qualia sunt illa sabbata
quae semper celebrat superna curia.
quae fessis requies, quae merces fortibus,
cum erit omnia Deus in omnibus.

Oh how many, how great are the Sabbaths
which the celestial court celebrates eternally;
which are the rest of the weary, the reward of the strong,
when God will be all things in all things.

The Easter sequence *Epithalamica* is one of the most complicated and beautiful compositions attributed to Abelard (see Anthology 15). The piece is composed in rhyming, accentual verse, exhibiting a variety of accentual patterns and incorporating a refrain. The sequence seems both to express Abelard's love for his wife and to praise God's redeeming love. Its very title, a rare Latin word which means "love songs," speaks of love. The poet fuses several images from Scripture: the lovers in the *Song of Songs*; the Wise and Foolish Virgins from the Gospel of Matthew, Chapter 25; and various female figures he associates with the Resurrection, including Miriam (who sings and plays a hand drum or tambourine in the Old Testament), the Virgin Mary, and Mary Magdalene, both at the tomb and in the garden where Magdalene encountered the risen Christ.

In this theological love song, the singers grieve when the beloved slips from their arms into the bonds of death, only to return for a joyful reunion. The textual refrain comes from Psalm 118 (117):24, "Haec est dies quam fecit Dominus" (This is the day the Lord has made), which is also the text of the Gradual chant for the Easter Mass (see Chapter 3 and Primer II.2). To cement the relationship to Easter, the poet also references the popular eleventh-century Easter sequence melody *Victimae paschali laudes*, bringing Mary Magdalene, who is mentioned there, into a new, more jubilatory context. The textual refrain used for the last four strophes of Abelard's poem, sung by the choir representing the bridesmaids, is set three times to three different melodies. The final line of the piece completes the biblical text of the refrain and, at the close on "Amen," repeats the melody of the first statement of the refrain (Ex. 7.2).

On yet another level, the sequence is an Easter drama that is powerfully intertextual with other elements of the Easter liturgy mentioned above. If *Epithalamica* was written for the Paraclete, the nuns played a significant role, as did Heloise, who lost her beloved husband but could regain him through a love that transcends and justifies loss. In the sequence, the bride is attended by the community, as represented by the choir. She has lost her husband and searches everywhere for him. She recovers him in the form of the risen Lord, heralded by the choir in the text of the Easter Gradual. The nuns of the Paraclete knew the story of their abbess's tragic marriage, and understood and welcomed the compositions of Abelard into their liturgical life. This chant, when sung on Easter at the Paraclete, would have united composer, solo singer, and choir of nuns, offering a joyful context for what

Example 7.2: *Final strophe of Abelard's* Epithalamica, *with the refrain "Haec est dies!" and the last line of the entire piece*

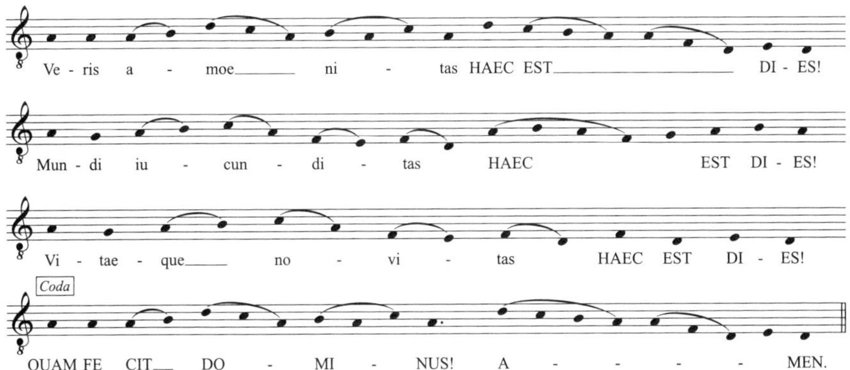

The delight of spring THIS IS THE DAY!
The joyfulness of the world THIS IS THE DAY!
And the newness of life THIS IS THE DAY!
WHICH THE LORD HAS MADE! AMEN.

was at first experienced as personal tragedy—a loss of love transformed through the sense of religious meaning and resurrection.

Heloise might have rebelled against this interpretation: in her letters to Abelard she recalled her passion for him and spoke about its control over her mind even while at prayer. Abelard may have hoped to comfort her, channeling this energy and redirecting it. Thin is the membrane that separates love of God from the passions that humans feel for each other, and religious composers of the twelfth century were skilled at exploiting the parallels and at fusing the one with the other.

Heloise was a different kind of nun than her contemporary Hildegard of Bingen, discussed below. Yet in their own ways, both were worldly. Heloise represents the type of woman many men thought made the best kind of abbess, one who had been married and had known the ways of the world. Hildegard was committed to the monastic life at an early age, yet she preached in various settings and welcomed consultation in her many letters. Both women were closely supported by male patrons, and this made possible the quality of life they enjoyed as intellectuals and artists.

THE MANY FACETS OF COURTLY LOVE

The first recorded repertory of love songs with vernacular texts was written in the twelfth century by poets from southern France in the language of Old Occitan (also known as Provençal). Love was a favored subject in part as a result of increased study of classical authors, especially the Roman poet Ovid, whose *Art of Love,* a book that describes how to meet Roman women and seduce them, was highly influential in the twelfth century. Ovid was known in bits and scraps by a range of poets who had read enough of him to adopt both his raw sexuality (and often make it even more explicit) and his duplicity and cynicism in matters of love. Views of love as expressed in well-known classical texts and in the contemporary world of twelfth-century Christians make understanding the emotion an intertextual exploration between several possible sets of meanings, some sexual, some courtly, some religious.

Perhaps because courtly singers were often patronized by wealthy women, this century also offered increased emphasis on the female perspective in literature, as well as a small body of poetry in the vernacular written by women. Queen Eleanor of Aquitaine (c. 1122–1201)—whose grandfather was an early troubadour, and who was married first to the king of France and then to his greatest military rival, King Henry II of England—managed an elegant court at various times in her tumultous life. So too did her daughters, one of whom, Marie, was married to the count of Champagne and was known for her support of poet-composers and the author Chrétien de Troyes.

Tailors were beginning to cut clothing to fit the body and reveal its contours, just in time for new attitudes toward women to emerge and songs about them to become popular, even as part of a written tradition. Style in language, clothing, and ideas was driven by the courts to a degree unknown before the twelfth century. Love too was subject to fashion, and depictions of it were built on the interplay between reality and fantasy, like the illusions created through the new attention to appearance. While women in earlier visual arts wore loose-fitting robes, the twelfth-century queens depicted at Chartres have slender figures with clinging garments that emphasize the lines of their bodies (Fig. 7.1).

Twelfth-century authors interpreted the complexities of romantic love across a range from the tragic to the comic. A framework for love songs can be found in many dramatic and quasi-dramatic literary works from the period, some of which may have been influenced by women or even written by them, and, as we will see, some of which have music interpolated within them. The *Council of Remiremont* sets the stage in a humorous way, exhibiting the playfulness that characterizes some literature from the period. It is a satirical poem that describes a mock church council; its ceremony is presided over and attended by nuns, who read from the "Gospel of Ovid" and debate which kinds of men make the best lovers, clerics, or knights (the clerics win hands down).

The Art of Courtly Love, a treatise attributed to the cleric Andreas Capellanus, was perhaps written at the court of Marie of Champagne at Troyes, and in the third quarter of the twelfth century. It is divided into three books, the first two describing love relationships between men and women of various classes. Andreas praises refined love in which the woman is treated magnificently, and depicts love itself as improving a man's very being, especially when it is unrequited. "Love . . . can endow a man even of the humblest birth with nobility

Figure 7.1: *Mid-twelfth-century jambs on the west facade of Chartres Cathedral:* from left, *a prophet, a king, a queen, and a king*

of character; it blesses the proud with humility; and the man in love becomes accustomed to performing many services gracefully for everyone. O what a wonderful thing is love, which makes a man shine with so many virtues."

In his third book Andreas turns the tables, exhibiting emphasis on argument and conflicting viewpoints. The noble flesh-and-blood Mary of the first two books reverts to a nasty Eve, a creature to be avoided at all costs: "Every woman . . . is envious and a slanderer of other women, greedy, a slave to her belly, inconstant, fickle in her speech . . . a liar, a drunkard, a babbler, no keeper of secrets . . . and never loving any man in her heart." With such ideas in circulation, it is no wonder that the nun Hildegard created a world in which triumphant souls had their own relationship with a gentle bridegroom—Christ—who would not violate or slander them.

THE FIRST VERNACULAR SONG REPERTORY

The love songs written in the twelfth century by troubadour composers are part of Andreas's courtly society. In such a setting, fraught with irony and multiple meanings, the several stages in a love relationship—seeing, conversation, physical contact, and consummation—could be either hurried or delayed. Relationships could stop at any stage from flirtation to sexual intercourse, but those that remained "pure" were capable of enduring longer. The emotions described in these love songs can turn inside out with the stroke of a pen, especially when the lover is rejected and needs to erect psychological defenses to protect a wounded heart.

In much vernacular poetry, the Virgin Mary and the country girl Marie—two women, one holy, pure, and unattainable, the other a shepherdess who can be conquered through seduction or force—grow closer in nature, and the interplay between them is often ironic. Troubadour songs must be understood within the context of these conventions, and the precise degree to which they depict the reality of their time, psychological or social, is difficult to ascertain. What is apparent, however, are the many interrelationships explored in this repertory between secular and sacred themes. This kind of interplay, which comes to the fore in the twelfth century, only increases in importance in the later Middle Ages, perhaps reaching its most elegant and provocative blending in the songs of Frauenlob (see Chapter 12).

The difficulties of recovering the music for twelfth-century vernacular songs are many; even the basic facts of composers' lives are hard to come by. Many poets did not sing their poetry themselves, but rather gave their texts to performers to sing, apparently using a repertory of adaptable songs that the performers held in memory; thus the poets' works often survive without melodies Every performance was some kind of re-creation, with great latitude for the artist working within an oral tradition particular to his or her own region.

Historians have often overlooked or even denied women's authorship of medieval song. Adding to the problem is the fact that only a small amount of music survives to go along with the poetry of the trobairitz (female troubadours), and none of it dates from the twelfth century. What we have, rather, are various thirteenth-century chansonniers, or collections of songs, some of which contain groups of twelfth-century works, sometimes accompanied by the *vidas*, or lives, of their composers. (These vidas were usually not compiled until generations later; the chansonniers are discussed in Chapter 8.)

Best known among the trobairitz is Comtessa de Dia, also known as Beatriz de Dia (fl. second half of the twelfth century). Of the five pieces attributed to her, one of them is a *tenso*, or debate. In fact, more than half of the poems attributed to trobairitz embody arguments of one sort or another. None of the details found in the Comtessa's vida can be verified, and it is possible that she is a created figure whose poetry cannot be securely attributed. Whatever the case, her shadowly figure helps us understand how the female voice was contextualized in the twelfth century. Her *A chantar* is the only trobairitz poem that survives with its music (Ex. 7.3). This love song, although not a full-fledged tenso, also references argumentation, as the woman makes the song her messenger, sent to her cold-hearted lover to define her noble love and describe her beauty, making her position strong although she has been rejected.

THE POETRY OF THE TROUBADOURS

It is always hard to trust the authenticity of a repertory written down so long after the fact, in this case only after the troubadour tradition was starting to decline. Scholars have developed various ways of judging quality and discerning the earlier layers of the music, including comparing surviving versions of single songs, many of which differ to significant degrees from one another. The textual traditions, too, are often so variable that even well-known poems such as Bernart de Ventadorn's *Can vei la lauzeta mover* (see below) have been reconstructed by modern editors from several varied sources.

Like the popular accentual Latin poetry of the twelfth century, the poetry of the troubadours was based on lines constituted of fixed numbers of syllables, although there was considerable variety in form from poem to poem. The particular forms of vernacular chansons that dominated the song repertory of Machaut and later fourteenth-century French composers had not yet been standardized (see Chapter 10). Unlike the sequence repertory created for the Abbey of St. Victor in Paris (see below), in which stock melodies were adapted for select

Example 7.3: *Last two lines of strophe 1 from* A chantar, *attributed to Comtessa de Dia*

6. C'a - tres-si sui en-ga- nad' e tra-hï - a 7. Com de-gr'es-ser s'ieu fos de-sa - vi- nens.

For I am deceived and betrayed, exactly as I should be if I were ungracious.

texts, many of the poems of the troubadours appear to have had unique melodies. It can be assumed that singer-composers each had their own repertories of tunes, only some of which survive. The rhythmic values of the notes are not known, nor are the various possible ways of adding ornaments or of accompanying the songs with instruments. Therefore, no two modern performances will be exactly alike.

In addition to the tenso, types of songs in the troubadour repertory include the *canso* (love song), *sirventes* (political song), *planh* (lament), *pastorela* (a simple courtly song involving a knight and a shepherdess), and *alba* (dawn song). Poet-composers often crossed these generic boundaries, which were not firm. The poems unfold in *coblas*, or stanzas. Stanzas may work in pairs that have the same rhyme scheme (*coblas doblas*), or the first line of each stanza may contain the rhyme word of the one before it, forming a different kind of linkage. Poems often close with a *tornada*, a shorter strophe directly addressing the lady or another patron. The genre of the song itself may have suggested to the performer the style of the melody.

THREE TROUBADOURS

The troubadour Marcabru, whose *Pax in nomine* we studied in Chapter 6, flourished in the second quarter of the twelfth century. His *L'autrier jost'una sebissa* (The Other Day Beside a Hedge; see Anthology 16), one of the most popular troubadour songs recorded today, represents the kinds of challenges this repertory offers to modern performers, who must make decisions ranging from fundamental issues regarding rhythm and the use of instrumental accompaniment to matters of pronunciation and mode of delivery. The simple reciting style of this *pastorela*, as illustrated in Example 7.4, allows the singer opportunities to create character and bring the drama of the dialogue to life, but does this mean that two singers might be involved? The knight's goal is to seduce the shepherdess through flattery, but she sees through his wiles when he claims that in the act of love they will become equals. She spurns his advances with wit and aplomb, even making them reverse roles so that she becomes the knight's master and wins a mock debate.

Example 7.4: *Opening of Marcabru's* L'autrier jost'una sebissa

The other day beside a hedge I found a humble shepherdess, full of joy and good sense, like the daughter of a peasant girl.

For modern sensibilities, this lighthearted story has disturbing overtones. As Andreas Capellanus writes of the relationship between a nobleman and a peasant woman, the man can take what he wants. In *L'autrier jost'una sebissa*, the saucy shepherdess wins the argument, but many twelfth-century women surely were not so lucky. The song, like so much in this poetic repertory, is a game, a back-and-forth, and it can be interpreted in many ways. But the male narrator tells the story and remains in control of the poem, even though he loses the match. Marcabru has laced a simple genre with high-flown ideals and intellectual word play.

For Bernart de Ventadorn, who flourished in the second half of the twelfth century, far more poems survive with music than for any other twelfth-century troubadour. Of around 41 poems, music is extant for nearly half. Bernart was born in southern France. That his vida is often attributed to the thirteenth-century troubadour Uc de Saint Circ suggests the ways poet-composers disseminated legends about each other and cultivated the history of the tradition. Troubadours engaged in repartee with each other, with members of courts they served, and with their patrons, some of whom could sing and play themselves. They were part of a loosely formed guild, and these relationships provided an intertextuality that helped create a sense of community among the artists.

Bernart's most famous song, a canso titled *Can vei la lauzeta mover* (When I See the Lark Beating; see Anthology 17), exists in many guises in the medieval sources and was clearly part of a lively oral tradition. The poem begins with the lark beating its wings for joy. Through analogy, the poet becomes a creature of nature who soars ecstatically at one moment, and then falls when he remembers his lost love. The tornada, which would normally be addressed to a patron, brilliantly transforms convention by addressing Tristan (Sorrow), who now owns the poet, instead of the lady who has broken his heart.

The expressive power of troubadour melodies and the force of their situational texts is represented in *Reis gloriós* by a contemporary of Bernart, Guiraut de Bornelh (see Anthology 18). The song, an alba, has seven short stanzas, each of which has a refrain to the words "and soon it will be dawn" (Ex. 7.5). In most dawn songs, the singer is a watchman who must announce the coming of daybreak—and the need for the lovers to part—to his friend who lies in the embrace (usually) of another man's wife. But this particular singing watchman is prayerful and mixes religion with his words of warning; he seems to lament the lovers' tryst as much as he fears for his friend. In the last stanza, the lover addresses the watcher, saying that he pays little heed to the dawn, to danger, or even, implicitly, to the loyal poet who has waited alertly throughout the night. Love becomes

Example 7.5: *Refrain from Guiraut de Bornelh's dawn song* Reis gloriós

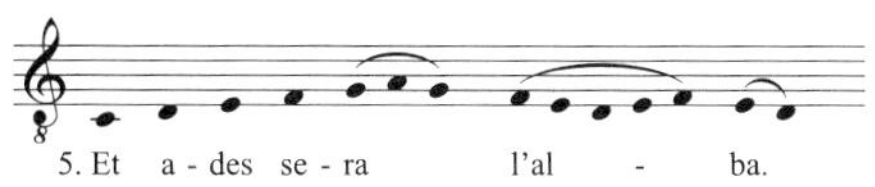

And soon it will be dawn.

an opiate, robbing a man of his senses, and a poet of his patron's affection and support.

THE AESTHETICS OF THE EARLY GOTHIC

In the Île de France (the area surrounding Paris) in the twelfth century, a new style of art, architecture, and music was born, today called Gothic. Throughout the late Middle Ages, Paris was the true cultural and educational capital of Europe. This was also the time that it first became a permanent home for the kings of France, and thus a center of political power.

Humanists of the fifteenth and sixteenth centuries thought of early Germans (Goths) as barbarians who destroyed the classical Roman civilization they valued so highly. They dubbed late medieval architecture "Gothic," and the name has stuck. It is used not only for art and architecture of the mid-twelfth through the fourteenth centuries, but also for a style of script and of music. The formal characteristics of the Gothic in architecture have to do with advanced building techniques—thinner walls and greater height, more-delicate carving, and pointed arches for doors and windows rather than the rounded ones of the Romanesque style (see Chapter 5). The ceilings in the naves of Gothic cathedrals have ribbed vaulting that makes for strength and height without adding weight and thickness. The beautiful uniform patterning of the vault ribs can be seen in the ceiling of Durham Cathedral, an Anglo-Norman church dating from the early twelfth century (Fig. 7.2).

Figure 7.2: *Twelfth-century ribbed vaulting in Durham Cathedral*

People reveled in the bold colors of large panels of stained glass designed to teach and to encourage prayer. The northern lancet window (a tall and narrow opening) of the west facade of Chartres Cathedral, one of the most famous surviving examples of an early Gothic window, dates from the mid-twelfth century (Fig. 7.3). As medieval decorative arts so often do, this window embodies musical meanings, in this case the *Stirps Jesse* responsory attributed to Fulbert of Chartres (see Chapter 4). The beholder of such a glorious window was directed upwards, from the bottom, where Jesse lies sleeping, to the lofty lineage of the house of David that sprouts from the patriarch's loins and includes the Virgin Mary and her son. It is possible that some sort of gallery at one time allowed visitors to gaze upon the glass from a closer distance than is possible today.

The Stirps Jesse window was designed for viewers whose minds were filled with the best-known melodies of the Chartrain liturgy. *Stirps Jesse* (see Anthology 5) was a signature chant of this community, sung at every Marian feast and on external processions throughout the year. The art has a powerful intertextual relationship with the liturgy and music of Chartres Cathedral. But it also can stand on its own, as a commentary on Old Testament texts. Jesse and his son, David the Psalmist, are types of Mary and Jesus, with a line of kings in between them. Prophets stand to the right and left, holding scrolls, and above seven doves surround Christ's head.

This window is governed by a kind of visual rhyme that comes from steady repetition of elements; it seems to have a beat that relies on the symbolic power of numerical groupings, especially as relates to the symbolic number seven. Seven represented time and history: the days of creation (including the day of rest); the lineage of Christ, which according to Matthew's Gospel proceeded in three groups of 14 (two times seven); the medieval belief in the seven ages of time; the days of the week; and the seven decades that were then seen as constituting the natural span of life. Seven related as well to the inner makeup of human beings: the seven gifts of the Holy Spirit extrapolated from Isaiah 11:2–3, frequently pictured as doves (as here), were seen as virtues (the matching seven vices are not found here).

In the window, each group of elements has seven units: the seven in the main "trunk" of the plant, the seven prophets to each side, the seven doves, the seven large floral groupings that sustain each figure in the plant, blooms of which they hold in their hands. This is art made for an individual to study and relate to other well-known things—in this case, to a familiar piece of music—and ultimately to use as an object of prayer. It allows the viewer to see through time, referencing layers of scriptural quotations and perhaps prompting thoughts about the viewer's own lineage: Who is your great-grandfather, your father, your mother? Can you remember them? Can you pray for them? The number seven is also embodied in various combinations in the mid-twelfth-century triple portal of Chartres Cathedral (Fig. 7.4).

Figure 7.3: *The Stirps Jesse lancet window in Chartres Cathedral, mid-twelfth century*

Figure 7.4: *The west facade of Chartres Cathedral, dating from c. 1145*

VICTORINE SEQUENCES AS AN ART OF MEMORY

The Victorine sequence repertory contains foundational elements that set the stage for our understanding of late medieval music, and for continuing to think about what it means that art and music in the Gothic period were designed for an age that was increasingly absorbed with individuals, and especially with their inner lives, their imaginations, and their communities.

The school of the Abbey of St. Victor, open to all students for much of the early 1100s, was an oasis that helped to account for the attraction that Paris began to have for young men seeking learning in the twelfth century. Resident there was one of the greatest theologians of the period, Hugh of St. Victor (c. 1096–1141), a contemporary of Peter Abelard and his intellectual peer (some would say rival). Hugh influenced the development of music at the abbey through his ability to use symbols to organize information, just as the idea of the *Stirps Jesse* organizes the lancet window at Chartres. In his book *The Moral Ark of Noah*, Hugh wrote that his students sighed over the "instability and restlessness of the human heart" and asked if "such a serious evil could be countered by any skill or the practice of some discipline." He then spent the rest of the treatise developing an enormous symbol of Noah's ark, one that organizes all of the information in the

Bible as a history with a Christian interpretation focused on the Cross, symbolized by the mast of the boat, and in turn representing the Church. The animals are treated allegorically. Seals, for example, represent people who can't make up their minds about religion; sometimes they swim in the water, and sometimes they clamber aboard the ark.

The repertory of sequences developed at the Abbey of St. Victor likewise used texts and music to fashion a musical ark of Noah, one that existed within individual minds even as it bound the community together through singing. Adam of St. Victor, another of the great poet-composers of the twelfth century, was instrumental in initiating both the large repertory of twelfth-century sequences written for the liturgy at the Cathedral of Notre Dame and the related but distinct Victorine sequence repertory. In the early 1100s Adam was the precentor (cantor) at the Cathedral of Notre Dame in Paris. A religious reformer, he left his position in the 1130s as a result of a theological dispute and joined the Abbey of St. Victor, where he died, probably in 1146.

Adam was the first in a long line of great musicians who flourished in Paris in the twelfth and thirteenth centuries, although it is difficult to attribute specific works to them. *Zima vetus* for the Easter season (see Anthology 19), probably by Adam, was part of an enormous cycle of 29 pieces sung at the Abbey of St. Victor, all based on a single work: the sequence *Laudes crucis* for feasts of the Cross (there are two of these in the calendar, one on Sept 14 and the other on May 3). As the repertory of Victorine sequences in this period was just over 70 works, the Cross cycle constituted nearly half of the entirety. A comparison of the opening of *Zima vetus* with the first notes of *Laudes crucis* (which may be too early to have been written by Adam) demonstrates how the Easter piece was ornamented and transformed, making the melody of the Cross used for the sequence *Laudes crucis* into a joyful Easter celebration in *Zima vetus* (Ex. 7.6). The music is "resurrected," showing one level of the symbolic system of compositions based on *Laudes crucis*. Each text set to some variation of *Laudes crucis* was engrafted into the huge symbolic structure created out of the music, and the musical cycle, in turn, relates to Hugh of St. Victor's commentaries on the meaning of the Church, the ark of Noah, and the Cross that he fashioned into a mast for the whole. The art of memory allowed each individual, depending on skill and intellect, to construct a sounding image of the Church within his or her mind.

Example 7.6: *Opening of the sequence* Laudes crucis (top line), *juxtaposed with opening of* Zima vetus (bottom line)

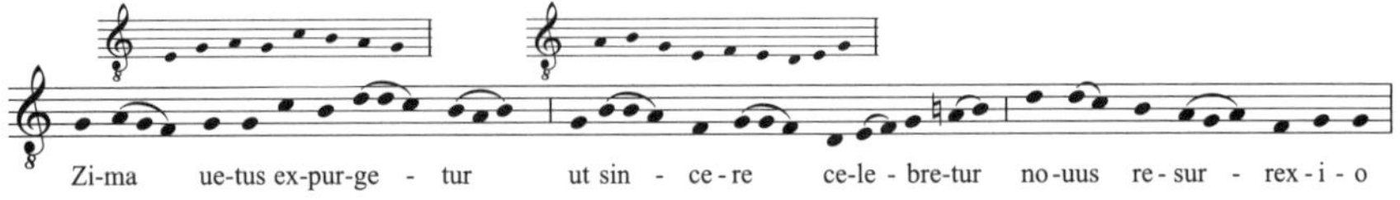

Let the old leaven be purged so that the new resurrection may be celebrated freely.

The repetitive lines of *Zima vetus* make a large-scale form whose steady "beat" is related to the repetitions found in Gothic architecture and decorative arts. The aesthetic that underlies such compositions compares in a variety of ways with that favored by the artists who created the Stirps Jesse window of Chartres Cathedral. In manipulating the individual segments of larger wholes as they counted out their poetry in the rhythms of set patterns of lines, Adam of St. Victor and his contemporaries laid the foundation for the attitudes toward rhythm and the compositional process that we will study in Chapter 9.

HILDEGARD OF BINGEN: LEVELS OF MEANING IN SONG AND DRAMA

The highly learned nun Hildegard (1098–1179) serves as a worthy representative of the dynamism of twelfth-century thought. Her long life encompassed work as a major theologian, poet, dramatist, composer, medical doctor, preacher, and administrator of a Benedictine priory she founded and had built near Bingen, in southwestern Germany. Her nearly 400 letters include much information about music and the arts, mixed with advice to people from many walks of life and from all over Europe, from local abbesses to Queen Eleanor of Aquitaine. Hildegard was renowned for her prophecies and visions concerning the central place of human beings in the creation and functioning of the cosmos. Her music can be viewed as an exploration of the role that praise and song play within communal life.

The importance of music to Hildegard is evident in that she was the first composer in the history of western European music known to have supervised the copying of her complete musical oeuvre. The nuns who copied Hildegard's works were part of a tradition of women copyists that continued in the later Middle Ages. Two manuscripts survive, one for use in her own monastery, the other produced for a male monastery in what is modern-day Belgium. Whereas many German manuscripts were still not copied in heightened neumes in the later Middle Ages, her chants are written in carefully heightened notation that can be read today. Hildegard surely realized that an art of memory would not serve to reconstruct these newly composed pieces; people would have to learn them from a written practice.

Hildegard wrote the text and music for some 72 songs as well as for a kind of morality play called *Ordo virtutum* (The Order of Virtues), considered below. These genres can be placed in the context of theological understanding through study of her *Scivias*, a record of Hildegard's visions completed around 1152. Incorporated into the final chapter of this treatise are the texts of some of her songs (the so-called *Scivias* songs) and an abridged version of the play. *Scivias* too was copied in her monastery, with illuminations probably inspired by Hildegard herself. Her work was part of an attempt in the Rhineland during this period to incorporate music into theological treatises. This can also be seen in the *Speculum Virginum* (Mirror of Virgins), written around 1140, and the *Hortus Deliciarum* by Herrad of Hohenberg (d. 1195), both of which include song texts, some of which have neumes.

What distinguishes Hildegard from all the other composers studied in this chapter is that she claimed to receive much of her music and her major theological treatises in visions that came directly from God. The portrait of her at the beginning of her monastery's copy of *Scivias* references both the Evangelists and Gregory the Great: as the Living Light pours down on her head, her lifelong friend and secretary, the priest Volmar, looks on, ready to transcribe what she says or sings (Fig. 7.5; compare the portrait of Gregory the Great receiving the chant in Fig. 3.1). Volmar, who was also the provost (the priest who served the sacramental needs of the community), was described by Hildegard as her *symmista*, a fellow sharer in the mysteries of the faith. The friendship between Hildgard and Volmar is an important kind of love that many religious men and women shared in the twelfth century. They worked together on common projects, and he was the likely person who taught her and members of her community how to notate music. *Mathias sanctus*, a sequence dedicated to Matthias, the patron saint of Trier, offers a vivid example of Hildegard's freely inventive and highly individual musical style (see Anthology 20). Trier, a major center not far from Bingen, is one of the places where Hildegard preached. The sequence also offers a sense of the kind of man Hildegard admired, one who was gentle and faithful, perhaps using her friend Volmar as a model.

Scivias unfolds in visions, each forming a chapter in one of the treatise's three books; after a vision is transcribed, Hildegard comments upon its meanings. The revelation that ends Book 3 is particularly suggestive: "Then I saw the lucent sky, in which I heard all kinds of music, marvellously embodying all the

Figure 7.5: *Portrait of Hildegard from a copy of a twelfth-century manuscript (now presumed lost) made by the nuns of the Abbey of Hildegard in Eibingen in the 1920s*

meanings I had heard before." The music Hildegard describes has three aspects: sounds of the saints, laments calling people back to rightful acts of praise, and the music of the *Ordo virtutum*, in which the personified virtues help secure salvation for those ensnared by the Devil.

The responsory *O nobilissima viriditas* was sung for saints who were virgins, an important group for a female monastery. In *Scivias*, Hildegard reveals where this song fits in her plan of the cosmos: she likens the virgins to a tree embraced by the divinity that shines in a brilliant sphere not touched by the earth. *O nobilissima viriditas* is a song of joy celebrating the undefiled Church that is powerfully allegorized by the Virgin Mary. The plant Hildegard designed through the texts and music of her songs for Virgins is a redefined Stirps Jesse; not surprisingly, the chant *Stirps Jesse* was popular in the region of Germany around Bingen, and various ways of depicting a tree with virtues and biblical figures in the branches are found in twelfth-century illuminated manuscripts.

As shown in Example 7.7, *O nobilissima viriditas* is an improvisation on the beloved eleventh-century Marian antiphon *Ave regina caelorum*. Hildegard quotes the antiphon directly in the first long melisma, on "O." She then takes off on an extraordinary set of variations, coming back to the parent chant fleetingly, and ever more rhapsodically, as she provides a sonic foretaste of paradise. In Hildegard's songs the Virgin Mary serves as a model for love between God and human beings. The Virgin's powers would find new manifestations in various sorts of secular works, both monophonic and polyphonic, beginning in this period and becoming more important in the thirteenth-century motets studied in Chapters 9 and 10.

Example 7.7:

(a) *The Marian antiphon* Ave regina caelorum

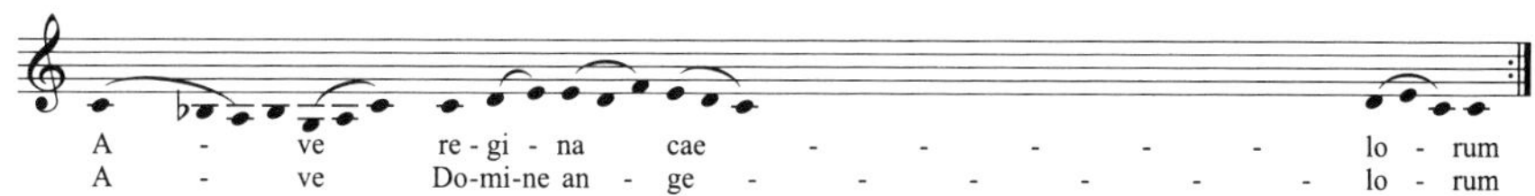

Hail, Queen of heaven. Hail, Lady of the angels.

(b) *Opening of Hildegard's responsory* O nobilissima viriditas, *based on the Marian antiphon* Ave regina caelorum. *Borrowed notes have white noteheads.*

O most noble greenness

THE *ORDO VIRTUTUM*

While the *Scivias* songs resound in the ether, Hildegard's play *Ordo virtutum* unfolds in the earthly center of the universe, a place of struggle. The leading character is Anima, a human soul, who has chosen worldly ways and is seduced by the Devil. The virtues, who would have been played by the members of Hildegard's community, sing to the lost soul of goodness, each allegorizing particular inner states. The Devil (perhaps played by Volmar) is the only character who merely speaks his part, as Satan challenges the soul to love the tangible goods of the world and ignore the unseen workings of faith.

When Victory binds the Devil, she sings from the middle section of the Marian antiphon *Ave regina caelorum* (Ex. 7.8), thus linking this virtue to the greatest of the saints and creating a bond with the *Scivias* song *O nobilissima viriditas* (see Ex. 7.7), which quotes from the same antiphon. Hildegard has fashioned an elaborate group therapy session for her nuns, who would learn to support each other in every performance of this drama, as they leaned on the Virgin Mary and the familiar liturgical music written in her honor and refashioned in many ways in Hildegard's new musical creations. Who knows how Hildegard assigned the parts for her play: in accordance with what a nun was good at, or what she lacked?

On another level, the *Ordo virtutum* is about love and the place of the individual within the community. Each Virtue has a lover, the bridegroom of the *Song of Songs*, who is also Christ. The idea is that each soul can relate to him in a special way, becoming a new Eve in the monastic garden of Eden, and embodying a particular virtue that is part of a larger understanding of community life, but also in the life of the world as well. The love that Christ had for his mother Mary, his virgin bride, is the model to which all the members of Hildegard's community, and indeed all readers of the treatise, are encouraged to aspire; the quote from a famous Marian antiphon in Victory's speech, for example, underscores this point.

The virtue Chastity has an important role in the play, exemplifying the special love life that Hildegard envisioned for the nuns in her care. In one scene,

Example 7.8: *Victory's song from Hildegard's* Ordo virtutum *(*bottom*), compared with a middle phrase from* Ave regina caelorum *(*top*)*

Top: *Rejoice glorious virgin, more splendid than all*

Bottom: *Rejoice, O companions, because the old serpent has been bound*

Humility tells the other Virtues that she will hold a place for them in the royal wedding chamber. When Charity promises to lead them into the radiant light of the flower of the rod (that is, Christ), they respond that they will run to him ardently. Chastity then describes the consummation of the Virtues' encounter: "Maidenhood, you remain within the royal chamber. How sweetly you burn in the King's embraces, when the Sun blazes through you, never letting your noble flower fall. Gentle maiden, you will never know the shadow over the falling flower."

Human sexuality is a metaphor for divine love in this scene: the nuns in Hildegard's community, like the Virgin Mary, are fruitful without intercourse. The portrait of Hildegard in Figure 7.5, with the sun's rays streaming onto her mind, is yet another symbol of this directly experienced encounter, and one that also made her works incarnate. Hildegard separated her community from the male monastery to which they were once attached; perhaps this reflects her wish for the nuns to be free to sing and pray as they chose. But the play is not only about nuns; it uses their state and their community to advocate for a particular state of the Christian soul, one in which that soul can come like a lover to God.

The parade of figures we have encountered in this chapter is diverse, yet all were concerned with the role of the individual, especially as a part of a community. In their works, many of these poet-composers explored human and divine love, and often the relationship between the two. Abelard and Heloise were a pair of lovers who became monastic reformers. Troubadours like Marcabru and Bernart de Ventadorn, whose works began to define romantic love, flourished in southern France and produced the earliest surviving repertory of vernacular songs. Adam of St. Victor, working in a city (Paris) that would become increasingly important in the history of European music, developed the new aesthetic ideals that were also being realized in early Gothic art and architecture. Hildegard of Bingen composed what may be the first musical play about inner psychological states. The play's remaking of religious symbols placed the struggles of humans at the center of the universe, addressing their needs for love, and using the state of monastic life and of the consecrated virgin as symbolic of a greater whole. The dynamism of the twelfth century is reflected in all these figures, and much of their music pulses with a new force and drive that would also find expression in the notational advances of the thirteenth century.

FOR FURTHER READING

Abulafia, Anna Sapir, "Intellectual and Cultural Creativity," in Daniel Power, ed., *The Central Middle Ages: Europe 950–1320* (Oxford: Oxford University Press, 2006)

Aubrey, Elizabeth, *The Music of the Troubadours* (Bloomington: Indiana University Press, 1996)

Chenu, M. D., *Nature, Man, and Society in the Twelfth Century*, trans. Jerome Taylor and Lester Little (Toronto: University of Toronto Press, 1997)

Constable, Giles, "The Place of the Crusader in Medieval Society," *Viator* 28 (1998): 377–403

Klinck, Ann Lingard, and Anne Marie Rasmussen, eds., *Medieval Women's Song: Cross-Cultural Approaches* (Philadelphia: University of Pennsylvania Press, 2002)

Leigh Choate, Tova, Margot Fassler, and William Flynn, "Hearing the Heavenly Symphony: An Overview of Hildegard's Musical Oeuvre with Case Studies" and "Hildegard as Musical Hagiographer: Engelberg, Stiftsbibliothek MS 103 and Her Songs for Saints Disibod and Ursula," in Beverly Kienzle, George Ferzoco, and Debra Stoudt, eds., *A Companion to Hildegard of Bingen* (Leiden: Brill, 2013), 163–220

Noble, Thomas F. X., and John Van Engen, eds., *European Transformations: The Long Twelfth Century* (Notre Dame, IN: University of Notre Dame Press, 2011)

Sweeney, Eileen C., "Abelard's *Historia Calamitatum* and Letters: Self as Search and Struggle," *Poetics Today* 28 (2007): 303–36

Szövérffy, Josef, "'False' Use of 'Unfitting' Hymns: Some Ideas Shared by Peter the Venerable, Peter Abelard and Heloise," in *Psallat chorus caelestium: Religious Lyrics of the Middle Ages: Hymnological Studies and Collected Essays*, 537–49 (Berlin: Classical Folia Editions, 1983)

PART III

Schools and Urban Sounds in the Thirteenth Century

The thirteenth century witnessed new developments in notation that transformed the composition, performance, and reception of music. Many of these developments were possible because the art of writing and copying music manuscripts no longer was the exclusive purview of the Church in general, and of monasteries in particular. At the same time, the rise of the mendicant (at first, wandering, non-property-owning) orders, both Franciscans and Dominicans (studied in Chapters 8 and 9, respectively), meant that there were large groups of traveling preachers moving throughout Europe. These itinerant friars lived close to the people and sought to inspire them through sacred songs with texts in vernacular languages. Such works, meant for singing not in church but rather in the town square or on the road, constituted a kind of interactive preaching through song.

It was in the 1200s that repertories of songs with vernacular texts, including those of the troubadours studied in Chapter 7, were first written down in present-day France, Germany, Italy, Spain, and Portugal. Latin song, both sacred and secular, continued to flourish as well. It is difficult to say if or how secular song repertories were supported by the accompaniment of instruments, but in some times and places singers and players must have collaborated (if indeed they were not one and the same). Contact with the Middle East and northern Africa influenced the development of European instruments in the thirteenth century, as can be seen in the marvelous depictions of instruments found in the Spanish *cantigas* manuscripts (see Chapter 8). Unfortunately, we don't know what these instruments played, as virtually no instrumental music survives from this period. One of the earliest collections of instrumental dances can be found in a late-thirteenth chansonnier, *Manuscrit du roi* (Paris, Bibliothèque Nationale fr. 844, ff.5*r*, 104*v*), and there is no indication of how many or what instruments were used, or even if these were melodies to be adapted for singing in choral dancing. Yet these 13 estampies (a poetic and music form for dancing) constitute over a quarter of the surviving pieces of instrumental dance music from 1250 to 1430. Unlike singers, many of whom trained at choir schools and other ecclesiastical establishments, few instrumentalists possessed the degree of learning required to notate music. Instead, they played by ear, employing an art of improvisation that cannot be securely recovered (although many modern performers try their hands at it). Wealthy households, including those of high-ranking prelates of the Church, supported one or more such entertainers (known as *jongleurs* or minstrels) as a matter of course.

In the sprawling, noisy city of Paris, minstrels and mendicants mingled on a daily basis with students and professors from the new university. Statutes of governance were drafted by 1215 for regulating teaching licenses and fees, and by 1221 the establishment was called "a university of masters and scholars at Paris." Populations of medieval urban centers are difficult to calculate because tax records were not yet kept, but Paris around 1200 was the largest city in Europe, with some 200,000 inhabitants. Its growth rate in the thirteenth century was

Major Universities and Their Dates of Founding

phenomenal, in part because it had become a true royal capital during the later twelfth century, and in part because the ecclesiastical schools and university drew students from throughout Europe. Parisian musical culture was characterized by a cosmopolitan blending of sacred and secular repertories, as well as the creation of new genres such as the motet, discussed in Chapter 9. The soundscape in medieval Paris was surely different not only from the quiet of most monasteries, but from anything medieval musicians had experienced before.

Music did not play a major role in the university curriculum at Paris, although Boethius was still taught. Nevertheless, surviving thirteenth-century music theory manuscripts show how important it was for musicians to be trained in the new arts of composition and notation. Moreover, music was deeply affected by the scholasticism that originated with the master teachers of the late eleventh and twelfth centuries, including Peter Abelard and Hugh of St. Victor. As we will see in Chapter 9, scholasticism denoted a system of argumentation designed to refute or prove a point. In a typical thirteenth-century classroom, the master teacher would provide a lecture on a topic and then engage the students in a debate of various assertions, following the model of rigorous disputation set forth by Aristotle, whose works had recently been rediscovered. The idea of the debate, which was important to twelfth-century vernacular song, was important in thirteenth-century repertories as well.

Aristotle's ideas had a strong influence on many musicians in the late 1200s; among them was Johannes de Grocheio, the first theorist to write about the meanings of both sacred and secular repertories. (Since Grocheio wrote in Paris around the turn of the fourteenth century, he will be considered in Chapter 10.) Just as Aristotle deduced the categories of things from close observation of the natural world, so musicians like Grocheio—and visual artists as well—were increasingly interested in expressing what they heard, saw, and experienced, rather than in preconceived ideals. This is yet another reason that the musical repertories of the thirteenth century are so varied and rooted to the places in which they were made.

CHAPTER EIGHT

"Then Truly Was the Time of Singing Come"

> Suddenly, as at sunrise, the whole earth had grown vocal and musical. Then truly was the time of singing come; for princes and prelates, emperors and squires, the wise and the simple, men, women and children, all sang and rhymed, or delighted in hearing it done. It was a universal noise of song.
>
> —Thomas Carlyle, 1831

Throughout the Middle Ages, the liturgy sustained a network of singing communities, including nuns, priests, and clerics, and, by degrees, laity. Each community of liturgical song rendered the music in accordance with local variants reflected in intoned texts and special chants for favored saints and festivals. But from the thirteenth century forward, there is substantial evidence for other kinds of singers and communities that existed alongside those of the Church, and often in interaction with them, in making the "universal noise of song" that James Joseph Walch, quoting Carlyle, described in his account of thirteenth-century Europe.

As we learned in earlier chapters, secular repertories employed patterns of repetition called refrains. Refrains often help define form, and their use would be increasingly important in the standardization of the most important chanson forms—the so-called *formes fixes* (fixed forms)—that were not fully standardized until the second half of the fourteenth century, and that are studied in Chapter 10. In its most usual meaning, a refrain is a section of a poem or song that recurs. In song forms, the recurrence may be text, melody, or both. In some instances, only a part of it repeats. "Haec est dies" in *Epithalamica* (see Anthology 15) is a textual refrain; the refrain "and soon it will be dawn" in Guiraut de Bornehl's *Reis gloriós* (see Anthology 18) is a repeating line of both text and music, falling at the end of each strophe of the song.

But the word *refrain* has a different meaning as well: it can also denote a quotation, a word, or, more commonly, a section of borrowed text (and music) used to make an intertextual connection to another work, set of works, or ideas, which may or may not relate to the formal structure of the song. The ending line of Marcabru's *L'autrier jost'una sebissa* (see Anthology 16) appears to be a proverb taken from the oral tradition and quoted in the song. Nearly 2,000 refrains (quotations or citations) of this type have been identified; they are found interpolated within literary works as well as in monophonic and polyphonic songs (see Chapters 9–11). We can see several types of refrains operating in the songs studied below, and with both meanings of the word, a repeating section or a citation.

Each region produced songs in a dazzling array of styles and genres. Regionality and language were increasingly important determinants of the way music was created and sounded in the thirteenth century. St. Francis of Assisi wrote popular songs in Italian; students turned clerical music into polemical and lewd Latin songs; clerics reset secular songs with pious texts; a great variety of trouvères (writers of secular songs in northern France) flourished, from the rich and powerful Thibaut, count of Champagne, to Adam de la Halle, an enterprising entertainer from Arras; and composers wrote vernacular texts and music in honor of the Virgin Mary at the court of King Alfonso the Wise, showcasing verse forms in Galician-Portuguese, the language of the Spanish court. (As we will see in Chapter 12, the minstrel tradition took root in Germany and other regions as well.)

Although much of the secular poetry from this period was still sung to melodies that circulated only in oral traditions, a more sustained effort was made to notate the music for such texts, largely as the result of changes in how and where scribes worked. By the early thirteenth century, the scribes of monasteries and cathedrals increasingly worked for hire outside of their institutions; the work of copying was also often farmed out to independent scribes who were not monks or clerics. The production of textbooks for the flourishing university culture in Paris also necessitated large numbers of readily available scribes. The music of the twelfth-century troubadours studied in Chapter 7 was, for the most part, first notated by thirteenth-century scribes working in northern France. As a result of these trends and various types of scribal exchange, music-writing skills expanded from liturgical repertories to those that flourished outside the Church.

ST. FRANCIS AND HIS FOLLOWERS

The thirteenth century was dominated by charismatic religious figures who were part of an ongoing transformation of thought, feeling, the arts, and music led by the work of the mendicants, officially sanctioned orders of wandering preachers. The religious fervor of the twelfth century studied in Chapter 6 had been stirred by traveling preachers whose teachings were unregulated by the Church and, in some cases, judged to be heretical. Yet ecclesiastical authorities recognized the ability of well-trained preachers to mix with the people and teach orthodoxy in engaging ways. Music was central to this evangelizing dynamic.

The mendicants (from the Latin verb meaning "to beg"), also called friars, joined a religious order, followed particular rules of life, lived within communities (although with freedom to travel), and had well-defined liturgical and musical practices. Two major groups of mendicants were founded in the early thirteenth century, both of which radically altered the face of European music. One was named for St. Francis and the other for St. Dominic: the Order of Friars Minor (Franciscans) and the Order of Preachers (Dominicans). Both orders quickly established major houses in Paris, an international crossroads that attracted students from all of Europe. The conditions were ideal for the new orders to become international themselves and to be leaders in the creation of new styles of song.

It is appropriate to launch our discussion of the thirteenth century with Francis of Assisi (1182–1226), a saint who was larger than life (Fig. 8.1). His influence spread throughout Europe, in preaching, in art, and in music, for, according to all reports, he was a wonderful singer. His story, rewritten many times, served as a model for new artistic viewpoints and for a powerful sense of spirituality.

Figure 8.1: *The earliest surviving portrait of Francis of Assisi, a fresco (early thirteenth century, retouched) found in the Benedictine monastery of Sacro Speco in Subiaco, near Rome*

Francis grew to fame just as enormous collections of miracle stories, many of which centered on the Virgin Mary, were being standardized and used as materials for public preaching. The people who wrote the various lives of Francis were all Franciscans themselves. They wanted his life to represent who they were and what they intended to achieve, and they were lavish in the recollection of miracles associated with his life story, some of which are recalled in the *lauda* (plural, *laude*), a type of vernacular spiritual song especially favored by Franciscans in Italy.

In most tellings, Francis, from a wealthy mercantile family in northern Italy, is depicted as a scoundrel in his youth. He was an entertaining performer of scurrilous songs. He tried soldiering as a career and was supposed to take over his father's business, once he had thoroughly sowed his wild oats. Francis's conversion story involves a trip past a dilapidated church. He entered, began to pray at a crucifix there, and it spoke to him: "Francis, go and repair my house, which, as you see, is completely destroyed." Dedication to the Cross and its call to sacrifice was paramount with him from this time forward. Later in life, he was miraculously imprinted with the five wounds, or stigmata, of Christ. Life was ever dramatic and action-filled for the Francis we encounter in his biographies. He tried unsuccessfully for martyrdom by joining the Fifth Crusade to Syria and crossed the battle lines to preach to Sultan Malik al-Kamil. As both men were fluent in French, they were able to converse, and the "jongleur for Jesus" was sent away unharmed.

An example of Francis's special gifts is found in the story of a spectacular Christmas drama he created for the Italian town of Greccio. He had an elaborate stage set constructed out of doors, wishing "to do something that will recall the memory of the child who was born in Bethlehem," and borrowing animals from a local farm to make a living tableau. The friars sang roles, and Francis preached and prayed the Mass liturgy, in a performance that must have resembled an early opera, but with a religious theme. The Christmas re-creation reminds us that Francis often did his work outdoors, as was appropriate for friars, and drew the liturgy out into nature. According to tradition, once when he was preaching outdoors and some swallows were chirping nearby, he said to them: "My sisters, the swallows, it's my turn to speak now, because you've already said enough. Listen to the word of God." His *Canticle for the Sun*, one of the best known of all medieval poems, is said to be the earliest preserved song text in Italian. In this song, composed as he was near death, Francis invokes the powers of God in nature, beginning with Brother Sun and Sister Moon:

Laudato sie, mi Signore cun tucte le Tue creature,	*Praised be You, my Lord, with all Your creatures,*
spetialmente messor lo frate Sole,	*especially Sir Brother Sun,*
lo qual è iorno, et allumini noi per lui.	*who is the day through whom You give us light.*

Et ellu è bellu e radiante cun grande splendore:	*And he is beautiful and radiant with great splendor,*
de Te, Altissimo, porta significatione.	*Of You Most High he bears the likeness.*

FRANCISCAN *LAUDE*

The compositions written by the learned Franciscan Julian of Speyer (d. c. 1250) for the Office of Francis followed in a tradition of music for rhymed Offices. But the Franciscan laude written for popular singing were very different in style from these Latin-texted liturgical chants. Most laude have a melodious refrain and multiple verses sung by a leader, telling the story of sacred events and creating characters. *Laude novella* (see Anthology 21) features a refrain that is a repeating section of two ten-syllable lines, with strongly marked caesurae in the middle of each line. Participation was encouraged in the early laude by preparing the refrain through musical foreshadowing at the end of each verse.

Laude also offered ways for people to imitate the thoughts and feelings of Jesus and Mary, creating song-playlets in the vernacular for every major season, a practice that expanded in the fourteenth century. Other songs in the repertory praise Francis himself. *Laudar vollio per amore*, for example, presents a musical biography of Francis in Italian (Ex. 8.1). In such pieces common people could enter the world of the miracle literature and of liturgical poets in their own everyday language.

The *laudesi* were loosely organized lay groups formed by the friars throughout Italy for the purpose of singing about the dramatic events of the Gospels and saints' lives. Every region evangelized by Franciscans would see the emergence of some kind of vernacular religious song; several types were composed and notated in the fourteenth century (see Chapters 10 and 11). Fourteenth-century laude were generally more musically challenging than their thirteenth-century counterparts, and the forces necessary for performance changed accordingly. In the fourteenth century, laudesi hired musicians to play instruments and do some of the singing; polyphonic settings of laude developed as the tradition was taken up by trained musicians and the singing fraternities that thrived in Italian cities, harbingers of the learned societies that would later encourage the rise of opera (as Wendy Heller describes in *Music in the Baroque*).

Example 8.1: *Opening of* Laudar vollio per amore *for St. Francis*

For the sake of love I wish to praise the first little brother.

THE FRANCISCANS AND THE LITURGY

In Rome, Franciscans helped the papacy with its goal of reforming and standardizing liturgical and musical practices. In the third quarter of the thirteenth century, Pope Nicholas III ordered the destruction of all Roman liturgical books that did not conform to the new Roman-Franciscan use. The liturgy of the papal court, of the Franciscans, and, gradually, of most churches in the city became one as a result of these efforts. One effect of this Franciscan reform was to help standardize out of existence the subtle dialects of the common Roman chant traditions found throughout Europe and to do away completely with the Old Roman chant tradition studied in Chapter 3. An era that began with the rise of Frankish chant in the ninth century culminated in an even greater desire for musical and liturgical uniformity, this time promoted within Rome itself.

THE LIVES OF STUDENTS IN SONG

The manuscript known as *Carmina burana* (Songs of Benediktbeuern) is a vast repertory of songs copied around 1230 in the Tyrol, a state of the Holy Roman Empire that comprised parts of modern-day Italy and Austria. This exceedingly valuable manuscript, much rearranged over the centuries, was found in the early 1800s in the library of the Benedictine monastery of Benediktbeuern, near Munich, and finally ended up in the Bavarian State Library. The main body of the manuscript represents the work of two scribes who probably belonged to the culture of semi-privileged, often disgruntled young men sometimes known as goliards, or followers of the mythical Bishop Golias, a lewd and bibulous cleric. The goliards traveled to the major educational centers of Europe in search of learning and positions in ecclesiastical or secular courts, often critiquing many aspects of student life. The Tyrol region was a crossroads for itinerant student populations, and this deluxe illuminated codex seems to have been prepared for a patron who had himself once been a student or a *magister* (professor).

The students who traveled by the thousands to medieval cities in the thirteenth century were good for business, but brought a host of problems. In many cases, they stood outside the jurisdiction of secular law and were subject only to officials in charge of the schools and universities. This situation created town-gown friction that sometimes resulted in violence. Students were, in most cases, clerics in minor orders; they were not priests or monks, and they were bound to the Church by loose tethers. Students all had to study Latin—still the language of learning—to do well in any career. It is no wonder so much Latin song from the period describes the lives, loves, and problems of students, as well as of their professors. *Carmina burana* is the greatest collection of student song that survives from medieval Europe, and many things about it bear witness to this vibrant singing culture.

The limited musical notation of the songs and plays of *Carmina burana* is unheightened, meaning that only those works surviving in still other copies with accurate pitches can be securely transcribed. Only around 40 of the more than 250 songs (including several dramas) are notated, and only around 30 of these can be transcribed today through consultation with other versions of what appear to be the same piece. (The twentieth-century composer Carl Orff, whose choral settings made the manuscript famous in modern times, chose 24 song texts and wrote his own melodies for them.) The compositions in *Carmina burana* (abbreviated *CB* below) are grouped by categories, showing how clerical musicians thought about their heritage in the early thirteenth century. The manuscript includes moral-satirical poems (*CB*, nos. 1–55); love songs, with much emphasis upon Ovidian themes of lustful longing (nos. 56–186); drinking and gaming songs (nos. 187–226); religious dramas; and some 24 song fragments at the end.

MORAL-SATIRICAL SONGS

In many ways the moral-satirical songs are the most traditional and learned of the entire collection. Many of the poets represented were well known from their activities in the twelfth century and wrote a variety of Latin lyrics, including love songs. The poems chosen for inclusion are highly critical of the Church, of the power of the curia (the papal administrative body) in Rome, of the paying of fees for all kinds of legal services provided by the papal court, and of the selling of ecclesiastical offices. Among them are several *conductus* (the plural and the singular forms are the same), strophic accentual Latin songs that developed from the more modest beginnings seen in Chapter 6 into a powerfully polemical and often sophisticated genre in the twelfth and thirteenth centuries.

How and where such pieces were sung is not known, but we can imagine that they were welcome in a range of settings, both liturgical and secular. An early conductus attributed to Philip the Chancellor (c. 1160–1236) of the University of Paris establishes the critical tone, especially in regard to paying money to the Church as fees for services. In this work there are two warring kingdoms, of good people and the other an evil Babylon; and the secular influence has come to hold sway: "The Church has become the den of corpse-thieves; the king of Babylon has entered the temple of Solomon" (*Deduc Syon*, *CB*, no. 34; Ex. 8.2). *In Gedeonis area* (no. 37) is a song about how the chaff is burying the grain, the moth is destroying Gideon's fleece, and lay inferiors are taking the places of priests. This song longs for the golden days of the monastic and cathedral

Example 8.2: *Opening of the conductus* Deduc Syon, *by Philip the Chancellor*

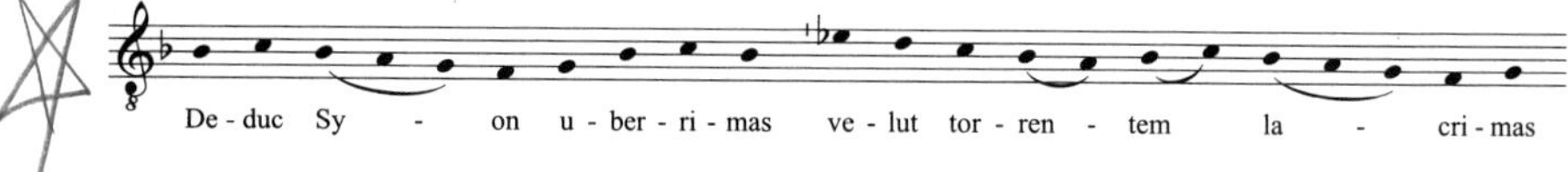

Weep, Syon, an overabundance of tears, like a torrent

schools, places that, with some exceptions, would never again be major centers of learning after the thirteenth century, when the universities would largely take over (see Chapter 9).

LOVE SONGS

In the love poems we find the mixing of traditions alluded to at the beginning of this chapter. By the early thirteenth century, when *Carmina burana* was copied, the songs of the troubadours had captured the imaginations of songsters throughout Europe, and their works were being collected by poets in northern France and elsewhere. The two main scribes through whose work we know these songs shared in this delight with things French, but were also interested in songs from east of the Rhine. Scribe One was an Italian speaker who knew a bit of Old French and also of Old Occitan (what we now call Old French was known as the langue d'oïl as distinct from Old Occitan, known in Old French as the langue d'oc) and German, and was probably from the town of Brixen in the South Tyrol, where the manuscript appears to have been compiled. Troubadour lyrics were well known in northern Italy, and this accounts for his familiarity with this repertory and its language. Scribe Two is from northern France and his Latin is less than good. He is very interested in German lyrics and adds stanzas in German to some poems, but his grasp of German is also not strong. Modern critical editions have corrected numerous errors in these texts, but before they were scrubbed clean of their difficulties, the songs reflected a stew of influences, showing the linguistic dynamism of thirteenth-century vernacular song and its interaction with Latin.

In many cases the scribes were apparently making new poems as they wrote, utilizing freely circulating bodies of texts and music, both written and remembered. German works were traveling westward, just as the influential music and poetry of troubadour and trouvère poets were being received in German-speaking lands and shaping the work of musicians there. Song-swapping is reflected in many aspects of *Carmina burana*, as many songs existed in intertextual relationships with each other. The lively musical and poetic exchanges taking place in the world of traveling students and musicians is captured just as it turns to writing. Several of the love songs in *Carmina burana* show a variety of linguistic influences, with refrains from one tradition incorporated into the poetry of another, or with versions of the same texts in two languages. Various musical bits wandered throughout the collection, too, adapted and readapted. Just as in the motet repertory (see Chapter 9), learned musicians were exploring their ideas about many subjects in both Latin and the vernacular within a repertory that mixed languages, as well as the sacred and the secular.

DRINKING AND GAMING SONGS

The third section of *Carmina burana* shows how medieval students delighted in parody, knowing as they did by heart an enormous repertory of sacred chant. A taste for parody through contrafactum is found in the so-called Gamblers' Mass, a spoof on the chants and texts of the Mass liturgy Many students, abandoned by the fickle goddess Fortune, whose wheel is depicted on a page tipped into the opening of the manuscript, lost their money and clothes in dice games in taverns like the one shown in Figure 8.2.

The unfortunate student gambler pleads for a winning combination in a Latin contrafactum *Victimae novali zynke ses* that fits the renowned melody of the Easter sequence *Victimae paschali laudes* very well (Ex. 8.3). The intertextual relationship between the two pieces is rich in meanings. Instead of the paschal lamb, the "victim" in *Victimae novali zynke ses* is the gambler who has lost to the Lord of the Die, Decius. The life-and-death duel described in the Easter sequence is replaced with luck and winnings. The address to Mary Magdalene to tell the apostles that the Lord has risen becomes a charge for Fortune to express her reasons for the gambler's misfortunes. The empty garments at the tomb become the lost clothing of the gambler, drawing a parallel between the dice throwers in a medieval tavern and those who gambled at the foot of the Cross.

Figure 8.2: *Students drinking and playing dice in a tavern, from* Carmina burana

Example 8.3:

(a) Victimae novali zynke ses *from the Gamblers' Mass; contrafactum of the Easter sequence* Victimae paschali laudes

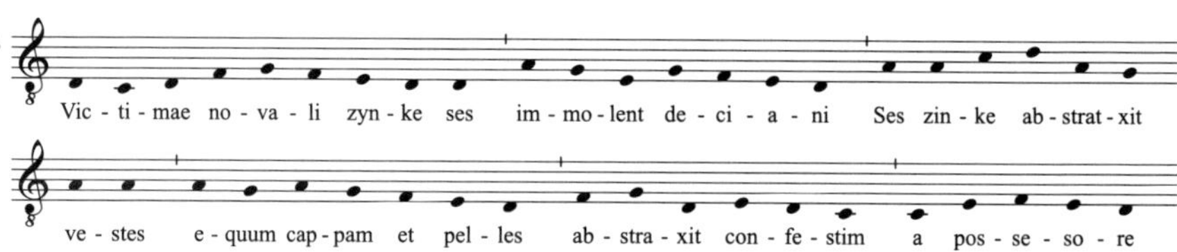

Let the dice pay homage to the new victim of five/six. Six/five took his clothing and robbed the owner in a flash of a horse, a mantle, and a pelt.

(b) *The Easter sequence* Victimae paschali laudes

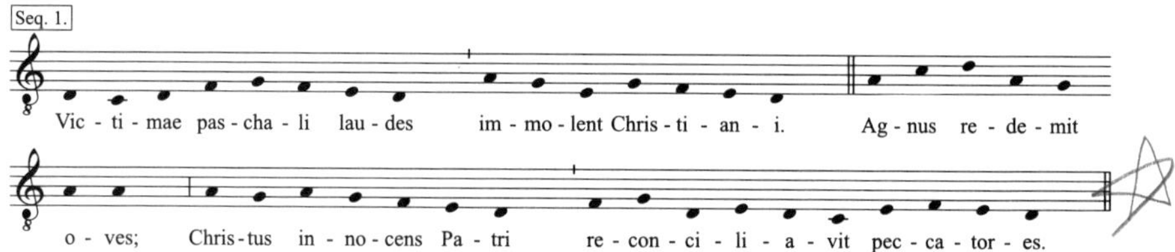

Let Christians offer praises to the paschal victim. The lamb redeemed the sheep; innocent Christ reconciled the sinners to their Father.

Bache bene venies, addressed to Bacchus, the god of wine, emphasizes the students' purported propensity to pick up women, get them drunk, and seduce or rape them (see Anthology 22). In monastic and cathedral schools, male students received educations comparable to those of their female counterparts in some convents. But women were excluded from the developing universities and missed out on the scholastic revolution taking place in the thirteenth century (see Chapter 9). Through their sophisticated use of language, these student songs transport us to a culture where women of comparable stature were neither present nor welcome, and those who were conjured up were objects of various kinds of sport and abuse. The women are part of the game engaged in by poets, as expressed in their playfully rhyming and accentual Latin verses.

The melody for the song text *Bache bene venies* quoted in Example 8.4 is not found in *Carmina burana*; it has been reconstructed using a melody found in the thirteenth-century *Play of Daniel* that fits the structure and sense of the text. Tellingly, although this work is sung in the *Play of Daniel* with a sacred Latin text, it is given to raucous Babylonians who have captured temple vessels from the Jews and are using them for drinking parties. The refrain of *Bache bene venies* shows the power of rhyme and repetition, a medieval version of that old standard *In Heaven There Is No Beer.*

Example 8.4:

(a) *Refrain from* Bache bene venies

Such a wine, a wine so fine, exquisite wine, makes a man of the curia honest and valiant.

(b) *Intertext with melody from* Ludus Danielis *(The Play of Daniel)*

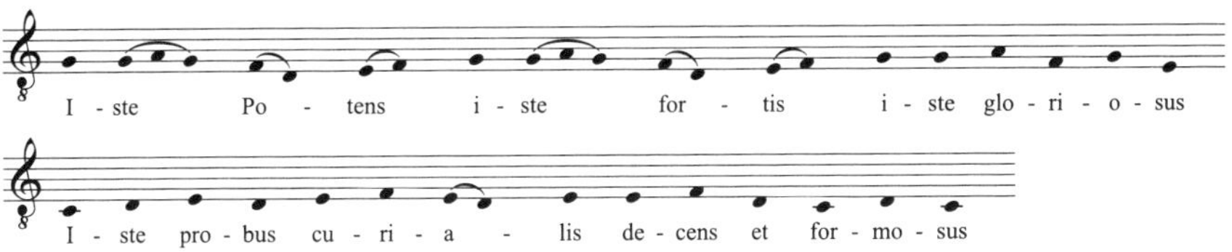

This man is powerful, this man is strong, this man is glorious;
This honest man of the curia is honest and handsome.

But *Bache bene venies* is more than a bawdy charge to drink and carouse. The song's verses abound with scriptural references to the stealing of the sacred vessels by the Babylonians from the Jewish temple during the period of captivity, the very situation found in the *Play of Daniel*. Clearly there was a powerful relationship between the drinking song and the music in the *Play of Daniel*, and both relate to a widely circulating oral tradition of student song. Indeed, the picture of student life found in *Carmina burana* presents youth who are themselves Babylonians, ravagers, dedicated, in this case, to the pagan god Bacchus, who will not treat them well. Singing between the worlds of their studies and their revelry, and in intertextual relationships with both, medieval students adopted an existential angst.

RELIGIOUS DRAMAS

The thirteenth century was filled with many kinds of dramatic works, from Easter plays of varying degrees of complexity—all featuring some form of the *Quem quaeritis* trope studied in Chapter 4—to full-fledged collections such as the Fleury Playbook, studied in Chapter 5, which includes saints' plays as well as plays for Easter, Christmas, and other holidays, to the *Play of Daniel*, which is filled with farcical shenanigans worthy of January 1 and the celebrations associated with that day. The extent to which the plays fit into the Mass or Office, or were affixed to some other ritual form, is often difficult to determine.

The several plays found in *Carmina burana* are unique works that stand somewhat outside the tradition of religious dramas, although many of their texts are borrowed from liturgical sources. Like the songs in the collection, many of the plays have German words and phrases incorporated into their Latin texts, and use comic effects that are surprisingly different from many contemporary liturgical plays. In the opening scene of the Christmas play, for example, St. Augustine argues with Archisynagogus, who is supposed to adopt Jewish mannerisms described in the rubrics (instructions). The two characters toss a line from the Christmas sequence *Laetabundus* back and forth, thus mocking the debating tradition that was then current in the schools, and referencing the debates sometimes arranged by Christian clerics between themselves and Jews. The compilers of *Carmina burana* saw fit to make fun even of the darker sides of life in the early thirteenth century.

SONGS AND SONG COLLECTIONS FROM NORTHERN FRANCE: THE TROUVÈRES

Carmina burana introduces a number of broadly construed song genres, each developing particular themes, but all situated in student culture. Very different, although surely related, is the culture of song that developed around the trouvères, the courtly poet-singers of northern France. The trouvères wrote in the Old French dialects of the north; Old French is a different language from the Old Occitan of the southern troubadours. The surviving trouvère repertory is roughly ten times the size of that of the troubadours; still, of some 1,500 trouvère song texts, we have music for only about 250.

Trouvère lyrics grew out of medieval romances. These tales of knights and their ladies emphasized the beauty of the women, the bravery and strength of the men, and the death-defying power of their love. The narratives are filled with trickery and magic, with themes adapted from folktales, and with a host of secondary figures who are often more admirable than the knights and ladies themselves. (The 1987 film *The Princess Bride* is one of many modern spoofs of these traditions.) Many trouvère poems are spoken from the female point of view, and some can be ascribed to women.

Flourishing beside the romances were stories of the miracles of the Virgin Mary, whose saving powers made her the greatest action figure of the thirteenth century. These parallel traditions interacted throughout the century in romances, plays, and the miracle literature, and poets enjoyed moving back and forth between them in the lyrics of their songs. Authors on both sides of the fence delighted in the parallels between sacred and secular themes. Gautier de Coincy (d. 1236), monk and abbot, says in his vast Marian miracle collection written in Old French: "I do not scorn the devices of the trouvères, but I am dressed in rough black serge, whilst they sport fur-trimmed garments; may my role be not displeasing to them, for I am no trouvère, save to my lady and friend; no common minstrel am I."

Trouvère songs (or *chansons*, to use the French name) exist in many guises. The forms of French chansons in the thirteenth century are exceedingly fluid, even more so than in the troubadour repertory studied in Chapter 7. The *grand chant courtois*, a modern term used to describe the most refined and complex type of French song, is commonly a strophic work with the structure **ABABX**, where the **X** section falls somewhat higher in range and contains no set number of lines. Such songs might have seven or more strophes, allowing room for development of character and theme. Refrains of various types were often added as well; the position of the refrain in the structure of the chanson was often of formal importance, as it was in many songs found in other vernacular traditions, the Italian laude, for example, and the Gallician cantigas.

The rondeau, a dance form, was fairly simple by comparison with the many more courtly works, and the refrain is a significant feature. In the text below, attributed to the late-thirteenth-century trouvère poet and painter Guillaume d'Amiens, the lines are somewhat irregular in their syllable count and the rhymes are not exact. Still, the musical form is roughly **ABaAabAB**, with the capital letters standing for refrains having the same text and music, as shown below. The **A** lines are "open" in that they do not cadence on the final; the **B** lines are "closed" in that they do end on the final of D (Ex. 8.5). The refrain is sung by a shepherdess who does not wish to be caught in the act of making love. The piece points to the many ways that medieval song was rooted in the dance and in the lives of women, real and imagined. The melody, which in modern performance is sometimes accompanied by clapping and rhythms worthy of dancing, is a medieval earworm; once heard, it is never forgotten.

Prendés i garde, s'on mi regarde!	**A**	*Be on guard, if someone is watching me!*
S'on me regarde, dites le moi.	**B**	*If someone is watching me, tell me.*
C'est tout la jus en cel boschaige:	**a**	*It is right over there in that woods:*
Prendés i garde, s'on mi regarde.	**A**	*be on guard if someone is watching me.*
La pastourele i gardoit vaches:	**a**	*The shepherdess who was watching the cows:*
"Plaisans brunete a vous m'otoi!"	**b**	*"Sweet brown-haired woman, I offer myself to you!"*
Prendés i garde, s'on mi regarde!	**A**	*Be on guard, if someone is watching me!*
S'on mi regarde, dites le moi.	**B**	*If someone is watching me, tell me.*

Example 8.5: *Refrain of the rondeau* Prendés i garde, s'on mi regarde

Be on guard, if someone is watching me! If someone is watching me, tell me.

The study of texts and melodies of citations or borrowed material (as distinct from "refrain" as repeating material in a song) offers an excellent introduction to a specialized repertory of quotations that are often difficult to identify, as is the case with *Chançon ferai que talenz*, discussed below. In fact, before the first major collections of trouvère songs were compiled in the mid- and late thirteenth century, there were already romances with sung citations interspersed within their texts, the earliest of which is *The Romance of the Rose* or *Guillaume de Dole* by Jean Renart (not to be confused with the later allegory by Guillaume de Lorris and Jean de Meung, also called *The Romance of the Rose*).

Renart (fl. 1200–1222) uses sung citations to establish characters or inform dramatic situations. He quotes from many trouvère songs in contexts that reflect his understanding of genre and meaning. For example, the courtly chanson is sung in intimate settings by the emperor or his personal minstrel, whereas more frolicsome songs for dancing involve the women and sometimes the entire audience. Singing was widespread in Renart's social world. Performers were expected to come not only from the ranks of jongleurs and minstrels, but also from the sons and daughters of the well-born, their servants, and even counts or dukes and their ladies; each would sing songs appropriate to his or her station in life; but delight was clearly taken in the mixing of expectations.

The early use of song quotation in romances demonstrates the free circulation of texts and melodies in northern France long before the first *chansonniers* (manuscript collections of songs) were compiled in the second half of the thirteenth century. The chansonniers themselves further attest to repertorial fluidity. Like the compilers of *Carmina burana*, the scribes of the texts and music for the chansonniers, working from various written collections and their own memories, contributed to an evolving sense of how to organize vernacular song. Citations—borrowed material from other works—provided a way of weaving commentary into the textual and musical fabrics of both monophonic and polyphonic chanson repertories. Some of this commentary was local and vernacular, and some of it was learned (see Chapters 9 and 10).

THE CHANSONS OF THIBAUT OF CHAMPAGNE

There are around 20 extant major chansonniers, and, with but one mid-thirteenth-century exception, all were copied in the late thirteenth or early fourteenth century, long after the first generations of trouvères were dead. Texts often circulated without their music, making it difficult to identify the early layers of music, and to know which melody is best suited to which text. Songs are usually grouped by composer; the most famous trouvère is Thibaut of Champagne (1201–1253), whose works open several collections, reflecting his high social standing as both count of Champagne and king of Navarre.

The music for Thibaut's poetry is uniquely well preserved. Thirty-two manuscripts contain song texts by him, and 14 of these sources are at least partially notated. The *Manuscrit du roi* (Paris, BN fr. 844, ff.5*r*, 104*v*, commonly known as Manuscript M among the chansonniers) contains 56 noted examples from Thibaut's 60 attributed works. Many of the songs were added to the source in a different but contemporary late-thirteenth-century hand, and in an ordering that was typical for Thibaut's works. As mentioned above, this precious source also contains one of the earliest collections of music believed to have been written for instruments, in this case, *estampies*, a kind of instrumental dance. Later additions are in a notation that sometimes allows for transcription with rhythmic values (see Chapter 9). Thibaut's *Chançon ferai que talenz* (see Anthology 23) demonstrates the flexibility of the grand chant courtois in combination with a variety of citations, a different borrowed quotation for each strophe.

ADAM DE LA HALLE

Adam de la Halle (c. 1240–c. 1285), one of the last trouvères, belonged to the guild of jongleurs that dominated the social landscape of the northern French commercial town of Arras (Fig. 8.3). All the world was a stage in this city, where the jongleurs wrote plays, led processions related to the healing cult of a miraculous candle supposedly given to them by the Virgin Mary, served as courtiers, sang for banquets, fairs, and jousting tournaments, and accompanied the lords of the region on the battlefield to keep spirits high.

Adam was a leading jongleur in a region that featured hundreds of singing entertainers and boasted a huge repertory of song in the Picard dialect, which

Figure 8.3: *Adam de la Halle at work (nineteenth-century drawing from an original thirteenth-century manuscript Arras MS G57)*

was distinct from the dialect of Old French spoken around Paris. The *puy*, or song contest, was a favorite activity, as was the sung *jeu-parti*, or debate. The word *puy* came to be used in the later Middle Ages for a society of jongleurs, characterized as they were by literary competitions. Adam's output was collected in a deluxe "edition" soon after his death, the first such collection devoted to a single poet-composer writing in the vernacular. It contained 36 chansons, 17 jeux-partis, 16 rondeaux, 5 motets, a *congé* (farewell poem), and 2 plays, one of which, *Le jeu de Robin et Marion*, became his most famous work.

Le jeu de Robin et Marion (The Play of Robin and Marion) is a dramatic *pastourelle*, the French version of the *pastorela* depicting an amorous encounter between a knight and a shepherdess, of which Marcabru's *L'autrier jost'una sebissa* (see Chapter 7) is an early example. In this case, the bourgeois composer mocks both the knightly class and the peasantry, the former as being crude and brutal, the latter as merry, dancing, and ineffectual. The heroine, the shepherdess Marion, triumphs over both the knight (who is intent on raping her) and her boyfriend, Robin (who blunders his way through the play in the company of loutish companions). The most important refrain, "Robins m'aime," is Marion's signature music, and it follows her throughout the work (Ex. 8.6). The young men, on the other hand, promote various kinds of gaming, just as many of Adam's fellow trouvères did; one of them even suggests a farting contest. Such self-mocking humor would have been appreciated in a region filled with professional entertainers.

Example 8.6: *Opening of Marion's song from* Le jeu de Robin et Marion *(The Play of Robin and Marion)*

Robin loves me, Robin has me. Robin asked for me, and he will have me.

Example 8.7: *Refrain from* Fines amouretes ai, *a polyphonic chanson by Adam de la Halle*

A tender love have I. God! I don't know when I shall see her.

Adam's three-voice rondeau *Fines amouretes ai* presents a courtly lover who does not trust himself: the speaker decides to stay away from his beloved rather than dishonor her through an inevitable pregnancy. Each statement of the refrain (in this case, a musical-textural line that repeats, and that may have been borrowed from an earlier source) shows his resolve in a new context: "A tender love have I. God! I don't know when I shall see her" (Ex. 8.7). Adam's rondeaux are the earliest surviving polyphonic chansons. Their static harmonies draw the melodies into their powerful sway. They also introduce us to a trouvère who was learned enough to write in a simple polyphonic style as taught in Paris (see Chapter 9), even though he was originally from Arras, a city that rivaled Paris in traditions of song and minstrelsy. It appears that Adam spent some days of his youth in Paris, and one of his plays seems to express a longing to return.

CANTIGAS FROM MEDIEVAL SPAIN

In this chapter we have encountered a variety of song collections, from the richly illustrated Latin songs of *Carmina burana* to a chansonnier containing the collected works of Adam de la Halle (which includes a portrait of the trouvère at his desk, looking like one of the Evangelists). But no song collection from the thirteenth century is as visually magnificent as those containing the musical miracles of the Virgin Mary composed at the court of King Alfonso the Wise of Spain (r. 1252–1284). How much influence Alfonso had on the tradition of *cantigas,* or Spanish songs, is a matter of debate. He may have been a compiler rather than a composer, although he surely welcomed poets and musicians to his court from far and wide.

The organization of the manuscript containing the *Cantigas de Santa María* (Songs of the Virgin Mary) in the National Library of Spain in Madrid (no. 10069, called To or Tol, as it was once in Toledo) seems to represent the original intentions of the compilers working in 1270–80 (contains 102 cantigas, with 26 more in appendices). Every tenth song is a *cantiga de loor* (song of praise); the rest are longer narrative songs describing the actual miracles. Two other major manuscripts are now found in the library of the Escorial in Madrid: Manuscript Escorial T.1.1, which has been expanded considerably beyond Tol (the poems have been rearranged, and there are 194 cantigas), and Manuscript Escorial B.1.2 (or simply Manuscript E). The latter is the richest of the three in music and musical information; it contains over 400 cantigas with notation.

Apparently, the king's initial intention was to write (or have written) 100 poems. In the three major manuscripts of the *Cantigas de Santa María*, every tenth song receives an illumination, and every one of these depicts a musician or musicians, making these sources the most significant for musical iconography from the entire thirteenth century. An opening illumination from Escorial T.I.1 (Fig. 8.4) shows Alfonso in the act of teaching, with a group of instrumentalists to our left, two with bowed vielles (medieval fiddles) and another with a lute (a plucked instrument with a long neck and a rounded belly), and a group of four singers to the far right who are tonsured (that is, have haircuts particular to clerics). At the king's feet to the left and right are scribes, perhaps taking down texts or music or both.

The troubadours of Spain wrote in Galician-Portuguese, the literary language of Alfonso's court. The *Cantigas de Santa María* offer an extraordinary display of poetic fireworks, representing every form and meter used in the late thirteenth century, and showing the triumph of the vernacular in verse. Each of the more than 400 texts in Manuscript E has its own music, most in scales built on either D or G. Although there is little to be sure about in matters of rhythm, the pitches of these songs can be securely transcribed. In this repertory, too, the refrain plays a major role, and as with the Franciscan laude there may have been singing that involved the interplay of groups and soloists. As we can hear from listening to *Rosa das rosas*, the first cantiga de loor from the collection (see Anthology 24), many modern performers are aware that the music and form of the cantigas may show Arabic influence, and delight in experimenting with ornamentation and phrasing that reflects this understanding.

The widely circulating body of Marian miracles employed in the cantiga collections made the Virgin the mother of all, a woman who forgives everyone, from

Figure 8.4: *King Alfonso the Wise* (center) *with instrumentalists and singers (National Library in Spain, MS Escorial T.I.1)*

Example 8.8: *Refrain from the cantiga* A Madre do que a bestia

Ay, the mother of him who made the beast of Balaam speak, also a sheep was made to speak.

a pregnant abbess to thieves and other criminals. Originally, the miracles were chosen from works that circulated north of the Alps, but later additions included miracle stories from Spanish regions as well. The nature of the texts, like the many sources of the melodies, testifies to the international flavor of court life. *A Madre do que a bestia*, for example, retells a twelfth-century story of a peasant woman whose sheep is kept by a shepherd who is supposed to give her the wool at shearing time. When she goes to get the wool, the shepherd says that thieves stole her animal, but the Virgin Mary gives her sheep the ability to speak and identify itself among all the other shorn members of the shepherd's herd. In celebration, the woman takes her wool to the Marian shrine at Rocamadour (in southwestern France). The rhyming stanzas are punctuated by a refrain that relates to the story (Ex. 8.8), and the dramatic nature of the cantiga is borne out in performances that create character through dialogue, often with comic overlays.

MARTIN CODAX

We close with a song by the obscure poet-composer Martin Codax (fl. c. 1240–1270) from the coastal region of Galicia in northwestern Spain. His work represents the thousands upon thousands of lyrics from medieval Spain and Portugal that survive without their music. Six of Martin's surviving poems have music; a seventh was added to the manuscript by a later hand. This messy leaf, now at the Morgan Library in New York City, was discovered in the early twentieth century, binding a copy of Cicero's works. It is the only copy of Martin's poems with music, and its very existence is a testimony to the role of chance in the transmission of medieval manuscripts.

The situation described in Martin's *Ondas do mare de Vigo*, the first song in the cycle, is mysterious: a woman stands by the sea looking out for a ship that will never return and longing for someone she once loved but can now only imagine (see Anthology 25). The poet is a ventriloquist, speaking, as Galician poets so often do, in the voice of a woman and imagining what she thinks; this genre was known as the *cantiga de amigo* (friend's song). Early in the cycle of six poems, her hopes rise; later she dances "on holy ground" in anticipation of a wedding; but in the end we see she is still awaiting the arrival of more news.

The age of song was experienced among many languages, cultures, and genres. It depicted high life and low life, great aspirations and brutal assaults. It was critical and full of praise, hating and loving, cold and hot. The way in which "real life" was represented in song is a matter of debate. Some scholars treat the poetry and music as evidence of the highest order; others feel that poets deliberately created an escapist world of dreams that did not depict the circumstances of the times. Both these views, and many others in between, accept the centrality of song to thirteenth-century culture.

The music of the songs itself provides a kind of reality, a sonic image of what people valued, from simple refrains to complex large-scale forms. We know little about the rhythms rendered in any of the repertories studied in this chapter. Most singers and accompanists today favor performances that allow for clear declamation of the texts, and take license in the development of character. They do their creative best to represent an era when text and music worked together, and melody was the stream that moved the mill wheel.

FOR FURTHER READING

Aubrey, Elizabeth, ed. *Poets and Singers On Latin and Vernacular Monophonic Song* (Farnham: Ashgate, 2009).

Bayless, Martha, *Parody in the Middle Ages: The Latin Tradition* (Ann Arbor: University of Michigan Press, 1996)

Butterfield, Ardis, *Poetry and Music in Medieval France: From Jean Renart to Guillaume de Machaut* (Cambridge: Cambridge University Press, 2002)

Katz, John, and John E. Keller, eds., *International Symposium on the Cantigas de Santa María (1981: New York, N.Y.)* (Madison, WI: Hispanic Seminary of Medieval Studies, 1987)

Nichols, Stephen G., "'Art' and 'Nature': Looking for (Medieval) Principles of Order in Occitan *Chansonnier* N (Morgan 819)," in Stephen G. Nichols and Siegfried Wenzel, eds., *The Whole Book: Cultural Perspectives on the Medieval Miscellany* (Ann Arbor: University of Michigan Press, 1996)

Page, Christopher, *Voices and Instruments of the Middle Ages: Instrumental Practice and Songs in France, 1100–1300* (Berkeley: University of California Press, 1986)

Rosenberg, Samuel N., Margaret Switten, and Gérard Le Vot, eds., *Songs of the Troubadours and Trouvères: An Anthology of Poems and Melodies* (New York: Garland, 1998)

Sayce, Olive, *Plurilingualism in the Carmina Burana: A Study of the Linguistic and Literary Influences on the Codex* (Göppingen, Germany: Kümmerle, 1992)

CHAPTER NINE

Music and Learning in the Thirteenth Century

In 1215, Pope Innocent III summoned lay and clerical leaders to the Lateran Basilica in Rome to hear him proclaim a series of statutes consolidating and centralizing papal authority in the governance of the Catholic Church. From this point on, the papal bureaucracy would swell as legions of enforcers mobilized to suppress heretical groups such as the Albigensians in the south of France. The Vatican moved against them not only by declaring the so-called Albigensian Crusade (1209–55), but also by promulgating new laws promoting devotion to the Eucharist, a sacrament which the Albigensians denied.

The Fourth Lateran Council also mandated a renewed emphasis on education: every church was to have a teacher in residence who could instruct the youth (and many of these teachers were musicians). Non-Christian groups were to be restrained from freely mingling within society; Jews, for example, were forced to wear badges or other distinctive clothing and were otherwise ostracized. Fresh attempts were to be made to retake Jerusalem, which had been lost to the armies of the Muslim sultan Saladin in 1187. Clergy were more tightly reined in than ever before, not only in regard to sexual practices, but also in their relationships to the laity. Religious women, whose ways of life were increasingly under suspicion, would also see their freedoms severely curtailed by the end of the thirteenth century.

At the same time, new knowledge was streaming into Europe as a result of translations made from the Arabic of Greek science and philosophy, discovered through contact with libraries and learning in the Near East. Especially important was work carried out in Toledo, known as "the city of translators," where from the middle of the twelfth century to the middle of the thirteenth, Jewish, Christian, and Muslim scholars translated many Arabic texts into Hebrew and Latin. The complete corpus of Aristotle's writings, containing knowledge that had to be reconciled with both Christian and Jewish belief, was slowly becoming available to scholars teaching in the recently founded University of Paris. Under the influence of Aristotle, philosophy became a newly systematic discipline, and careful modes of reasoning propositions, most of which are still in use today, came to dominate in schools. The scholasticism that developed in the thirteenth and fourteenth centuries was marked by debate, rhetoric, and encyclopedic overviews, the *summa*, or compendium of all knowledge, being a favored form of expression for scholarly writing. The love of proving theological propositions was fostered especially by the Dominicans, who are studied below. Their founder, St. Dominic (1170–1221), had preached in southern France and was especially dedicated to converting heretics. His followers in the thirteenth century arranged public debates on theological issues, forcing people under suspicion of heresy to attend.

These currents of thought and action were manifested in thirteenth-century repertories of music. We examine several of them in this chapter, beginning with music written by the women who brought new modes of fervent devotion to the Eucharist; their piety was transformed by learned Dominican exegetes in the development of the Feast of Corpus Christi. It was in northern France that square notation (see Primer II.1) and the four-line staff were standardized; these innovations laid the foundation for notating the rhythmic dimensions of polyphonic practices at the Cathedral of Notre Dame in Paris. A thirteenth-century gradual from the Abbey of St. Victor (Paris BN lat. 14819) contains an earlier section dating from 1140–60 that shows a fully developed four-line staff with nascent square notation, the kind of notational understanding that made the rhythmic modes possible.

Yet the scholasticism prevalent in the Parisian schools soon left women behind, making it nearly impossible for them to compose in new genres, such as the motet, that increasingly required learning they did not possess. As improvised polyphonic repertories were written down using formulas expressive of rhythmic values, musicians, like philosophers, had to master new rules and techniques. The writings of music theorists from the second half of the thirteenth century are permeated with the vocabulary of the Aristotelians, and the concepts used to explain music were also conditioned by teaching found in the schools.

MUSIC AND THE MIRACULOUS

The only new feast of the temporale—the cycle of feasts that celebrated events in Jesus's life, suffering, and resurrection—established in the thirteenth century was Corpus Christi (Body of Christ). It served to address the problems posed by the Albigensians and other heretical groups, especially regarding denial of the Eucharist. From 1215 forward, Christians were required to take communion once a year, at least at Easter, and were to be confessed of their sins beforehand. The new emphasis on the communion service would transform sacred music: the Mass increasingly became the occasion for new musical composition, and the Office slowly faded in musical importance, although new rhymed offices continued to appear. The Feast of Corpus Christi also set the stage for new dramatic works that employed incidental music and that fostered devotion to the communion host and miraculous stories associated with it. In addition, the allegorical expositions of the Mass that related parts of it to stages in history or in the life of Jesus were replaced by commentaries that saw the inner meanings of the Eucharist displayed in every segment of the service.

ST. DOMINIC AND SCHOLASTICISM

The newer kind of exegesis is represented by members of the Dominican Order, whose founder, St. Dominic, presents a contrast to St. Francis, whom we studied in Chapter 8. Francis was a jongleur for Christ, a lover of nature, a dramatic preacher, and a bearer of the Five Wounds in his own flesh. Dominic was a preacher too, and, like Francis, was devoted to poverty and the simple life. But he was better educated in theology, establishing houses of his followers near the universities of Paris and Bologna, and setting up an early form of centralized governance for the Dominican friars with headquarters in Paris. While the Franciscans standardized chant in Rome, the Dominicans, working in Paris, shortened the liturgy they inherited for practical reasons of constant travel and created a huge compendium of music for their services. They expected all Dominicans to follow the same liturgy and use the same music, and established approved exempla for copying, thereby spreading the use of square notation throughout Europe. (We'll have more to say about this and other notational innovations below.)

Like the Franciscans, Dominicans often preached out of doors. They instituted a popular procession featuring the Marian antiphon *Salve Regina* (Ex. 9.1). In this practice, the Dominicans would walk from Compline in their own church to the church of the laity, singing the antiphon with the people and praying to the Virgin Mary for protection. Special services for the Virgin, and the increasingly elaborate music associated with them, would mark the lives of musicians throughout late medieval Europe. As a result, *Salve Regina*, an antiphon written in the eleventh century, became one of the most beloved pieces of music in Europe. It would be set multiple times, was thought to call down miraculous

Example 9.1: *Opening of the Marian antiphon* Salve Regina, *the music featured in Dominican* Salve *processions throughout Europe*

Hail, Queen, mother of mercy; hail, life, sweetness, and our hope. To you we sigh, weeping and groaning in this valley of tears.

intervention from the Virgin Mary, and formed the basis for many works in the Renaissance, Baroque, and Classical periods. Several of the hundreds of miracle stories that circulated in late medieval Europe feature the singing of this famous piece.

Scholasticism, with its complex arguments made in the classroom, had as its foil the miraculous elements of popular devotion, especially as they related to the host and the powers of the Virgin Mary. In much art and music of the thirteenth century, the mystical fervor of Francis meets the scholastic intellectualism of Dominic, two sides of a common coin.

RELIGIOUS WOMEN

A key chapter in Dominic's life occurred during the Albigensian campaign. Wishing to bring heretical women to the Catholic faith, he took a group under his wing, and they eventually became Christian nuns. Dominic thus helped to establish a pattern that enabled religious women to function in the midst of suspicion and repression: throughout the thirteenth and fourteenth centuries, they worked alongside supportive male mentors who protected them—Augustinians, Cistercians, and Franciscans, but above all, Dominicans. Under the mantles of their friends and spiritual guides, women in some religious communities (such as the Bridgettine nuns of Sweden or the Dominicans of Paradies bei Soest studied in Chapter 12) flourished as composers of chant, artists, liturgists, scholars, and community leaders.

The thirteenth century also witnessed the rise of the beguines, laywomen who lived in community but were not governed by a formal monastic rule. Some religious men who served as advisors to nuns and beguines believed that women taught them things about faith that could not be learned in schools, and that the female perspective could be useful in combating heresy. Accordingly, women were given a role in religious instruction, but they often went too far in the eyes of clergymen. The Flemish beguine Marguerite Porete was burned at the stake in Paris in 1310 for her apparent refusal to cease teaching from her proscribed book *The Mirror of Simple Souls.* It was a Dominican who condemned her, but another Dominican, the mystic Meister Johann Eckhart, was influenced by the writings of Marguerite and other beguines, and was himself put on trial (although posthumously cleared). Although the mystical dimension of late medieval piety was hardly a gendered phenomenon, some of the most significant writing about the Middle Ages in recent decades has centered on women, especially beguines and mystics, and it is crucial to bring them into the discussion of music.

Many examples demonstrating the powers of religious women from the thirteenth century involve music. Marie d'Oignies, often called the first beguine, is described while singing about her mystical devotion to the Eucharist. And it was two women from the Low Countries, Juliana of Cornillon and Eve of St. Martin in Liège, who finalized the work of establishing the Feast of Corpus Christi. Juliana's biographer portrays her as jubilizing rapturously when she prayed, her soul bathed in the wordless melodies of her voice. When she was a girl, Juliana spoke of seeing the moon with one part of it darkened as she gazed on the altar. This moon symbolized the elevated host that was becoming the centerpiece of late medieval Christian piety. God revealed to Juliana that the darkened spot signified a feast that was missing from the calendar, one celebrating the sacrament of the altar. It was her task both to create the chant and liturgy for the new feast, and to ensure that they were accepted.

The Abbey of Cornillon was a house of Augustinians with a hospital for lepers. It was a double monastery, men and women living separately while working in close proximity. Juliana, who had become the prioress of the women's community, worked for years on the theology of the new feast, discussing it with religious leaders of Liège. When she felt prepared, she collaborated with a young canon named John to create the Mass and Office of Corpus Christi. Juliana was often persecuted and had to flee Liège more than once, but she had the backing of both Hugh of St. Cher, a leading Dominican theologian in Paris, and his friend and fellow believer in the goodness and importance of religious women, Jacques Pantaléon, at one time archdeacon of Liège, who would later become Pope Urban IV. The feast was declared in the diocese of Liège in 1247, and the Church of St. Martin became the liturgical center of its first celebration.

THE FEAST OF CORPUS CHRISTI

After Juliana died in 1258, the anchoress (a woman enclosed for life in an individual cell) Eve of St. Martin continued to press for bringing the Feast of Corpus Christi to the universal Church. When Pope Urban IV declared in 1264 that the feast was to be celebrated throughout Christendom, he sent a copy of the papal bull to Eve. Although it was not accepted in most places until the early fourteenth century, Corpus Christi—celebrated on the Thursday after Trinity Sunday, marking the final feast in the temporal cycle—was the most influential feast of the late Middle Ages. Significantly, it is the first festive musical phenomenon in the Latin West known to be directly inspired by women.

The Feast of Corpus Christi, with special music for the Mass and Office, celebrates the power of communal veneration of the host. As a result, a moment of elevation in the second part of the Mass—when the host is lifted on high by the celebrating priest and is transformed by ritual power—became the high point of the liturgy, and people sometimes believed that seeing the consecrated host brought special grace (Fig. 9.1). The feast was imported into every community in Europe, miracles were associated with it, and some of the music became the most beloved and popular of the entire repertory, with long-lasting influence on the history of Western thought and expression.

The texts and music created by John and Juliana for Corpus Christi did not become standard. The Dominicans who had supported the feast became involved in the work of providing and establishing other texts and music, and the complexity of the sources is a case study for the difficulties posed by the introduction of new feasts in the later Middle Ages. Today, historians usually ascribe the most

Figure 9.1: *Elevation of the host at Mass, from a legal manuscript dated to 1241 (Bodleian Library, University of Oxford)*

widespread set of standardized texts and chants to the Dominican theologian Thomas Aquinas of Paris (1225–1274), although the texts and music were not attributed to him until the early fourteenth century. Scholars point to parallels between St. Thomas's eucharistic thought and the texts of the new liturgy to establish his authorship. In this way, the miracles associated with the host and the embodiment of Christ's real presence, which became central to popular understandings of the Mass liturgy, were joined to the intellectualism of scholasticism.

One of the most beloved of all medieval melodies and texts is the hymn *Pange lingua gloriosa* for the Feast of Corpus Christi. This piece—attributed, like most of the texts for this feast, to Thomas Aquinas—formed the heart of late medieval piety and eucharistic devotion; set repeatedly by Renaissance and Baroque composers, it would form a kind of musical battle cry for the anti-Protestant Counter-Reformation. The final two stanzas of the text, beginning with the words "Tantum ergo," were the most beloved part of the hymn and came to stand on their own (Ex. 9.2). *Tantum ergo* was set by composers from all periods, including several from the nineteenth century.

The reverential piety underlying some sections of the Renaissance Mass is directly connected to late medieval devotional practices as reflected in the Mass and Office for Corpus Christi and their reception. This can be seen especially in the Benedictus section of the Sanctus in polyphonic settings of the Mass ordinary. The Benedictus was associated with the coming of the real presence into the host at Mass, and so often takes on a particularly different cast from the rest of the Sanctus, and indeed from all other parts of a polyphonic setting.

Example 9.2: Tantum ergo, *the final two strophes of the Corpus Christi hymn* Pange lingua

Strophe 5: Therefore let us venerate such a great sacrament with bowed heads, and let the ancient teaching submit to this new rite; let faith furnish the rest for the failure of the senses.
Strophe 6: To the Begetter and the Begotten, let there be praise and jubilation, a good wish, honor, might, too, and blessing: let there be comparable praising to the One proceeding from Both. Amen.

LEARNED MUSIC IN THIRTEENTH-CENTURY PARIS

Musical developments in late-twelfth- and thirteenth-century Paris have long been understood as transformative, and the innovative techniques behind them certainly required training in the schools to be mastered. Although the teaching of polyphonic practices according to the theorists encountered in this chapter had no significant role in the liberal arts curriculum at the University of Paris, we can assume that theoretical treatises were among the many books chained and ready for consultation in the Chapel of St. Ursula at the Sorbonne. The religious music emanating from the Cathedral of Notre Dame praised God while it magnified clerical roles and the powers of the kings of France, who were loyal to the pope and to the dictates of the Fourth Lateran Council. The highly wrought polyphony developed at Notre Dame often reflected the strategies of scholastic debate and rhetoric, and the rules fundamental to scholastic thought more generally. Musical motives are tossed back and forth between the voices, creating a well-regulated argument sustained by the power of a slower-moving chant that, in some genres, drones beneath the musical interplay characteristic of the upper voices.

The Parisian corpus was the first large multi-voice repertory to be organized liturgically and written down, a worthy successor to the polyphonic repertory of the Winchester Troper studied in Chapter 5, which supplied polyphonic voices in single lines (and these, in turn, had to be fitted to the appropriate plainsong). As we will see below, by the mid-thirteenth century the Parisian polyphonic repertory was being transcribed in new forms of notation that expressed not only relative pitch but also rhythm. Such sophisticated music, especially if it were to be taken to other regions, had to be taught, and several music theorists of the period left treatises giving a sense of how musicians learned to sing, notate, and compose in the Parisian style.

THE CATHEDRAL OF OUR LADY

The music of the so-called Notre Dame School was created in a rarified place: the royal capital of France, with its schools and fledgling university, and its houses of Dominicans, Franciscans, and other religious orders, including the famous Augustinian Abbey of St. Victor on the Left Bank of the Seine and the great Benedictine Abbey of St. Denis on the outskirts of the city.

At the heart of all this activity was a building project. The old cathedral of Paris, dedicated to St. Stephen, had fallen into decrepitude by the early twelfth century. Near where it once stood, on the island known as the Île de la Cité, a new cathedral rose up beginning in the early 1160s, during the tenure of King Louis VII. Louis's son, Philip Augustus, was born during the Octave of the Assumption (the week following the feast) in 1165, when the king was 45 years old. Up to that point he had produced only daughters, at that time not suitable successors to the throne. When his young third wife became pregnant (after five years of marriage), he begged for divine intervention. When Queen Adela went into labor, the population prayed that it would be delivered from the inevitable disasters that attended kingdoms without kings. The next morning every bell in the city pealed out the good news, and the feasting began. The tympanum of the right portal of the west facade of Notre Dame survives from this period, and may celebrate what many believed to be a miracle: Louis VII, having tried for decades, had produced an heir. In this part of the portal above the entrance, the king pays homage to the Virgin Mary of Chartres; his wife, Adela, was a native Chartrain (Fig. 9.2), and legend has it that the king and his wife had prayed to her for help in conceiving and bearing a male child.

The cathedral Louis VII planned would be dedicated not to Mary only, however, but to the Assumption of the Virgin (Mary's rising to heaven after death). Because Philip Augustus was born near this feast, it had special significance for father and son, and the church, its liturgy, and its music became an offering from the preserved royal lineage. The architecture of the new cathedral bespoke the tastes, history, and extraordinary power of the Capetian kings of France and their posture as defenders of the Roman Catholic Church throughout Europe and in the Holy Land. When the late Gothic phase of the cathedral was completed in the 1250s, Louis's great-grandson, Louis IX, was on the throne. The cathedral was taller, longer, and wider than any church in Europe (Fig. 9.3). Music created at Notre Dame shaped taste at courts and churches throughout the Continent, just as Paris set the fashion for clothing and court life. The surviving manuscripts and manuscript fragments of Parisian music demonstrate that many clerical and secular leaders throughout Europe desired not only French architecture, but also Parisian polyphonic magnificence and musicians capable of providing it.

The architecture of the choir (the section in the east end of the cathedral where the polyphony studied here was performed), walled off as it was by an enormous choir screen, made it a contained and relatively small space well suited to sumptuous chamber music. The singers of the most complex repertory were two to six in number, the most senior and capable of around sixteen choristers hired each year. All these singers were fired at the close of their contracts every year and had to go through auditions once again. The days immediately after Christmas gave them an opportunity to show off their skills: it was the time when all the canons of the cathedral came back for a week of feasting and entertainment, culminating in the plays and much-criticized frivolities of the Feast of the Circumcision, January 1 (sometimes called the Feast of Fools; see also Chapter 6).

The abundance of Christmas music from the Middle Ages reflects these traditions. During this week, the clerical orders celebrated their respective identities: December 26 was the Feast of St. Stephen, patron of deacons; December 27, the Feast of John the Evangelist, patron of priests; December 28, the Feast of the Holy Innocents, the patrons of acolytes; and January 1, the

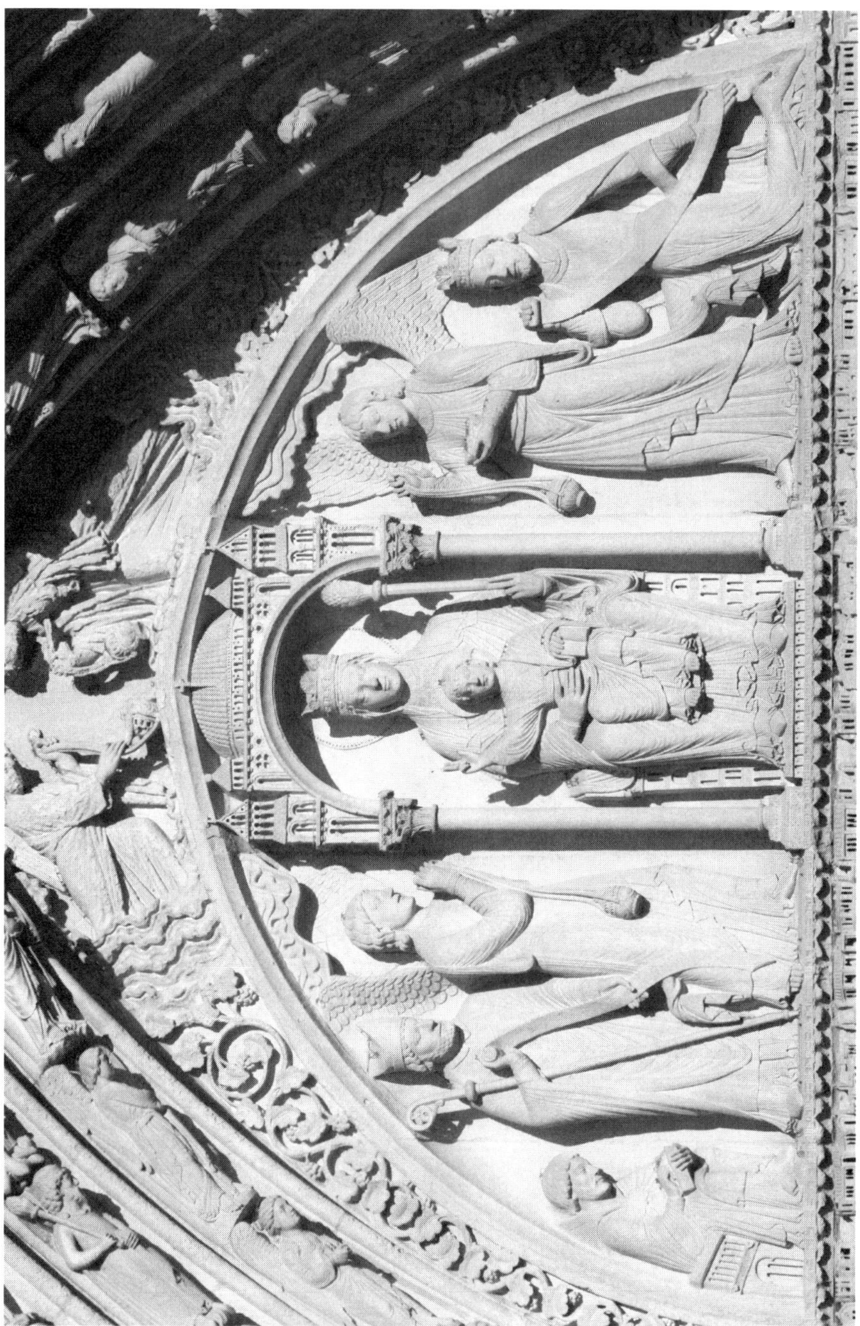

Figure 9.2: *A king (Louis VII?) paying homage to Our Lady of Chartres, from the so-called St. Anne Portal, Cathedral of Notre Dame, Paris*

Figure 9.3: *The choir of the Cathedral of Notre Dame, Paris, thirteenth century*

Feast of the Circumcision of Jesus, dedicated to the subdeacons. Each of these feasts had special music associated with it, making the Offices of Christmas week the most elegant of the entire church year. *The Play of Daniel* (see Chapter 8) from Beauvais Cathedral was performed on the Feast of the Circumcision (January 1), along with a special Office stuffed with extra music. In the play we experience a sense of the frivolities often associated with the end of the week after Christmas and the beginning of a new year.

THE NOTRE DAME SCHOOL

Like the cathedral itself, the Notre Dame corpus and the notational practices used to transcribe it were created over the course of several generations. Scholars have established an unbroken chain of prominent musicians who served at the cathedral, beginning with the sequence composer Adam of St. Victor (see Chapter 7), who was the cantor (precentor) of the cathedral until at least 1133 and seems to have retained the office even after he was removed to the Abbey of St. Victor, where he died, in around 1146. Adam was succeeded as precentor by Albertus Parisiensis (Master Albert, fl. c. 1146–1177). The compilers of the Codex Calixtinus attributed to him the polyphonic *Benedicamus* setting *Congaudeant catholici*, which, if it is indeed a three-voice work, is the first surviving such composition (see Chapter 6). We cannot say for sure that it is by Magister Albertus, but the attribution in the Codex Calixtinus does prove his fame in the third quarter of the twelfth century, and that of the Parisian school as well.

Names of other composers in the two generations after Albertus are known from a late-thirteenth-century treatise on music compiled by an Englishman who had studied in Paris. This work's author is now known as Anonymous IV, the number assigned to the treatise in a compendium of music theory treatises made in the nineteenth century. Anonymous IV seems to have acquired his knowledge as part of an orally transmitted history of Parisian music, a project that must have been especially meaningful to a man who was trying to master the practical work of transcribing and teaching notation in England.

Anonymous IV identifies Léonin (Leoninus, c. 1135–c. 1201) as "the best composer of organum," and credits him with compiling the *Magnus liber organi* (Great Book of Organum). He reports that this large collection of liturgically organized polyphony (and some monophony) was used at Notre Dame until the time of Pérotin (Perotinus Magnus, fl. late twelfth and early thirteenth centuries), who edited or abridged it. According to Anonymous IV, Pérotin was "the best composer of discant." (Discant is basically note-against-note polyphony, as distinct from organum, in which the chant is set against faster-moving notes in the upper part or parts; see Chapter 6.) Indeed, it can be demonstrated from the liturgical use reflected in the *Magnus liber* and the variants of the various chants foundational to the polyphony within it, that it was first designed for singing at the Cathedral of Notre Dame in Paris, although adapted for other churches as well. Scholars now agree that Léonin was a well-known poet, at one time a canon at the Cathedral of Notre Dame, who lived out the end of his life at the Abbey of St. Victor, dying around 1201, this date putting the initial compilation of the *Magnus liber* in the late twelfth century. Some believe that Pérotin was Petrus, a subcantor who served at the Cathedral of Notre Dame in the early thirteenth century, in any case the *Magnus liber* was apparently under revision in the early decades of the thirteenth century.

Another prominent poet associated with the development of the repertory was Philip, chancellor of the Cathedral of Notre Dame (c. 1160–1236) and de facto head of the nascent University of Paris, which grew out of the cathedral school. He composed many conductus texts, some of which were included in the *Carmina burana* collection (see Chapter 8). Some scholars think he worked directly with Pérotin, and composed motets as well as melodies for his conductus texts, and so was doubtless a contributor to the *Magnus liber* as it was revised in the early thirteenth century. Whoever composed them, many of the carefully wrought monophonic songs with Latin texts produced in this time of great musical exuberance were settings of Philip the Chancellor's poetry. The unusually lavish ornamentation at the ends of lines in *Sol oritur in sidere* (see Anthology 26), a monophonic conductus attributed to Philip, could only have been rendered by the finest singers in Paris, who must have been adept at performing both monophonic and polyphonic repertories. With such skilled musicians in residence, the performing forces at the Cathedral in the twelfth and early thirteenth centuries doubtless constituted a kind of workshop for new genres, styles of singing, and even for thinking about ways of notating the repertory of the Cathedral of Notre Dame.

MODAL NOTATION IN THE *MAGNUS LIBER ORGANI*

Each of the Parisian composers discussed above was involved in the musical developments and aesthetic ideals that culminated in the creation of the *Magnus liber organi*, although, as we'll see, the collection had no fixed form or contents, and few of the surviving pieces can be securely attributed to any one person. It was at this time that the first notational system expressing precise rhythmic values evolved in Paris as well. This evolution, which took place in several stages, was a product of numerous innovations that went hand in hand in Paris in the second half of the twelfth century. Foundational to all of them was the new song (sometimes called the *cantica nova*), the accentual sung Latin verse that had been developing from the eleventh century, but culminated in its most overwrought manifestation of the style in the Parisian sequence as championed both at the Cathedral of Notre Dame and the Abbey of St. Victor.

As we saw in Chapter 7, the large-scale accentual grid provided by the texts of these very long chants led to a kind of motivic development not witnessed before in the history of Western music (see *Zima Vetus*, Anthology 19). These new songs of substantial length were being composed and sung in great numbers in twelfth-century Paris. It is clear from surviving liturgical books and the new sequences organized within them by the early thirteenth century, that accentual patterns featured in the poetry dominated musical sensibilities and productivity during this time. It was in the second half of the twelfth century that fully developed square notation appeared in Paris as well (see Primer II.1).

Unlike the early St. Gall neumes studied in Chapter 3, square notation is not cursive. Rather, even within the compound neumes known as ligatures (shown as brackets in modern transcriptions of polyphonic works), every note is discrete, a crucial factor in the development of a notation capable of expressing rhythm in patterns of long and short notes. A direct relationship between Parisian sequences and the development of the rhythmic modes cannot be proven, but we do know that the two came from the same place and time, and involved the same musical personnel at the Cathedral of Notre Dame and the Abbey of St. Victor. Accentual patterns based on the metrical feet of Latin poetry, by some as-yet-not-understood process, eventually were recast into patterns of long and short notes, patterns that came to be superimposed onto the ligatures of square notation used for writing down polyphonic works. Over the course of the first half of the thirteenth century, the notation evolved again from ligature patterns that represented the rhythmic modes (but have nothing to do with individual note shapes), to mensural notation in which particular note shapes came to have assignable rhythmic values. Although the rhythmic modes still matter in early mensural notation, as individual note shapes became increasingly capable of expressing rhythmic values on their own during the late thirteenth and fourteenth centuries, the importance of the modes diminished (see Part IV). But as we will see, the rhythmic modes hung on in the slow-moving tenors of Latin-texted polyphonic works, even in the fourteenth century.

Parisian singers surely displayed their most elaborate improvisational skills in the soloistic sections of chants for the Mass and Office, and it is within them that the written tradition of Notre Dame polyphony was born. The "new" polyphonic music was first an improvised practice created to decorate plainsong, and this connection to chant remained crucial in the early stages of development. In the early thirteenth century, two- and three-voice settings of conductus were the only polyphonic genres that were entirely newly composed.

By the late twelfth and early thirteenth centuries, the ligatures used to express melismas in the soloistic portions of the chant had became associated with the six patterns known as the rhythmic modes (see Primer II.3). As can be seen in the treatise *Discantus positio vulgaris* (Common Position on Discant; SR 29:218–22; 2/21:108–12), written by an anonymous theorist around 1230, and in Anonymous VII, who probably wrote around 1240, the initial understanding was that each of the rhythmic modes is made up of feet consisting of three beats or *tempora*. *Modus* is the level of counting that governs the long, and *tempus* is the level of counting that governs the breve. In the beginning, a regular long consisted of two beats or tempora and a breve of one, making the foot characteristic of mode 1, long-breve, of mode 2, breve-long; and of mode 6, a foot made up of three breves. Modes 1, 2, and 6, then were considered "correct," whereas modes 3, 4, and 5 were considered "beyond measure" because they had notes that exceeded two tempora. A major difficulty in studying the rhythmic modes from the earliest theorists is that they already were writing long after the system developed, and, furthermore, even their works have been revised and edited (see below); our only copy of *Discantus positio vulgaris*, for example, is in the edition of Jerome of Moray.

Discantus positio vulgaris describes the rhythmic modes as follows (with the conventional modern transcription given in parentheses):

mode 1: long, breve (half note, quarter note)

mode 2: breve, long (quarter note, half note)

mode 3: long, breve, breve (dotted half note, quarter note, half note)

mode 4: breve, breve, long (quarter note, half note, dotted half note)

mode 5: long, long, long (three dotted half notes)

mode 6: breve, breve, semibreve, semibreve (two quarter notes, two eighth notes) (equivalent to three breves)

The six rhythmic modes (also discussed in the Primer II.3) were expressed in phrase groupings called *ordines* (singular, *ordo*). Each ordo should begin and end with a note of the same value. Mode 1 predominates in the literature, especially in the early layers of the repertory, with its repeating "trochaic" patterns falling in feet consisting of a long plus a breve. For example, the following pattern consists of a secundus ordo in mode 1 because it has two full feet before the rest:

long-breve/long-breve/long-rest

As the examples discussed below from the *Magnus liber organi* show, the character of much early-thirteenth-century polyphonic music is driven by its expression in the rhythmic modes. To medieval thinkers, the modes were a way of retrieving time through music and making it live once again, in both pitch and rhythm. St. Augustine argued that time existed only in the human memory. For recall, he used the idea of the patterns of rhythmic verse, the same patterns used for the rhythmic modes. The degree to which Augustine's theories were important in the development of the modes is a matter of debate.

THE MANUSCRIPTS OF THE NOTRE DAME REPERTORY

As noted above, the *Magnus liber organi* was not a specific "book" but an evolving repertory of liturgical music linked both historically and through the liturgy and chant sources to the Cathedral of Notre Dame in Paris. Most of the pieces that constituted the fullest Notre Dame corpus are found in three major manuscripts that were copied in the mid-thirteenth century. (In the discussion below, these sources are identified by letters corresponding to their present-day locations.) These vast compendia thus preserve the polyphonic practice of the two generations after 1198, when Odo of Sully, the bishop of Paris, first mentioned the singing of organum in three or four voices on Christmas and St. Stephen's Day in the Cathedral of Notre Dame; the four-voice *Viderunt omnes* setting ascribed to Pérotin (see below) is the most famous example.

Manuscript W1, now in the library of Wolfenbüttel, Germany, is the earliest of the three sources of Notre Dame polyphony. The manuscript was copied around 1230, probably at and certainly for the Augustinian Cathedral of St. Andrew, the leading ecclesiastical establishment of Scotland. It contains early examples of the writing of polyphonic repertories using the rhythmic modes. Manuscript W2, also in Wolfenbüttel, is believed to be from Paris, although its specific origin has not been determined. It represents the work of many scribes and includes a great number of motets, some with French texts. W2 is the latest of the three major manuscripts containing the *Magnus liber* and subsequent additions; its notation is the easiest to transcribe, as it is in the most advanced state of the three manuscripts.

The third source, known as Manuscript F (for its location in Florence's Biblioteca Medicea Laurenziana), falls between W1 and W2 chronologically. We will concentrate on it for the earlier layers of the Notre Dame repertory; significant sections have been transcribed in an authoritative new edition of the *Magnus liber organi*. The Florence Codex is a deluxe manuscript, decorated with painted initials to begin each section and a frontispiece depicting three zones, each of which contains a queen pointing to one of the types of music described by Boethius: of the spheres, of the body, and of instruments. The most recent theory is that F was presented to King Louis IX for the dedication of his new royal chapel, the Sainte Chapelle, in 1248. Perhaps F was offered to win the king's favor for Notre Dame Cathedral and its clergy: its conductus repertory presents a history of his family's memorable deeds.

A distinguishing feature of this manuscript fit for a king is its size: it includes more than twice the number of pieces in either W1 or W2. Like them, the Florence Codex is divided into sections focusing on particular genres, with attention to numbers of voices as well. Its contents include four-voice and three-voice organa (*organa quadrupla* and *tripla*, or simply *quadrupla* and *tripla*) and conductus; two-voice organa (*dupla*) for the Office; two-voice organa for the Mass; two-voice *clausulae* (we'll discuss these little "paragraphs" of musical development below); two-voice conductus; three-voice "conductus motets"; two-voice Latin motets; monophonic Latin conductus; and monophonic Latin refrain songs and related works. Each genre has its own relationship to the liturgy, and stylistic and notational characteristics unique to it.

NOTRE DAME ORGANUM

The organa found in the *Magnus liber* are essentially in two styles, *organum purum* (see below) and discant (see Chapter 6), which would become (in some instances) *clausulae*; a third, transitional texture was represented by *copulae*, which might feature repetitions of several short phrases on a variety of pitch levels. Foundational chants, those pieces that were commonly set polyphonically at the cathedral and elsewhere, were numbered long ago by the musicologist Friedrich Ludwig and are labeled either M or O, depending on whether a chant comes from the Mass or the Office. *Stirps Jesse*, for example, is O16, and this is why pieces based on it are so labeled in editions of the *Magnus liber*. This information is crucial for those who might want to do further research on the repertory.

The interaction between the voice sustaining the chant in long notes and the florid line or lines above it is sophisticated and has to do with the ways that consonant and dissonant intervals are expressed. Octaves, fifths, and fourths were the major consonances in this practice, just as in earlier polyphonic repertories, and their use produces the requisite perfect intervals at the ends of musical phrases. In fact, many two-voice organa in Manuscript F are not that different harmonically from polyphonic settings found in the Codex Calixtinus. The parts of the chant that would be sung by a soloist are set polyphonically, while the parts traditionally sung by the choir remain in plainsong. When the soloistic parts are sung in a decorated line above a slow-moving chant (called a tenor, from the Latin verb meaning "to hold"), the musical style known as *organum*, *organum purum*, or *organum per se* results. If the upper voice or voices entered with pitches that would be dissonant against the tenor, the tenor (the voice singing the original chant notes) might delay its entrance. Later the tenor might briefly drop out, once again because of dissonance, although the singers often seem to have piled on the dissonances right before main cadences. The musical fabric is made up of developing motives, often exchanged between the upper voices.

The three- and four-voice organa found in manuscripts F, W1, and W2 are the rarest of musical birds and may be among the oldest layer of pieces in the repertory. Most of them were created especially for Christmas week, decorating chants for Christmas and the Feast of St. Stephen. A page from the Florence Codex containing a four-voice setting of the Christmas Gradual *Viderunt omnes* (Fig. 9.4) shows that it resembles a modern score, with the parts lining up above the tenor. The "upper" voices explore what is essentially the same range as the tenor. In triple and quadruple organa for major feasts, such as the setting from the Marian responsory *Stirps Jesse* (see Anthology 27), the rhetorical use

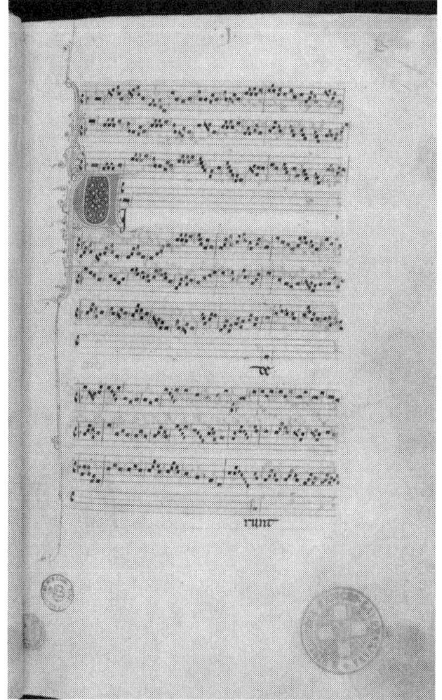

Figure 9.4: *Organum quadruplum: the opening of the Gradual* Viderunt omnes, *from the Florence Codex*

of melodic sections creates a display of musical fireworks. The singers wanted to be rehired, and those who sang such grand, festive works before the largest and most influential audience in all of Paris could put their best foot forward. In Paris in the thirteenth century, the foundation was laid for the notational system and scoring that we still use today.

The opening of *Viderunt omnes* in Example 9.3 is essentially in rhythmic mode 1, and displays many of the musical features characteristic of the style: short, neatly composed melodic phrases that are developed in a variety of ways, exist on several pitch levels, and can be tossed playfully from one voice to another. Below these shapely upper voices, the plainchant (see Anthology 3.2) drones on, and every shift of a single pitch in the tenor causes the entire musical fabric to change gears. Theorists of the time, such as the anonymous author of the so-called Vatican Organum Treatise (Ottoboni lat. 3025 in the Biblioteca Apostolica Vaticana), reveal that musicians understood how to move for each possible circumstance offered by the tenor, both in organum purum and in discant. The scribes were writing down a practice that was still being improvised within the liturgy.

A two-voice setting of the opening of the responsory *Stirps Jesse* in Manuscript F (see Anthology 28) illustrates the two polyphonic styles of organum and discant. It also reminds us that notation of the rhythmic modes was an evolving practice. In fact, we might say that the discant section of this piece is premodally trochaic—that is, it tends toward mode 1, but is not there yet. In fact, Johannes de Garlandia (John of Garland, fl. c. 1270–1320; not to be confused with the English grammarian of the same name), seems to have edited an anonymous treatise on mensurable music (SR 30:223–26; 2/22:113–16) to produce the *De mensurabili musica* now associated with his name. So although he was a contemporary of the important later theorists and compilers Lambertus, Anonymous 4, the St. Emmeram Anonymous, Franco of Cologne, and Jerome of Moray, the work he edited is somewhat earlier and foundational. It is the first known work

Example 9.3: *Opening of a four-voice setting of the Gradual* Viderunt omnes, *as found in the Florence Codex*

They have seen

to lay out in full the rhythmic nature of music in the Notre Dame repertory and its notation, compiled over two generations after the death of Leonin.

Organa pura from the slightly later Manuscript W2 can be transcribed in rhythmic modes, as the notation is more consistently applied than in F, showing that new styles of thinking about music and its notation were coming into this venerable style. In spite of its musical sophistication, however, organum purum was not the wave of the future. Rather, discant sections were the fertile soil from which the musical plants would grow that came to dominate the landscape of the most forward-looking music throughout Europe in the later thirteenth century.

These discant sections were called clausulae or *puncta*, both words meaning a "section" in literature. Composers of clausulae not only placed them within works of organum purum; they also extracted the famous chant melismas that formed the basis of the clausula repertory and wrote new polyphonic settings of them, some of which could be substituted for other clausulae within the larger pieces. Composers created clausulae of many shapes and styles for liturgical use, as well as for study or recreation. The first series of "substitute clausulae" in manuscript F are all in two parts, and there are around 200 works in this section; a later part of the manuscript contains three-voice clausulae. (Anthology 29 contains a two-voice and a three-voice clausula on the same chant tenor, *Flos Filius eius*.)

THE THIRTEENTH-CENTURY MOTET

We have seen that medieval composers delighted in providing melismas with texts, no matter what the genre. Notker the Stammerer set "very long melodies" with words, helping to create a new genre called the sequence (or prose); prosulae were written for the melismas of Kyries and Glorias; *Benedicamus Domino* chants—usually famous melismas borrowed from elsewhere in the liturgy—were fitted to these closing words with more texts added, creating what are known as *Benedicamus* tropes (many of which, in turn, are called versus or conductus). These troped *Benedicamus* chants were further expanded by the addition of a second or even a third extra line of music when sung polyphonically.

It is no wonder that clausulae, those short, vocalized polyphonic gems set into the fabric of organa (but also coming to exist as a genre in their own right), were soon supplied with words. When clausulae were texted, a new polyphonic genre was born: the motet. But it would be a mistake to oversimplify the development of the motet, for the earliest examples could only be written in square neumes with modal significance called "cum littera" (with words) notation. In order to indicate rhythmic values, it was necessary to express the clausula in the ligatures of square notation that contained the modal patterns. The addition of words meant that the ligatures were broken up, and the notation was no longer able to express rhythms. There was clearly a need for a new kind of notation.

THE DEVELOPMENT OF MENSURAL NOTATION

As we have seen, the rhythmic modes had developed in the context of melismatic vocalizations and were expressed in ligatures. What would happen when the addition of words to clausulae made the music predominantly syllabic? How could the rhythms of the music be expressed after the ligatures were dissolved?

At first, in fact, rhythm wasn't expressed in the notation of the motet genre. It was not possible to discern the rhythms of a motet without knowing the modal clausula on which it was based, given that its rhythms were revealed through ligature patterns in melismatic chant notation. Some early clausulae—for example, the three-voice clausula on *Flos Filius eius* (see Anthology 29.2)—were surely created expressly to solve this problem: that is, to be used as guides to the rhythms of early motets.

At the same time that motets were being created from clausulae, monophonic conductus were being composed in two- and three-voice settings; for instance, the conductus *Deduc Syon* attributed to Philip the Chancellor (see Ex. 8.2) existed in Paris in a two-voice version as well. Polyphonic conductus, with their homophonic textures, were the first multi-voice works without liturgical tenors, but some of them, too, were reshaped to unfold above a tenor, creating what is often called the "conductus motet." Polyphonic conductus offered one solution to the notational crisis provoked by the early motet, perhaps allowing the rhythms of the texts to suggest how to sing the piece. The long melismatic "tails" of conductus such as *Sol oritur in sidere* (see Anthology 26) were often written in ligatures that expressed the modes, and the relationship between "cum littera" conductus and their modal "tails" *(caudae)* is much debated by scholars today.

It was mensural notation, in which individual ligatures and note shapes stood for durational values (rather than patterns superimposed on ligatures, as in the rhythmic modes), that provided the ultimate solution to the dilemma. Mensural notation is also called Franconian notation, after a Dominican theorist called Franco of Cologne (fl. mid- to late thirteenth century), a German writing in Paris who described these rhythmic innovations around 1280. In his treatise *Ars cantus mensurabilis* (The Art of Mensurable Music), he describes notation with a Trinitarian spin, making the perfection of the number three foundational to the system (see SR 31:226–45; 2/23:116–35). Accordingly, a long is perfect *(modus perfectus)* if it has three beats (now usually transcribed as a dotted quarter note), and imperfect if it has two beats. A breve is perfect if it has one beat, and altered if it has two beats.

A version of Franco's rules for the values of note shapes is set forth in Primer II.4. He also had rules for the shapes of ligatures and for rests, which are indicated by lines drawn vertically through the staff. In addition to his discussion of longs and breves, Franco describes the semibreve: a breve can be replaced by two semibreves, the second (the major semibreve) being worth twice the count of the first (the minor semibreve), or by three semibreves of equal worth. The values of semibreves still belong to Franco's world of perfection as expressed through the number three.

The theorist Anonymous IV realized that notational practices had changed dramatically in the decades leading up to his work in the late thirteenth century. A musical revolution was taking place, as modal notation slowly gave way to mensural notation. Subsequent innovations in the fourteenth century would result in notation that expressed rhythmic values with ever greater precision and increasingly smaller divisions of the beat. As the sounds of written music changed in response to these notational developments, a higher level of expertise on the part of the scribes who wrote the music down was required.

POLYTEXTUAL MOTETS BASED ON *STIRPS JESSE*

The best way to study the motet in its many guises is to take one famous melisma and trace several of its settings. Through such study, one encounters many experiments with polyphonic textures and sees the changes taking place in the motet in the mid-thirteenth century,

In this most Marian of centuries, a Marian chant serves well as the foundation for a large complex of interrelated pieces. When the familiar *Flos Filius eius* melisma lifted from the responsory *Stirps Jesse* was used as the tenor of a motet, the many meanings of the chant were symbolically present; poet-composers could experiment with the interplay between the Virgin Mary and the shepherdess Marie, divine love and romantic love, chastity and sexual encounters. The possibilities for glossing were many, as were the chances for humor and irony. We have seen that the thirteenth century witnessed the mixing of the sacred and the secular in several understandings of art and music. The polytextual motet was the perfect vehicle for such mixing: by allowing two or more texts, even in different languages, to unfold simultaneously, motets derived their meanings from both the individual voices and the interaction between them.

Stirps Jesse produced a thicket of sonic shoots. It is clear from the varied uses of chant in polyphonic settings, in Paris and elsewhere, that medieval musicians and their listeners knew and loved the chants that were decorated in these ways; indeed, some of the melismas were so universally familiar as to be like the standard "changes" (chord sequences) of popular songs that modern jazz musicians know by heart and that form the basis of so many of their improvisations. In the responsory *Stirps Jesse*, music used for the words "Flos filius eius," at the "e-" of eius, was sung to some 30 notes. The *Flos Filius eius* melisma (or some part of it) provided the foundation for around 40 pieces of polyphonic music.

Stirps Jesse was set as two-voice organum in manuscripts F and W2, and as three-voice organum in F and W1. There are ten clausulae based on various sections of the parent chant in F, and some of these clausulae were used as the bases for motets. The modal notation of the clausulae from F on which many motets are based is traditionally analyzed by counting perfections—that is, rhythmic cells of three beats each; these are marked in the score of the parent clausula, numbering 36 (see Anthology 29.3). In Franconian notation, a perfect long was worth three beats, so patterns in the tenor set up the number of perfections, using rests and sometimes repeated phrases. In order for the music to work, the transcriber has to pay attention to the perfections in the tenor, and to consonances and dissonances at the ends of phrases to make sure everything moves in accordance with the patterning of the tenor.

The clausulae and the motets based on them are exercises in sounding numbers; this gives them an overriding intellectual power that relates to long-held beliefs about music as an art of proportion. *Plus bele que flor* (quadruplum)/*Quant revient* (triplum)/*L'autrier joer* (duplum or motetus)/*Flos Filius* (tenor) (see Anthology 30.1) is a triple French motet (three voices above a tenor) based on the parent clausula. The quadruplum sings of the Virgin Mary; the triplum is about the courtly aspect of love; the duplum reveals a dramatic scene of love and sorrow; and all three are sustained by the familiar *Flos Filius* melisma in the tenor. There are four levels to this miniature exploration of love (Ex. 9.4).

Example 9.4: *Opening of* Plus bele que flor/Quant revient/L'autrier joer/Flos filius

Quadruplum: More lovely than a flower, I believe, is she to whom I give myself.

Triplum: When leaf and flower come back with the approach of the summer, Lord!

Motetus: The other day I was wandering in a lonely place, and into an orchard I went.

Tenor: The flower, her son

The two Latin text lines of *Castrum pudicicie/Virgo viget/Flos Filius*—a double motet (two voices above a tenor)—are glosses on the meaning of the tenor, quoting directly from the parent chant (see Anthology 30.2). The piece is closely tied musically to the parent clausula, yet putting words to the vocalise changes many surface details of the piece. The rhythms of phrases are different, and there is now more dissonance. But there are also more ways than one to transcribe such a piece, either by following the rhythm of the clausula closely or by experimenting with other ways of conceptualizing individual phrases. The beautifully shaped melodies and their forceful rhythmic texts have great appeal for contemporary audiences, as shown by the numerous recordings made of motets belonging to this family of works.

Two-voice Latin motets were, in general, the most closely tied to the clausulae. But Manuscript W2 contains many motets with French texts. New collections of motets were created throughout the later thirteenth century, and in addition to these major sources, a great number of fragments have been located. Motets were everywhere by the turn of the fourteenth century, far outpacing the small collections in manuscripts W2 and F, yet still tied to the traditions these sources represent. The many layers of textual meanings and the different languages are further manifestations of the medieval love of glossing—expressing ideas about a subject in many guises. In that sense, thirteenth-century motets were an antidote to the times, allowing for the expression of joy and delight in a world that was increasingly fragmented and difficult.

The thirteenth century itself is something like a motet, filled with singing and crying, cruelty and joy, mysticism and learnedness, transparently lyrical music and complex poetic illusions. The music of the thirteenth century has occupied two chapters of our book and will open Chapter 10 as well, where a variety of innovations in music are seen to characterize the late thirteenth and early fourteenth centuries. This was an epoch when some musicians became increasingly critical of the difficult times in which they lived and anxious, even self-conscious, about their roles within society. There was perhaps never a time in the history of Western music when so many aspects of music and musical life witnessed dramatic transformation.

For Aristotle, the master philosopher of the Parisian schools, time was an attribute of motion and was continuous and related to number, measurement, and the natural world. According to the Christianized interpretation of Aristotle's physics that was taught during the time of Franco, the tempora are qualities of time rather than quantities. Thus while an imperfect long may have the same count as an altered breve, they are not the same thing and do not occupy the same space in a metrical foot. Ultimately, however, it would come to pass that beat would underlie all levels of music, and all notes would be defined in accordance with it.

This understanding of how to measure the passage of time is reflected in the nature of mechanical clocks, which were invented in the late thirteenth century and would transform how people lived and worked, as well as how they perceived music—or at least some of it—in the fourteenth century. Clock time is very different from hourglass time, and even more different from time as told by a sundial. So too is measured music different from chant in its view of time (and of eternity). The many levels of time demanding a unifying beat can first be seen in the development of the late-thirteenth- and early-fourteenth-century motet, a subject of our next chapter.

FOR FURTHER READING

Baltzer, Rebecca A., "The Polyphonic Progeny of an *Et gaudebit*: Assessing Family Relations in the Thirteenth-Century Motet," in Dolores Pesce, ed., *Hearing the Motet: Essays on the Motet of the Middle Ages and Renaissance* (New York: Oxford University Press, 1997), pp. 17–27.

Farmer, Sharon, *Surviving Poverty in Medieval Paris: Gender, Ideology, and the Daily Lives of the Poor* (Ithaca, NY: Cornell University Press, 2002)

Haines, John, "Anonymous IV as an Informant on the Craft of Music Writing," *Journal of Musicology* 23 (2006): 375–425

Huot, Sylvia, *Allegorical Play in the Old French Motet: The Sacred and the Profane in Thirteenth-Century Polyphony* (Stanford, CA: Stanford University Press, 1997)

Maurey, Yossi, "Heresy, Devotion, and Memory: The Meaning of Corpus Christi in Saint-Martin of Tours," *Acta Musicologica* 78 (2006): 159–96

Minnis, Alastair, and Rosalynn Voaden, eds., *Medieval Holy Women in the Christian Tradition c. 1100–c. 1500* (Turnhout, Belgium: Brepols, 2010)

Pesce, Dolores, "The Significance of Texts in Thirteenth-Century Latin Motets," *Acta Musicologica* 58 (1986): 91–117

Roesner, Edward H., "Who 'Made' the 'Magnus Liber'?" *Early Music History* 20 (2001): 227–66

Rothenberg, David, *The Flower of Paradise: Marian Devotion and Secular Song in Medieval and Renaissance Music* (Oxford: Oxford University Press, 2011)

Simon, Walter, "Beguines, Liturgy, and Music in the Middle Ages: An Exploration," in Pieter Mannaerts, ed., *Beghinae in cantu instructae: Music Patrimony from Flemish Beguinages (Middle Ages–Late-18th Century)* (Turnhout, Belgium: Brepols, 2009), 15–26

PART IV

Musicians and Patrons in the Fourteenth Century

The history of music in the fourteenth century unfolds in a climate of political intrigue, turmoil, and fear. Every musical repertory reflects its times, but in this period the lives and productions of many composers were deeply affected by their patrons in increasingly diverse ways. In Chapter 10 we examine the machinations of the French court in the early 1300s, with all its lavishness, as well as the critique of it and of the Church created by a small group of highly skilled poets, artists, and musicians. Musicians supported by the courts (both sacred and secular) were virtuosi who could notate and perform the rhythmically intricate music of the day. An Ars Nova (new art), born in France in the early fourteenth century, moved to both Italy and England, where, as we will see in Chapter 11, local traditions reshaped the French Ars Nova into something quite different. Later in the fourteenth century, various extremes in Ars Nova techniques ushered in an era of increasing refinements and subtleties, sometimes known as mannerism in music and the visual arts.

In Chapter 12, an epilogue devoted to musical developments in institutions and places not frequently studied, we find the first transcribed repertory of folk music, examine the work of nuns who reflect ever more inwardly on liturgical song, and encounter styles of folk polyphony, one of which was transposed from Spain to Iceland, where our book ends, midway to the New World. Fourteenth-century Europeans became more adventurous in their explorations of distant lands, inspired by the reports of extraordinary journeys to the Far East written by the Venetian explorer Marco Polo (c. 1254–1324) and the Dominican Jordanus (fl. 1321–1330), and wherever they went, music traveled along, as unfortunately did fleas carrying disease.

Fourteenth-century Europe also witnessed dramatic cultural, political, and religious upheavals. As a result of land clearing, a long period of warmth, and favorable conditions for crops, there had been significant population growth in the thirteenth century. By around 1300, Europe had, by some estimates, 80–100 million people, as compared to 50–60 million a century earlier. Significant numbers of these people left the land for the towns, in search of better lives. This demographic—large numbers of people newly moved to urban areas—made Europe particularly susceptible to the ravages of famine and plague, both of which struck with a vengeance in the fourteenth century.

The worst famine began in 1310 in northern Europe (southern Europe was hit less hard) and raged for some ten years. Many older people starved themselves to provide for the young, and children were often abandoned in macabre Hansel and Gretel scenarios. There was an increasing gap between rich and poor. Landlords, whose incomes were falling due to a devalued currency, squeezed the peasants mercilessly, and there were peasant revolts in England and elsewhere during this period. The weather was wet and cold, seeds produced very little, and people were forced to eat their seed grain, blighting the future. At least those living close to the land had a chance to survive; in the towns and cities food went to the highest bidders, rather than to the poor and

Europe in the Restless Fourteenth Century

the rising mercantile class. Famine weakened people, making them susceptible to disease.

The horrors of starvation faced throughout the century were surpassed by those of the bubonic plague, which originated in China, was carried by ship into Africa, and from there migrated to Europe, where it struck in 1348 and spread rapidly, sparing no region. In two years, the population diminished by a third to a half. For the rest of this century and into the next, plague broke out sporadically, killing children in particularly high numbers. Famine and plague destroyed the already fragile bonds of civil society. Minority groups were increasingly blamed for problems that seemed to have no solutions; Jews, in particular, were scapegoated for the plague and subjected to savage pogroms in many cities. Ingmar Bergman's 1957 film *The Seventh Seal*, in which a knight returns to his Scandinavian home to play chess with Death, depicts a culture ravaged by fear and suffering.

As if that weren't enough, the fourteenth century was also wracked by seemingly endless warfare, notably the ongoing struggle between France and England known as the Hundred Years' War (1337–1453), but many other major conflicts as well (see map). The ways of war were becoming ever more cruel. Instead of knights battling each other and then releasing those they conquered for ransom, the new goals were to kill and maim as many of the enemy as possible. Much of the fighting was done by mercenaries without ties to the land. Crops and villages were burned, livestock slaughtered, and tributes extorted from the people.

The Church was involved as well in the turmoil of the century. The papacy was "captured" by France and removed from Rome to Avignon between 1309 and 1378. There the papal establishment acted much like a secular court, spending extravagantly and engaging in political intrigue, with an ever-growing bureaucracy to collect fees and determine who held offices in the Church.

At the same time, the fourteenth century saw an epidemic of "measure mania" as mathematicians, astronomers, and other scientists made great strides in understanding the mechanisms of the natural world. By the end of the century, town clocks constructed throughout Europe had come to regulate the hours and keep everyday life humming to an increasingly steady beat. The most sophisticated fourteenth-century musicians, proponents of the Ars Nova, were fascinated by rhythms and counter-rhythms, and by the expression of multiple layers of time. We have seen that many composers of the twelfth and thirteenth centuries were highly skilled poets; several composers of the fourteenth century were astronomers and mathematicians. So we come full circle, back to the kind of thinker we encountered in the early fifth century in the philosopher and mathematician Boethius, whose writings continued to be studied in fourteenth-century Europe.

CHAPTER TEN

Music and Narrative in Fourteenth-Century France

Despite the political and social difficulties outlined in the introduction to Part 4, the late thirteenth and fourteenth centuries were unparalleled times for musical creativity. Paris was a major center, as it was a hub for university life and sustained a sumptuous court that was the envy of Europe. Parisian music, literature, philosophy, and visual arts were often interdependent, and several individuals moved in more than one sphere of activity. Many of the most skilled musicians were civil servants who were tied, in one way or another, to the kings of France or their close associates.

In 1328, France saw one line of kings, the Capetians, replaced by another, the Valois (Table 10.1). Although the country was engaged in ongoing wars with England, by the end of the century the dukes of Burgundy, the cadet line of the Valois kings (the lineage of the king's brother), would begin to exert their powers, emerging as leading patrons of music. The dramatic stories of fourteenth-century life, love, and piety are reflected in the use of music to underscore narrative works, several of which we will encounter in this chapter and the next. Music was also linked to large-scale artistic designs or productions of manuscripts, such as those of poet-composer Guillaume de Machaut. Pieces studied in this chapter often unfold within or alongside the literary works

Table 10.1: *Kings of France and England in the Thirteenth and Fourteenth Centuries*

FRANCE	ENGLAND
Capetian Dynasty (987–1328)	
Philip II (Augustus) r. 1180–1223	John Lackland r. 1199–1217
Louis VIII (the Lion) r. 1223–1226	Louis VIII of France, claimed from 1216–1217
Louis IX (St. Louis) r. 1226–1270 (canonized 1297)	Henry III r. 1216–1272
Philip III (the Bold) r. 1270–1285	Edward I r. 1272–1307
Philip IV (the Fair) r. 1285–1314	Edward II r. 1307–1327
Louis X (the Difficult) r. 1314–1316	Edward III r. 1327–1377
John I (the Posthumous) r. November 15–20, 1316	Richard II r. 1377–1399
Philip the V (the Tall) r. 1316–1322	
Charles IV (the Fair) r. 1322–1328	
Valois Dynasty (1328–1589)	
Philip VI (the Fortunate) r. 1328–1350	
John II (the Good) r. 1350–1364	
Charles V (the Wise) r. 1364–1380	
Charles VI (the Mad) r. 1380–1422	

they accompany in the manuscripts, and many of these composite sources are directly reflective of the political and social circumstances of their times.

MUSIC AND COURT LIFE AT THE TIME OF THE LAST CAPETIANS

Several musical sources copied in Paris date from the era of the last Capetian kings. Two manuscripts of special importance were apparently created for and within the court by musicians, poets, and artists who worked (at least some of the time) in the service of the kings. These manuscripts—Montpellier Bibliothèque Interuniversitaire, Section Médecine, H 196 (Mo) and Paris BN fr. 146 (the interpolated *Roman de Fauvel*)—provide windows onto the musical lives of the best composers of the age, as well as demonstrating the gradual transition between the "old" and "new" musical styles.

Mo, the earlier of the two sources, has been associated with Marie of Brabant (c. 1254–1321), the young queen of Philip III ("the Bold"). Married in 1274 and crowned at Sainte Chapelle in 1275, Marie was a great patron of the arts and a relative of and friend to several trouvères. Her coronation is said to have been heralded by women and maidens singing "diverses chançons and diverses motés." Among these diverse chansons may have been a *carole*, a round dance. The dancing of the carole (English, carol; Italian, *carola*) and other types of song out of doors, which clearly involved women, was characteristic of Parisian musical life in Marie's time. (No music for the carole survives from this period, but see Chapter 11 for discussion of an early English carol.) Some clerics condemned the widespread practice; others thought it offered young people an activity that might distract them from more dangerous possibilities. The joys found in the natural world and the pleasures of physical love as celebrated in the song literature, belong to the world of the dance as well (as we saw in the song of trouvère Guillaume d'Amiens in Chapter 8). Decoration, both larger paintings and marginalia, as found in Mo encourage the reader to observe human beings as a part of nature (Fig. 10.1). The idea of Marie as patroness or recipient of this book suggests another way that women influenced the composition, copying, and design of works—both individual pieces and collections—that pleased them and suited their tastes.

All was not dancing and joy for Marie of Brabant, subject as she was to the intrigue that often characterized court life during the late Capetian era. The queen was estranged from King Philip early in their marriage through the machinations of the powerful chamberlain Pierre de la Broce, who ran the king's household. He detested Marie and her influence, and managed to have her accused of poisoning Philip's oldest son by a previous marriage. Fortune's wheel rotated once again when a dying friend of the king sent letters apparently incriminating Pierre, who was summarily hanged. Perhaps Mo was a gift in honor of the royal couple's reconciliation, a celebration of love and courtly pleasures as well as of hunting, King Philip's favorite pastime (depicted in the bottom register of Fig. 10.1). At least it can be said with assurance that whoever compiled the manuscript knew this court and its life.

THE MUSIC OF THE MONTPELLIER CODEX

An enormous collection of motets in many styles, the Montpellier Codex documents the development of the genre from the later thirteenth to the early fourteenth century. It comprises eight divisions or fascicles. Fascicles 2–6—the ones linked to Queen Marie—were most likely copied around 1280; the first and seventh fascicles of the manuscript may date from somewhat later, and the eighth fascicle from the early fourteenth century. The shift in musical styles is paralleled by a shift to mensural notation, with the first layer of the codex being quasi-Franconian, the second nearly completely Franconian, and the last fascicle showing the complete triumph of Franconian notation.

Motets expressed in modal and Franconian notation, as well as the other music of the Notre Dame School studied in Chapter 9, were dubbed Ars Antiqua (old art) by some musicians of the early fourteenth century. The most forward-looking fourteenth-century French polyphony, by contrast, represented the so-called Ars Nova (new art) that would spread to Italy and England (see Chapter 11). The latter featured the possibility of ever-smaller note values, which could be combined freely with longer values, treating all as belonging to the

Figure 10.1: *Opening of fascicle 7 of the late-thirteenth-century Montpellier Codex (Mo)*

same notational system. The transition between the two styles can be seen in the polytextual motet *S'amours eüst point de poer/Au renouveler/Ecce*, attributed to Petrus de Cruce (fl. c. 1290) by the early-fourteenth-century theorist Jacques of Liège, which occupies pride of place at the opening of fascicle 7 in the Montpellier Codex (see Anthology 31) (see Fig. 10.1). In it, Petrus uses from two to four semibreves in the time of a breve; in other works attributed to him, there are as many as nine.

Petrus was in Paris from around 1260 to 1290, first as a student and then as a teacher. He served much of his later life in Amiens, where he participated in the liturgy of the bishop's chapel, and he is recorded as leaving a book of polyphonic music to the chapter upon his death. *S'amours eüst point de poer/Au renouveler/Ecce* is a highly sophisticated work and reveals many of the characteristics associated with motets in the Petronian style. The triplum is a true "upper" voice and stands out not only because of its higher range, but also because it is extremely active musically, proclaiming a far longer text with a greater number of notes than the duplum (Ex. 10.1). The duplum of *S'amours* explores a similar range of pitches as the tenor and moves comparatively slowly; both lower voices are dominated by the rhythmic modes. The top voice, meanwhile, is free to move about in a higher register and with freer rhythms. The duplum and tenor catch up to each other periodically, forming sonorous chords with the triplum to underscore the text on particular words or at breaking points in the line.

Example 10.1: *Opening of the motet* S'amours eüst point de poer, *by Petrus de Cruce*

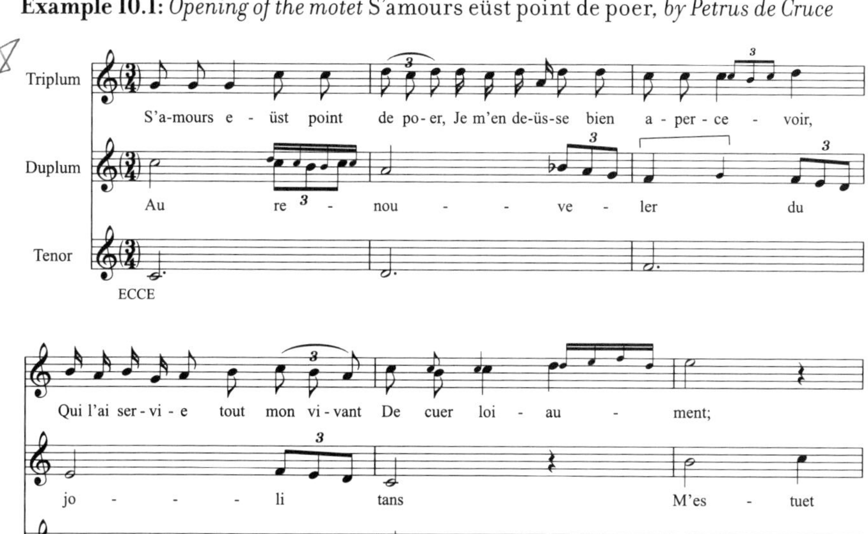

Triplum: If Love had any power, I would have noticed, for I have served him my life long with a faithful heart.
Duplum: When the merry time returns
Tenor: Behold

The three-voice motet *S'on me regarde/Prennés i garde/Hé mi enfant*, contained in the last fascicle of the Montpellier Codex, transports us to the era of the last Capetians, studied below. It is the first polyphonic work we have seen with a French tenor, and many of its features point to a musical future dominated by the polyphonic chanson first championed by Adam de la Halle (see Chapter 8). *S'on me regarde* is based on the text and music of the monophonic rondeau *Prendés i garde* studied in Chapter 8, a tuneful piece that, although ascribed to Guillaume d'Amiens, is so simple as to sound like a folk song (with an inconsistency typical of medieval orthography, there are different spelling of the word "prennés"). A certain uniformity characterizes the three lines of the motet: the tenor, with its repeating notes, and the upper two voices, with their frequent crossings and imitations, as well as a tenor-like motive of three repeated notes. In some places, such as measure 4, all three voices pound out the rhythms in unison, while in others they dovetail (Ex. 10.2). Each voice is a singable entity, yet together they create something new and powerfully unified—a polyphonic setting of an earlier monophonic song. The nervous, chattering character of the music reminds us of the tense situation that prevailed in court at the time, when many people wondered who was watching whom.

A rapacious genre, the motet absorbed many kinds of music in the thirteenth century, recombining textual and musical genres in a variety of ways. In the early fourteenth century, as we'll see below, it would give birth to various styles

Example 10.2: *Opening of the three-voice motet* S'on me regarde

Triplum: If someone sees me, if someone sees me, tell me! I am too [ardent].
Motetus: Keep guard, if someone sees me; I am too ardent. Do tell me.
Tenor: Oh, my child.

of polyphonic chansons on the one hand, and on the other hand to a complex late scholastic genre, the so-called isorhythmic motet.

THE END OF THE CAPETIAN DYNASTY

The enigmatic Philip IV ("the Fair") was the last Capetian king to remain on the throne for more than half a dozen years (see Table 10.1). His character presented an unfortunate combination of utter ruthlessness and excessive piety, coupled with a desire for a well-organized administration that could collect the taxes levied to pay for his wars and other lavish expenses. The king was an ambitious builder, reconstructing the palace complex in Paris, essentially remaking the heart of the city, and creating a well-appointed group of buildings that served to magnify his power.

The magnificent Sainte Chapelle, constructed by Philip's grandfather, Louis IX, and consecrated in 1248, was retained as the centerpiece for the younger king's new group of buildings. The walls of his palace were said by a contemporary "to have so much space between them that they could contain an infinite populace." His extravagant building campaign was not the only drain on the treasury; even more expensive were Philip's wars against England, Spain, and Flanders. He expelled all Jews from his kingdom in 1306 and confiscated their wealth and property. He also attacked the Knights Templar, the wealthy defenders of the crusaders, taking their lands and riches, and having them condemned on trumped-up charges that led to the torture, imprisonment, and public burnings of nearly 200 men.

Philip the Fair was followed by a succession of sons, all of whom died young and without surviving male issue. His daughter Isabella married Edward II, king of England; claims to territories in France by their son, Edward III, would launch the long period of devastation known as the Hundred Years' War (1337–1453). The situation at the French court was filled with charges, countercharges, and sudden gains and losses. The wives of two of Philip's sons, Louis and Charles (later King Louis X and Charles IV), were accused of adulterous affairs in 1314; their alleged lovers were executed and the women imprisoned for life. After acceding to the throne, Louis X had his wife strangled while she was shut away to enable his speedy remarriage. It is hardly to be wondered at that the most famous musical work of this period is a study in politics and expresses delight at revenge taken against a powerful figure in the court of Philip the Fair.

POLITICS AND THE *ROMAN DE FAUVEL*

The *Roman de Fauvel*, a book of allegorical and satirical poetry interpolated with music during the last years of the reign of Philip the Fair and the rule of two of his three sons, Louis X and Philip V, mirrors the troubled politics of the times. The interpolated version survives in a single manuscript, Paris, BN fr. 146, dating from around 1317–18. Although the form of the work grows directly from that established in Jean Renart's *Romance of the Rose* (see Chapter 8) and other thirteenth-century vernacular romances, the sophisticated interaction between text, art, and music found in this particular manuscript is unique in the later Middle Ages.

The *Roman de Fauvel* relates the exploits of a greedy and lustful horse that comes to occupy the throne of France. Fauvel—whose name is an anagram of the vices Flatterie, Avarice, Vilainie, Variété (fickleness), Envie, and Lâcheté (cowardice)—courts Lady Fortune, hoping to ensure that he will remain in power. Instead, Fortune offers him Pride, the queen of all vices, for a bride. After Fauvel's marriage and its consummation (accompanied by noisy, mocking music-makers singing puerile songs), a joust is declared between the Virtues and the Vices. The Virtues are seen as the untainted guardians of France. Accordingly, their song in the battle is the late sequence *Virgines egregie* (Outstanding Virgins), expressed in mensural notation. Indeed, whenever they appear, the Virtues are accompanied by Latin texts. They win the battle, but the many offspring of Fauvel and Pride ensure that the larger war will continue.

In music, poetry, and the art of manuscript illumination, BN fr. 146 manifests the hatred felt toward the king's trusted administrators who abused their powers. Philip the Fair had just such a man in his employ: Enguerrand de Marigny, a Norman and the son of lesser nobility, who got his start as a butler to the queen of France and eventually became the head of Philip's household. In this context, the energy that went into preparing fr. 146 is easy to understand. The manuscript must have been created by a group of well-educated and artistically talented young men, all members of the royal chancery or some other local institution, and so in the employ of the king and his immediate relatives. They resented being lorded over by a person with little education, whose bloodlines were at best the equal to their own.

Some of this large coterie (including the composer Philippe de Vitry, discussed below) moved in the circles of Charles of Valois, the king's brother. Profoundly ambitious, Charles detested the chamberlain and was a major player in plotting his demise. Within months after Philip's death, Enguerrand was tried for malfeasance, and then, when his accounts proved in order, for sorcery. He was hanged on the royal gibbet of Montfaucon on April 30, 1215; the choice of the Feast of the Ascension for his "elevation" reflects the same gallows humor that pervades fr. 146. In a parody of Ascension iconography, his body, with its dangling feet, remained suspended on the gibbet for two years, the rope being replaced as necessary.

Like the rotting body of Enguerrand, the *Roman de Fauvel* is a warning, issued to royal administrators by a group of chancery clerks and their friends. This group may have included highly placed noble patrons to Philip V, newly crowned during the years that the musical version of the *Roman de Fauvel* was compiled. In spite of its comic and satirical overtones, *Fauvel* is a deadly serious work, a lament for just and good governance, a plea for a Christian king who cares about and for his people, and a marveling at the swiftly turning wheel of Lady Fortune, a character in many narratives with music from the fourteenth century. The rage inspired within subjects of the crown and Church during the fourteenth century by mismanagement of secular and religious institutions crackles on every carefully planned page.

The two volumes of the poem may have been created in stages. If one believes the inscriptions, the author of the first book is unknown, but his work was completed in 1310. The second book is signed by Gervais du Bus, a Norman who was active from 1300 to 1348, and who at the time *Fauvel* was composed was employed as one of the most highly placed of the 40 or so notaries in the French royal chancery. He was Enguerrand's chaplain and had received many favors from him. The attribution may be ironic, as perhaps is the date of the second volume, December 6, 1314, one week after the death of Philip the Fair and the beginning of the end for Enguerrand; it was the moment when Lady Fortune's wheel turned.

THE MUSIC OF *FAUVEL*

Although the core text of the *Roman de Fauvel* survives whole or in part in 15 manuscript sources, only fr. 146 was interpolated with 2,000 new lines of text, created to work interactively with the musical "glosses." In addition to its narrative power, the music provides a compendium of the practices of the most talented young composers of the age. Plainchant (much of it modified to suit the circumstances), conductus, monophonic vernacular songs, and several styles of polyphonic works—from rearranged thirteenth-century motets to cutting-edge compositions that are early representatives of the Ars Nova—were all part of these composers' world, and were manipulated by them in ways that are both learned and musically astute. The music theorist Johannes de Grocheio, writing in Paris around 1300, identified three kinds of music: ecclesiastical, mensural, and popular. All three are mingled in *Fauvel*, which surveys the varied musical soundscape of early-fourteenth-century Paris.

Considering its multifaceted nature, the production of fr. 146 must have been a group project. The supposed head of the team, whose name is found in the manuscript as "mesire Chaillou de Pesscain," has been tentatively identified as Geoffrey Engelor, also known as Chalop of Persquen, a Breton and a notary of the kings of France from 1303 to 1334. The patron of the manuscript remains a matter of speculation (some have proposed Charles of Valois), but with all the means of production at their disposal—from parchment and inks (*Fauvel* marks the introduction of musical notation in more than one color) to the most skilled scribes, illuminators, and composers of the day—it is possible that the notaries and their friends worked on this magnificent compilation with no one sponsor and, in part at least, for their own delight.

The brilliant intertextuality of the interpolated *Roman de Fauvel* is apparent on every page, beginning with the first folio (Fig. 10.2). The Old French text of

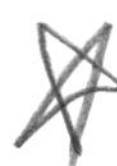

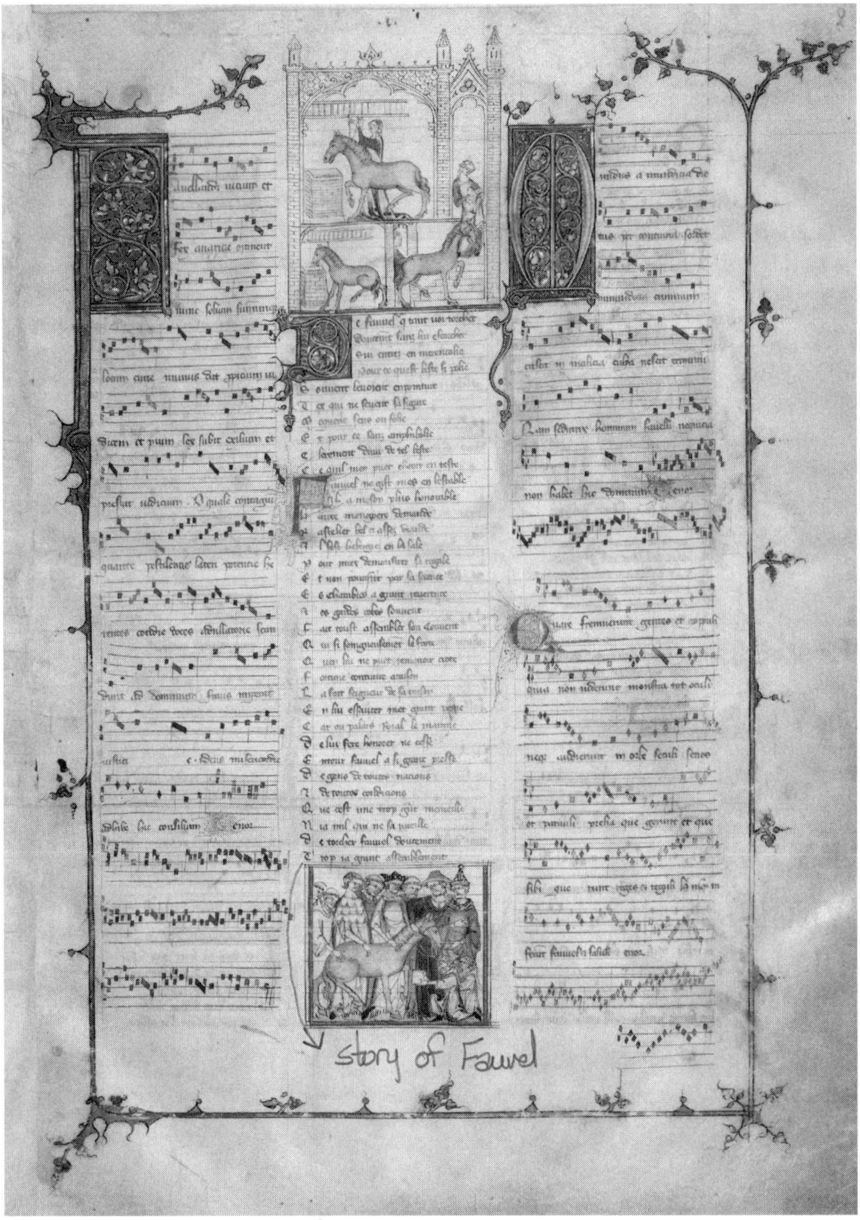

Figure 10.2: *Opening of the interpolated* Roman de Fauvel *(Paris, BN fr. 146, fol. 1r), showing Fauvel being led by a rope (*top*), and being praised by all classes of wealth and privilege (*bottom*)*

story of Fauvel

12 surviving copies

in color

F - flattery
A - attery
U - villany
V - varite
E - envy
L - lachete

Pope Gregory + dove story - mocked later in story?

the poem is found in the middle of the page, with the music and illuminations around the edges, functioning like a gloss. The artist shows Fauvel at the top being led by a rope, an allusion to the hanging of Enguerrand de Marigny, whose character is embodied by the equine usurper. *Quare fremuerunt*, one of the two-voice motets on the page, offers fleeting dissonance in its opening and middle sections (as with the opening in Ex. 10.3, which features B against A in the first measure). The voices move in sprightly organum throughout, with occasional Petronian groupings of semibreves.

The text and the music of *Quare fremuerunt*, like the illumination, foreshadow Fauvel's imminent demise. The text is modeled upon the opening of Psalm 2, but draws upon the meanings of the entire psalm and its contemporary exegesis. Psalm 2 is a poem about the nature of kingship and was commented on at length by Thomas Aquinas and other scholars whose writings were well known to the compilers of the *Roman de Fauvel*. Psalm 2 was also identified with the Capetian kings in courtly circles: it was sung in the Office commissioned by Philip the Fair for his sainted grandfather, Louis IX.

Quare fremuerunt is about leaders who rage against the anointed (translated as the Christ), and contains a warning near the end: "Serve ye the Lord with fear: and rejoice unto him with trembling." Wrath is coming, and blessed are those who follow the Lord. The music embodies the extensive number symbolism related to the disciples of Christ in the Bible, who number 72, a number incorporated within other musical compositions in the *Roman de Fauvel*. There are 6 lines of text, with 12 per line, equaling 72; there are a total of 72 breve tempora. By using this mystical number within works describing the need for good people to triumph over evil rulers, the musicians express their own hopes for change. Not only do the varied elements on the page relate to events, texts, and music outside of the manuscript, and to the unfolding narrative enacted later in both texts and music; they also interrelate on the page itself, demonstrating that various people involved were in conversation as the work was planned, including most likely Philippe de Vitry, to whom some motets in fr. 146 have been ascribed.

Example 10.3: *Opening of the two-voice motet* Quare fremuerunt, *from the* Roman de Fauvel

Why do tribes and nations rage?

JOHANNES DE MURIS, PHILIPPE DE VITRY, AND THE ARS NOVA

"In this year [1291], on the vigil of All Saints, that is the last day of October, I, Philippe de Vitry, was born." This marginal note was penned by the composer in his own copy of a work by the popular chronicler Guillaume de Nangis. It appears alongside a passage describing a military victory by citizens of the northern French city of Arras, near the hamlet that gave him his name (Vitry-en-Artois). The fourteenth century was the first period in which people began to show interest in their actual birth dates and wished to record the information. This change took place as it became possible to measure time more accurately; the first mechanical clocks came into regular use in the fourteenth century, establishing hours of the day with a precision that had not been possible before. In the mid-thirteenth century, the longest note in common use was the perfect long, worth three beats, and the shortest possible note was the semibreve, worth a ninth of a perfect long. In the Ars Nova, a longer note, the maximodus, worth three perfect longs, was commonly used in tenors, and each of the longs could be divided into breves, semibreves, and minims (see below).

Time was a subject of great interest to musicians who had studied the Aristotelian corpus at the University of Paris, and who knew mathematics and the sciences well enough to integrate and even modify Aristotelian thought. Among these scholars was Johannes de Muris, or Jehan des Murs (c. 1295–c. 1350), a music theorist, astronomer, and mathematician whose copious notes in the books he owned allow us to reconstruct a fairly full biography. Among Johannes's writings on music was the much copied and highly influential *Libellus cantus mensurabilis* (Little Book of Mensurable Song), compiled for the use of performing musicians. The innovations in notation that he describes surely reflect the cutting edge of musical practice in the chanson and motet from around the time of the *Roman de Fauvel* through the mid-fourteenth century.

Johannes allowed for several levels of time, but unlike those of earlier mensural notation, they are all interrelated as part of the same system (see Chapter 9). As shown in Table 10.2, there are four levels of mensuration. Except for the minim, each note can be divided into either two or three parts. The basic beat no longer falls on the breve, but on the semibreve. Prolation, or division of the semibreve into minims (which have tails to distinguish them from semibreves), determines the shaping of musical lines, as beats could be freely grouped into patterns of two or three, now that there was an underlying sense of time to regulate the whole. In the writings of Johannes, we find the fourteenth-century equivalent of the modern time signature, with **c** serving to represent duple time. Mixing of meters and an emphasis on duple time was something that would not have been allowed in the thirteenth century. Duple time could not be expressed in earlier forms of modal notation, which by the middle thirteenth century depended upon the idea of perfection embodying the number three.

Table 10.2: *Levels of Mensuration in* Libellus cantus mensurabilis *and Their Signatures*

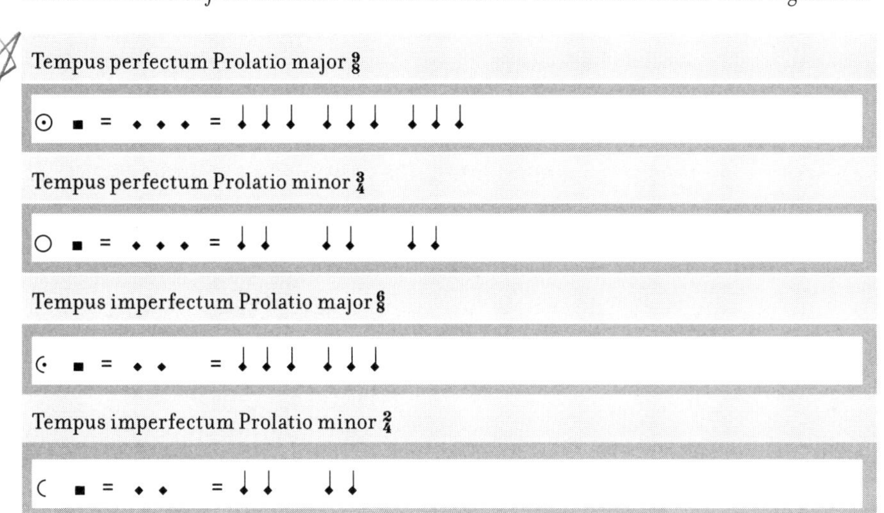

THE MOTETS OF PHILIPPE DE VITRY

Johannes de Muris surely knew Philippe de Vitry (1291–1361), and although the treatise once ascribed to Philippe has been shown to lack a firm textual tradition, a number of musical works are attributable to him, whereas none can be securely assigned to Johannes. Philippe's motets, a few of which seem to have been composed for the *Roman de Fauvel,* belong to the varied musical world of early-fourteenth-century Paris, in which new systems of notation and thought gave music the power to organize texts, words, and syllables in a precise temporal relationship that used ever-smaller note values.

Philippe used the technique of isorhythm ("same rhythm"), a term invented in the early twentieth century to describe pieces (motets and eventually polyphonic movements of the Mass Ordinary) governed through the use of identically repeating rhythmic patterns. At first the patterns were confined to the tenor voice, but in the late fourteenth and early fifteenth centuries they spread to other voices as well. Pitches of the tenor were involved too; medieval theorists distinguished between *color* (a repeating melodic unit) and *talea* ("cutting," denoting a repeating rhythmic unit). Even in the earliest isorhythmic motets, the other voices respond to the patterns of the tenor in a variety of ways.

One of the five motets attributed to Philippe in the *Roman de Fauvel*, *Tribum/Quoniam/Merito* (Anthology 32), provides an excellent illustration of the techniques favored by innovative poet-composers around 1320 and embodies ideas that exemplify the early Ars Nova. The isorhythmic tenor is laid out in a formal grid of repeating patterns, and two statements of the color divide the piece into two nearly equal parts. This creates a dependable framework for the upper voices. The tenor of *Tribum/Quoniam/Merito* is in modus imperfectus, each long being worth two breves. There are two statements of the color (the chant melody quoted in the tenor), and each is equal to 36 longs, or 72 breves. The latter number, as noted above, has symbolic importance throughout the *Roman de Fauvel*.

The upper voices of Vitry's motet interweave in similar repeating patterns above the structured tenor, giving their entrances a kind of rhythm as well. The triplum line has the nervous quality that is characteristic of much Ars Nova polyphony: a measure or two of rapidly moving semibreves are frequently bracketed by (in this case) imperfect (two-beat) longs, which allow for constant catching of the breath, as it were. These ongoing stops and starts may have been useful for singers who had to make sure they were together before moving on. Modern transcriptions use bar lines to help guide the eye; motet notation had no bar lines, nor was polyphony written in score in France in this period. Musicians had to put the polyphonic lines together from a page that displayed the parts in individual blocks, as can been seen in the example from the Montpellier Codex (see Fig. 10.1).

In manuscript fr. 146, Vitry's motet comments upon an elaborate illumination that shows a group of older men (representing Fauvel's minions) walking through a baptismal font that spews filth and mire. This reverse sacrament turns the aged into youths, zombie evildoers who will not die. The motet works in opposition to the illumination, offering hope as well as condemnation. Its texts describe the "gallows" that raging Fortune has prepared "openly before all as an eternal mirror" (triplum), and the fate that awaits "the fox which chewed on the cocks [French]" (*gallus* means both rooster and Frenchman) and his "band of thieves" (duplum). An apt quotation from Ovid (*Ex Ponto*, IV.3.35–36) provides a kind of refrain: "All human affairs hang on a slender cord; and with a sudden fall what once flourished comes to ruin."

These images refer to the public hanging of Enguerrand de Marigny. In fact, *Tribum/Quoniam/Merito* is part of a retrospective narrative: the three motets that relate specifically to the death and notorious career of Enguerrand begin at the point in the poem when Lady Fortune rejects Fauvel's proposal of marriage. The motets' texts chronicle the events in reverse order: the story in the poem goes forward chronologically, while the story embodied within the three motets moves backward in time. In the first of the three motets *(Aman novi/Heu Fortuna/Heu me)*, Enguerrand has been hanging on the gallows for two years. In *Tribum/Quoniam/Merito*, the second motet, King Philip is no longer alive and Enguerrand has just been killed. In *Garrit Gallus/In nova fert/Neuma*, the last of the three, both Philip (the "blind lion" mentioned in *Tribum*) and Enguerrand are still alive; but the palindromic tenor, which reads the same forward and backward, suggests an impending reversal of fortune. Lady Fortune is often depicted as having a wheel within a wheel, one moving backward, the other forward in time, and the motets in conjunction with the narrative embody this understanding.

FROM MOTET TO INSTRUMENTAL MUSIC

An instrumental version of Vitry's motet is found in the Robertsbridge Codex, the first surviving source of keyboard music. Copied in England in the second third of the fourteenth century, this two-leaf fragment—which apparently belonged to the Cistercian monastery that gives it its name—also includes a small set of dances (estampies) and another motet from the *Roman de Fauvel* with accompaniment. The keyboard arrangement of *Tribum/Quoniam/Merito* illustrates the exchange of music between different media—in this case, vocal ensembles and organ. This is how complex instrumental music was born in the late Middle Ages.

The piece was written by and for an instrumentalist of great skill, and the music reflects contemporary developments in organ building. Keys had become narrower so that organists could accommodate a wider range of pitches and play sustained chords. Here a fluid and rhythmically complex decorative voice unfolds above the earlier isorhythmic piece. The Robertsbridge version uses the isorhythmic motet, with its patterned scaffolding, as a foundation for dramatic instrumental display played by the right hand. As can be seen, the motet has been transposed in this version, and the left hand accounts for most of the notes in the two lower voices of the motet, while the freer right hand either adds a new part or ornaments the top line of the motet (Ex. 10.4, on p. 212).

The lively rhythmic characters of the upper voices in both versions of *Tribum* are made possible because very long rhythmic values and very short ones can be combined in close proximity. This disregard for the thirteenth-century ideal of perfection was attacked by the influential theorist Jacques of Liège (c. 1260–c. 1330). In an enormous compendium of music theory called *Speculum musicae* (The Mirror of Music), Jacques criticized Vitry and his fellow *moderni* (modern composers) for abandoning organum and concentrating instead on motets and chansons. He complained that conductus, "a song that is so beautiful and gives such pleasure," had also been ignored by the proponents of the Ars Nova. Why, Jacques wondered, were the moderni thought to be the subtle ones—they who used semibreves singly, provided them with tails, and allowed them to make longs and breves imperfect? "Wherein does this lasciviousness in singing so greatly please, this excessive refinement, by which, as some think, the words are lost, the harmony of consonances is diminished, the value of the notes is changed, perfection is brought low, imperfection is exalted, and measure is confused?" (SR 35:278; 2/27:163).

GUILLAUME DE MACHAUT: NARRATIVE AND MEMORY

The extraordinary achievements of poet-composer Guillaume de Machaut (c. 1300–1377) belong to a tradition of narrative works with music running from Jean Renart's romances with sung refrains and the lyrical entertainments of Adam de la Halle (see Chapter 8) to the *Roman de Fauvel*. In fact, Machaut may

Example 10.4:

(a) *Opening of Philippe de Vitry's motet* Tribum/Quoniam/Merito

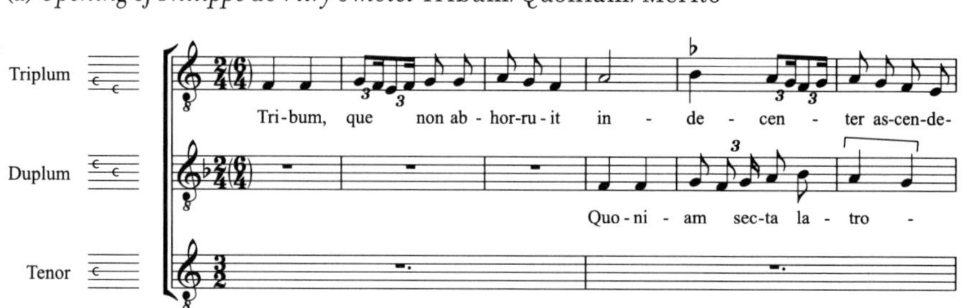

Triplum: The tribe that did not abhor to ascend indecently

Duplum: Since a band of thieves

Tenor: We suffer these things justly.

(b) *Opening of keyboard arrangement from Robertsbridge Codex*

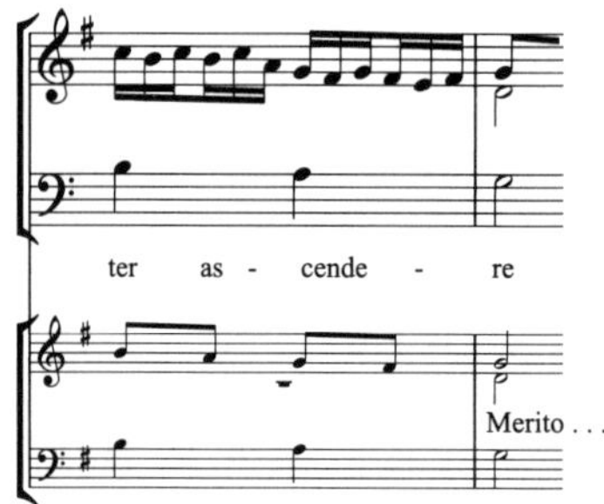

have been in contact with Philippe de Vitry in his youth and would have been aware of, and perhaps drawn into, the circles of court scribes, musicians, and illuminators who created new kinds of musical narratives in Paris around 1320.

In the mid-1300s, Machaut began producing collections of his own works. The poems of earlier poets, from Boethius to Philippe de Vitry, resonate clearly through these compositions. It is probable that Paris, BN fr. 1586 (c. 1356, also known as Manuscript C), the earliest source containing part of Machaut's corpus, was supervised by the poet-composer himself, and that he had a hand in the placement and design of the illuminations as well. In most of his manuscripts, the music is separated from the poetry and organized by genre. In fr. 1586, for example, there are five *dits* (first-person narrative poems), and then a section of lyric texts without music, followed by lyrics with music. But in one of the dits, the *Remède de Fortune* (Remedy of Fortune), the music is interpolated within the text of the poem; its style, and even its notation, are crucial to understanding the meanings of the narrative as a whole.

In the *Roman de Fauvel*, music provides a remedy to Lady Fortune's ups and downs by allowing for a biting critique of social ills. Machaut's *Remède*, by contrast, offers solace through cultivating an art of memory, one that nurtures the composer while also commemorating a loved one lost to the plague. The work was apparently written in memory of Bonne of Luxembourg, the daughter of John of Luxembourg, Machaut's first patron. As the first wife of king-designate John II of France, the second of the Valois monarchs, she bore ten children but died of the plague in 1349, just before John was crowned. Machaut enjoyed a generous income as a canon of Reims Cathedral, arranged by members of the royal family. This benefice would sustain him all his mature life and establish his close relationship with the cathedral, where he was in residence half of every year.

THE *FORMES FIXES*

Machaut's *Remède de Fortune* incorporates three long-established song forms that were becoming standardized at this time: the rondeau, the ballade, and the virelai. Their manifestations from the fourteenth century forward are known as the *formes fixes*, or fixed forms, because they are fairly predictable in structure; the naming of the voices, too, changed in this period, so that eventually the top voice was called the cantus, the middle voice, the contratenor, and the lowest voice, the tenor. All three song forms are defined by the position of refrains within their structures. Refrains—repetitions of text with music (shown below as uppercase letters)—could be used to establish beginnings and ends of strophes, and to link successive strophes as well. The changing stanzas of text also used musical repetition (lowercase letters):

Rondeau: **ABaAabAB**
Ballade: **aab(C)**
Virelai: **AbbaA**

The formes fixes developed directly out of the various song and dance-song forms found in the twelfth and thirteenth centuries. The rondeau is characterized by a two-line refrain falling at the beginning and end of each strophe, but half of the refrain (**A**) falls in the middle of the strophe as well. The virelai features a single-line refrain at the beginning and end of each strophe. The ballade, Machaut's favored form, may have a refrain that is distinguished from the text and music of the rest of the work. Below, we'll take a closer look at Machaut's handling of these forms.

THE *REMÈDE DE FORTUNE*

In the *Remède de Fortune,* Machaut creates something new, while remaining grounded in earlier works of literature that would have been well known to his audience, notably Boethius's *Consolation of Philosophy* and the thirteenth-century *Romance of the Rose* by Guillaume de Lorris and Jean de Meun. Like his predecessors, the speaker in the poem must learn to deal with Fortune. But, unlike the scholar Boethius, whose consolation is Lady Philosophy, or Fauvel, who attempts the outrageous stunt of trying to marry Fortune, the narrator in the *Remède* takes his solace from Lady Hope, the inspiration of many a courtly lover. The narrator moves as in a dream through elegant gardens and buildings peopled with courtly characters who include powerfully drawn allegorical figures. When he loses his nerve as he is about to sing for his beloved, Hope seeks him out and persuades him to try again. Unlike *The Romance of the Rose*, this love story is the journey of an artist discovering his voice, a kind of fourteenth-century *Portrait of the Artist as a Young Man* (James Joyce, 1916).

Lady Hope inspires the lovesick narrator to rise above his fear of mutability and the ravages of Fortune, who is depicted as a fickle and untrustworthy hag. As long as he does not forget Hope, he will be protected. She sings to him again, this time something with "new words and music." It is a ballade, and the notation is that of the Ars Nova. The narrator quickly learns the song and vows to store it in his memory. Now he is free to create "new music" himself and can use his memory in dark times to restore the equanimity nurtured by Lady Hope's messages and song.

The first piece the narrator sings after Lady Hope departs, *Dame, de qui toute ma joie vient*, is also a ballade, but now the narrator follows her example, and composes and notates in the style of the Ars Nova (Anthology 33.1). He returns to his beloved and to the community as a new man, just as the music is in a new guise: he has shifted from Ars Antiqua note values (of the earlier music used for the poem) based on modus to an abundance of small Ars Nova note values based on tempus. Likewise, he has shed his melancholy, is able to control his trembling and tears, and sings the sprightly virelai *Dame, a vous sans retollir* before the assembled company (Anthology 33.2). In a larger sense, the narrator—and through him

Machaut—has learned to accept the social role of the poet-composer; he performs willingly, the force of his creations binding members of community together through a common experience. (In Chapter 11, we will see a similar theme arise in Boccaccio's *Decameron*.) The poem with its interpolated chansons celebrates the importance of the refined dance forms with texts in the vernacular as capable vehicles for high art and serious expression. From Machaut forward, the polyphonic chanson would be an increasingly intellectual endeavor, worthy of the attention of the most skilled composers.

Dame, a vous sans retollir, the piece Machaut presents to the company for dancing, is a tuneful song and remains in the memory long after it has been heard. Through its place in the narrative of the *Remède de Fortune*, and its expression in a different notation from music interpolated earlier in the story, it demonstrates that the new style was appropriate for Machaut's own voice as a public artist. *Dame, a vous sans retollir* is grounded in an aesthetic of joy in music and poetry, one that could give life and hope to its fourteenth-century listeners. Then as now, music encouraged the remembering of better times and strengthened those many who needed it in difficult times, including composers themselves. It embodies Hope, the remedy for Fortune, and the appropriate offering for the mid-fourteenth century.

MACHAUT'S MOTETS AND MASS

Machaut adopts a different, but equally innovative, approach to large-scale narrative structures in his cycle of 17 motets. Taken as a group, which he surely meant them to be, the motets represent the mystical journey of a pilgrim soul toward a sense of union with the triune God. Most have emotionally charged Latin liturgical tenors and French texts in the upper voices. With such texts and their intertexts (primarily the Bible, the liturgy, the *Romance of the Rose*, the *Consolation of Philosophy*, and the writings of contemporary mystics), Machaut aligns the quest of the courtly lover with the search of the believer for wisdom, seen in Christian theology as Christ himself. The hearts of both kinds of pilgrims are enflamed, they are willing to suffer for love, and they learn to hope for joyful union with the beloved. The cycle is yet another way in which the "courtly" becomes serious business in the hands of this great poet-composer.

The motets in the middle of the cycle of 17 works introduce familiar allegorical figures, such as Lady Fortune (motet 8) and Pride (motets 7 and 9). Motet 9 (*Fons totius/O livoris/Fera pessima*) is the only motet with a first-person voice and the only one completely in Latin. It represents the pilgrim's struggle with the Devil—the "most evil beast" referred to in the tenor, a kind of fourteenth-century *Thriller* (Michael Jackson, 1982). The full text of the Lenten chant from which the tenor was taken (Genesis 37:20, 33) describes Jacob seeing the bloody clothing of his son Joseph and believing him to be dead. But the singer and listener know better: the tenor offers hope and foreshadows a good ending for the pilgrim's journey.

The text of the duplum features the cruel, deceiving vice of Envy, which was an inspiration to Lucifer, the angel who wanted to usurp God's powers and instead fell from heaven to rule his own ghoulish counter-kingdom. Envy is a personification that still stalks its prey. The triplum text, on the other hand, speaks about the Devil himself, seen in the fourteenth-century Christian imagination as the promoter of vices to torment people. We encounter him all alone in a long introduction before the other voices enter, the duplum finally joining in a long, wailing "O" of pain, which, with its C♯, is highly dissonant against the D that sometimes sounds in the triplum, as well as with the G in the triplum and tenor. (Ex. 10.5).

If both the *Remede* and the motet cycle are about journeys and transformation, Machaut's six-movement setting of the Mass Ordinary commemorated the end of a very personal journey—that of his own life. It, too, raises the subject of music and memory, for Machaut wrote this work to be sung in his own remembrance after death. The *Messe de Nostre Dame* (Mass of Our Lady) is a milestone in the history of Western music: the first known complete polyphonic setting of the Ordinary, the movements of which are musically unified, in this case, by the

Example 10.5: *A cry of pain in an excerpt near the opening of Machaut's motet* Fons totius/O livoris/Fera pessima

Triplum: You were established in the highest place, elevated above the angelic thrones, now called the ancient, ferocious dragon
Motetus: O fierceness of Envy
Tenor: Most evil beast

use of Marian musical materials and common formal characteristics. Four of the movements—the Kyrie (see Anthology 34), Sanctus, Agnus Dei, and *Ite missa est*—are isorhythmic, motetlike structures. The other two movements, those with longer texts—the Gloria and Credo—are set so that the voices "move in parallel", but conclude with isorhythmic "Amens."

More important for understanding the purposes Machaut had in mind in composing the work are the ways in which the musical quotations found in the Mass relate to a consistent Mariological program. This program connects the assembly of movements directly to Reims Cathedral, dedicated as it was to the Virgin Mary. Characteristics of local plainchants appear in several of the tenors. The tenor of the Kyrie, for example, is borrowed from Kyrie IV, often troped with *Cunctipotens genitor* (see Chapter 4), a work sung at Marian feasts in the Sainte Chapelle in Paris in the fourteenth century; this same Kyrie was sung in Reims with the Marian trope *Rex virginum* (King of virgins). Moreover, the melody of the chant, which begins with a repeated D, was characteristic of Reims practice, as distinct from that of many other northern French centers.

The Virgin Mary was the lady of Machaut's own life of learning and courtly love, and the patron saint of the cathedral that supported him. His instrumental piece *Hoquetus David* (David Hocket), probably written for the coronation of King Charles V in 1364, sets the *Laudes regiae* melody known in Reims. It delights with the hiccup-like effect produced by two voices alternating in rapid succession, each singing while the other rests. The joyful hocketing that characterizes the musical texture of Machaut's artful Mass in honor of the Virgin symbolizes the joy of a well-lived life, one marked with regular performances of the Mass both before and after the composer's death (Ex. 10.6). Machaut was increasingly careful in the preparation of his works to create a legacy of remembrance; he is the first composer we know of who built his own musical monument and arranged

Example 10.6: *A bit of hocketing decorating the end of Machaut's Kyrie II*

Lord, have mercy.

for its endowment and performance after his death. His influence on composers in the generations to follow was powerful, and depended to a degree on his own attention to his legacy.

THE ARS SUBTILIOR: MUSIC AT THE CLOSE OF THE FOURTEENTH CENTURY IN FRANCE

The Ars Nova, the musical style foreshadowed by the motets of Petrus de Cruce and making an early appearance in the *Roman de Fauvel*, predominated throughout the fourteenth century in the most sophisticated musical circles in Europe. It offered composers a set of well-known chanson templates in the fixed forms, as well as notational and theoretical practices to sustain their works. Ars Nova musicians in the second half of the fourteenth century were beholden to a master, Machaut, who was instrumental in regularizing the formes fixes; to courts in France, the Low Countries, Spain, Cyprus (the French court), and northern Italy; and to the wealthy establishment of the popes at Avignon in southern France between 1309 and 1378, where the musicians' services as singers in chapels and as entertainers at secular gatherings were highly valued.

During this time, composers played upon the traditions they had inherited and created chansons that were more rhythmically and notationally sophisticated than anything seen before or after, at least until the twentieth century. Modern historians have dubbed this ornate musical texture the Ars Subtilior (more refined or precise art); it compares in its overwrought complexity to late scholastic thought and to the florid artistic and architectural styles known as Flamboyant. All of these are characterized by the manipulation of patterning in heavily detailed surfaces, as seen in fourteenth-century windows in which the elaborate tracery blocks out the pane (Fig. 10.3). The composers, artists, and scholars who created works in this style straddled the worlds of late scholasticism and early humanism, pushing on the details of their works or arguments until they engulf the whole. The exuberant display of technical sophistication in rhythm and notation of rhythm suggests the coming triumph of humanism as well. Just beginning its ascendance in fourteenth-century Italy, humanism emphasized the works of man over those of God. As discussed in Richard Freedman's *Music in the Renaissance*, it was an intellectual movement grounded in Petrarch's view that philosophy—especially as shaped through reading and writing—could bring wholeness to the soul.

THE CHANTILLY CODEX

The Chantilly Codex provides a good introduction to the Ars Subtilior. This manuscript, probably copied in Italy in the early fifteenth century, contains 100 songs and 13 motets, most thought to date from the 1380s and 1390s. The Chantilly

Figure 10.3: *A flamboyant window showing detail overwhelming function and design*

Codex shows that there was an international repertory of advanced and difficult chansons, predominantly French but with contributions from other regions as well. Whoever sponsored the preparation of the manuscript wished to have the very best and most up-to-date collection possible. The Chantilly Codex shows how misleading it is to give 1400, or any other single date, as a division between musical styles. Rather, there was an ongoing and fluid transformation of the most sophisticated chanson repertory from around 1380 to 1420. The interconnectedness of the songs in the manuscript and the many indications of personal contact between their composers helped to breed the kind of sophistication embodied within the most ornate songs in the repertory.

The Ars Subtilior, at its most complex, emphasized the use of multiple groupings of minims and *semiminims*, notes with stems and seraphs (flags) that divided the minim in half. Colored notation (which first appeared in the *Roman de Fauvel*) is commonly featured in the codex: red notes are to be read as indicating a change in prolation (the relationship between the minim and the semibreve), reducing their black equivalents by a third or a half in value. Some of the notational innovations of the Ars Subtilior make transcription difficult today, even for experts. In at least some instances, multiple solutions to these rhythmic riddles created by learned singers (a group that would have included the composers) are possible.

As discussed earlier, in motet notation the singer can only see his own part, and singers must adjust as they work together from the score, using an art of memory to recall the appropriate motion from one interval to another. As music became more rhythmically complex, performers found themselves needing to

Example 10.7: *Opening of the refrain from the ballade* Je me merveil/J'ay pluseurs fois

Because everyone is getting involved [in forging]

work more closely together, with each person a quick and able interpreter not only of his own part, but of the ways in which his work fit into the whole. The sense of when to add variations in pitch (a practice known as *musica ficta*, to be discussed in Chapter 11) was learned by practice, as composers often assumed that the musicians would know whether to add a sharp or flat necessary to make the parts work together harmoniously.

The double ballade *Je me merveil/J'ay pluseurs fois* (see Anthology 35) by the composer-theorist Jacob, or Jaquemin, de Senleches (fl. 1382–1383) is a classic example of a work that requires skilled performing artists; the piece and its notation play with the interaction between musicians, but in ways that only they could understand. The tenor has no words and would have been sung on a single vowel, with *sol-fa* syllables, or performed on an instrument. The upper voices have different texts, but a common refrain. The refrain, which repeats three times, once for each of the stanzas, is written in canon, one voice following the other with the same musical material at the distance of a breve (Ex. 10.7). But there is a further trick to the music that is not visible in the transcription: the two upper parts are expressed on the page using different mensuration signs (see Table 10.2); only an experienced musician would be able to correctly "solve" the canon. Inept musicians who were not quick to understand how the different rhythmic levels intersected could not read the piece without creating a howling mess. Well-trained singers, on the other hand, could demonstrate their own skillfulness throughout and mock those who could not keep up with the best of them. Such music is for teaching, for learning, and for gamesmanship. Nevertheless, the lines are often elegant and exquisitely crafted.

Music in fourteenth-century France displays new ways of understanding the art of memory and demonstrates that intertextuality in the most sophisticated works often involved musicians from different locales. Musicians from a variety of regions knew each other, coming into contact through common employers and through having spent at least some time in Paris. Yet French music in the 1300s was more than a steady march of newness; there was considerable continuity with the past. The narratives studied in this chapter are tales crafted through dependence on earlier works, from the Bible to Boethius to the popular stories of the thirteenth century. Frankish chant was still sung in every parish church and monastery, and many repertories of Ars Nova music depended on it, for both their musical and intellectual foundations. Nor did music in the style of the Ars Antiqua disappear: late chant and genres of chant continued to flourish, especially through the composition of sequences and rhymed offices. Machaut himself composed a great quantity of monophonic chansons, many of them of the highest quality, although he was the last major French composer to do so. Most significant chansonniers containing the troubadour and trouvère repertories, along with stories about their composers, were copied in the late 1200s and 1300s, demonstrating an ongoing interest in the music and texts of the twelfth- and thirteenth-century chanson in the fourteenth century.

Just as French fourteenth-century music was part of a historical and stylistic continuum, so its composers and performers belonged to an international community of musicians. Although France led the way in musical innovation, the best musicians from Italy and England, in particular, were the equal of any. As we will see in Chapter 11, a guild-like camaraderie united this group of peers, with frequent exchanges both across the Alps and across the English Channel.

FOR FURTHER READING

Bent, Margaret, "Words and Music in Machaut's Motet 9," *Early Music* 31 (2003): 363–88

Bent, Margaret, and Andrew Wathey, eds., *Fauvel Studies: Allegory, Chronicle, Music, and Image in Paris BN Ms. Fr. 146* (Oxford: Oxford University Press, 1998)

Briggs, Charles F., *The Body Broken: Medieval Europe, 1300–1520* (London: Routledge, 2011)

Huot, Sylvia, *From Song to Book: The Poetics of Writing in Old French Lyric and Lyrical Narrative Poetry* (Ithaca, NY: Cornell University Press, 1987)

Leach, Elizabeth Eva, *Guillaume de Machaut: Secretary, Poet, Musician* (Ithaca, NY: Cornell University Press, 2011)

Leech-Wilkinson, Daniel, *Machaut's Mass: An Introduction* (Oxford: Oxford University Press, 1990)

Robertson, Anne Walters, *Guillaume de Machaut and Reims: Context and Meaning in His Musical Works* (Cambridge: Cambridge University Press, 2002)

Roesner, Edward H., François Avril, and Nancy F. Regalado, eds., *Roman de Fauvel in the Edition of Mesire Chaillou de Pesstain: A Reproduction in Facsimile of the Complete Manuscript, Bibliotheque Nationale, Fonds Français 146* (New York: Broude Bros., 1999)

Tanay, Dorit, *Noting Music, Marking Culture: The Intellectual Context of Rhythmic Notation, 1240–1400* (Holzerlingen, Germany: Hänssler, 1999)

CHAPTER ELEVEN

Italy and England in the Fourteenth Century

The most advanced compositional strategies employed within the polyphonic chanson and motet repertories evolved steadily in fourteenth-century France. Various features of the late Ars Antiqua inspired the innovations of the Ars Nova, which in turn made possible the complexities of the Ars Subtilior. The history of notation in French music fits especially well into this developmental arc. Yet this apparent linear evolution is misleading, for it encompasses only a rarified strand of fourteenth-century music created by a small group of highly skilled musicians, many of whom knew each other by reputation, if not personally.

France's leadership in the musical arts was not universally acknowledged, particularly in parts of Europe where French avant-garde musical traditions were hardly known at all. Moreover, France did not have a monopoly on musical innovation, and even when it was influential, there were always fresh "translations" of French forms in new guises. The music of the Trecento has its own genius, as does the music of fourteenth-century England, and of other European regions even less influenced by the Notre Dame School and the Ars Subtilior (to which we will turn in Chapter 12). Italian song forms were written under varying amounts of French influence: the madrigal was conceived of as an Italian form from the beginning; the *caccia* (plural, *cacce*), on the other hand, seems to have had its origins in the French *chace* (chase), and the *ballata*, the song form that takes over in the later fourteenth century (or Trecento, to use the Italian term), was heavily influenced by the French formes fixes. To appreciate this plethora of regional repertoires requires an understanding of folk music and folk culture as well, both of which will play an increasing role in the pages that follow, but which are not documented in a written tradition for the most part (see Chapter 12 for the first instance).

MUSIC OF THE TRECENTO

It is difficult to trace out the history of secular Italian Trecento music. The ascendancy of Franco-Flemish musicians in the courts and chapels of Italy in the fifteenth and early sixteen centuries (as discussed by Richard Freedman in *Music in the Renaissance*) further obscures the legacy of fourteenth-century Italian music. As we will see, the sources are fragmentary and, for the most part, were copied decades after the music they contain was composed. Unlike the kingdom of France, Italy was a loose-knit collection of independent courts and city-states. The universities were dedicated not to theology and the liberal arts, as in Paris, but to medicine and law. They were shaped and regulated by student groups rather than by professors; as a result, Italian universities were different in character from those of Paris and Oxford. Profitable trade across the Mediterranean and to the east gave rise to a large and flourishing bourgeois class in urban areas. The bourgeoisie was especially powerful in the Republic of Florence, which was a major musical center by the middle of the century.

MARCHETTO OF PADUA

The story of the Trecento is usually considered to begin in northern Italy with Marchetto (fl. 1305–1319), an Italian singer in charge of teaching choristers at the cathedral in the thriving university town of Padua. He is primarily known not for his compositions (although a few can be attributed to him), but rather for his work as a music theorist. Marchetto wrote two significant treatises, one on monophonic chant (*Lucidarium in arte musice plane* [Elucidation of the Art of Plainsong], 1317–18) and a companion work concerning mensuration in polyphonic repertories (*Pomerium in arte musice mensurate* [The Garden of Mensural Music], 1318–19), written at the court of Robert of Anjou in Naples, where Marchetto had contact with learned French theorists and musicians. Both are suffused with a knowledge of practical music-making. The *Lucidarium* was copied 15 times between its completion and the early sixteenth century; the *Pomerium*, although laying the foundation for the understanding of Italian mensural theory, was copied only 7 times, the practice it describes being essentially dead by the early fifteenth century.

Marchetto was interested in how musicians thought about musica ficta (or *musica falsa*), those pitches that fall outside the common gamut as expressed in the Guidonian concept of range found in the "hand" (see Chapter 5). For the most part, the only accidental used in the plainsong repertory is B♭, which was sometimes employed as a signal for the singer to know what hexachord he or she was in, and sometimes to avoid a tritone. The term *musica falsa* does not appear until the late twelfth century, and understandings for how to use such pitches outside the gamut evolved slowly, with significant contributions made by theorists from the late thirteenth and early fourteenth centuries. Johannes de Grocheio (see Chapter 10) cautions that concepts of mode relate to plainsong and not to other types of music, and the extent to which the church modes are useful for analysis of polyphony in the fourteenth century is a matter of debate. Rather than looking for rules that fit all conditions, it is useful to think in terms of tendencies governing the ways in which intervals, especially at cadences, are approached in polyphonic works, sometimes through the addition of accidentals, and let each source speak on its own terms. It is crucial not to superimpose rules made for sixteenth-century counterpoint onto the music of the thirteenth and fourteenth centuries.

Marchetto's theoretical works demonstrate that the musical and notational innovations he describes were part of a vibrant early-fourteenth-century musical culture in northern Italy, one that involved both sacred and secular repertories. In the *Lucidarium*, he transcended principles of hexachord mutation by contemplating ways of "permutation," that is, motion involving chromaticism. He wanted to allow the half step falling between *mi* and *fa* on specific pitches (traditionally B–C and E–F) to be placed on any pitch in the gamut. Marchetto was also not content with the Pythagorean division of the step, or whole tone, that came from thinking of it as the ratio 9:8. Instead, he thought of the whole tone as a quantity rather than a ratio, and divided it into five equal parts; this was useful for musicians who wanted to make their intervals slightly smaller or larger, without engaging the complex mathematics of Pythagorean semitones. Marchetto also adopted a flexible view of modes, envisioning melodies that exceeded their normal ranges or that employed melodic formulas other than those in common use. His *Pomerium* was the first treatise on mensural music that allowed for systematically worked-out divisions of the breve into both duple and triple meters, down to the smallest note values, which forms something of a contrast with the way these durations were understood in the French Ars Nova (Ex. 11.1).

Marchetto's theoretical thought is reflected in the music he composed during his tenure at the Cathedral of Padua. *Ave regina celorum/Mater innocencie/Ite Joseph* (see Anthology 36), a Latin double motet for the Virgin Mary, is thought

Example 11.1: *Comparison of Italian and French Ways of Reading Groups of Semibreves*

to have been composed for the dedication of the Scrovegni Chapel in Padua on the Feast of the Annunciation, March 25, 1305. The chapel is decorated with a brilliant cycle of frescoes about Mary's life by the painter Giotto di Bondone. Marchetto's motet embodies Giotto's plan in some detail. For instance, there are 39 frescoes in the apse of the church and 39 perfections in the motet. The triplum text references the glorious fresco of the Virgin Mary en route to her wedding, with instruments playing to accompany her journey (Fig. 11.1). Giotto painted his own portrait among the Elect; not to be outdone, Marchetto included himself in the motet through an acrostic spelling out the letters of his name.

Figure 11.1: *Giotto's depiction of the Virgin Mary en route to her wedding (Scrovegni Chapel, Padua, early fourteenth century)*

In a more general sense, the sounds of the Trecento reflect understandings of music found in the treatises of Marchetto. The Italian propensity for duple divisions of the smallest note values allows the florid upper lines of many polyphonic works to unfold without the jerky stops and starts characteristic of melodic lines in some early-fourteenth-century French motets and chansons. Trecento music makes frequent use of chromatic notes, usually allowing for efficient and smooth upward or downward melodic motion at cadences. The three medieval hexachords each contain one half step *(mi-fa);* Marchetto not only wanted the half steps to be smaller or larger according to the quality of melodic motion, but to allow the hexachords to have more half steps, moving outside the traditional system of hexachords. Both of these features, rhythmic and melodic, can be heard in Marchetto's motet.

SOURCES OF TRECENTO MUSIC

The sources containing Trecento music can be divided into two broad categories: the ten major manuscripts, all of which were copied in the second half of the century or later; and numerous fragments of varying types, from stray leaves to parts of codices that are now lost. Altogether, these sources contain more than 750 works in the following genres: madrigals (167), ballate (409), cacce (25), liturgical pieces (110), and nonliturgical Latin works (45 motets, 38 of which survive only in Trecento manuscripts). We will encounter these genres throughout discussions of sources below.

MADRIGALS IN THE ROSSI CODEX

The earliest layers of the Trecento repertory are best represented in the Rossi Codex, which may have been put together in the 1380s in or around Padua. The Rossi Codex is the only surviving large-scale source of music from the first half of the fourteenth century in Italy. It comprises two substantial fragments, perhaps of a once even-greater collection. The madrigal, an unaccompanied song for two or three voices, is the predominant genre in the Rossi Codex. The Trecento madrigal, not directly related to the later musical genre of the same name, flourished through the first three quarters of the fourteenth century and then, for the most part, fell out of favor. The florid melodies of the upper voices offer a taste of the soloistic prowess that would reemerge in the rise of opera in the seventeenth century.

Trecento madrigals are commonly settings of nature poetry. Their forms vary a great deal, although by the third quarter of the century works usually unfold in two or more stanzas called *terzetti*, each of which has the same music, and conclude with a ritornello. The ritornello is not a recurring refrain as the name (and its later usage) might suggest, but is simply another stanza that is deliberately constructed to provide poetic, musical, and thematic contrast with the preceding stanzas. The poetry most often is organized in 11-syllable lines, with melismatic decorations at the beginnings or ends of lines.

Quando i oselli canta, an anonymous madrigal found in the Rossi Codex, is a parody of courtly love as expressed in a pastoral setting (see Anthology 37). In the opening terzetti, the narrator wanders in a bucolic reverie amid twittering birds and shepherdesses weaving their garlands. In the ritornello, which is different in both musical style and poetic meter, he leans over for a kiss from his beloved, and the young woman smacks him on the head with her distaff, rudely awakening him and the listener from the world of the early strophes (Ex. 11.2).

POLYPHONIC SONGS IN THE SQUARCIALUPI CODEX

As far as can be told from the surviving sources, the most prolific Trecento composers lived in Florence for at least part of their lives. Florence was a city of bourgeois merchants and brilliant monasteries, but it had no major university and, being a republic, lacked a resident ruling family and an elegant ducal court. Nevertheless, music thrived there among its cultural elite, so it should not be surprising that the greatest repository of Trecento song, the Squarcialupi Codex, is Florentine. An enormous volume, it contains 353 polyphonic songs by 14 composers, mainly, but not exclusively, Florentine. Each composer has a separate section with his own portrait and unique marginalia, in the way of a French chansonnier.

The painting style and handwriting suggest that this book was produced in the scriptorium of the monastery of Santa Maria degli Angeli in Florence and illuminated principally by a disciple of the well-known painter Lorenzo Monaco

Example 11.2: *Contrasting textures from the madrigal* Quando i oselli canta

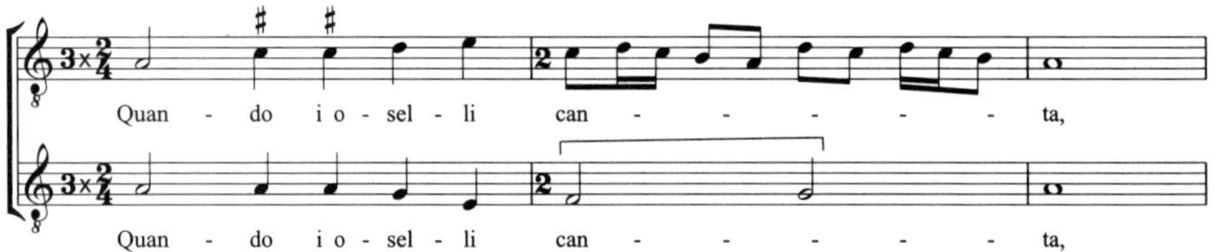

Opening of terzetto: When the birds sing . . .

Opening of ritornello: I turned to kiss her and

(who worked in the monastery for much of his life). But the Squarcialupi Codex remains perhaps the most tantalizing mystery in all medieval music sources. Who commissioned this deluxe manuscript, and why? Who was the audience for such a book? And where and how did the four musical scribes who worked so carefully to produce this magnificent "edition" obtain the different copies of the pieces they worked from?

The Squarcialupi Codex is testimony to the musical greatness and variety of the Trecento. Members of the Florentine cultural elite were well-informed about French life, finance, arts, and culture, and many of them lived for extended periods in France. In the early fifteenth century, some person or group of people apparently wanted to demonstrate that Italian composers of secular songs were as worthy as their French counterparts, and to feature them in a magnificent "chansonnier" made in Italy. Moreover, the codex featured a distinctively Italian genre, the ballata. Corresponding to the French virelai, this strophic form surpassed the madrigal in importance in late-fourteenth-century Italy. Whereas madrigals predominate in the Rossi Codex, in the Squarcialupi Codex the ballata is far and away the most popular form.

MUSIC IN BOCCACCIO'S *DECAMERON*

To understand the repertory the Squarcialupi Codex contains, and musical life in later Trecento Florence, we head for the hills surrounding the city as Giovanni Boccaccio (1313–1375) describes them in his *Decameron.* Many of the tales in this collection were previously in circulation, but Boccaccio reworked them and set them in Florence in 1348, while the Black Death was raging in Europe. The opening scenes of the *Decameron* are so ghastly as to resemble a sci-fi thriller. In the plague-ridden city, institutions no longer sustain social norms; parents run from their suffering children; mad wretches cavort in the midst of unblessed corpses. To escape death's loud rattle, a group of ten young men and women (Boccaccio calls them a *brigata*, or brigade) take refuge in the countryside, seeking solace and hoping to preserve their lives a bit longer. All have apparently lost everything, including their entire families.

To restore some semblance of order, these refugees organize a ten-day rural retreat, naming a king or queen from among themselves for each day and creating a daily structure of ten recited tales, ranging from the hagiographical to the outrageously bawdy. The stories are punctuated by singing, much of it accompanied by instruments and dancing. One of the supposed remedies for the plague was to avoid morosity, to remain calm, to conjure up pleasant thoughts, and to recreate with music. These ten youths, imagining order on the edge of a world that has been destroyed, remember as they try to forget. In Machaut's *Remède de Fortune* (see Chapter 10), memory made an artist hopeful and productive; in the *Decameron*, the brigata reconstructs life, love, lust, and joy through story and song (Fig. 11.2).

Figure 11.2: *Two scenes from a fourteenth-century copy (c. 1390) of the* Decameron: top, *the* brigata *in a circle telling tales;* bottom, *Death flying with a scythe into a woman's bedchamber (Paris, BN Ms. it. 482, ff.4*v *and 5*r*)*

Boccaccio presents the *Decameron* as a guidebook for women seeking to learn the ways of the world, removed as they were from university life. The music and music-making throughout the day offer a picture of what repertory the upper levels of society in Florence at midcentury played and sang for self-amusement. Music also distinguishes characters throughout the book: the elegant youths play a lute and a vielle, for example, whereas their servant plays the bagpipes. The end of every day is given over to a particular kind of song, the ballata (from the Italian *ballare*, to dance). Unlike the complex ballate found in the Squarcialupi Codex, the ballate mentioned in the *Decameron* are monophonic and had to be simple enough for the dancers to sense the beat.

FRANCESCO LANDINI AND THE BALLATA

Although ballate vary in structure, their basic underlying form is the same. The classic ballata is a strophic piece characterized by a *ripresa* (refrain), followed by two *piedi* (feet) set to different music. The music of the ripresa is then sung again to a new text, the *volta*, which is repeated to conclude the strophe. The musical structure of a strophe is thus **AbbaA**, with small letters representing the same music with a different text; this single unit repeats depending on the number of strophes to be sung. Such a work demanded only two sections of music:

TEXT	Ripresa (1–4 lines)	Piede (2–3 lines)	Piede (2–3 lines)	Volta (1–4 lines)	Ripresa (1–4 lines)
MUSIC	A	b	b	a	A

In the *Decameron*, the entire group is described as joining in with the singer on the refrains. In this social context, improvisation was assumed and the length of the ballata would have been determined by the dynamics of the group. None of the 11 ballata texts that Boccaccio provides (one inside a novella, the rest at the close of each day) survives with a musical setting from the fourteenth century. In fact, there is a disconnect between what must have been a local, highly popular repertory of song and the more musically advanced ballate that appear in the Squarcialupi Codex. It is likely, however, that the simple ballate described in the *Decameron* were linked to the rich tradition of sacred spiritual songs found in the laude repertory. Several later laude are contrafacta of Florentine ballate, showing that the influence could work both ways.

The most prolific composer of ballate was a blind organist named Francesco Landini (c. 1325–1397). His portrait in the Squarcialupi Codex shows him holding a small portative organ while Lady Musica does the same at the bottom of the page, creating a parallel that announces his prowess as a player and composer (Fig. 11.3). In addition to singing, playing, and teaching, Landini was an intellectual who delighted in discussing theology and philosophy. The esteem

Figure 11.3: *Portrait of Francesco Landini from the Squarcialupi Codex, with Lady Musica in the lower margin*

extremely rich in color illumination

in which he was held is reflected in a contemporary description of a meeting in 1389 by group of Florentine intellectuals to which Landini belonged:

> The whole company remained in the pleasant shade, as a thousand birds sang among the verdant branches. Someone asked Francesco to play the organ a little, to see whether the sound would make the birds increase or diminish their song. He did so at once, and a great wonder followed. When the sound began many of the birds fell silent and gathered around as if in amazement, listening for a long time. Then they resumed their song and redoubled it, showing inconceivable delight, and especially one nightingale, who came and perched above the organ on a branch over Francesco's head.

The upper line of the ballata *De sospirar sovente* (see Anthology 38) demonstrates Landini's characteristic falling melodic line, which avoids parallel fifths by moving back up to the final instead of arriving on the fifth, and decorates the final pitch of a line by the third below (Ex. 11.3). This sound at the cadence, which became prevalent from his time and into the fifteenth century, is often called the "under-third" or "Landini cadence." It developed first in the monodic ballate of the generation before Landini, and was brought by him and others into polyphonic pieces. Unlike the madrigal *Quando i oselli canta* (see above), which is a study in contrasts, *De sospirar sovente* is marked by musical similarities not only between lines and within each section, but also between the two sections. However, the sections of this and other ballate differ from one another harmonically: the soloistic piedi have open cadences, and this sense of incompleteness pushes back to the refrain, a characteristic of many songs with refrains studied in this book.

Landini's ballata also had another life as a lauda, one of the spiritual songs discussed in Chapter 8. Laude poetry of the period was often published without music; for example, a text for John the Baptist, *Batista da Deo amato*, is annotated: "Cantasi come *De sospirar sovente*" (It is sung like *De sospirar sovente*). To sing the laude, musicians were required to fit their texts to the top voices of the corresponding polyphonic ballate. This process of reworking is typical of a musical culture on the cusp between written and oral traditions and of a time

Example 11.3: *A cadence from the opening of Landini's ballata* De sospirar sovente

5. To sigh often

4. And so much you confuse me

when most skilled musicians were also editors. It is yet another of the infinite ways medieval musicians had of creating intertexts.

THE CACCIA AND TRECENTO SACRED MUSIC: ANTONIO ZACARA DA TERAMO

The caccia is the third popular genre of Trecento secular song, and in many ways the most musically appealing to modern sensibilities. Composers learned to write imitative polyphony in the late twelfth and early thirteenth centuries, and became more skillful over time. Melodic lines unfolding in strict imitation often made for a static harmonic sense, as illustrated by the late-thirteenth-century *Alle psallite cum luia* transcribed in Primer II.4. The famous canon *Sumer is icumen in*, written in England in the late thirteenth century, was set to two texts, one secular, the other a hymn of praise for the Virgin Mary. As can be seen in Example 11.4, the upper voices chase each other in canon (that is, exact repetition), while a steadily repeating phrase in the tenor known as a *pes*, or foot, sustains the whole. This wonderful music is utterly without harmonic variety yet the early imitative part writing offers the listener a sonic sense of play that can be heard right away and appreciated on several levels.

Although the caccia has much in common with the *Sumer* canon, it is more fully developed both in the imitative part writing and in its harmonic dimension. Like its French counterpart, the *chace* (chase), the caccia is a lively embodiment of the

Example 11.4: *Opening of the round* Sumer is icumen in, *adapted for four voices in canon over a two-voice* pes

Upper voices: Summer is a'coming in. Loudly sing cuckoo!

Pes: Sing cuckoo! Now sing cuckoo!

spirit of the hunt: one voice chases the other. Caccia texts always offer a narrative of a particular moment in time. They are about dogs or men on horses chasing deer or birds, often with thinly veiled references to sexual conquest. The text of a much-anthologized piece set by Maestro Piero (c. 1300–c. 1350), *Con dolce brama*, contains an opening line dripping with double entendre: "With sweet longing and great desire I said to the master, when I was in his galley: 'Let's go to my lady's harbor.'"

Antonio Zacara da Teramo (c. 1350/60–after May 19, 1413), one of the most beloved composers of the late fourteenth and early fifteenth centuries, is among the last composers included in the Squarcialupi Codex; the pages designated for his music have not been completely filled in. Antonio, who spent much of his life working in Rome, composed what is perhaps the last known caccia, *Cacciando per gustar*, a lively parody of the hunt, set in a marketplace (see Anthology 39). The speaker begins in a sylvan reverie, about to pick a flower in a garden of delight. All of a sudden he is rudely awakened by urban commercial life; here what is being hunted are not foxes or hares, or even flowers that represent women (although there is much double entendre at play), but rather bargains. The chase is on, with buyers seeking after goods and sellers pressing hard upon the buyers. The top two voices are in canon, one chasing after the other at a distance of 22 measures. The tenor has its own text, filled with barkers' cries about everything from fish, to cheese, to oil, to offers of tooth extraction. The interplay between the three voices offers a lively, noisy setting, with the repetitions of the canonical chase giving the buyers and sellers opportunities for varied conversations as they wrangle over various wares.

The characteristic genres of Trecento popular song—madrigal, ballata, and caccia—are a repertory that seems to disappear as Johannes Ciconia (c. 1370–1412) and other Franco-Flemish composers began to import their own styles and sounds into Italian courts and cities, working in the employ of wealthy Italian aristocrats. In turn, northern composers were influenced by what they found in Italy. Italian song may well have flourished in the fifteenth century, but we will have to await its reappearance in northern and southern repertories of *frottole* (simple strophic songs of the sixteenth century) and later laude to get a taste of it.

Italian Trecento sacred music, on the other hand, continued to thrive in the early fifteenth century. Unlike the secular song repertory, it has more obvious native antecedents in the thirteenth century. The repertory includes motets and many polyphonic settings of individual Mass Ordinary movements. Here, too, Antonio Zacara da Teramo was a major innovator who anticipated the full flowering of Renaissance music. He is the first known composer to use parody in his Mass movements—that is, to use a secular song as the basis of a sacred composition. He paired a few Mass movements (the Gloria and Credo) by matching ranges, texture, mensural structure, and cadential patterns. He is also given credit for pairing the voices of polyphonic textures into duets that answer one another, a technique that would become important in later generations.

There are a great number of known surviving Trecento Glorias—57 at latest count. Most date from the twilight of the century, spilling over to around 1420. Antonio Zacara wrote six Glorias, one of which is found in the Old Hall Manuscript,

Example 11.5: *A phrase from Antonio Zacara's "English" Gloria*

For you alone are the Holy One

that most English of surviving late medieval polyphonic compendia (see below). There is also reason to believe that the influence traveled both ways, as one of Antonio's Glorias is labeled "Anglica" in two manuscripts, one Italian (Bologna, Q15), the other a collection of sacred works in the Polish National Library in Warsaw. This piece shows that Antonio knew about the characteristics of English sound: the work is filled with sonorous thirds and sixths (discussed below). Near the opening, for example, he adds a sixth in the cantus on the word "pax," also creating a third below the contratenor, A–F–A. As shown in Example 11.5, "Quoniam" is set to a vertical triad, F–A–C, and in fact the entire phrase is dominated by such triads.

ENGLISH SONG IN THE LATE THIRTEENTH AND FOURTEENTH CENTURIES

In a royal statute from 1549, shortly after King Henry VIII broke with the Roman Church and joined the Protestant Reformation, his successor Edward VI and Archbishop of Canterbury Cranmer commanded English bishops to take all liturgical books and "so deface and abolyshe" them "that they never after may serve eyther to anie soche use, as they were provided for." In accordance with this and later decrees, huge bonfires were set for the burning of liturgical and other books; the larger ones were torn asunder, their leaves sometimes used for book binding and other purposes. Books that offended those in power were not just burned: often they were publicly executed, with hooded hangmen present for the dramatic ceremonies of their "deaths."

If one includes churches of all types in England, Wales, Scotland, and Ireland, all of which were once required to have a set of Office books, the number of medieval English office books extant at the time of the 1549 decree would have been between 30,000 and 50,000; of these, barely 20—less than a tenth of 1 percent—have survived. The destruction involved literary works as well as liturgical books and theological treatises. Especially in the north of England, some wealthy families (known as recusants) remained Catholic and even refused to attend Protestant services. They retained medieval musical and liturgical practices in their private chapels, occasionally employing furnishings with secret backs and hidden compartments that could be turned into altars. The better part of remaining medieval English literature survived in the libraries of recusant Catholic families, who treasured their old books as much as they did the sacraments and the chant. Artworks and architecture suffered from similar acts of destruction, leaving England dotted with what Shakespeare called "bare ruin'd choirs" (Fig. 11.4) and obliterating much of medieval culture from the collective memory.

Unlike in France, Italy, or Spain, there is little surviving vernacular song repertory from late medieval England. No collection remains comparable to those of the cantigas, the French chansonniers, or the Squarcialupi Codex. Nor are there figures who emerge to integrate music and poetry in fourteenth-century England. What might our view of songs with English words be like had Chaucer been a poet-composer like Machaut? As it is, a mere three dozen religious and secular songs with English texts, both monophonic and polyphonic, survive from the twelfth century through 1400.

FROM SECULAR TO SACRED

Byrd one Brere (Bird on a Briar; Ex. 11.6) demonstrates the challenges in uncovering and understanding this fragile repertory. The text and melody are thought to have been scrawled on the back of an early papal document by a man from

Figure 11.4: *Ruins of Fountains Abbey, Yorkshire, England*

Example 11.6: *Early-fourteenth-century melody with two sets of English words* (a) *and* (b) *and a Latin contrafactum* (c)

(a) *Bird on a briar, bird, bird on a briar*

(b) *Maid in the moor lay, maiden in the moor lay*

(c) *A virgin gave birth, a queenly virgin*

Norfolk in the early fourteenth century. Like many English fragments, this can be linked to no other document by handwriting or notational style, yet there are possible interrelationships between it and some other pieces. The melody of *Byrd one Brere* perfectly fits another English lyric, *Maid in the Moor Lay* (The Maid Who Slept in the Moor), a text that is probably Irish in origin and may date from as early as the thirteenth century (see below). It is an early carol, a song meant for dancing.

Another text for this melody survives in the *Red Book of Ossory*. In this record book Richard de Ledrede, a Franciscan who became bishop of Ossory in Ireland in 1316, wrote out the words of 60 songs, texts he wanted his clerics to sing in lieu of songs that were "dramatic, lewd, and secular in nature." In some cases, Richard indicated the familiar tune to which the new text was to be sung; *Peperit virgo, virgo regia* (A virgin gave birth, a queenly virgin) was paired with *Maid in the Moor Lay*. So in this interrelated complex of three song texts, the bird on the briar sings intertextually about the maid in the moor. And the regal virgin has been brought in to do away with them both, while keeping the tune alive in a new guise.

Like his Franciscan counterparts on the Continent who created laude in Italy and spiritual songs in German lands (see Chapter 9), Richard de Ledrede was promoting the practice of transforming secular songs into sacred ones. Polyphonic English carols with religious meanings, a central repertory surviving from the fifteenth century, have their beginnings in thirteenth- and fourteenth-century popular traditions of singing and dancing, as reflected in *Maid in the Moor Lay*. Through the action of memory, multiple meanings abounded when this tradition was reshaped, especially in music for processions. Such a group of interrelated texts is reminiscent of the motets studied in Chapter 10, which created yet another conglomeration of sacred and secular meanings, each the richer because of the other's presence.

LATE-FOURTEENTH-CENTURY SACRED MUSIC, WITH AN EMPHASIS ON ENGLAND

The rite of Salisbury Cathedral, known as the Sarum rite, predominated throughout England, Wales, Scotland, and Ireland in the later Middle Ages, and representatives of the Sarum chant dialect survive in Office and Mass books. Yet all the collections that surely existed of English sacred polyphonic works from before 1400 have been lost, with the exception of the Winchester Troper (see Chapter 5) and an early-thirteenth-century copy of the *Magnus liber organi* prepared at St. Andrews, Scotland, known as Manuscript W1 (see Chapter 9). In spite of the wholesale destruction of institutional records, evidence has been found of around 180 manuscript collections of varying formats and lengths from before 1500 in England containing polyphony; there were doubtless many more. The Worcester fragments, a collection of stray pages, apparently from Worcester, comprises nearly 100 years of compositional activity—from the early thirteenth to the early fourteenth century—and a wide variety of styles. Some of the fragments are more complete than others, and the most damaged are only scraps. For the most part, the leaves had been used for book binding and the creation of flyleaves.

The earliest extant collection of late medieval English polyphony is the Old Hall Manuscript (British Library, Additional MS 57950), copied in the second quarter of the fifteenth century, but including earlier layers of compositions. The fragments of polyphonic works found in it and other sources are often difficult to date, to associate with particular places, or even to fit back into their liturgical contexts. Moreover, sorting out what is English from what is French is a daunting task in light of the frequent exchanges across the English Channel that took place during the Hundred Years' War.

The surviving English repertory contains works that are marvelously mellifluous, harbingers of the sounds that would delight fifteenth-century sensibilities in both sacred and secular polyphonic repertories on the Continent. The "English sound" often features a polyphonic texture that doubles pitches at intervals of thirds and sixths before ending phrases on the traditional open fifths and octaves. Initially an improvised practice, this style was not named or theoretically standardized until the fifteenth century, but it must have flourished in various guises in the thirteenth and fourteenth centuries.

That the English sound was striking to fourteenth-century continental ears is evident in the words of Netherlandish theorist Johannes Boen (d. 1367), who, when visiting Oxford as a student, found that the English "laymen and clerics, young and old" sing entirely "in 3rds and 6ths, ending on 5ths and octaves." Example 11.7, from the first third of the fourteenth century, shows the sequence-like text *Christi messis* set in three parts. It is written in score, a tradition of music writing that dominated in England throughout the fourteenth century, in contradistinction to the motet notation favored on the Continent, in which the each voice was written separately on its own set of staves (as with *Alle psallite*, Primer II.4).

Example 11.7: *Opening of the English cantilena* Christi messis

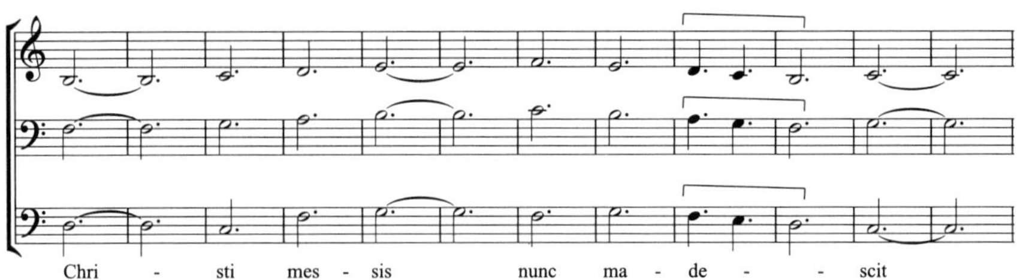

Now the harvest of Christ grows damp

This piece is what has come to be called a *cantilena*: a work with a sequence-like text, usually dedicated to the Virgin Mary, and notated in score (see Ex. 11.7).

Indeed, the majority of the surviving fragments of fourteenth-century English polyphony were written in honor of the Virgin. Many were works created for the liturgical celebration of a Mass that also incorporated Marian texts and a Vespers or Compline hour of prayer dedicated to the veneration of Mary. English cathedrals and monastic churches featured Lady Chapels, as did royal and other noble households. In these exquisite places, music, liturgy, art, and architecture were synthesized to create a sense of beauty befitting the Rose of all Virtue. Surviving fragments of polyphonic music must be reimagined in these resonant spaces, staffed by the finest young singers in England. In the texture of this music, one can see the desire that texts be declaimed and heard clearly, however skillfully ornamented they might be.

CANTILENAS AND MOTETS

The smoothly resonant harmonies and homophonic texture of the cantilena are evident in the three-voice *Singularis laudis digna* (see Anthology 40). The sequence-like text praises Edward III, king of the English, who had declared himself king of France in 1340. The piece commemorates Edward's conquest of the French seaside city of Calais in 1347; at the behest of his consort, Queen Philippa, he stayed the sentence of execution he had imposed upon its leaders. The piece was doubtless written for one of the king's chapels, either of his own household or of one of the collegiate churches he founded. Traditionally devout, the king had an enormous collection of relics, a deep devotion to the Virgin Mary, and a desire to use religion to strengthen his rule and legacy. He endowed the chapels he founded with six choristers each, so we can imagine this piece may have been originally sung with two to a part.

The prominence of musicians in the chapels of Edward III and his son, the Black Prince, is suggested by the isorhythmic motet *Sub Arturo plebs*, which contains a catalogue of men who played and composed in England in the late fourteenth and early fifteenth centuries (Ex. 11.8). The motet testifies to the numbers

Example 11.8: *Opening of the English composers' motet* Sub Arturo plebs

Triplum: Let the people encamped with Arthur

Duplum: The source of playing on the lyre

Tenor: Their sound has gone out through all the earth and to the ends of the world.

of composers reflected in the first layer of the Old Hall Manuscript and in surviving fragments from the later fourteenth century. It gives a taste of what must have been one of the most extraordinary schools of composition from the entire Middle Ages, and is one of several late-medieval compositions that catalogue musicians and their works, paying homage to the craft and its practitioners.

More than 30 motets survive from fourteenth-century England. They generally exhibit a somewhat wider voice range than continental motets and employ four voices more frequently than the standard three found on the Continent. The fourth voice may provide harmonic filler as a kind of counterpart to the tenor, or it may function as a second tenor of equal importance. English motets make more frequent use of the repeating *pes* in their tenors, and of characteristically English sonorities emphasizing the intervals of the third and sixth.

Just as Machaut adopted techniques used in his motets for individual movements of his *Messe de Nostre Dame* (see Chapter 10), English composers based their polyphonic Mass movements on techniques found in motets like *Sub Arturo plebs*. The Gloria of Richard Queldryk (fl. c. 1400), found in the earliest layer of the Old Hall Manuscript, was written for a Mary Mass. Like some late-fourteenth-century English motets, it is a four-voice, isorhythmic piece in duple meter. The top two voices are texted and move more quickly than the two lower voices in the first half, forming a kind of duet above a harmonic scaffolding (Ex. 11.9). The two lower voices move twice as fast in the repeat of the color, creating a sense of urgency as they nearly match the upper voices in their fast-paced character. The upper voices unfold sometimes in staggered entrances and sometimes in parallel, their frequent thirds giving the music its honeyed "English" sound. In several instances, isorhythmic patterns were used to make pairs of pieces for liturgical performance in the Old Hall repertory; this Gloria, for example, is paired with Queldryk's three-voice isorhythmic Credo in the manuscript.

Example 11.9: *From Richard Queldryk's Gloria, illustrating the setting of a Marian Gloria trope text*

Triplex 1: You who take away the sins of the world, receive our prayer.

Triplex 2: Mary, Virgin Mother, you who take away the sins of the world, have mercy on us.

MASS ORDINARY CYCLES

We have seen that in the thirteenth century, the establishment of the Feast of Corpus Christi brought renewed emphasis on the meanings of the communion service. This emphasis had a great effect on the composition of music for the Mass, and on the ways liturgical music was performed. Indeed, among the elite chapels of Europe there seems to have been a shift in the nature of liturgical singing. The soloistic work required for responsorial psalmody gave way to choral performances of the Mass Ordinary, a change that went hand in hand with the development of polyphonic settings of these texts.

In addition to the greater devotion to the act of communion, other developments encouraged an understanding of the Mass Ordinary chants as pieces that could be combined musically into some sort of set. The English Franciscan Haymo of Faversham (c. 1175–1244) produced a widely used ordinal (a book describing a particular set of ritual practices) that streamlined and standardized the liturgy. The gradual (a collection of chants for the Mass) promulgated by the Franciscans in 1251 became the norm after Pope Nicholas III ordered all Roman books not in conformity with it to be destroyed (see Chapter 8). The Franciscan gradual was written in square notation, and its promulgation also helped establish this kind of notation, originally championed in Paris, throughout Europe. In concert with Haymo's work, liturgical reformers in Rome began to create cycles of Ordinary chants for feasts of particular rank in the Kyriale (a collection of Ordinary chants). Ordinary tropes were removed, and groups of chants became associated with particular occasions; these changes helped to make ordinary chants more prominent, at the same time the Kyriale was becoming a standard liturgical book in all churches and chapels. Chants assigned to special feasts and seasons in some of these books formed an early stage in the development of organized sets of Mass movements, although there were not intrinsic musical relationships between the individual pieces themselves.

The earliest known plainchant Mass cycles, each of which was composed in a single mode, were copied in the early fifteenth century in a manuscript from French Cyprus. This same manuscript contains paired individual polyphonic Mass movements, as do the more recent layers of the Old Hall Manuscript, but in general such ideas do not belong to the fourteenth century. Some early polyphonic Mass movements were once thought to form nascent cycles, but this is now considered to be true only for Machaut's extraordinary *Messe de Nostre Dame* (see Chapter 10).

Throughout much of the Middle Ages, the terms *cantus planus* and *cantus firmus* were used to indicate medieval chant, as opposed to other kinds of music. By the fifteenth century, cantus firmus had also come to mean chant moving in long notes, often of equal value, upon which a polyphonic composition could be based. The cantus firmus Mass would reach its fullest development in the fifteenth and sixteenth centuries, but early examples of this fledgling genre can be found in the fourteenth century, including Machaut's Mass and some of the works of Antonio Zacara da Teramo discussed above.

The flowering of the polyphonic Mass ordinary was also hastened by the further development of the private Mass. Fears of the fires of purgatory increased dramatically in the fourteenth century, so much so that wealthy patrons often wished commemorative Masses to be sung for them and their family members to speed souls on their ways to better places. Private Masses did not fall under official regulating rubrics for the Mass liturgy. Hence composers who created works to commemorate the anniversaries of their patrons' deaths or other occasions were free to be more creative. Machaut wove Marian allusions into the texture of his Mass, and Antonio Zacara da Teramo and later Old Hall composers used musical features to link one movement to another. Musical and textual references to people, places, and events occurred in dedicatory motets and festive pieces such as *Singularis laudis digna*, the cantilena in honor of Edward III studied above. Honorifics of all sorts would frequently find their ways into the masses and motets of the fifteenth century. Such works reflected the increasing dependencies of the best composers upon their wealthy patrons, many of whom were Italian.

The musical innovations that would become prominent in the fifteenth century have their beginnings in France, with a highly sophisticated understanding of rhythm and of multilayered polyphonic works; in England with its own version of the Ars Nova and the Ars Subtilior, especially as found in the Old Hall Manuscript, but always with a harmonic texture that expanded the sonic palette; in the Lowlands, where an Ars Nova presence reminds us that the knowledge and skill of fifteenth-century Netherlandish and Belgian composers operating in Italy did not come out of thin air; and, of course, in Italy itself, where the experiments characteristic of the Italian Antonio Zacara da Teramo were every bit as crucial to the development of fifteenth-century polyphonic writing as were those of his northern contemporaries. There would be a new style favored among the musical elite of the fifteenth century, but it would be a hybrid.

FOR FURTHER READING

Bennett, Judith M., "Ventriloquisms: When Maidens Speak in English Songs, c. 1300–1550," in *Medieval Woman's Song: Cross-Cultural Approaches*, ed. Anne L. Klinck and Ann Marie Rasmussen (Philadelphia: University of Pennsylvania Press, 2002), 187–204

Bowers, Roger, "Fixed Points in the Chronology of English Fourteenth-Century Polyphony," *Music and Letters* 71 (1990): 313–35

Duncan, Thomas G., "The Maid in the Moor and the Rawlinson Text," *Review of English Studies*, ns 47 (1996): 151–62

Haar, James, and John Nádas, "Antonio Squarcialupi: Man and Myth," *Early Music History* 25 (2006): 105–68

Haggh, Barbara, "Foundations or Institutions? On Bringing the Middle Ages into the History of Medieval Music," *Acta Musicologica* 68 (1996): 87–128

Lefferts, Peter, *The Motet in England in the Fourteenth Century* (Ann Arbor: UMI Research Press, 1986)

McDonald, Nicola F., and W. M. Ormrod, eds., *Rites of Passage: Cultures of Transition in the Fourteenth Century* (York: Medieval Press, 2004)

Morgan, Nigel, "The Sanctorals of Early Sarum Missals and Breviaries," in G. H. Brown and L. E. Voigts, eds., *The Study of Medieval Manuscripts of England: Festschrift in Honor of Richard W. Pfaff* (Tempe: Arizona Center for Medieval and Renaissance Studies, 2010), 143–62

Wathey, Andrew, "The Production of Books of Liturgical Polyphony," in Jeremy Griffiths and Derek Pearsall, eds., *Book Production and Publishing in Britain, 1375–1475* (Cambridge: Cambridge University Press, 2007), 143–61

Williamson, Magnus, "Liturgical Polyphony in the Pre-Reformation English Parish Church: A Provisional List and Commentary," *Royal Musical Association Research Chronicle* 38 (2005): 1–43

CHAPTER TWELVE

On the Edges

Rather than ending with a grandiose summary joining strands of polyphonic development on the eve of the Renaissance, we will close with a look at select music and processes for creating music that relate only peripherally to the "central" repertories studied in fourteenth-century France, Italy, and England. In addition to these complex polyphonic core repertories, the fourteenth century provides a variety of simpler genres, styles, and understandings best appreciated through regional case studies, many of which relate to folk rather than learned traditions, or continue to promote earlier genres of sacred music, especially among women. There are many regions in western Europe where the Ars Subtilior never arrived and the Ars Nova was extant only in the occasional court of the wealthy. All of this music bears the trademarks of the regions in which the evidence survives. Many of the sources date well into the fifteenth century, demonstrating how long medieval techniques of composition and notation survived in western Europe.

The extraordinary range of musical styles throughout western Europe in the fourteenth century makes a fascinating parallel with that of the plastic arts, both architectural and representational: some churches were built with French models in mind; in other regions late-medieval French innovations appear only in decorative details, or not at all. On Gotland, a large island off the coast of Sweden, architecture continued to be built in the Romanesque style until 1361, when the Danes conquered the island and ambitious building campaigns

Figure 12.1: *The fourteenth-century church at Stanga, Gotland:* left, *Romanesque tower;* right, *Gothic art and portal*

ceased. In the more than 90 Romanesque-style churches extant on the island, Gothic details began to appear in the fourteenth century, especially in the design of portals (Fig. 12.1). But the churches of Gotland are no less superb in their craftsmanship than those of other, more complicated styles, as in France. It is fascinating indeed to consider some of the ways that the developments studied in Chapters 10 and 11 bypassed entire regions of fourteenth-century Europe, and earlier forms and compositional techniques continued to fire a range of musical imaginations.

FRAUENLOB AND GERMAN MINSTRELSY

Wagner's opera *Die Meistersinger von Nürnberg* (The Mastersingers of Nuremberg, completed in 1867) celebrates the creativity and vitality of the German song tradition. Its leading character is Hans Sachs (1494–1576), in real life a middle-class Meistersinger, or poet-composer, who wrote more than 6,000 songs. The tradition to which Sachs belonged is usually said to begin with Heinrich von Meissen (c. 1260–1318), also known as Frauenlob ("Praise of Our Lady") because of his songs in praise of the Virgin and of women in general. Frauenlob was a Minnesinger, the courtly German equivalent of a trouvère or minstrel. In a painting from the mid-fourteenth century, reproduced on the cover of this book, he is shown instructing a group of musicians playing four-string vielles, an oboe-like shawm, a psaltery or zither (far right), a bagpipe (in front of the psaltery), a duct flute (left), and several percussion instruments.

Like the jongleurs we met in Chapter 8, minstrels were professional secular musicians, usually instrumentalists, both male and sometimes female. Schools for minstrels, such as the one associated with Frauenlob, were established in many urban centers in the thirteenth and fourteenth centuries. Some musicians were outfitted with horses and instruments by their patrons and were able to attend for weeks; the less well funded doubtless walked to school and participated for shorter periods. It seems that the ability to sing and play well was a way of gaining preferment, even for knights. Very little instrumental music from this period survives (see the introduction to Part III). It lived primarily in an oral tradition, each musician stocking his memory with tunes, much as country fiddle players do today; but the many songs of Frauenlob give us a sense of what the most sophisticated German minstrel music sounded like. Whether or not he knew Hildegard's songs from two centuries earlier (see Chapter 7), their works share stylistic, cultural, and regional features.

As a well-paid minstrel, Frauenlob traveled widely and earned great renown in his lifetime. A chronicler says of his funeral procession that "women carried his body from his lodgings to the sepulcher with loud lamentation and great mourning, on account of the infinite praises that he heaped on the whole feminine sex in his poems." His vocal music was written down a century after his death in neumes that can be transcribed (most importantly in Vienna, Österreichische Nationalbibliothek, Cod. 2710). Although the songs are monophonic, they were surely sometimes sung with instrumental accompaniments, and perhaps even with some sort of improvised polyphonic elaboration.

Frauenlob's devotion to the Virgin Mary is indicated by her picture in the upper-right-hand corner of the painting referenced above: he teaches music under the protection of her mantle. Well might she honor a poet who composed a monumental *Leich* (lyrical narrative poem) in her honor, a work of 20 strophes and 508 lines. The Virgin Mary in Frauenlob's *Marienleich* serves as the goddess Natura, giving form to the cosmos and its creatures in the poet's idealistic and imagistic universe.

The smith from the high country
hurled his hammer in my womb
and I forged seven sacraments.
I carried him who carries earth and sky
and yet am still a maid.
He lay in me and took leave of me without labor.

Most certainly—
I slept with three—
till I grew pregnant with God's goodness,
pierced by sweetness upon sweetness.
My ancient lover kissed me,
let this be said:
I gazed at him and made him young—
then all the heavenly hosts were glad.
(The proud Maid's praises must be sung—
let none take it ill!)
he said my breasts were sweeter than wine
and drank his fill—
my Beloved is mine.

Frauenlob shaped the poem with heavy reliance on the biblical *Song of Songs*; its grand design depends on many levels of number symbolism. In the poem he said of his compositional process: "I act like a workman who guides his work with his carpenter's square without interruption. By his skill he shapes its height and length, as wide and broad as he means to structure it; and once he has encompassed it at right angles according to his desire, then he works on it as best he can." The music is formulaic, and Frauenlob, like many German poet-composers, used a group of individual melodies, or *Töne* (singular, *Ton*), that served well for a variety of texts in German circles, where the art of making contrafacta was finely honed.

The *Marienleich*, unlike Frauenlob's shorter poems, consists of a series of 20 Töne. Each contains a variety of melodic cells and, depending on the needs of the irregular poetic lines, many cells develop only one or two ornamented pitches (Ex. 12.1). Each Ton is also repeated in the second half of the strophe, as would be the case in a sequence. The 20 strophes in this Leich are arranged so that the modes are cycled through two and a half times. This is not the only reference to the modal Office: each strophe ends with a *differentia*, connecting it not to a psalm but to the next strophe (see Chapter 4). Strophe 20 closes out the piece with a grand "Amen." Many German minstrels of the period were intellectuals who combined the sacred and secular in their works.

Another influential German musician of the period was Hugo Spechtshart of Reutlingen (c. 1285–1359/60), a parish priest who, among other works, wrote a treatise on plainchant and singing that goes by several titles, most commonly *Flores musice* (Flowers of Music). His keen observations of the musical world around him are revealed in his chronicle. In the plague year of 1349, Hugo described the actions and music of the flagellants, groups of people who paraded publicly, completing acts of penance in hopes of inspiring divine compassion. Hugo's interests make him a kind of early ethnomusicologist, a student of music and culture, and the first to provide a small repertory of

Example 12.1: *From strophe 11 of Frauenlob's* Marienleich, *with melodic cells indicated by brackets*

The smith from the high country threw his hammer in my womb, and I forged seven sacraments.
I carried him who carries the heavens and earth, and yet am still a maid.
He lay inside me and took leave of me without labor.

Example 12.2: *Song of the flagellants during time of plague, recorded by Hugo Spechtshart*

Now here comes the wave of evil; flee from hot hell. Lucifer is an evil companion. Whomever he catches, he smears with pitch. Therefore we intend to flee him.

mid-fourteenth-century German folk songs, put in the context of ritual behavior. *Nu tret herzuo der boessen welle*, for example, was sung when the flagellants stripped down to their underwear and used their whips to draw blood (Ex. 12.2). By 1350, another group had adapted these songs for drinking, in parodies that foreshadow the head-bashing flagellants in the 1974 film *Monty Python and the Holy Grail*.

RELIGIOUS WOMEN IN THE LONG FOURTEENTH CENTURY

Like Hugo's flagellants, musicians and artists in many regions of Europe were engaged in the production of what we might call folk art. Many of the books women copied and illuminated in late medieval Germany were liturgical books that included music. The drawings they contain are too often dismissed as *Nonnenarbeiten* (nuns' work). Even when it is less than skillfully rendered, such art can be imaginative and possess a freshness of approach that transcends iconographic stereotypes. The books created by some communities of nuns present a complex interiority not seen elsewhere, giving a new understanding of their artistic and musical activities. Richly illuminated liturgical books clearly were highly prized by northern German women in the later Middle Ages. Nuns were the patrons of such productions; but further, in some cases they were involved in planning and designing the books. They also served as scribes, notators, and illuminators, and composed some of the music as well.

THE NUNS OF PARADIES BEI SOEST

The most fabulous among the surviving northern German liturgical manuscripts are those that belonged to the Dominican convent of Paradies bei Soest in Westphalia. These women developed ways of decorating the letters of their liturgical books that created a profound personal and communal exegesis of the chants and their meanings, often hiding passages of Scripture, prayers, and even portraits of themselves within the ornately flourished initials. For many fourteenth-century women, both nuns and beguines, John the Evangelist was a saint who had special meaning. In Scripture he is described as the beloved disciple: in the Crucifixion scene, it is he to whom Jesus entrusts the care of his mother. St. John was believed to have lived as a virgin and to have been assumed into heaven at the end of his life, making a parallel with the Virgin Mary in life and death. As such, he resonated with religious women as both protector and model.

A long sequence for John the Evangelist, *Verbum Dei, Deo natum*, originally written in the twelfth century, was highly favored in several houses of Dominican nuns east of the Rhine. The piece was adapted for liturgical books from Paradies bei Soest with extraordinary decoration. Every verse has an initial, and every initial is "embroidered" by pen with filigree, figures, and text scrolls, chosen and added by the nuns. John's connection to the Virgin Mary was expressed through musical contrafacta as well. In the thirteenth century, Dominicans had created a new sequence by adding texts in praise of the Virgin to the well-known eleventh-century Easter sequence *Victimae paschali laudes*. The nuns of Paradies bei Soest went one step further, composing yet another variation, *Virgine Johanne laudes*, a sequence for John the Evangelist, using music to fuse their beloved John with Mary and Jesus. Newly discovered fragments from this and other houses of Dominican nuns show that they collected and even copied polyphonic works as well.

In a Paradies gradual from the late fourteenth century, John is depicted in a flourished initial beginning *Virgine Johanne Laudes*, with the eagle, his symbol, resting on his breast. A few folios later, the nuns copied the tones for the Introit psalms. Each initial contains a commentary on the word "Gloria" (the Doxology being the words used for the tones) in tiny scrolls in the margins and woven into the letters (Fig. 12.2). Depicted in the first G is Jesus, in the second Mary, and in the third John; this is yet another strategy for joining them, this time employing visuals and the modes of recitation. Clearly these large choir books were meant for both singing and study. Their preparation was an art in which liturgical commentary and musical understanding were joined.

BRIDGET OF SWEDEN (1303–1373)

A musical and liturgical practice, newly construed and different from anything seen before, is associated with the Bridgettines (Order of the Most Holy Savior), a religious foundation established in the fourteenth century by Bridget of

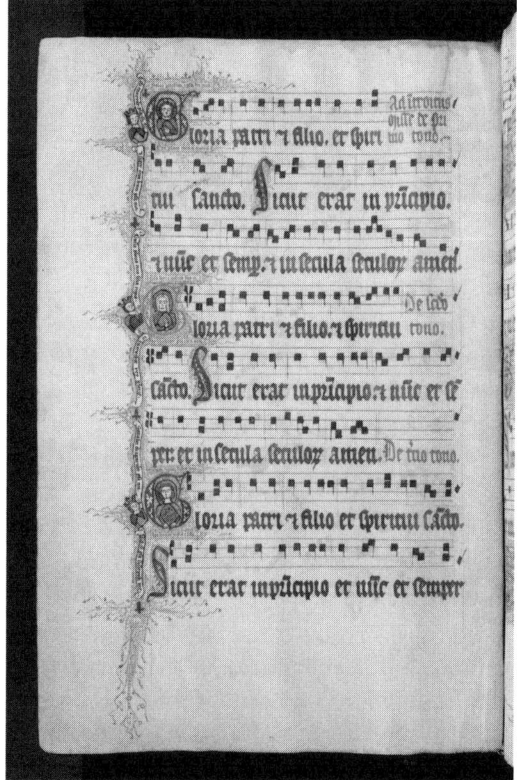

Figure 12.2: *Tones for the Introit as decorated by the nuns of Paradies bei Soest in the early fourteenth century (Düsseldorf, Universitäts- und Landesbibliothek, MS D11)*

Sweden. A married woman with eight children, St. Bridget was a pious woman. Like well-to-do men and women (and, increasingly, bourgeois people as well), Bridget would have used a book of hours, a set of readings for the Office said by laity throughout the day; this was the first type of book owned by medieval laity in any significant numbers. Books of hours are some of the most common late medieval codices, and those prepared for the wealthy can be exquisitely illuminated. The prayer books themselves reflected regional liturgical uses—for example, of Rome, of Paris, of the Low Countries, and of Salisbury Cathedral (the Sarum rite). Most typically, among other series of prayers, such a book would contain the Little Hours of the Blessed Virgin Mary, an Office that allowed the person praying to enter into Mary's joys and sorrows throughout her life, along with other cycles of prayer. (A leaf from a late medieval book of hours showing Mary at the time of annunciation by the angel Gabriel is reproduced as Fig. 1.2.) St. Bridget used the Little Hours of the Virgin as the basis for a new liturgical form of prayer for women, moving a familiar practice of private devotion (based on the earlier practices of monasteries and cathedrals, as studied in Chapter 4) back into a communal sphere.

St. Bridget founded her order of religious men and women upon the death of her husband, soon after they returned from a pilgrimage to Compostela. Assisted by several men and her daughter Catherine, she established the Bridgettine motherhouse, the Abbey of Vadstena, on Lake Vattern in the Diocese of Linköping, Sweden. It was a double monastery (both men and women), and the order spread to several places in the late fourteenth and early fifteenth centuries, most notably to England, where Syon Abbey was founded in 1415.

Hard hit by the Protestant Reformation, Syon Abbey was closed in 1539 and the surviving members relocated to various sites in the Lowlands, Rouen, and finally Lisbon. Some nuns and brothers took personal books with them. In addition, part of the original library of some 1,400 books has survived. These 80 or so volumes contain several liturgical books that document the liturgical and musical practices of the English Bridgettines. Architecture both separated and unified the male and female contingents of the congregation, and drew the laity in as well. The nuns sang from a gallery, so they could not be seen. From on high, they were able to observe the altar and the actions of the priest better than the laity in the nave of the church, who in turn could hear the women sing.

St. Bridget's liturgy and the music written for it, created with the help of several male collaborators, worked in alternation with the liturgy of the male monastics. The men of Syon sang the full Office (Sarum rite), while the women sang the texts that any pious layperson would have known by heart, the Little Hours of the Virgin. Thus the laity attending Bridgettine services could replay in their memories a sounding version of the prayers they said at home every day. The readings for Matins (scaled down in number) were meditations by St. Bridget, and the main Mass of the day was that for the Virgin Mary. The music the women sang was carefully regulated, as instructions from their own liturgical sources tell us: "Their singing should be serious, sober, and simple, without breaking of notes and gay releasing [that is, without hocketing], and with meekness and devotion; they should never have any organs; their psalmody should be distinct and clear and everything should be measured and added by the nuns themselves, moderated with discretion."

LATE MEDIEVAL MUSIC IN SPAIN AND ICELAND

Two manuscripts from Spain, one from the early fourteenth century and the other from the later fourteenth century, bear witness to polyphonic repertories removed from those of France, England, and Italy. The Monasterio de Santa María de la Real de Las Huelgas, a royal foundation in Burgos in northern Spain, was established in the late twelfth century by King Alfonso VIII of Castile and his wife, Eleanor of England, a daughter of Eleanor of Aquitaine and Henry II of England. In the later Middle Ages the monastery was a training ground for women of the upper classes, both those who would be consecrated as nuns and those who would not, as well as a royal mausoleum. Several liturgical books survive from Las Huelgas from the twelfth through the sixteenth centuries, including a major collection of music, much of it polyphonic, used to supplement missals and antiphoners.

THE LAS HUELGAS CODEX AND THE *LLIBRE VERMELL*

The Las Huelgas Codex, dating from the early 1300s, is the most significant repertory of polyphonic music from a late medieval monastery anywhere in Europe, and the only major polyphonic codex from medieval Spain. It is also the only truly retrospective anthology that survives, drawing as it does from every genre of music created during the thirteenth century, from organum to various kinds of motets. Las Huelgas was a Cistercian monastery (it still functions today) where the use of polyphonic works generally was not encouraged. However, it would seem that the rules could be bent for the sake of instructing noblewomen in the finest repertory that money could buy. It is not to be wondered at that French polyphonic traditions were adapted in northern Spain in a monastery where the daughter of Queen Eleanor would be buried, and her granddaughter would serve as abbess.

Visual evidence indicates that this manuscript was written by only one music scribe and one text scribe (they may have been the same person). It would seem that the scribe worked from a variety of smaller collections, which may have dated from various times in the twelfth and thirteenth centuries. He (or she) must have edited the music on the spot, updating the notation in the process of copying and carefully organizing the repertory. In the motets, the French texts are often translated into Latin, for the sake of propriety, liturgical or otherwise (see, for example, *Castrum pudicicie/Virgo viget/Flos Filius*, Anthology 30.2). The Las Huelgas Codex contains nearly 200 pieces, grouped as follows:

Polyphonic Kyries; a Gloria trope (*Spiritus et alme*); Alleluias; one Offertory; Sanctus, Agnus, and Benedicamus settings
Sequences (both polyphonic and monophonic)
Motets (one in four voices, the rest in two and three voices)
Conductus (both polyphonic and monophonic)

These are the same kinds of pieces that were composed and copied in Paris throughout the thirteenth century. The scribe-editor expresses monophonic sequences and conductus in modified Franconian notation, so that the rhythms can be read—a rarity in the period. Around half the pieces are unique to the Las Huelgas Codex, suggesting either that northern Spain had a strong indigenous musical culture or that many of the works are from French sources that have been lost. A statement in the monastic commentary on the rule of life encourages polyphonic singing by the women of the community. In addition, the codex includes a delightful exercise in solfège syllables—addressed to "you cloistered virgins, gold-plated nuns, suited for these things by birth"—to demonstrate various techniques, including hocket. Musical expectations for the women of Las Huelgas were far different from those for the Bridgettines!

Another source from Spain sheds light on a world apart from that of the Las Huelgas Codex. The *Llibre vermell* (Red Book) of Montserrat, named for a red-velvet cover provided in the nineteenth century, was compiled at the Benedictine Abbey of Montserrat, where there was a Marian cult that inspired pilgrimage, similar in popularity to that of Compostela (see Chapter 6). The celebrated Black Madonna of Montserrat, a statue said to date from the twelfth century (Fig. 12.3), is honored in the texts of the manuscript. This image, and others like it elsewhere in Europe, can be viewed as embodying the feminine ideal from the *Song of Songs* 1:5: "black but comely." (It is not clear how these statues acquired their color, whether by long exposure to smoke or by design.)

The *Llibre vermell* was copied no later than 1400 and is a kind of shrine book, including miracle stories about the Virgin of Montserrat, petitions, prayers, and other devotional texts. It also contains ten songs in Latin and Catalan intended to regulate the pilgrims' behavior in the courtyard of the monastic church. The introduction says: "Because many pilgrims, when they keep vigil at night in the church of Blessed Mary of Monserrat, want to sing and dance as they do all day in the street, and therefore because in church they ought to sing only virtuous and devout songs, these songs have been written here."

The collection is meant for popular singing; three pieces are specifically designated for dancing out of doors, probably with accompaniment by drums

Figure 12.3: *The Black Madonna of Montserrat, in the monastery of Santa María de Montserrat, Spain*

and instruments, performed by the pilgrims. (Frame drums were ubiquitous in Spanish culture. They were played by Christians, Muslims, and Jews alike, but when women played them, it was deemed bad for their reputations.) The monks who composed and wrote down this small collection adapted traditions of folk polyphony, music consisting of a few notes that people sang in canon. *Laudemus virginem*, for example, consists of a single repeating phrase that is found in each

Example 12.3: *Imitative polyphony in honor of the Virgin Mary, from the* Llibre vermell

Let us praise the Virgin. She is the mother and Jesus is her son.

voice (Ex. 12.3). With such a simple, resonant work, great numbers of untrained singers could sing in parts, through voice exchange and use of contrary motion.

CROSSING THE ATLANTIC

The extraordinary popularity and vitality of polyphonic folk music is demonstrated by another version of *Laudemus virginem*, recently discovered—modified and set to an Icelandic text—in four different Icelandic manuscripts. In these contrafacta, the two voices unfold not in canon but simultaneously, thus showing another way the texture of the song can work harmonically. The copying of the piece well over 1,000 miles from the Black Madonna of Montserrat and her shrine suggests that the vast and complicated strains of music circulating in an oral tradition included both monophonic and polyphonic families of songs.

The example of *Laudemus virginem* probably illustrates the folk technique of improvising rather than the transmission of a particular piece. An Icelandic traveler named Björn Einarsson is known to have gone from Venice to Compostela in the early fifteenth century. His travels may have taken him through Montserrat, where he would have heard this kind of vocal music. Icelandic intertexts for a piece in the *Llibre vermell* depended on a lively art of memory, one that had not diminished over the long centuries of learning to notate and transcribe, and one that involved improvisation and adaptation of new texts. Ironically, however, the proof of this mode of oral transmission is in the manuscripts. As we have seen repeatedly throughout our study, dependence on written sources for evidence of our musical past is nearly absolute, and remains so throughout the history of Western music until the twentieth century and the development of the recording industry.

THE GLOBAL MIDDLE AGES

The music we have encountered in this Epilogue comes from far-flung regions, and the distances between them are indicative of differences in language and culture. Much has inevitably been left out of our account of medieval music, most notably—as this is a book about western Europe—the music of eastern Europe and the Byzantine Empire, which produced chant and chant notation that can be securely transcribed as early as the tenth century. By the same token, our survey has not done justice to the notion of a global Middle Ages. After all, people made music in every continent in the medieval world, not just Europe. It is not possible in a short book to cover all these traditions. Yet we can mention some of the ways in which medieval music can be studied as a global phenomenon.

In spite of the fact that there is little written music to recapture, every medieval musical culture has tuning systems, instruments, and, in some cases, forms of notation and theoretical treatises that remain available for study. This evidence opens up possibilities for many kinds of work on the history of sound and sensibility. The work of Laurence Picken and other scholars on music of the T'ang dynasty, as preserved in manuscripts found in Japan, is perhaps the best example of the ways in which repertories from medieval China, once thought to be lost, have once again been partially recovered. Richard Widdess's study of early Indian theoretical treatises attempts to bring the notation to life, thereby drawing closer to early systems of sound. Although these musical forms and muscial systems may have little or nothing to do with musical practices in the West, there is much to be learned from comparing medieval systems of musical thought, from the Byzantine Empire, to India, China, Japan, and the classical civilizations of Latin America (whether reconstruction of sounding phenomena is possible or not).

The way the cosmos incorporates an understanding of music also has much to tell us through comparative study, from the Greeks to the Chinese and various cultures of Africa and South and Central America. For example, the parallels between a twelfth-century Western Christian understanding of sound and the cosmos, as found in the works of Hildegard of Bingen (see Chapter 7), and twelfth-century Chinese cosmology through study of Chu Hsi, a Confucian scholar who lived from 1130 to 1200, are fascinating, and may depend on the various ways an Aristotelian view was understood and transmitted.

People of the global medieval world told their tales in song, and there is much to be learned from comparisons of narrative styles and various uses of language for singing and proclaiming, even when the notes themselves are lost. Recent studies engage with such comparative work on the arts in the global Middle Ages, covering topics such as sacred objects (books, cloth and clothing, shrines) in various cultures or different strains of visual culture. This kind of comparative study suggests methods of working that might be adapted for music, although we have only begun to fathom what they might be.

Ironically, one thing that emerges from study of the global Middle Ages—which for many subjects extends to around 1500—is the central importance of European and Byzantine music and music theory. Owing to the sophisticated ways in which many of these traditions were preserved, especially those of refined and highly trained musicians, Europeanists can often adduce evidence that is not available from other parts of the world. Most non-European cultures never learned to write their music down, at least not with the precision found in the West. In one sense, this makes the global study of music difficult, but it also means that a knowledge of western and eastern European traditions is an excellent starting point for many kinds of global historical studies.

Our book speaks for 1,000 years of music in as many cultures. It speaks for thousands upon thousands of voices, of tunes and families of tunes, of ways of making music, of processes for storing music in the mind, of constantly relating one melody to another (and another and another) by both individuals and communities. This is the loam of Western music, encompassing lands and peoples from Iceland to Hungary and from Scandinavia to northern Africa. It nourished the growth of the many European traditions that developed in unique ways in the centuries after 1400. The story of music in the medieval West is both an epic saga and a repressed groaning of muffled voices. Its cast of characters includes those who had the power and the inclination to preserve their music, as well as those who lacked the means to let us know how they sang and played. We celebrate even as we lament.

FOR FURTHER READING

Attinger, Gisela, "Sequences in Two Icelandic Mass Books from the Later Middle Ages," in Lori Kruckenberg and Andreas Haug, eds., *The Sequences of Nidaros: A Nordic Repertory and Its European Context* (Trondheim, Norway: Tapir, 2006), 165–81

Bell, Nicholas, *The Las Huelgas Music Codex: A Companion Study to the Facsimile* (Madrid: Testimonio Compañía Editorial, 2003)

Heng, Geraldine, "The Global Middle Ages: An Experiment in Collaborative Humanities or in Imagining the World, 500–1500 C.E.," *English Language Notes* 47 (2009): 205–16

Jeffery, Peter, "Popular Culture on the Periphery of the Medieval Liturgy" *Worship* 55 (1981): 419–27

Jones, Malcolm, *The Secret Middle Ages* (Westport, CT: Praeger, 2003)

Matthews, Alastair, "Literary Lives in Medieval Germany: The Wartburg Song Contest in Three Hagiographical Narratives," *Deutsche Vierteljahrsschrift für Literaturwissenschaft und Geistesgeschichte* 84 (2010): 44–59

APPENDIX

A Medieval Music Primer

IV. THE LITURGY OF THE ROMAN CATHOLIC CHURCH

Medieval music is imperfectly comprehended from modern scores and notation alone. Performers of the repertoires studied in *Music in the Medieval West* and the accompanying anthology, and the scholars who write about them, learn to read from the manuscripts themselves and make their own decisions based on their knowledge of and close contact with medieval musical artifacts, theory, and practice. This Primer is designed to give all students of medieval music a basic tutorial in using these primary sources.

I. SOURCES

I.1. DATABASES AND REFERENCE TOOLS

Many libraries throughout the world—including such major repositories as the French National Library (Bibliothèque Nationale de France) in Paris and the Bavarian State Library (Bayerische Staatsbibliothek) in Munich, the Beinecke Rare Book and Manuscript Library at Yale University, and the Morgan Library and Museum in New York City—have digitized many of their medieval manuscripts to ensure broad public access. As a result, every teacher and student can work with original sources, bringing a wealth of codices and manuscript fragments into the classroom for group projects and discussions, as well as for individual study. Several online databases have been created as guides to finding and using these manuscripts.

Because the digital landscape is in constant flux, these online resources can only be referenced here in a general way. Many are listed on the author's website, which will be updated periodically (see link in the Study Space). CANTUS is a database for Latin liturgical chant, with a focus on the chant texts for the Office. CANTUS is searchable by textual incipit (the opening few words of a chant text), keywords, saints' names or liturgical occasion, and "chant identification numbers" (drawn from standard chant research resources). CANTUS has many image links, taking the user directly from a chant text to a picture of a medieval source containing that chant. *Oxford Music Online* contains articles with bibliography on every topic covered in *Music in the Medieval West*. In addition this fundamental reference work contains descriptions of the most important medieval manuscripts, including sources for the study of chant, music theory, polyphonic repertories, and vernacular songs.

Although many sites are available for locating digitized manuscripts, printed reference books remain crucial for the study of medieval source materials. An important resource for scholarly purposes is the *Répertoire international des sources musicales* (International Inventory of Musical Sources, or *RISM*), an extensive catalogue of sources, including many medieval books containing the genres studied in *Music in the Medieval West*: tropes, sequences, music theory, polyphonic works, and music for processions.

Another print resource that you will encounter repeatedly in the study of medieval chant is the *Paléographie musicale* (Musical Paleography), a series of noted manuscripts in facsimile with introductions and other materials, including indexes. (Many of the volumes can be read online as well.) The series is published by the monks of the Benedictine Abbey of Solesmes in northern France (see §§I.3 and I.4 below), and includes basic sources from several traditions of Western chant, including various dialects of the Frankish (Gregorian), Milanese (Ambrosian), and Beneventan (southern Italian) traditions.

I.2. MANUSCRIPT DESIGNATIONS AND SIGLA

With so many libraries and other repositories possessing medieval manuscripts and manuscript fragments, librarians and scholars have developed ways of referring to sources and to pages within them. A recently developed system based on the *RISM* catalogue creates uniformity: each country has a unique code, and each city and library within that country has its own siglum (identifying letter or symbol). This information is linked to the library's shelf marks, the catalogue numbers associated with individual manuscripts. But most great libraries in the world have long used their own systems of manuscript designations; these are often easier to read than the *RISM* sigla and are commonly used in many fields of study, not just music (the only field in which the *RISM* designations are widely used).

Many medieval manuscripts are numbered not by pages but by folios (abbreviated ff., or fols.; singular, f., or fol.), that is, the front and back of a given page. To identify a source, then, you must in most cases use the folio number followed by *r* or *v*, to indicate whether you are referencing the front (recto) or back (verso) side of the folio.

Two manuscripts may serve to illustrate the differences between the two ways of referencing sources. The first is a twelfth-century Italian antiphoner (a book containing music for the Office) now in the French National Library in Paris, one of the sources catalogued in CANTUS. To indicate this source according to *RISM*, we would say: F-Pn n.a. lat. 1411. F-Pn is the siglum for France (F), Paris, Bibliothèque Nationale de France (Pn), Département des Manuscrits

(Department of Manuscripts); n.a. lat. stands for "nouvelle acquisition latine" (new Latin acquisition). Another way of referring to this same manuscript is Paris, BN n.a. lat. 1411, which is what would be found in many scholarly works of all fields. Once a source has been fully designated, it is common to refer to it thereafter by an abbreviated siglum, such as n.a. lat. 1411.

A manuscript that you will encounter in these pages is D-Mbs Clm 4660 (in the *RISM* designation). This book is in Germany (D, for Deutschland) in the Bayerische Staatsbibliothek in Munich (Mbs), where it is catalogued as Clm (Codices latini monacenses, or Latin Manuscripts) no. 4660. Most English-writing scholars refer to this manuscript as Munich, Bavarian State Library, Clm 4660. In informal discussions, however, it is called *Carmina burana*, a nickname with a history of its own (as discussed in Chapter 8).

In this book and the accompanying anthology, we refer to manuscripts by their more user-friendly designations, rather than by their *RISM* sigla. We also use the common nicknames for the famous sources we will be studying, as this is how scholars and performers who work with them know them.

I.3. THE *LIBER USUALIS*

The best known and most widespread of modern chant books is the *Liber Usualis* (Book for Common Use, abbreviated *LU*). It contains the chants for Masses of Sundays throughout the year and for major feast days of the temporal and sanctoral cycles in the Roman Catholic Church, following liturgy dating from before the reforms of the Second Vatican Council in the 1960s. It also includes Offices or hours of prayer for a handful of feasts. The first cycle (*temporale*) consists of feasts of the Lord, that is, feasts that commemorate events in the life, suffering, and resurrection of Jesus; the second cycle (*sanctorale*) comprises feast days for the saints.

The musical repertory in the *Liber Usualis* was restored from medieval manuscripts in the late nineteenth and early twentieth centuries by the monks of Solesmes mentioned above. It is worth going to your music library and spending time with the *Liber Usualis*, or downloading the book from the Internet.

Because many of the chants sung on modern recordings are taken from the *Liber Usualis*, we often do not hear the variety of dialects that were present in the medieval repertory. When you work with the *LU* and other modern chant collections, therefore, you should also consult Fr. Jerome Weber's Chantdiscography, an online resource of great value. He provides an index of recorded chant that is continually updated, and, when he is able to ascertain it, the source information as well.

The contents and pagination of editions of the *LU* differ slightly, but all are divided into the same ten sections:

1. Introduction to notation and to calendars
2. Chants for the Mass Ordinary (see §IV.2 below). In this section, the chants are organized by classification of feast, and by genre following the order in

which they are sung in the Mass. Kyries, for example, come first because they are the first of the Ordinary chants to be sung. The numbers are often used to designate the pieces, for example, Kyrie *Cunctipotens Genitor* is also known as Kyrie IV, its number in the *LU*.

3. Tones for the psalms (see §III.3) and other formulas for reciting texts, followed by plans for three hours of prayer: Lauds, Vespers, and Compline (see §IV.3)
4. The temporale cycle of feasts, running from Advent (the season before Christmas) to Sundays in "ordinary time." Chants found in this section are "proper" to the feasts (see §IV.2).
5. Feasts for commons of saints; for apostles, martyrs, and others; for church dedications; and for votive Masses. (Common chants are those used for particular categories of saints.)
6. The sanctoral cycle of feasts, beginning with saints whose feasts fall in Advent. (At the end of the *Liber Usualis* you will find an index of feasts, with all the saints represented in the book listed by name.)
7. The Mass and Office for the Dead, including the sequence *Dies irae* (Day of Wrath), dropped from the Roman rite in the reforms of the Second Vatican Council (1962–65)
8. Appendix, including the Te Deum and other miscellaneous chants
9. Indexes (very useful, for example, for finding incipits of psalms)
10. Later supplements, which vary according to region

I.4. THE *GRADUALE TRIPLEX*

The Solesmes editions were officially endorsed by the Catholic Church in 1903. Since the Second Vatican Council of the 1960s and its attendant liturgical reforms, a new series of chant books has come out, some of which are useful for the study of medieval repertory. An introduction to these books is found in Peter Jeffery, "The New Chantbooks from Solesmes," *Notes* 47 (1991): 1039–63. Among the most important of these newer collections is the *Graduale Triplex* (*GT*).

The *Graduale Triplex* juxtaposes older chant editions with hand-drawn reproductions of the medieval notation, following some of the most important early chant manuscripts. The three Mass Propers for Easter found in Anthology 3 are taken from this source. Example P1 shows two Easter chants expressed in the square notation associated with the Solesmes method of chant interpretation (see §II.1 below for an overview of chant notation). Above and below it the monks have provided the neumes of early medieval manuscripts for the sake of comparison. The following manuscripts, indicated by their common abbreviations (see §I.2 above), are as listed found in the preface to the *GT*, the first three being the sources most commonly used for the neumation supplied for the chants. The *PM* references are to facsimiles in the *Paléographie musicale* series:

L Laon 239, early 10th century; *PM*, vol. 10

C St. Gall 359, early 10th century; *PM*, series 2, vol. 2

E Einsiedeln 121, early 11th century; *PM*, vol. 4

G St. Gall 339, first half of the 11th century; *PM*, vol. 1

H St. Gall 390–91, late 10th century (Hartker Antiphoner); *PM*, series 2, vol. 1

B Bamberg 6, late 10th century

Working with your teacher, or by yourself (if you are feeling adventuresome), use the *GT* as a guide to locate chants in some of the earliest manuscripts in this list (the most commonly referenced of them are online). Every medieval chant in the *Graduale Triplex* is supplied with the following information: the sigla of the manuscripts from which the neumes have been taken, and the page and folio number of the chant in those manuscripts. Using these numbers to find particular folios within medieval manuscripts online, it is easy to compare early versions of the chants to those in modern books. There are many differences. For example, Offertory chants have verses in the early sources, a feature that had died out in most regions by the twelfth century. There are no Offertory verses in the *GT*, nor would there be in most medieval chant books from the early twelfth century forward. Also in early books, the temporal and sanctoral cycles are mixed rather than separated out, as in later medieval books and in the *Liber Usualis* and the *Graduale Triplex*.

We can use the *GT* to compare a chant featured in both Chapter 3 and Anthology 3 to medieval versions of the chant. Already in the ninth century, the Easter chant *Resurrexi* was categorized as an Introit in the fourth mode, which has its final on E, and a reciting tone of A (see §III.2 below). In the score as given on pages 196–97 of the *GT* (Ex. P1), most of the music necessary to sing this chant is written out. The introit (the opening chant of the Mass liturgy) for Easter Sunday includes several parts—first the Introit antiphon (an antiphon is a short chant, usually sung with a psalm or a psalm verse), then its psalm verse ("Domine probasti me," Psalm 139 [138]: 1–2). The performer must know that the verse should be followed by the intoned Doxology, or *Gloria Patri*, a short prayer text addressed to the members of the Trinity which always forms the last verse of an intoned psalm or canticle ("Glory be to the Father, and to the Son, and to the Holy Spirit; as it was in the beginning now and forever, Amen" [Gloria Patri et Filio et Spiritui Sancto; Sicut erat in principio, et nunc, et semper, et in saecula saeculorum. Amen), followed by a repeat of the antiphon. To sing the *Gloria Patri* here, the performer would fit the words to the same tone used for the psalm verse. The *GT* provides other useful information as well. For instance, it gives the psalm and the verses from which the chant text is taken. For each

Example P1: *The Introit* Resurrexi *and the Gradual* Haec dies, *from the* Graduale Triplex, *pp. 196–97*

I have arisen and am still with you, alleluia: you have put your hand on me, alleluia. Your knowledge has become wonderful, alleluia, alleluia. Lord, you have tested me and known me; you have known my sitting down and my rising up.

chant it shows which of six very early collections of chant texts contain the piece, and it provides notation from medieval manuscripts. In the case of *Resurrexi*, the neumes in black are as found in Laon 239, and below the line in red as found in Einsiedeln 121, with folio or page numbers for each manuscript provided in a small box along with the manuscript sigla.

Medieval musicians in the early Carolingian period would not have written down as much information as is found in the *Graduale Triplex*. It is instructive to find this same piece in St. Gall 359 from the early tenth century, and compare it to the example in the *GT*. The psalm is not written out in St. Gall 359. It can be surmised that the cantor was expected to have a *tonary*, a book listing the modes of chants (see Chapter 3), from which he could determine how to sing the psalm. As he knew the psalm tones (see §III.3 below) by heart, he would be able to fit the words to the appropriate memorized tone, and could generate new pieces from this information as well, if he wished. It can be seen by comparing the contours of the Introit antiphon that the same melody is found in all sources represented here. *Resurrexi* belongs to one of the oldest layers of the chant repertory and is fairly fixed in its text and pitches, compared to some of the repertory we will study from the tenth century and after.

II. MEDIEVAL NOTATION

II.1. NEUMES AND SQUARE NOTATION

The version of the hymn *Ave maris stella* studied here, from the *Liber Usualis*, is written in square notation (Ex. P2; see Chapter 1). This is a modern version of the notation that evolved in Europe in the twelfth and thirteenth centuries and came to be used in many regions, especially west of the Rhine. For anyone who reads modern musical notation, square notation is not difficult to transcribe or sing from. The staff has four lines and two clefs are used, C clef and F clef, indicating which line stands for C or F. Medieval musicians used both of these clefs, depending on the range of the chant they were notating, helping them make efficient use of the valuable parchment on which the music was copied. Even if the music moved up or down dramatically, they might keep the notes within the same area of parchment just by using a different clef.

The hymn is in mode 1, designated by the number written below the word "Hymn" (see §III.2 for a discussion of the church modes). In this version, the first thing you see on the staff is a C clef, followed by a succession of square neumes. The shapes of the neumes found in square notation developed out of earlier ways of writing music, more specifically out of French neumes. Very early neumes, which probably evolved out of signs used by grammarians, are directional, with the acute accent, or upward sign, slanting up to the right, and the *gravis* or grave

Example P2: *Square-note version of* Ave maris stella *from the* Liber Usualis

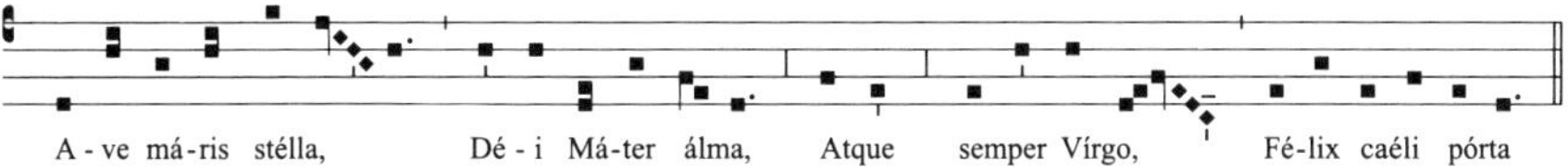

Hail, star of the sea, tender mother of God and ever virgin, happy door of heaven.

accent sign, which means "lower," slanting downward to the right. Hence the acute directionality came to be expressed by the *virga* ("rod"), representing a relatively higher note. The *punctum* (dot) and *tractulus* (dash) represented notes of the same or lower pitch. Many neumes of two, three, or more notes appear to be derived from combinations of these foundational note shapes: acute and *gravis* or *virga* and *punctum* or *tractulus*. These signs developed differently in each region; below, after the discussion of square notation, we will look at the notational style from the area around the Swiss monastery of St. Gall.

Example P2 is written in square notation. The first note is a *punctum*, a simple square representing a single note over the syllable *-la* in *stella*, the first note is a *virga*, which looks like a *punctum* with a downward stem. This represents the highest note in a grouping known as a *climacus* (from the Greek for "ladder"), since the *virga* is followed by three descending *puncta*, shown as lozenge-shaped notes. Neume shapes that are created by combining two or more signs are known as ligatures (from the Latin verb *ligare*, to unite). Ligatures or ligated neumes were necessary when a vowel was sung to more than one note. Hence a melodic style in which many of the syllables are set to ligatures of two or more notes is called "neumatic." When the average syllable is set to a single note, the style is called "syllabic." When some syllables are sung to a great many notes, the style is called "melismatic."

The two most important ligatures consist of two notes each. The *pes* or *podatus* (from Latin and Greek words for "foot") can be seen on the syllables *-ve*, *-ris*, and *Ma-*. The lower note is sung first, then the higher one. It was originally formed by a *gravis* joined to an acute, meaning "lower, then higher," and looking like the shape of a foot. In *Liber Usualis* notation it looks like a *punctum* with a *virga* connected to it above. The *clivis* (possibly from a Latin word for "hill" or "incline") is the opposite of the *pes*, a higher note followed by a lower note. It was originally formed from an acute joined to a *gravis*, forming a hill-like shape. An example can be seen on the syllable *al-* in the second phrase. A somewhat jazzier note is the *quilisma* (from a Greek word for "rolling"). It originally resembled a sign used in medieval Latin to represent a question mark. The *quilisma*, a special type of *pes*, originally represented a quivering or trembling sound, which usually ascended a half step to the note following. In modern recordings following the Solesmes method, however, it is usually sung merely as a short, light note, with some lengthening of the note before. The first example in *Ave maris stella* is the second, jagged note over the syllable *-go* of *Virgo*.

You can now transcribe *Ave maris stella* from the *Liber Usualis* or sing it directly from the score. Other versions of this same melody abound in the medieval sources. (See Example 1.3 in Chapter 1 for a version of the chant as sung at the Cathedral of Notre Dame in Paris.)

Other commonly used neumes in square notation appear in the score of the Easter Introit *Resurrexi* (see Ex. P1, and Anthology 3). In addition to the two-note *pes* and the *clivis*, it includes several three-note neumes. The *torculus* (on the syllable "-sur-" of "resurrexi") looks like a *punctum*, a *virga*, and a *punctum*; the *porrectus* looks like a *virga*, a *punctum*, and a *virga*. (The word "sum" is set to a melisma consisting of a *pes* and a *porrectus*.) A three-note neume that occurs often, for example on the first syllable of *isti* and the second syllable of *super*, looks like an ornamented form of the *scandicus* (see Table P1). But in the St. Gall neumes it is actually a *tractulus* followed by a *quilisma-pes*. The *climacus* is sometimes joined

Table P1: *Square neumes and equivalents in modern notation and in St. Gall neumes and French neumes*

NAMES OF SYMBOLS	BASIC ST. GALL NEUMES	SQUARE NOTATION	MODERN NOTATION
1. ***virga***	a/		
2. ***tractulus***	-		
3. ***punctum***	•		
4. ***gravis***	\		
5. ***clivis***	/\		
6. ***pes***	✓		
7. ***porrectus***	N		
8. ***torculus***	S		
9. ***climacus***	/:		
10. ***scandicus***	.:/		

with other neumes to make a smooth grouping, for example on "-cta" of "facta," where the *climacus* begins with a *pes* instead of a *virga*.

Like *Ave maris stella*, most well-known pieces of medieval music have come down to us in varied forms. As a result of this, and of the nature of the notation and the loss of direct contact with medieval practice, many decisions must be made by the performer, even with the simplest of pieces. Medieval square notation as used for most chant repertories tells us little about the rhythm, for example. (Not until the development of the rhythmic modes in the thirteenth century, as described in §II.3 below, did it become possible to notate the relative durations of notes.) The performance practice most widely used in the twentieth century, developed by the monks of Solesmes in France (see §I.4 above), assigns approximately equal value to every note. The classic "equalist" or "Solesmes style" of singing chant also groups the notes into units of two and three pulses. It has no basis in medieval practice, but it does achieve the softly undulating line that can be heard on numerous recordings. An accessible introduction to this approach is *A Gregorian Chant Master Class* by Theodore Marier, a handbook and CD featuring the singing of the nuns of the Abbey of Regina Laudis in Bethlehem, Connecticut. The film *Work and Pray: Living the Psalms with the Nuns of Regina Laudis* offers many examples of singing in the Solesmes style.[1] The *Liber Usualis* also contains a useful introductory section titled "Rules for Interpretation."

Today, singers experiment with alternative approaches to rhythm and expression. Although the ways of interpretation are many, in general performers try to use the ligatures of the notation to group the notes, and pay close attention to the accentuation and other features of the texts as well. The singing of Richard Crocker, featured in the recordings for Anthology 3, is based on his interpretation of medieval neumes. It is especially interesting to follow his recordings along with the *Graduale Triplex*.

II.2. ST. GALL NOTATION

The early-tenth-century manuscript St. Gall 359 is a cantatorium, a book containing the chants for soloists at the Mass liturgy. The notation in this source demonstrates how neume shapes appeared at the Abbey of St. Gall in modern-day Switzerland, a major center for the production of musical manuscripts in the Middle Ages. The Easter Gradual *Haec dies*, as presented in the *GT*, is written in square notation. But above the staff are neumes from the tenth-century MS Laon 239, from northeast France; below the staff of square notation are St. Gall neumes, as found in St. Gall 359, which will be discussed here. (A portion of

[1] *Work and Pray: Living the Psalms with the Nuns of Regina Laudis*, written and produced by Margot Fassler (New Haven: Yale Institute of Sacred Music, 2004), distributed by W. W. Norton & Company.

Haec dies is shown in the original notation from St. Gall 359 in Fig. 3.2 of this volume; or you can find the digitized manuscript online and enlarge the neumes for close study.) As can be seen by examining the neumes from St. Gall 359, the notation functioned only for singers who already knew the chant by heart, as the neumes are not "on the line"—that is, they are not precisely heightened so that specific intervals and pitches can be read from them. The early-tenth-century cantor-scribe who prepared St. Gall 359 doubtless sang softly as he wrote, or at least heard songs he knew well in his mind.

The very first neume in *Haec dies* is a *clivis*. As can be seen in Table P1, a *clivis* represents two notes, moving downward. To make a *clivis*, the scribe drew an upward-slanting *virga* and then went down to make a *gravis*; this created a hairpin shape that says "higher to lower." The opposite kind of neume, the *pes*, reverses the procedure: *gravis* then *virga* for "lower to higher." A *pes* appears above the word "quam" in the chant *Haec Dies* (see Example P1). The scribe began by drawing a short, downward-moving *gravis*, then hooked around and slanted upward to the right in a *virga*: the result is two notes, the second of which moves upward from left to right and is therefore higher in pitch.

Three major three-note neumes are used in *Haec dies*, as found in the *GT*. The *climacus* ("ladder") indicates three notes progressing downward in pitch; this shape occurs right after the *clivis* of "Haec," the first word in the chant. As you can see by following along in the St. Gall notation below the staff of Example P1, or in Figure 3.2, to draw this neume, the scribe made a *virga* (the higher note) followed by two lozenge-shaped *puncta* (lower notes). On the "di-" of "dies" we have another *climacus*, followed by a *porrectus*, which is made of a *virga*, a *gravis*, and a *virga*, so it represents a higher note followed by a lower note, followed by a higher note. On the "-cit" of "fecit" one can see a *torculus* ("twisted") after the two comma-like notes (clearly visible in Fig. 3.2). How did the scribe make this neume? He began with a *pes* (lower to higher), and then descended again with a *gravis*, keeping his pen on the parchment throughout. The result is a group of three notes, the second of which is higher than both the first and the last.

Notice the little "t" above the initial *clivis* of *Haec dies* in the St. Gall notation; it indicates the Latin word for "sustain." Above the next group of notes is a small "c" with a very long tail; this means "quickly," and the scribe lengthens the tail to show that all five notes—those of the *climacus* and the next *clivis*—should be speeded up. He can also use a nearly horizontal bar called an *episema* to express holding a note longer in order to emphasize it. One of these can be seen at the end of the *virga* on the "-es" of "dies," another above the last *clivis* of "exsultemus," just before "et laetemur." The ability to indicate that some notes should be held longer provided a way to mark musical phrase endings, but also a way to emphasize certain words while proclaiming the text, as in the word "bonus" in *Haec dies*. Clearly, at St. Gall in the early tenth century, chant was not sung with every note having the same duration. But what the precise rhythmic values were, neither this scribe nor any other tells us. In manuscripts from other regions of

Europe, away from St. Gall, the opening few notes of *Haec dies* suggest several possible performance practices. There was no one way.

In order to transcribe *Haec dies*, you will need a version that is written in heightened (diastemic) neumes, as in the square notation found in the *GT*. In general, heightening did not happen in western Europe until the early eleventh century, although there were earlier attempts to use letter notation to express pitches and intervals (as in the pair of ninth-century theoretical treatises studied in Chapter 3). When the diastematic neumes of a chant are compared with the earlier neumes that are not heightened (adiastematic), we can usually tell that the melodic contour is the same. Like the square-notated version of *Haec dies* in the *GT*, later versions are guides for deciphering the earlier ones, and we are able to transcribe the earlier notated works because of the fixity of the repertory and the survival of later copies in heightened neumes. With *Haec dies*, comparison of the square notation in the *Liber Usualis* to the unheightened neumes found in St. Gall 359 proves that this is the same melody. Only the heightening in later manuscripts allows transcription from the earlier notation. Thus the repertory of Old Spanish chant, which survives in unheightened neumes alone, has been lost because it was never recorded in a later, precisely heightened version. For further study of the many dialects of chant notation, students are referred to the excellent collection of plates from medieval sources, with discussions and some transcriptions, in David Hiley, *Western Plainchant: A Handbook*.[2]

II.3. THE RHYTHMIC MODES

The rhythmic modes are patterns of long and short notes first embodied in the ligatures of square notation. The modes are expressed in feet, each of which has three beats. Melodies written in the modes fall into phrases called *ordines* (singular, *ordo*) that characteristically (when "perfect") begin and end with the same note value (Table P2). Thirteenth-century theorists classified the ordines by the number of complete statements or feet of a modal pattern they contained (not counting the rest). So, for example, the third ordo of mode 1 contains three complete long-short feet, as can be seen in Table P2. At first, the rhythmic modes appear to have been understood in the same patterns that underlie accentual Latin verse, but use long and short notes to create the patterns, as can be seen in Table P2. The patterns found in the ligatures of the first layers of Notre Dame polyphony from the early thirteenth century (see Chapter 9) have nothing to do with note shapes.

The ordines and their rhythmic interpretations as found in ligature patterns drive the aesthetic of early modal repertory. In the beginning, the characteristic foot of modal notation was a two-beat long followed by a single-beat breve. The idea of a ternary long being "perfect" came later in the thirteenth

---

[2] *Western Plainchant: A Handbook*, David Hiley (Oxford: Oxford University Press, 1993); see pp. 405–41.

Table P2: *The Modal Patterns, with Characteristic Ordines*

MODE	METRICAL PATTERN	PERFECT ORDO	PATTERN OF LIGATURES	MODERN EQUIVALENT
1	Trochaic: long-short	Third		
2	Iambic: short-long	Third	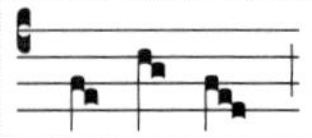	
3	Dactylic: long-short-short	Second		
4	Anapestic: short-short-long	Second	 or	
5	Spondaic: long-long	First	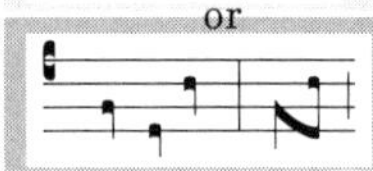	
6	Tribrachic: short-short-short	Third		

century, and would be a crucial concept for the development of mensural notation. The notation of the thirteenth century, and its movement from modal to mensural, added a crucial element to western notation: the ability to express rhythm precisely.

In the middle of the thirteenth century, notators began to think of expressing the modes and the values of which they are composed in terms of notes with particular shapes, long (*longa*) and breve (*brevis*), corresponding to the *virga* and *punctum* of square notation and particular ligature shapes as well. This innovation was born of necessity when texts were added to melismatic passage of music originally expressed exclusively in ligatures. As the ability of note shapes to stand for longs, breves, and even shorter notes increased, mensural notation was born (see §II.4 below).

II.4. MENSURAL NOTATION

Early mensural notation is also called Franconian notation. The name Franconian comes from the German theorist Franco of Cologne, who worked in Paris in the third quarter of the thirteenth century, and was one of several who categorized and explained mensural notation. As will be seen in our transcription exercise below, the rhythmic modes are also fundamental to mensural notation in this period. As the notation developed in the fourteenth and fifteenth centuries, however, the rhythmic modes no longer mattered.

Franco tried to embody the rhythmic modes through use of individual longs and breves as well as by particular ligature patterns. Rests also become codified in the system, depending on how many lines of the staff they cover. By the end of the thirteenth century, Franco's innovations had developed even further, so that longs, breves, and semibreves all had particular shapes. The following rules apply to the transcription of the note shapes, especially as regards a group of breves between two longs. In the third quarter of the thirteenth century, the idea of perfection became very important: feet were seen as perfections, and a perfect long as a three-beat note. Each of these beats is called a *tempus*; and a perfect long has three *tempora* (plural of *tempus*). Rules for transcribing Franconian notation include the following:

1. A long is perfect (three beats) if followed by another long, or by two or three breves.
2. If a long is followed by one or by more than three breves, then it is made imperfect (worth two counts) by the first breve.
3. If there are several breves between two longs, they must be placed in groups of three. If there are two left over, then the second of these is altered, to be worth two counts.
4. If one breve remains, it will make the following long imperfect.

Perhaps the most famous motet in the so-called Montpellier Codex (Montpellier HS 196) is the much-performed and recorded *Alle psallite cum luia* (Ex. P3). The piece is actually a polyphonic Alleluia with an added text (a trope). It probably originated in England, where the composition of Ars Antiqua liturgical polyphony continued unabated in the second half of the thirteenth century (see Chapter 11). With its abundant repetition and imitation, *Alle psallite* is a good piece to practice transcribing from mensural into modern notation, since if you get a bit of it right, you can transcribe the entire piece.

To be able to render late-thirteenth-century mensural notation in modern form, remember that everything is calculated in feet, or groups of three *tempora*, each of which constitutes a perfection. The shapes of the noteheads (longs and breves) matter, but so too do whether or not they have stems, and the sides on which the stems are placed. Semibreves are indicated by an upward stem on the left of a square note, and relate to breves in the same ways that breves relate to longs. To transcribe *Alle psallite,* start with the tenor. Set up your page in $\frac{6}{8}$ time, so a perfect long is worth the value of a dotted quarter note and a breve has the value of an eighth note (unless the principle of alteration applies). The piece on the manuscript page is expressed in motet notation, with the triplum voice on the left, the duplum (or motetus) on the right, and the tenor across the bottom of the page. You will need a score of three staves. Although the manuscript uses both C clef (for the upper voices) and F clef (for the tenor), you can transcribe the music using a G clef, if you like. the first note of the tenor is a D. It is a perfect long, followed by a Franconian ligature shape indicating long-breve-long, hence the first long of the ligature is imperfected by the breve and the second long is perfect. Next come two longs on E and D, both of which

Example P3:

(a) Alle psallite *in mensural notation from the Montpellier Codex*

corde uoto deo toto psal
alleluya
lite cu lira alleluya
Balam inquit uatici
nans iam de iacob
Balam inquit uatici

(b) *Transcription by Yvonne Rokseth*

are perfect and thus worth the value of a dotted quarter note. Then a line slashes through three lines of the staff; this is a rest, and because it covers three lines, it is perfect—that is, a dotted-quarter rest. This pattern repeats throughout most of the tenor, forming a kind of foundational foot (*pes*) for the entire work, with the two more-rhythmically lively voices unfolding above in imitation.

Now you basically know all that is necessary to transcribe the tenor of *Alle psallite*. (Use Yvonne Rokseth's transcription of the piece in Example P3 as a guide.) As the two upper voices are imitative, if you get one right, you have the piece nailed. The first line gives you everything you need to do the entire piece. Since the upper voices are written with C clefs, the first note of the triplum is D, an octave above the tenor. Having transcribed the tenor, you should be able to do this line in the following feet: perfect long; perfect long; imperfect long and a breve; imperfect long and a breve; perfect long; two semibreves and an altered breve; perfect long; and perfect rest. What follows should come fairly easily, and again you have Rokseth as your guide.

III. MEDIEVAL MUSIC THEORY AND PRACTICE

III.1. THE GREATER PERFECT SYSTEM

In *De institutione musica* (Fundamentals of Music), Severinus Boethius (c. 480–c. 524) explains the Greater Perfect System with the lowest pitch at the top and using a set of four tetrachords to make up a two-octave scale, or gamut. As shown in Example P4, the Greater Perfect System illustrates some of the common theoretical terms. Beginning with B above A (at the top of Ex. P4), each tetrachord has four pitches, and the relationship of pitches within each tetrachord is always semitone-tone-tone (STT). The first two tetrachords in the system are conjunct, that is, they share a pitch (E). (The transcription of Boethius's system of tetrachords given here is conventional: in early medieval music, pitch is a relative concept and is not associated with absolute frequencies.) The next tetrachord is disjunct, beginning with B an octave higher. The final tetrachord is once again conjunct, E being shared. Each tetrachord has a Greek name describing its position relative to the others.

The journey from Boethius's exposition of the Greater Perfect System, to the modes used by music theorists in the ninth century (see §III.2 below), to later understandings of pitch and scales is long and complex. However, the concepts of tetrachord, tone, semitone, disjunct, and conjunct are fundamental to understanding medieval music. According to Pythagorean number theory, the whole tone has a specific ratio (9:8), but the semitone does not. To this day, tonal systems and understandings are governed by how one measures the semitone. In Boethius's system, it comes out to 256:243—not a ratio easy to calculate on a monochord (see

Example P4: *Boethius's view of the Greater Perfect System (adapted from Charles M. Atkinson,* The Critical Nexus: Tone-System, Mode, and Notation in Early Medieval Music *[New York: Oxford, 2009], 12)*

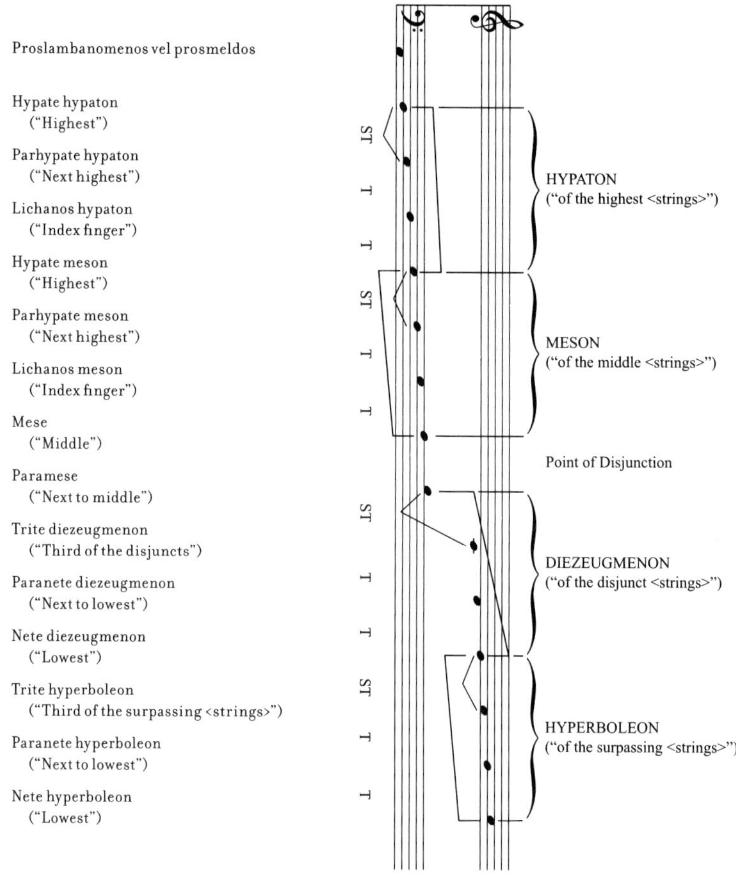

Chapter 2). Diatonic scales are made up of a combination of whole steps (each one tone) and half steps (each one semitone), but the precise measurement of the steps (tones) and half steps (semitones), as well as the relationships between the steps of particular scales, depend on theories of tuning.

Boethius defined another important concept, *species*, as an arrangement of tones and semitones having "a unique form according to one genus" of tetrachord (either diatonic, chromatic, or enharmonic), based on the arrangement and size of steps. This concept, which was part of Greek music theory (see Chapter 2), allows for steps larger than a whole tone and smaller than a semitone. However, the four tetrachords in Boethius's Greater Perfect System are of the same diatonic species, STT, as can be seen in Example P4. This is a diatonic system.

III.2. THE CHURCH MODES

The medieval modes, often known as the church modes today, are a system of scales whose character, like that of the tetrachords in the Greater Perfect System, is determined by a unique relationship between tones and semitones. As can be seen in Example P5, the eight modes are arranged in pairs (and later in the Middle Ages, these came to be called *maneriae*; singular, *maneria*); the higher and lower modes of each pair are called authentic and plagal, respectively. Every mode has a principal note, or final. The pairs of the scales are usually numbered as follows: protus (modes 1 and 2; final of D); deuterus (modes 3 and 4; final of E); tritus (modes 5 and 6; final of F); and tetrardus (modes 7 and 8; final of G). Each mode has a commonly used pseudo-Greek name: Dorian and Hypodorian (modes 1 and 2), Phrygian and Hypophrygian (modes 3 and 4), Lydian and Hypolydian (modes 5 and 6), and Mixolydian and Hypomixolydian (modes 7 and 8).

In addition to the final, each mode has a characteristic octave pitch range, which may be exceeded by one or two notes, and a reciting tone, to be used in intoned psalmody of various types in both the Mass and the Office (see §IV.2 and §IV.3 below), and in both antiphonal and responsorial psalmody. Note that the scales break at the fifth and fourth above and below the finals, putting great emphasis on the "perfect" intervals of octaves, fifths, and fourths. Medieval music theory is a reflection of the sonic ideas of the age, as is the music itself.

As shown in Example P5, the reciting tones of authentic modes generally lie a fifth above the final, and those of plagal modes are a third below the reciting tone of the corresponding authentic mode. However, exceptions are made to deal with the pitch B, which forms a tritone with F and so was deemed unsuitable as a reciting tone. This is particularly true of deuterus scales, where the expected reciting tone is B, the fifth above E. Instead, it has been moved up to

Example P5: *The modes and maneriae*

MANERIA	CATEGORY	RANGE AND RECITING TONE		MODE/GREEK NAME
Protus final of d	Authentic	D to d	a	1 (Dorian)
Protus final of d	Plagal	A to a	f	2 (Hypodorian)
Deuterus, final of e	Authentic	E to e	c	3 (Phrygian)
Deuterus, final of e	Plagal	B to b	a	4 (Hypophrygian)
Tritus, final of f	Authentic	F to f	c	5 (Lydian)
Tritus, final of f	Plagal	C to c	a	6 (Hypolydian)
Tetrardus, final of g	Authentic	G to g	d	7 (Mixolydian)
Tetrardus, final of g	Plagal	D to d	c	8 (Hypomixolydian)

C and the reciting tone of the corresponding plagal scale has been moved to A, the third below. Tetrardus scales present a problem as well. The reciting tone for the authentic scale of the pair is D, the fifth above G, but the third below D is B. Hence the reciting tone of the plagal scale with a final of G has been moved to C.

III.3. THE PSALM TONES

Each of the eight modes is associated with a psalm tone, a formula for singing psalms in the Office and antiphonal chants of the Mass, although the Introit tones are slightly more elaborate. Each of the psalm tones used for the Office is based on its reciting pitch (or *tenor*), the note that is used for proclaiming most of each verse of the text. However, just as a sentence requires punctuation, so do the recitation of psalm verses to their tones. Accordingly, there are formulas for openings (intonation), midpoints (mediant), inflections of the tenor to cover especially long texts (*flex*), and endings (termination) of each verse, and these are slightly different for each of the tones (Ex. P6).

Example P6: *The psalm tones*

In medieval monasteries and cathedrals, there were two basic ways of singing psalms, antiphonally and responsorially. Two sets of tones were used for both ways of singing in the Office, and these constitute the workhorses of medieval music: one set is for the antiphons, another for the verses of great responsories (to distinguish them from the short responsories also sung in the Office). Only the tones for the antiphonal psalms of the Office are discussed here (see §IV.3 for discussion of the great responsories).

The tones for antiphonal Office psalmody are slightly simpler than those used for Mass Introits and Office canticles, and each tone offers singers a way of inflecting the verses of the text—a kind of musical punctuation. Example P7, which shows verses from medieval poems adapted by Peter Jeffery, offers an easy way to memorize the eight psalm tones, their reciting pitches, and their formulaic

Example P7: *Verses from medieval poems adapted to the psalm tones by Peter Jeffery*

inflections. The first tone, for example, is memorized using a verse from Matthew 6 that has the word "first" in it. Present in this little exercise is the opening intonation formula (on "first seek"), the reciting pitch (A), the mediant (on "kingdom of God"), and the termination formula (on "added unto you"). The ninth psalm tone is the *peregrinus* or wandering tone, which was used for Psalm 114 (113), the first two verses of which are illustrated here. It can be seen that the reciting pitch wanders: it is A in the first half of the verse and G in the second half. The two verses remind us that in Office psalmody the opening intonation is only used for the first verse of the psalm.

In both medieval manuscripts and modern books, you will see the letters EUOUAE, with pitches above them, following the psalm intonation. These are the vowels of the final words of the Doxology ("s*e*-c*u*-l*o*-r*u*m *a*-m*e*n"). They provide the termination formula, or *differentia*, used to end each verse and to connect the tone to its antiphon at the end of the psalm. This is the same kind of information provided in the psalm tone poems of Example P7, but those give just one end formula for each tone, whereas for most tones there are several possibilities, and the EUOUAE designation tells the singer which one to use. The tones are varied just enough to keep the singer alert, and are related to the accents of the Latin as well as to counting back from the final accents. You can see how this intonation process works in Anthology 4, which pairs the Office psalm *Laudate Dominum* with the mode 7 antiphon *Ecce apparebit Dominus.* The nuns of the Abbey of Regina Laudis sing this entire psalm with *Ecce apparebit* in the film *Work and Pray*, demonstrating the alternation between the two sides of the choir, verse by verse, that is a crucial features of the performance practice (see §II.1 above).

III.4. A LESSON WITH HUCBALD

According to Boethius's description (see §III.1 above), the Greater Perfect System was built out of tetrachords. Medieval theorists took the tetrachord as the basic building block of a system of their own, loosely modeled upon the Greater Perfect System, but they related that tetrachord to the modes. The theorist, poet, and composer Hucbald of St. Amand (c. 850–930) attempted to give authority to the pairs of scales found in the church modes by using their finals (D, E, F, and G) as the basis of a system also mentioned in the *Enchiriadis* treatises (see Chapter 3). He gave each pitch what he thought was its Greek name. Thus, in Hucbald's account the new system seemed to be constructed out of the elemental pitches of the scales used for Gregorian chant, as found in the four pairings (he uses the word "tones").

> Passing over the first three notes [of the Greater Perfect System, A, B, and C] , the next four, namely the lichanos hypaton [D], the hypate meson [E], the parhypate meson [F], and the lichanos meson [G], are

> used in constructing the four modes or tropes. These nowadays are called "tones" and are the protus, deuterus, tritus, and tetrardus. This is done in such a way that each of these four notes reigns over a pair of tropes subject to it, namely a principal one, which is called the "authentic," and a collateral one, which is called the "plagal."[3]

Imagine yourself in the classroom of a Carolingian music teacher. He has just explained that the relationship between Hucbald's four "reigning" notes is TST, as opposed to the STT arrangement of pitches in Boethius's tetrachords. Hucbald believed that the Greek system began on A. If you build upward from A, making tetrachords using the pitch relationships TST, you can construct the system that Hucbald describes, provided you understand the difference between conjunct and disjunct tetrachords. Conjunct tetrachords share a note; that is, the last note of one group of four pitches and the beginning note of the next-higher tetrachord are the same. Disjunct tetrachords do not share notes.

Now we can see how Hucbald uses the "tetrachord of the finals" to construct a two-octave scale, or gamut. He believed his system was consonant with Greek theory as inherited from Boethius, but was also made from the most basic building blocks of Gregorian chant. In Example P8, you can see Hucbald's tetrachords, identify which are conjunct and disjunct, and locate the whole-step and half-step patterns. Hucbald's system enables us to begin to understand how early medieval musicians thought about the church modes, the pairs of scales that are fundamental to understanding medieval music theory (see §III.2 above).

Example P8: *Hucbald's tetrachord of the finals (from Fiona McAlpine,* Tonal Consciousness and the Medieval West *[New York: Peter Lang, 2008], 46)*

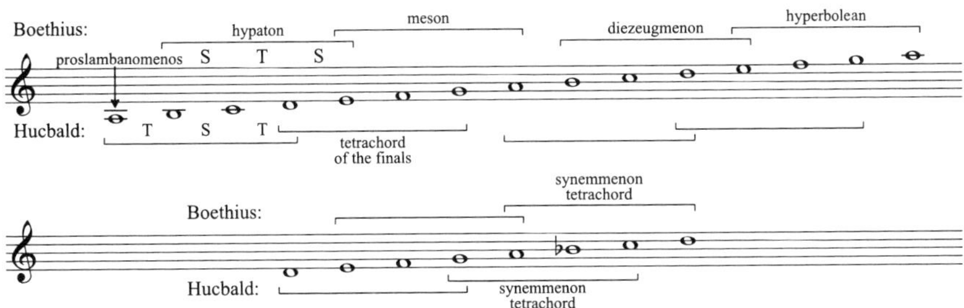

[3] *Melodic Instruction (De harmonica institutione)*, Hucbald of St. Amand, in *Hucbald, Guido, and John on Music: Three Medieval Treatises*, ed. Claude V. Palisca, trans. Warren Babb (New Haven: Yale University Press, 1978), 13–46, at 38.

IV. THE LITURGY OF THE ROMAN CATHOLIC CHURCH

IV.1. THE CAROLINGIAN (FRANKISH) MASS

The medieval high Mass, the kind celebrated on Sundays and major feasts, was a major musical production that unfolded in every church, cathedral, and monastery. It required architectural spaces, furnishings, books (increasingly), vestments, candles, and above all people to sing, for every part of it was proclaimed in song, including the intonations of the texts. Table P3 depicts the Mass as celebrated in Carolingian times, from the ninth century forward, with additions representing later developments. In the right-hand column, a brief statement concerning the allegorical meanings of liturgical action is given, following the early-ninth-century commentator Amalar of Metz, who was the most copied and influential commentator on the liturgy and its meanings from the entire Middle Ages. (Musical additions were usually not extant for the entire lives of each chant genre; for example, introits were troped in many regions in the ninth through eleventh centuries, but after this time most introit tropes died out.)

The Mass has two major sections, the Liturgy of the Word and the Liturgy of the Faithful. The chants sung in these two parts are listed in the leftmost column, with the kinds of musical additions or commentaries traditionally added to them in italics.

There were also two kinds of antiphons, both highly ornate, sung at Mass in some churches: processional antiphons and antiphons before the Gospel (not listed in Table P3). These antiphons are not sung with a psalm, and are free-standing pieces meant to accompany some sort of action.

IV.2. THE MASS PROPER AND ORDINARY

Liturgical chants fall into two major categories, Proper and Ordinary. Proper chants are those whose texts change in accordance with particular feasts and seasons; they constitute the oldest layer of chant in the Frankish repertory. Proper chants are primarily sung with psalmodic texts, but they proclaim the texts in three different ways: antiphonally (Introits and Communions), responsorially (Graduals, Alleluias, and Offertories) and *in directum* (verse by verse, as in the Tracts). Several of these genres of chant has a way of being *troped*, or supplemented by additional texts to comment on their meanings, (the Graduals and Tracts are not troped). Each genre of Proper chant whas its own way of employing the modes, and many have particular formulas that are characteristic of the genre. The Alleluias constitute the youngest layer of Proper chants, and the sequences that developed out of them are even later. In the sequences, which were composed from the ninth through the fifteenth centuries and even later, we find the only chant genre that can be seen to change over time, as musical taste and

Table P3: *The Mass of the Roman Rite, as Understood in the Ninth and Tenth Centuries*

Sung Parts of the Mass in Francia, c. 850 and Select Commentary on Chants and Readings by Amalar of Metz

PROPER CHANTS (TYPE OF PSALMODY) *NATURE OF COMMENTARY*	ORDINARY CHANTS *NATURE OF COMMENTARY*	PRIEST'S PRAYERS	READINGS	AMALAR'S COMMENTS SUMMARIZED (FROM HIS COLLECTED WRITINGS)
		LITURGY OF THE WORD		
Introit (antiphonal) *interlinear tropes*				Prophetic voice announcing the coming of Christ
		Collect		
	Kyrie (*primarily prosulae*)			Like Isaiah 33:2 "Lord, have mercy on us who wait for you"
	Gloria (*primarily interlinear*)			The priest intones the chant, and suddenly a multitude of angels replies (Luke 2:13)
			Epistle	Compares to voice of John the Baptist: a forerunner to the Gospel
Gradual (responsorial) *only rarely troped*				The choir of apostles responds to Christ
Alleluia (responsorial) *primarily prosulae*				The angel of great council Isaiah 9:6; a "new song" to the Lord
Sequence (developing in the ninth century)				
Tract (in directum); substitute for Alleluia in solemn times *no tropes*				May be penitential (Moses in Exodus 19:32) or joyful (Daniel in Daniel 6)
			Gospel	Christ address the people
		Credo *not troped*		After Scripture, a confession of faith

LITURGY OF THE FAITHFUL				
Offertory (responsorial) *Some introductory Prosulae for some melismas*				The bread and wine to be offered are like the clothing and vestments offered by people in Jerusalem, and the chant is like their song
		Preface		
	Sanctus *interlinear tropes*	Canon (spoken by the celebrating priest)		Sanctus from Revelation; Benedictus means that Christ will come to judge the living and the dead
		Pater Noster		
		Peace		
	Agnus Dei *interlinear tropes*			A chant for the people about to take the body of the Lord
Communion (antiphonal) *interlinear tropes*				A reciprocal voice, responding as in Luke 24:30–35: the disciples return from Emmaus and recall seeing the Lord as they broke bread
		Post Communion		
	Ite missa est *some tropes; some prosulae*			When this is sung by the deacon, the people's minds turn to that fatherland where the Lord has gone, and long for it

styles changed. Yet some of the oldest and best-established sequences remained in the repertories of some regions for centuries, and even after the reforms of the sixteenth-century Council of Trent.[4]

Ordinary chants are chants whose basic texts do not change throughout the year, although they may be commented upon with various kinds of tropes. Ordinary chants do, however, have different melodies, and these are often seasonal, or became so in the later Middle Ages. Some portions of the Ordinary

[4] *Music in the Renaissance*, Richard Freedman (New York: Norton, 2012).

have fairly large repertories of melodies, and others, especially the Credo, very few. But whatever the case, the Ordinary chants are a younger repertory in general than the Proper chants. The style of music they use is, for the most part, later than that employed in some genres of Proper chants. They tend to have been born after the modes were well established, and so use the full range of modal theoretical understanding. Moreover, they are more likely to be regional in their melodic uses and in the ways they are commented upon.

IV.3. THE DIVINE OFFICE

In *Music in the Medieval West,* we explore several ways in which the nature of the Mass chants suited the action of the medieval liturgy, with chants designed both to explain Scripture and to express the meanings of the eating of a ritual meal at the altar. The medieval Office was very different in character from the Mass. There were far fewer types of music in general, the main ones being antiphons for the singing of psalms and canticles, and responsories, elaborate chants sung at the close of an intoned reading. Responsories consist of a respond, sung by the choir (and made up of a psalm verse, part of which also acts as a refrain), and a verse, sung by a soloist. In manuscripts, these two parts are labeled R and V. Sometimes they are also performed with half of the Doxology, depending upon their position within the Office liturgy. The Office was also used as a narrative vehicle, and many parts of the Office for major feasts are arranged to express the story of an action in the life of Christ or of one of the saints (or a group of saints). Many Office responsories were versified, employing various poetic strategies. In the earlier Middle Ages the poetry was accentual, but not usually rhyming. In the later Middle Ages, new Offices might also be made up of rhyming stanzas of various types. Rhymed Office chants were written by the thousands—so abundant are they that many have never been studied or even catalogued.

The eight hours of prayer, which collectively constituted the Divine Office, were a central part of the daily liturgy in both monastic churches (overseen by an abbot or abbess) and secular churches (regulated by a bishop and his entourage of administrators). Devoted to prayer and the singing of psalms, the hours were celebrated at specific times of the day as follows: Matins (early morning), Lauds (sunrise), Prime (6 a.m.), Terce (9 a.m.), Sext (noon), None (3 p.m.), Vespers (sunset), and Compline (9 p.m.).

The outline that follows depicts the Office as sung for Sundays and major feast days in cathedrals. Although the basic structure of the Office, like that of the Mass (see §IV.2 above), was fixed, certain elements of the singing and intoned readings varied in accordance with the rhythms and themes of the church calendar. So the definitions of Proper and Ordinary discussed in relation to the Mass liturgy and its music relates to the Office as well, although in somewhat different ways. The ferial Office consisted of those psalms and antiphons sung during days when no major feast was being celebrated; you can find the ferial psalms for Lauds, Vespers, Compline, and the so-called Little Hours (Prime, Terce, Sext, and None), as well as for Sunday and all the other days of the week, in the *Liber Usualis* (see §I.3).

First Vespers (identical in structure to Second Vespers, but with different chants and psalms, as appropriate to the feast)

Matins

OPENING

1. Versicles: *Domine, labia mea aperies,* with response Psalm 51 (50):17, *Et os meum annuntiabit laudem tuam* (Lord, open my lips, and my mouth will declare your praise); and *Deus in adiutorium meum intende* (God, come to my assistance), with response *Domine ad adiuvandum me festina* (Lord, make haste to help me)
2. Invitatory psalm: Psalm 95 (94), *Venite exultemus Domino* (Come, let us praise the Lord), sung to a tone
3. A hymn

THREE NOCTURNS

1. Three psalms with antiphons and three lessons from Scripture, each prefaced by a blessing and followed by a great responsory. The third responsory, at least, was sung with half of the *Gloria Patri*.
2. Three psalms with antiphons and three lessons from the lives of church fathers or saints, each prefaced by a blessing and followed by a great responsory. The third responsory, at least, was sung with the first half of the *Gloria Patri.*
3. Three psalms with antiphons and three lessons from a church father or pope, each prefaced by a blessing and followed by a great responsory. The third responsory, at least, was sung with the first half of the *Gloria Patri.*

TE DEUM LAUDAMUS

(Monastic use would have a total of 12 psalms with antiphons and 12 lessons with great responsories)

Lauds (main musical elements)

Versicle/response: *Deus in adiutorium*, etc., and *Gloria Patri* (the Doxology)
Five psalms with antiphons (or with one antiphon for all five)
Hymn
Canticle: *Benedictus*, with antiphon (Song of Zachariah, Luke 1:68–79)
Prayer
Benedicamus Domino

Prime (main musical elements)

Versicle/response: *Deus in adiutorium*, etc., and *Gloria Patri*
Hymn
Psalms with one antiphon
Chapter (three texts according to season)
Short responsory
Kyrie, Pater noster, Credo
Collect
Benedicamus Domino

Terce, Sext, and None (main musical elements)

Versicle/response: *Deus in adiutorium*, etc., and *Gloria Patri*
Hymn
Psalms with one antiphon (three portions of Psalm 119 [118] for each hour)
Reading
Short responsory (sung to a tone)
Prayer
Benedicamus Domino

Second Vespers (main musical elements)

Versicle/response: *Deus in adiutorium*, etc., and *Gloria Patri*
Five psalms with antiphons (or with one antiphon for all five; might share the Lauds antiphons)
Great responsory (for major feasts in some churches)
Hymn
Versicle and response
Magnificat with Proper antiphon (Song of the Virgin Mary, Luke 1:46–55)
Kyrie, Pater noster
Prayer
Benedicamus Domino

Compline (main musical elements)

Versicle/response: *Converte nos deus salutaris noster/Et averte iram tuam a nobis* (Change us God, our salvation; and turn your anger from us); *Deus in adiutorium*, etc., and *Gloria Patri*
Psalms 4 (3), 31 (30):1–6, 91 (90), and 134 (133), with a single antiphon
Reading
Short responsory
Hymn
Versicle

Nunc dimittis (Song of Simeon, Luke 2:29–32)
Kyrie, Pater noster, Credo
Prayer
Benedicamus Domino
Antiphon for the Blessed Virgin Mary

The celebration of Matins is more complicated than Laudes, Vespers, and the Little Hours. For each Sunday, there was a particular set of psalms, readings, and responsories, and these were divided into units known as *nocturns*, as can be seen in the outline above. For any ferial day of the week following, Matins would consist of three readings and responsories and three psalms with antiphons, taken from one of the three nocturns of the preceding Sunday. But on major feasts, instead of the ferial Office, Proper readings and chants would be sung throughout. There were elaborate rules for dealing with the clash of feasts that sometimes happened, especially given that many feasts of the temporal cycle moved as they depended upon the ever-changing date of Easter. Sometimes when two major feasts collided, one would not be celebrated but would instead be commemorated by giving it a memorial, perhaps consisting of a three-lesson Matins. The canticles of Lauds, Vespers, and Compline were fixed, but the antiphons were Proper, giving the reciting of these important texts a festive coloring. The fixity of the canticle texts in the medieval Office helps to explain their great popularity as texts for choral music.

GLOSSARY

Advent—The four-week season leading up to Christmas on December 25.

alba—(pl. *albe*) A dawn song in the TROUBADOUR and TROUVÈRE repertories; usually, the singer takes on the role of a watchman who announces daybreak to a pair of illicit lovers.

Alleluia—A RESPONSORIAL chant of the MASS LITURGY, sung before the intoning of the Gospel.

antiphon—(1) a short chant that opens and closes the singing of PSALMS and CANTICLES in the OFFICE; (2) a chant for the ANTIPHONAL genres of the MASS: INTROITS and communions; (3) a long and ornate chant used for processions; (4) a type of chant sometimes sung before the Gospel of MASS.

antiphoners—Books containing the music for the OFFICE and organized by the church year. Also called *antiphonales.*

antiphonal singing—A performance practice, featuring alternation between two groups of singers.

Ars Antiqua—A term representing a fourteenth-century view of the POLYPHONIC repertory of the thirteenth century, most significantly the ORGANUM, CLAUSULAE, MOTETS, and CONDUCTUS of the NOTRE DAME SCHOOL.

Ars Nova—The term refers to French POLYPHONIC repertories from the fourteenth century, the notation in which they were expressed, and their theoretical underpinnings. Music of the *Ars Nova* (also called *Ars Modernorum* or *Ars Moderna*) was distinguished in the fourteenth century from the *Ars Antiqua* (or *Ars Vetus*), the POLYPHONIC music of the NOTRE DAME SCHOOL and its expression in FRANCONIAN NOTATION.

Ars Subtilior—A modern term designating the most rhythmically advanced late medieval POLYPHONY (chiefly CHANSONS, but also MASS movements and MOTETS) composed from around 1380 to 1420, and applied to the exceedingly complex notation in which this repertory was expressed.

authentic modes—The higher of the four pairs of scales making up the eight church modes.

ballade—One of the FORMES FIXES, a STROPHIC song form, the REFRAIN of which is distinguished from the rest of the stanza: aabC

ballata—An Italian song form from the fourteenth to the sixteenth centuries, similar in structure to the French VIRELAI, and like it, having a strong connection to the dance. Most ballate have a single stanza with the form, AbbaA : A (ripresa); bb (two piedi); a (the volta); and A (the ripresa). When there are multiple stanzas, the refrain may or may not be repeated between.

beguine—Women (beginning in the twelfth century) who wished to live a religious life in community without joining a formal order or professing vows. By the late thirteenth century, beguines were often persecuted and were steadily brought under control and supervision, whereas their male counterparts (the beghards) often became FRANCISCANS (third order).

Benedicamus Domino—Half of a versicle that finishes with *Deo gratias* (Let us praise the Lord; thanks be to God). This VERSICLE was used to close the hours of prayer (except Matins) of the Divine OFFICE, and was used in place of *Ite missa est* in MASSES without the Gloria.

Benedictine—A monk or nun living by the *Rule of St. Benedict*.

Benedictus—The song or CANTICLE of Zechariah, father of the Christian prophet John the Baptist (Luke 1:68–79), sung at LAUDS.

Breve—From Latin *brevis* (short). In the RHYTHMIC MODES, a note with a rhythmic duration between that of a LONG and a SEMIBREVE; two or three breves make up a long.

caccia—TRECENTO song form, featuring conversational dialogues concerning some aspect of contemporary life, most commonly the hunt, and most often composed in three voices, of which at least the top two are in CANON; the TENOR may be textless (presumably played on an instrument) and provides a harmonic foundation.

cadence—From the Latin verb *cado* (to fall or end). A point of musical repose, coming at the conclusion of a PHRASE, section, or entire piece.

caesura—A pause in a line of verse.

canon—A compositional procedure in which a voice (or voices) imitates another at some precise interval of time and pitch.

Canso—A love song in the TROUBADOUR repertory.

cantatorium—A book containing chants to be sung by the soloist or CANTOR.

canticles—Texts drawn from biblical passages in which characters burst into song; in addition to the fixed canticles (the BENEDICTUS of LAUDS, the MAGNIFICAT of VESPERS, and the NUNC DIMITTIS of COMPLINE), canticles were sung primarily during weekdays at Lauds, one assigned to each day. Generally sung to formulas like the PSALM TONES.

cantiga—Spanish or Portuguese monophonic song, often involving a refrain, and possibly the interplay of groups, soloists, and instrumentalists. Secular forms include the *cantiga de amigo* ("friend's song") and love songs in the voice of a woman. Sacred *cantigas* narrate miracles, whereas the *cantiga de loor* is a song of praise.

cantilena—A genre of English POLYPHONIC sacred music, written in score, usually with three voices, and a SEQUENCE-like Latin text.

cantor—Also known as the armarius or librarian in medieval rules and customaries. Cantors traditionally planned the LITURGY and its music, supervised the copying of books, and kept the roles, or records of death. In a CATHEDRAL chapter, the cantor was the second ranked authority after the dean. Also called a precentor; his immediate subordinate was called a subcantor or SUCCENTOR. Female, cantrix.

cantus (voice part)—In late medieval and renaissance POLYPHONY, the top voice, corresponding to superius, discantus, or triplex in earlier repertories.

cantus firmus—A melody (usually from liturgical chant), often chosen for its symbolic properties, and used as a basis for POLYPHONIC MOTETS and MASS movements.

carole/carol/carola—A complex term with many meanings, depending upon time and place. Early in its history a popular social dance, often sung in a ring, and later, especially in England, a religious song with a REFRAIN, set POLYPHONICALLY in the fifteenth and sixteenth centuries with various degrees of musical complexity.

cathedral—The place where a bishop has his throne or *cathedra*, hence the main church of a region (diocese). A group of priests (canons) associated with the governance of a cathedral is called a "chapter."

cauda Latin, "tail."—A long MELISMATIC section of a CONDUCTUS; sometimes early examples were expressed in MODAL NOTATION, whereas the worded sections might be "cum littera," that is not expressed in rhythmic values represented by ligatures.

Chancery—Episcopal or royal office responsible for the production of official documents.

Chanson—French, "song."—Any of a variety of secular French musical and poetic forms, including the music of the TROUVÈRES and TROUBADOURS, but also the POLYPHONIC songs of the thirteenth and fourteenth centuries.

Chansonnier—French, "songbook." A thirteenth or fourteenth-century collection of song poetry and (frequently) its music, and usually organized by composer. Some manuscripts contain portraits of composers at the heads of sections.

chansons de geste—French, "Songs of great deeds." A type of epic poem, organized into laisses, or strophes, each of which was sung to a simple melodic formula. None survives complete with its music.

choir—(1) a group of singers; (2) the eastern section of a CATHEDRAL, where such a group would sing, provided with CHOIR STALLS; in the later Middle Ages, commonly walled off by a choir (or rood) screen.

chromatic—In ancient Greek music, a way to describe the TETRACHORD made up of a minor third and two half steps or semitones.

Cistercians—A reformed order of BENEDICTINES, begun in the early twelfth century, and soon spread throughout Europe. Cistercians had the restoration of the LITURGY and music from the time of St. Benedict as a goal, and this impossible ideal played a major role in the ways they transformed both liturgical and musical practices.

clausula (pl. clausulae)—A self-contained section of DISCANT contained in, or substituted into, a work of ORGANUM purum. Also called punctum (pl. puncta). Some clausulae were given texts, turning them into MOTETS.

Clivis—A notational sign that indicates two notes, the second of which is lower. Also called *flexa*.

cobla—Stanza of a TROUBADOUR song.

codex A book bound at the spine, in double-sided pages, in contrast to a scroll.

color—See ISORHYTHM.

Compline—The last OFFICE of monastic or cathedral hours, sung before retiring.

conductus (pl. conductus; but some say conducti)—A song, usually sacred and STROPHIC, for one or more voices, setting a rhymed accentual Latin text; called a versus in some regions. Some conductus include refrains.

consonance—Interval or sonority considered stable in medieval musical practice; in opposition to dissonance.

contrafactum—From the medieval Latin verb meaning "to imitate" or "counterfeit," and so a piece with new words provided for pre-existing music.

contrary motion—In POLYPHONIC texture, when two voices move simultaneously in opposite directions.

contratenor—In fourteenth and fifteenth century POLYPHONIC works, a part written "against the tenor," and so often serving to work with the TENOR to form a harmonic foundation for the other voices or to otherwise fill out the more important duet between the TENOR and the superius (upper voice).

copula—A POLYPHONIC texture featuring repetition of short phrases at different pitch levels and frequently found at the close of a section of ORGANUM.

Corpus Christi—Feast of the Body of Christ, established in the thirteenth century as part of an increasing devotion to the EUCHARIST.

diapason—An octave (eight notes), or the interval of an octave.

diatonic—In ancient Greek music, a TETRACHORD made up of two whole steps and one half step.

differentia—The formula used to end a PSALM TONE and provide a smooth connection with the ANTIPHON to follow.

in directum—A performance practice in which each verse of a PSALM follows another all the way through, with no intervening responses or ANTIPHONS (TRACTS of the mass liturgy are sung this way).

discant—A style of singing ORGANUM in which all the voices move at nearly the same speed; to be distinguished from organum purum in which the voice singing the chant moves far more slowly, sometimes with the quality of a drone, than the voice or voices that decorate it.

dit—A medieval narrative poem, spoken, not sung, but perhaps with songs inserted at appropriate places.

Dominican—Member of the Dominican order, the Friars Preachers, founded by St. Dominic in the thirteenth century.

Doxology—A formula of praise to the Trinity, used as the final two verses of intoned office PSALMS and CANTICLES, as well as in the performing of the MASS INTROIT. The first half of the doxology was chanted at the close of some RESPONSORIES of the night office.

duplum—(1) A piece of ORGANUM in two voices; (2) a second voice part ornamenting the TENOR.

enharmonic—In ancient Greek music, a way to describe the TETRACHORD made up of a major third and two quarter tones.

estampie—A poetic and musical form for dancing; the music is textless, and so is thought to have been instrumental.

Eucharist—Section of the MASS commemorating the Last Supper through the use of blessed bread and wine; communion; from the Greek, meaning "thanksgiving." Sometimes used to mean the whole of the Mass liturgy.

Exegesis—An exposition or explanation, usually of biblical or liturgical texts.

Fascicle—From Latin *fascis* ("bundle"). A gathering or group of pages making up part of a CODEX.

ferial—Nonfestive, as in the ferial OFFICE, or the weekly and Sunday PSALMS and ANTIPHONS sung when no major feast intervenes.

final—A tonic pitch, usually found as the final pitch of a chant. See MODE.

flagellants—Bands of itinerant laypeople in the later Middle Ages, who processed through urban areas and preached warnings, whipping themselves to atone for the sins of all and to beg divine intervention, especially during times of plague and other disasters.

flex—A short line, like a kind of comma, used when a verse of a PSALM is especially long.

florid organum—A style of POLYPHONY in which one voice sustains long notes of a melody (often borrowed from PLAINSONG) and one or more voices ornaments by singing several notes for each sustained pitch, the voices forming PERFECT INTERVALS at CADENCES.

formes fixes—Long-established patterns for three genres of French songs, formed in the twelfth and thirteenth century, but not standardized until the second half of the fourteenth century. All three forms—RONDEAU, BALLADE, and VIRELAI—are defined by the position of refrains within their structures. Such structure is often designated by scholars by letters denoting textual and musical sections; uppercase letters indicate the repetition of both music and text, and lowercase letters the repetition of music to new text.

Franciscan—A member of the Friars Minor, a religious order founded by St. Francis of Assisi in the thirteenth century.

Franconian notation—A type of early MENSURAL notation, described by Franco of Cologne in the late thirteenth century. In Franconian notation, the shape of a note helps to indicate its duration.

friar—A MENDICANT.

gamut—Short for gamma-ut, the lowest note of the medieval solmization system, and which came to signify the entire range of pitches shown on the GUIDONIAN HAND.

Gloria Patri—The DOXOLOGY.

glosses—Comments inserted next to the biblical text, either between lines or in the margins; glosses served a variety of purposes, all the way from simply defining words or grammatical structures to more complicated commentaries that expanded upon the meanings of scriptural texts.

goliards—Itinerant scholars of the thirteenth century, associated with a repertory of poetry and song critiquing or satirizing student and clerical life and celebrating drinking and love.

Gothic—An originally pejorative term designating a style of art and architecture arising in the Île de France in the twelfth century.

gradual—A RESPONSORIAL chant of the MASS liturgy (meaning sung on the steps, or gradus, leading to the altar) and one of two chants sung between the intonation of the two Mass readings from Scripture.

grand chant courtois—The most refined and complex type of French song, usually a STROPHIC work with the form ABABX. The X section had no set number of lines, and the overall structure of the song was fairly fluid.

great responsories—Long chants following readings in the medieval OFFICE. These chants are RESPONSORIAL, that is their verses were sung by a soloist, and to a series of tones, one for each of the church modes.

Gregorian chant—A name taken from Pope Gregory the Great, and often used for the PLAINSONG tradition that developed north of the Alps during the Carolingian period.

Guidonian hand—Named for the Italian theorist Guido of Arezzo (although seemingly post-dating him), a hand-shaped diagram, assigning a pitch of the GAMUT to each joint, knuckle and fingertip. The hand was used in teaching and as an aid for memorization.

harmonics—The ancient Greek science of harmonics investigates the nature of pitches, their arrangements, and the underlying principles that govern them; because of a dependence on ancient Greek theory, harmonics is a basic component of medieval music theory.

Hebrew Bible—The canonical collection of Biblical texts fundamental to Judaism, known in Hebrew as the Tanakh; the term "Old Testament" is used to refer to Christian versions of this collection of texts.

hexachord—A collection of six pitches. In the Guidonian system, there are three fundamental hexachords, each comprised of the successive intervals tone-tone-semitone-tone-tone, and one beginning on C (natural), on F (soft, contains b-flat) and on G (hard, contains b-natural).

hocket—A texture found in thirteenth and fourteenth-century POLYPHONY in which the music is divided between two or more voices so that one voice sounds while another falls silent, in rapid succession. Hocketing can work within a PHRASE or group of phrases, as a section of a larger work, or as a free-standing composition.

homophonic—A texture in which several musical lines move together in a similar rhythm.

Humanism—Movement of the fourteenth, fifteenth and sixteenth centuries, concerned with the revival of ancient culture.

hymn—From Greek, *hymnos*, meaning a song for a god. In the medieval Latin tradition, hymns are STROPHIC songs of praise, sung throughout the hours of the OFFICE; their texts are found in collections, often without music.

iambic tetrameter—Lines of text consisting of four metrical units stressed short-long.

introit—The opening chant of the MASS LITURGY, an ANTIPHONAL genre that consisted of an ANTIPHON, a PSALM verse, the DOXOLOGY, and the repeat of the antiphon. In the ninth through the eleventh centuries, the most popular introits were TROPED interlinearly.

isorhythm—From the Greek, "iso," meaning "same," a term first introduced in the modern period. In a piece of music containing isorhythm one of more of the voices contains repeating patterns of the same rhythm. The device is most usually found in the TENOR of MOTET and MASS movements of the fourteenth and fifteeth centuries: a particular repeating rhythmic pattern is called a talea (Latin for cutting), and a repeating melodic phrase or segment is called a color. Late medieval composers delighted in creating tenors that contained combinations of color and talea patterns, to form foundations for large-scale works.

jeu-parti—A sung debate, popular among JONGLEURS, TROUBADOURS, and TROUVÈRES, similar to the TENSO.

jongleur—An entertainer, sometimes an instrumentalist, whose music was often improvised; the term is interchangeable with MINSTREL.

jubilus—From Latin jubilare, "to jubilate, shout for joy." Can mean any joyful MELISMATIC song of joy; from Carolingian times has been applied to the long melisma at the end of the ALLELUIA of the MASS liturgy.

Lady chapel—In late medieval CATHEDRALS, churches, monasteries, and castles, especially in England, a special place dedicated to the Blessed Virgin Mary, with artwork, music, and liturgical celebrations for her veneration. In an English cathedral, the

Lady Chapel would have been the largest and most deluxe of all chapels, and was frequently located to the east of the high altar, as can be seen, for example, at Salisbury cathedral.

Landini cadence—A CADENCE type frequently occuring in late medieval POLYPHONIC works; it consists of the use of a "escape tone." Instead of progressing smoothly from the leading tone to the final, one of the voices "escapes" after the leading tone to the sixth scale degree, and then leaps up a third to the final; also called a "lower third" cadence.

***lauda* (pl. *laude*)**—Italian religious song for popular singing, associated with the FRANCISCANS. In the thirteenth century, they tended to have a participatory refrain, and verses telling a story. In the fourteenth-century, *laude* began to be taken up by trained musicians, and became more musicially complex. Groups who sang *laude* were called *laudesi*.

Lauds—The hour of prayer traditionally sung at dawn in the monastic and CATHEDRAL OFFICE.

Leich—German narrative poem (either sacred or secular) that unfolds in unequal stanzas, each of which was sung, and probably accompanied by an instrument.

Lent—In the medieval church calendar, the forty-day season of fasting preceding the celebration of the Resurrection of Jesus at Easter.

Liber usualis—Latin, "Book for Common Use." A modern book containing the restored melodies of medieval chants organized to provide music for the major feasts of the Christian calendar and for Sunday services throughout the year.

ligature—A symbol designating a grouping of discrete notes; used in MODAL NOTATION to denote particular rhythmic patterns.

liturgy—The prescribed set of texts to be either spoken or sung to accompany the ritual actions of the MASS, OFFICE, or other occasions of worship, including processions and incidental services.

long—In the RHYTHMIC MODES of the thirteenth century, the longest time value, equal to two or three BREVES.

lute—A plucked-string instrument with a fretted neck (like the modern guitar), a rounded back, and a flat front, generally with about ten strings set in pairs.

madrigal—A poetic and musical genre of the TRECENTO, with a text exploring pastoral themes, and consisting of several stanzas, followed by a REFRAIN.

magister—Latin "master." A teacher or professor in a medieval monastery, cathedral school, or university.

Magnificat—The song or CANTICLE of the Virgin Mary sung at VESPERS (Luke 1: 46–55) to a tone, and with an ANTIPHON proper to the feast or season.

mannerism—A term once applied to music of the late fourteenth century, signifying excessive complexity; by extension, the term is also used to describe late sixteenth and seventeenth century repertory in which magnification of particular details seems to triumph over the sense of the whole.

Mass—The main service of the Roman Catholic Church, divided into two parts, a liturgy of the word, and a liturgy of the faithful, the latter commemorating the Last Supper through Eucharist (communion). The word can also be used to name the musical setting of the texts of the Mass Ordinary: the *Kyrie*, *Gloria*, *Credo*, *Sanctus*, *Agnus dei*, and *Ite missa est*.

Mass Ordinary—Those six MASS chants whose texts remain the same throughout the year, although inflected by their TROPES or PROSULAE in the Middle Ages.

Mass Proper—MASS chants that shift their texts and music every day in accordance with the themes of the feast or season.

maximodus—In ARS NOVA theoretical understandings, accounts for the division of maxima into LONGS, necessary for the workings of some ISORHYTHMIC TENORS.

mediant—A formula for the CADENCE of the middle phrase of a PSALM or canticle TONE.

meistersinger—Musicians from several classes in Germany (the successors to the MINNESINGER), organized into guilds, who used texts and music to educate and edify, sponsoring concerts and singing contests to promote their poetic and musical art;

their period of greatest influence was the sixteenth century.

melisma—A portion of a melody in which a single syllable is vocalized to several notes.

mendicants—From Latin, *mendico*, "to beg." Officially sanctioned orders of wandering preachers; the FRIARS, FRANCISCANS, and DOMINICANS.

mensural—A system of notation that developed in the second half of thirteenth century, and that (unlike MODAL NOTATION) assigned rhythmic values to particular note shapes.

minim—In the ARS NOVA, notes that divided the SEMIBREVE into two or three parts. This level of division was known as prolation.

minnesinger—Courtly poet-musicians that flourished in Germany from the late twelfth to the early fourteenth century.

minstrel—Any sort of professional entertainer of the Middle Ages, but particularly a musician, usually an instrumentalist; they could be itinerant street musicians, members of guilds, or employed by courts or towns.

modal notation—See RHYTHMIC MODE.

mode—One of eight theoretical categories that could be understood as a scale or set of conventionalized melodic patterns. Each mode is characterized by distinctive intervallic relationships and its own final (tonic) pitch. The eight modes or octoechos first developed in sixth-century Jerusalem and spread from there through much of the Eastern Christian world, from where the system was adopted by the theorists of Frankish chant.

modus—The length of a LONG in relation to a BREVE. In modus perfectus, the long contains three BREVES; in imperfectus, the long contains two breves.

monochord—A single-stringed instrument, used for teaching and study by ancient Greek theorists and crucial to Western music theory treatises as well; particularly useful for showing the relationship between sounded notes and string lengths. The string was tuned to whatever pitch was most suitable to the users and a bridge was used to mark off the intervals.

monophony—Music that sounds out a single line, sung either by a soloist, a CHOIR, or a congregation.

motet—In the Middle Ages, a short, texted work, usually with two to four voices, one of which is a TENOR drawn from PLAINSONG or some other source. Motetus is a term often used for the second voice of a motet.

musica ficta (musica falsa)—In music theory, signifying notes that are outside the Guidonian GAMUT. Rules governing musica ficta were not standardized in the Middle Ages, and yet most performers and editors introduce musica ficta to avoid tritones and to allow for smooth voice progressions, especially at CADENCES.

mutation—The modulation from one HEXACHORD to another.

neuma—A loan word from Greek meaning sign or gesture; *neume* is the French translation of *neuma*. In the Middle Ages, the term also meant a MELISMATIC portion of a song or chant.

neume—A notational sign that symbolizes a specific number of notes and an overall melodic direction of one or more particular pitches.

notational dialects—Regional families of NEUME shapes indicating the basic directions of pitch and melodic contours.—

Notre Dame school—A tradition of composition and improvisation flourishing in Paris in the late twelfth and thirteenth centuries, centered at the Cathedral of Notre Dame, encompassing ORGANUM, DISCANT CLAUSULAE, and CONDUCTUS, and expressed in the RHYTHMIC MODES.

Nunc dimittis—The canticle of the prophet Simeon (Luke 2:29–32) sung at COMPLINE.

oblique motion—In POLYPHONIC music: one voice stays stationary while another moves.

offertory—A RESPONSORIAL chant of the MASS LITURGY, characterized by verses sung by soloists before the eleventh century, after which time the verses were commonly dropped.

Office—Daily hours of prayer, sung in the Middle Ages in monasteries, CATHEDRALS, and related churches.

oratorio—Beginning in the Baroque, a large-scale sung work with religious meanings and/or references to biblical or other sacred texts.

ordo (pl. "ordines")—A phrase grouping in a RHYTHMIC MODE, generally consisting of several repetitions of the rhythmic foot between two rests, and beginning and ending with notes of the same duration.

organal voice—*Vox organalis*, a voice that decorates the PLAINSONG sung by another voice, sometimes called the *vox principalis* (principal voice).

organum—A generic term for various POLYPHONIC textures featuring the adding of one or more voices, often to a preexisting melody.

Ovidian—Relating to Ovid (Publius Ovidius Naso), a Roman poet (43 B.C.E.–17 C.E.) whose poems were much studied in medieval schools; love was a frequent theme of his, both in myth (the *Metamorphoses*) and in more practical terms (the *Art of Love).*

partial signature—A signature not used in all the voices, designating that some form of transposition is in play. Also called a conflicting signature.

pastorela/pastourelle—A simple song involving a knight, a shepherdess, and an attempt at seduction.

perfect interval—A unison, fourth, fifth, octave, or the combination of these with an octave (e.g. an eleventh is an octave and a fourth).

Perfection—In thirteenth-century notation, a three beat rhythmic cell.

pes—(1) A NEUME that indicates two notes, the second of which is higher. Also called *podatus.* (2) In POLYPHONY, a short repeating rhythmic phrase in the TENOR, predominating in English music.

Petronian—Referring to Petrus de Cruce and his style of MOTET, featuring multiple SEMIBREVES of various durations in the upper voice.

phrase—A term borrowed from linguistics to connote a short melodic unit, a section of a larger musical sentence.

plagal modes—The lower of the four pairs of scales making up the eight church MODES.

plainchant—The monophonic unison music of Christian liturgies, usually referring to the Western traditions. Also called plainsong.

planh—A lament in the TROUBADOUR repertory.

polyphony—A sung piece with two or more voices sounding simultaneously.

polytextual motet—A vocal composition in which two or more individual voices sing distinct texts, sometimes in the same language, and sometimes not.

prefatory tropes—TROPES (texted lines of music) added to the openings of pieces of PLAINSONG to introduce them both musically and thematically.

prosula—A text set to a preexisting MELISMA.

Psalms—150 Hebrew poems (tehillim, "songs of praise"), representing, at least to some degree, the liturgy and prayer traditions of the Second Jewish Temple; the psalms were translated into Greek by Jewish scholars for the Septuagint bible (3rd century B.C.E.); early Latin translations were made from the Septuagint. Most famous was one of Jerome's three translations, included in the Latin Vulgate, and known as the Gallican psalter. The psalms in Latin are the primary sources of texts for early medieval chant repertories.

psalm tone—A melodic formula for reciting the verses of the PSALMS; each MODE has its own tones, with inflected openings, midpoints, and cadential teminations called differentiae.

Psalter—A collection of 150 PSALMS; in the Middle Ages, some psalters were prepared for liturgical use, and may reference the texts of appropriate ANTIPHONS.

punctum—A fine point-shaped notational sign that indicated the same or a lower pitch. Also called *tractulus.*

puy—A song contest, favoured by the JONGLEURS; eventually the word came to be used for societies of jongleurs.

quadruplum—The fourth voice up from the TENOR in a four-voice POLYPHONIC work.

refrain—(1) A repeated verse of a poem or other text that is set to the same musical material; (2) a textual citation (sometimes with music) borrowed from another work.

responsorial singing—A performance practice, used in both the MASS and OFFICE, that features a soloistic verse and a choral respond.

responsory—A chant used in the OFFICE, sung responsorially, often following a reading.

rhythmic modes—Primarily six rhythmic patterns used by notators, singers, and composers of the thirteenth-century NOTRE DAME SCHOOL, and imported from there to several major European centers. Often notated through specific patterns of LIGATURES_ borrowed from SQUARE NOTATION.

romances—Narratives of knights and their ladies, often centered on the strength of their love; frequently involve magic and folkloric themes.

Romanesque—Architectural style of the tenth through twelfth centuries, inspired by that of ancient Rome, characterized by large blocks of stone, thick walls, round arches, and small windows.

rondeau (pl. rondeaux)—One of the FORMES FIXES, a STROPHIC song form characterized by use of the REFRAIN both at the beginning and end of each strophe, and half of it in the middle: ABaAabAB.

St. Gall neumes—Notation used at the monastery of St. Gall and the region surrounding it from the later ninth century forward, which shows melodic gestures but not pitch, and includes signs signifying interpretation.

sanctorale—Latin, *"of the saints."* The LITURGICAL cycle of feasts commemorating the days on which particular saints died.

Sarum rite The chant and LITURGY of Salisbury_ CATHEDRAL, which came to dominate in England, Scotland, and Ireland in the course of the thirteenth and fourteenth centuries.

scale—A series of at least three different ascending or descending pitches arranged in a particular pattern.

Scholasticism—A movement in late medieval higher learning characterized by a love of systematic categorization and logical argumentation.

scriptorium—A place for copying manuscripts; often in a monastery, the cloister was used as a place for copying.

sedes—A bishop's throne-like chair in a CATHEDRAL.

semibreve—A note, generally lozenge-shaped, that is shorter than a BREVE. Either three (equal) or two (unequal) semibreves make up a breve in the thirteenth century.

sequence—(1) A genre of chant (also called a prose) featured in the medieval MASS LITURGY and sung before the intoning of the Gospel. (2) A melodic sequence is a pattern of notes repeated at successive pitch levels.

Septuagint—The Hebrew Bible translated into Greek in the 3rd century B.C.E.

sirventes—A political song in the TROUBADOUR_ repertory.

solfeggio—Use of syllables to stand for particular pitches of a HEXACHORD or the gamut. Also called solmization, sol-fa, or solfège.

square notation—Notation using predominantly square shapes, developed in northern France from the mid twelfth century.

strophic—A poem in which each stanza has the same number of lines, meter (or accentual pattern), and rhyme scheme, and by extension, the same music for each strophe.

summa—A compendium of all knowledge (or all knowledge on a topic), favoured by SCHOLASTICS.

Syllabic—A text sung with one note assigned to one syllable.

symphonia—Symphony, from the Greek meaning "sounding together;" the term has many meanings in the Middle Ages, including "interval."

talea—See ISORHYTHM.

temporale—Latin, *"of the time."* Liturgical cycle of events commemorating the advent, birth, life, suffering, Resurrection and Ascension of Jesus.

tempus—(pl. "tempora") The basic duration of a BREVE; the beat.

tenor—A slower-moving voice that sounds out the pitches of a phrase of PLAINCHANT, while one or more voices ornament the chant.

tenso—A TROUBADOUR song in the form of a debate.

tetrachord—Grouping of four consecutive pitches.

tetraktys—A Pythagorean figure that recalls the first four natural numbers, whose sum is 10: 1 + 2 + 3 + 4 = 10. Used as a guide for remembering the ratios of the most important intervals: the unison (1:1), octave (1:2), fifth (2:3), and fourth (3:4).

through-composed—A musical work in which the music develops and changes throughout, as opposed to STROPHIC, where each unit of text often has the same music, repeating throughout the entire piece.

tonary—A book that groups chants (or the texts of chants) according to MODE.

tonus peregrinus—A PSALM TONE with two reciting pitches, one for the first and the other for the second half of the verse.

tornada—A closing strophe of a TROUBADOUR song which directly addresses the subject of the song or a patron.

tract—A Proper chant sung in place of the ALLELUIA on especially solemn feast days and throughout the season of Lent.

Trecento—The fourteenth century in Italy.

triplum—(1) A three-voice piece of ORGANUM. (2) The third voice from the bottom (TENOR) in a three or four voice texture.

trobairitz—Female troubadours.

trochaic—Following the pattern of a trochee, a poetic foot consisting of a long syllable followed by a short.

trope—An addition of a sung phrase of music (or a set of phrases) to comment upon a pre-existing chant.

troubadours—Poet-composers of MONOPHONIC songs of the twelfth and thirteenth centuries, writing in the language of southern France (Old Occitan, also known as Provençal), especially on the topic of courtly love. The term is also used for the Spanish and Portuguese poet-composers who wrote in Gallician.

trouvère—A courtly poet-singer of the thirteenth or fourteenth century, writing in some dialect of Old French.

tympanum—The arch-shaped niche above a doorway, especially of a major church; frequently contained sculpture, carvings, or other forms of art.

unheightened notation Musical notation in which the NEUMES are not precisely spaced on the page, so they do not designate specific intervallic relationships, but do indicate general melodic contour. Also called adiastemmatic.

verse—A line of poetry, stanza of a hymn, or a sentence within a PSALM.

Vespers—The hour of prayer sung at sunset.

vida—Mythic life of a composer, sometimes included in a CHANSONNIER.

vielle—Often used as a generic term for bowed string instruments of the Middle Ages; the most typical form is five-stringed, and played on the arm.

virelai—One of the FORMES FIXES; a STROPHIC song form, featuring a single-line REFRAIN sung at the beginning and end of each strophe: AbbaA.

virga—A rod-shaped notational sign that indicates rising pitch.

ENDNOTES

CHAPTER 1

3. The hymn text *Ave maris stella*, celebrating the Virgin Mary: The hymn text is discussed and read aloud (on the accompanying CD) in Clive Brooks, *Reading Latin Poetry Aloud: A Practical Guide to Two Thousand Years of Verse* (Cambridge: Cambridge University Press, 2005), 162–63.

5. how a medieval singer . . . as the text unfolded: See Howell D. Chickering and Margaret Louise Switten, eds., *The Medieval Lyric*, vol. 1: *Monastic Song, Troubadour Song, German Song, Trouvère Song*, 3rd ed. (South Hadley, MA: Mount Holyoke College, 2001).

5. Example 1.2: Chickering and Switten, *The Medieval Lyric*, 24.

7. each strophe has different music: The entire sequence, with translation of the complete text and study of other texts set to this same melody in twelfth- and thirteenth-century Paris, is found in Margot E. Fassler, *Gothic Song: Victorine Sequences and Augustinian Reform in Twelfth-Century Paris*, 2nd ed. (Notre Dame, IN: University of Notre Dame Press, 2011), 320–34.

8. Example 1.3: Fassler: *Gothic Song*, 436.

8. Example 1.4: Michael Anderson, "Enhancing the 'Ave Maria' in the Ars Antiqua," *Plainsong and Medieval Music* 19 (2010): 35–65.

9. *Ave beatissima / Ave Maria / Ave maris stella*: For a transcription of this motet, a translation of its texts, and a full discussion of the complex of meaning related to *Ave Maria* in thirteenth-century repertories, see Anderson, "Enhancing the 'Ave Maria' in the Ars Antiqua," 35–65.

9. Example 1.5: Giulio Cattin and Francesco Facchin, eds. *Polyphonic Music of the 14th Century*, vol. XXIIIB (Monaco: Oiseau-Lyre, 1991), p. 360.

9. Example 1.6: Kurt von Fischer and F. Alberto Gallo, *Polyphonic Music of the Fourteenth Century* XII: *Italian Sacred Music*, p. 183.

10. the time and place in which it was made: For an exploration of the re-creation of medieval music in contemporary pop music, see John Haines, "Living Troubadours and Other Recent Uses for Medieval Music," *Popular Music* 23 (2004): 133–53.

12. the intertextual mansions of the medieval imagination: See Mary J. Carruthers, *The Book of Memory: A Study of Memory in Medieval Culture*, 2nd ed. (Cambridge and New York: Cambridge University Press, 2008).

PART 1

16. SR 11; 2/3: Throughout the text, these paired SR citations refer to *Strunk's Source Readings in Music History*, Leo Treitler, general editor (New York: Norton, 1998). The first reference is to the one-volume edition; the second is to the volume in the seven-volume set

and the selection in that volume. In the reference SR 16:149; 2/8:39, the source is page 149 of selection 16, or page 39 of volume 2, selection 8 of the seven-volume set.

16. Calcidius commented on Plato's *Timaeus*: Calvin M. Bower, "The Transmission of Ancient Music Theory into the Middle Ages," in *The Cambridge History of Western Music Theory*, ed. Thomas Christensen (Cambridge: Cambridge University Press, 2002), 136–68.

16. "corrected the discipline of reading and singing most carefully": Einhard and Notker the Stammerer, *Two Lives of Charlemagne*, trans. with notes by David Ganz (London: Penguin, 2008), 37.

CHAPTER 2

20. ancient Greeks . . . once knew how to notate music: An overview of the various types of early notation and their growth and development around the world can be found in Ian D. Bent et al., *Notation*, §II: *Notational systems*, New Grove Online.

20. surviving taste of this repertory from late antiquity: See William A. Johnson, "Musical Evenings in the Early Empire: New Evidence from a Greek Papyrus with Musical Notation," *Journal of Hellenic Studies* 120 (2000): 57–85.

20. Example 2.1: Egert Pöhlmann and Martin West, eds. *Documents of Ancient Greek Music* (Oxford: Clarendon Press, 2001): 190–91.

23. prayers in which the people joined: *Egeria's Travels*, trans. John Wilkinson, 3rd ed. (Warminster: Aris and Phillips, 1999), 144.

23. system of eight modes . . . oldest monophonic chants in the Catholic Church: See Peter Jeffery, "The Earliest Oktoechoi: The Role of Jerusalem and Palestine in the Beginnings of Modal Ordering," in *The Study of Medieval Chant: Paths and Bridges, East and West* (Woodbridge, Suffolk: Boydell, 2001), 147–209, esp. 207–9.

25. Christian liturgy in Jerusalem . . . in Greek, Syriac, and Latin: On the early history of psalmody, see Peter Jeffery, "Musical Legacies from the Ancient World," in Thomas F. Kelly and Mark Everist, eds., *The Cambridge History of Medieval Music* (Cambridge: Cambridge University Press, 2012).

25. all the major languages of Christian antiquity: See Catherine Nolan, "Music Theory and Mathematics," in Thomas Christensen, ed., *The Cambridge History of Western Music Theory* (Cambridge: Cambridge University Press, 2002), 272–304.

29. visualizations of tones, scales, and intervals: On "geometric imagery" in music theory, see Nolan, in Christensen, *Cambridge History of Western Music Theory*, 280–84.

29. the world of Boethius and of early medieval music theory: An eleventh-century Italian copy of Boethius's treatise is found in the collection of the State Library of Victoria in Melbourne, Australia.

32. "a single consonance from differing sounds": Boethius, *Fundamentals of Music*, trans. Calvin M. Bower, ed. Claude V. Palisca (New Haven: Yale University Press, 1989), 17–19.

32. enharmonically, chromatically, or diatonically: The categorization of the tetrachords into three genera is attributed to Aristoxenus (fl. 335 B.C.E.), a pupil of Aristotle. His treatise on music survives in part. For a succinct discussion of his work and that of other Greek theoretical writers, see Thomas J. Mathiesen, "Greek Music Theory," in Christensen, *Cambridge History of Western Music Theory*, 109–35.

CHAPTER 3

37. first complete repertory . . . within the context of Christian ritual: For background to the period before the formation of Frankish chant, see Peter Jeffery, "Monastic Reading and the Emerging Roman Chant Repertory," in Sean Gallagher et al., eds., *Western Plainchant in the First Millennium: Studies in the Medieval Liturgy and Its Music* (Aldershot: Ashgate, 2003), 45–130.

38. chant manuscript copied . . . by a monk named Hartker: Hartker's Codex (St. Gall 390–391) is published in a facsimile with an index and commentary: *Paléographie musicale*, 2nd ser., *Monumentale*, vol. 1, ed. Jacques Froger (Bern: Herbert Lang, 1970); it has also been digitized.

39. first fully neumed Old Roman Mass book . . . in the early tenth century: Brief discussions are found in all the general introductions

to Gregorian chant. More detailed arguments are laid out in Kenneth Levy, "Gregorian Chant and the Romans," *Journal of the American Musicological Society* 56 (2003): 5–41.

43. the Gospel of the day . . . disciples and other holy people: There are four Gospels in Christian Scripture: Matthew, Mark, and Luke, called the Synoptics because of the shared material between them, and John, which is considered later than the other three. The Epistles consist of the letters assigned to Paul and a few other canonical letters.

44. the verses of the Offertory chants: See Rebecca Maloy, *Inside the Offertory: Aspects of Chronology and Transmission* (Oxford: Oxford University Press, 2010), for a study of the use of formulas within this genre and of its several layers.

45. Psalm 91 (90): Where two numbers are given, the second, in parentheses, indicates the Vulgate (based on the Greek), where it differs from that of the New Revised Standard Edition and many other English Bibles (based on Hebrew). The differences in psalm numbering can be summarized as follows:

Hebrew/English	Greek/Vulgate
1–8	1–8
9–10	9
11–113	10–112
114–15	113
116	114–15
117–46	116–45
147	146–47
148–50	148–50

45. Example 3.1a: Emma Hornby, *Medieval Liturgical Chant and Patristic Exegesis: Words and Music in the Second-Mode Tracts* (Woodbridge, Suffolk: The Boydell Press, 2009), 29.

45. Example 3.1b: Hornby, *Medieval Liturgical Chant and Patristic Exegesis*, 295.

46. *cantatorium* . . . solo chants sung by the cantor himself: See Michel Huglo, "The Cantatorium from Charlemagne to the Fourteenth Century," in Peter Jeffery, ed., *The Study of Medieval Chant: Paths and Bridges, East and West* (Bury St. Edmonds: Boydell, 2001), 89–103.

49. Sandwiched in between are two short theoretical treatises: An easy-to-read discussion of the Metz Tonary and its parts can be found in Peter Jeffery, "The Earliest Oktoēchoi: The Role of Jerusalem and Palestine in the Beginnings of Modal Ordering," in Jeffery, *Study of Medieval Chant*, 167–71.

49. hold melodies together like "a kind of glue": See David E. Cohen, "Notes, Scales, and Modes in the Earlier Middle Ages," in Christensen, *The Cambridge History of Western Music Theory*, 307–63, at 310.

49. *Resurrexi* . . . the contrast is clear: See David Hughes, "The Musical Text of the Introit Resurrexi," in Terence Bailey and Alma Santosuosso, eds., *Music in Medieval Europe* (Aldershot: Ashgate, 2007), 163–80.

51. combine the treatise *De octo tonis* with other early sources: See Barbara Haggh (Huglo), "Aurelian's Library," in *Cantus planus: Papers Read at the Ninth Meeting* (Budapest: Magyar Tudományos Akadémia, 2001), 271–300. She demonstrates what sources Aurelian had access to and says that he relied on books as well as on memory and oral tradition.

52. "operate with a notationless music culture": Charles M. Atkinson, *The Critical Nexus: Tone-System, Mode, and Notation in Early Medieval Music* (Oxford: Oxford University Press, 2009), 93. Atkinson offers a thorough discussion of Aurelian as well as all other Carolingian music theorists. See also Calvin Bower, "'*Adhuc ex parte et in enigmate cernimus . . .*': Reflections on the Closing Chapters of *Musica Enchiriadis*," in Andreas Giger and Thomas J. Mathiesen, eds., *Music in the Mirror: Reflections on the History of Music Theory and Literature for the Twenty-first Century* (Lincoln: University of Nebraska Press, 2002), 21–44.

52. "a multiplication of a single tetrachord": Atkinson, *The Critical Nexus*, 123.

53. Example 3.3: *Harvard Anthology of Music*, vol. 1 (Cambridge: Harvard University Press, 1968), 24.

54. "whether it is composed of fast or slow phrases": *Musica and Scolica Enchiriadis*, trans. Raymond Erickson, ed. Claude V. Palisca (New Haven: Yale University Press, 1995), 53.

CHAPTER 4

57. chess . . . in northern Europe at this time: An early witness to chess in the region is found in a late tenth-century manuscript in the Swiss Abbey of Einsiedeln; see Helena M. Gamer, "The Earliest Evidence of Chess in Western Literature: The Einsiedeln Verses," *Speculum* 29 (1954): 734–50.

59. music theory as received through Boethius: See Sarah Fuller, "Interpreting Hucbald on Mode," *Journal of Music Theory* 52 (2008): 13–40.

60. Musical events . . . inflected by the passing of time: See Bonnie J. Blackburn and Leofranc Holford-Strevens, *The Oxford Companion to the Year* (Oxford: Oxford University Press, 1999).

66. Example 4.2: *Gothic Song* (Notre Dame: University of Notre Dame Press, 2011), 415.

69. if the prosula was composed at the time . . . or was added later: See Richard Crocker, "The Troping Hypothesis," *Musical Quarterly* 52 (1966): 183–203.

69. Example 4.3b: David Bjork, *Aquitanian Kyrie Repertory of the Tenth and Eleventh Centuries*, ed. Richard Crocker (Aldershot: Ashgate, 2003), 221.

72. "most assiduous in illuminating, reading, and composing": Ekkehard IV, "The Three Inseparables," from Ekkehard's *History of St. Gall*, in George Gordon Coulton, ed., *Life in the Middle Ages* (Cambridge, Cambridge University Press, 1967), 50–57, at 51.

73. the very long melody *Occidentana*: See Calvin Bower, "From Alleluia to Sequence: Some Definitions of Relations," in Gallagher et al., *Western Plainchant in the First Millennium*, 351–98, esp. tables 15.1 (melody ID) and 15.2 (melody ID). The very long melodies were sometimes called "sequentiae," or by the modern term "sequelae"; *Occidentana* was also known by the title *Cithera*.

73. East and West Frankish sequence . . . a kind of geographical barrier: See Lori Kruckenberg, "Making a Sequence Repertory," in Kruckenberg and Andreas Haug, eds., *The Sequences of Nidaros: A Nordic Repertory and Its European Context* (Trondheim: Tapir Academic Press, 2006), 5–44.

74. Example 4.6a: Richard L. Crocker, *The Early Medieval Sequence* (Berkeley and Los Angeles: The University of California Press, 1977), 190.

75. map the intervallic spaces . . . a technological advance of great magnitude: See James Grier, *The Musical World of a Medieval Monk: Adémar de Chabannes in Eleventh-Century Aquitaine* (Cambridge: Cambridge University Press, 2006), 24.

76. In Paris, BN lat. 1121 . . . just before the Introit cue: See Paul Evans, *The Early Trope Repertory of Saint Martial de Limoges* (Princeton: Princeton University Press, 1970).

76. Example 4.7: Evans, *The Early Trope Repertory of St. Martial de Limoges*, 155.

77. the dialogue was sung . . . before Easter Mass: See David Bjork, "On the Dissemination of *Quem quaeritis* and the *Visitatio sepulchri* and the Chronology of Their Early Sources," *Comparative Drama* 14 (1980): 46–69; and Gunilla Iversen, "Aspects of the Transmission of the *Quem Quaeritis*," *Text* 3 (1987): 155–82. On the origins of *Quem quaeritis*, see C. Clifford Flanigan, "The Roman Rite and the Origins of the Liturgical. Drama," *University of Toronto Quarterly* 43 (1974): 263–84.

77. The nun Hroswitha . . . in this period: See James H. Forse, "Religious Drama and Ecclesiastical Reform in the Tenth Century," *Early Theater* 5 (2002): 47–70; and David Chamberlain, "Musical Imagery and Musical Learning in Hrotsvit," and Jonathan Black, "The Use of Liturgical Texts in Hrotsvit's Works," in Katharina M. Wilson, ed., *Hrotsvit of Gandersheim: Rara Avis in Saxonia?* (Ann Arbor, MI: Medieval and Renaissance Colloquium, 1987), 79–97 and 165–81.

77. "on His sacred mountain": Hroswitha, *Ascensio*, trans. by M. Gonsalva Wiegand in "The Non-Dramatic Works of Hroswitha" (Ph.D. diss., St. Louis University, 1936), 75–86, at 79, lines 97–103.

PART 2

80. traditional ideas about how to interpret Scripture: Marie-Dominique Chenu, "The Symbolist Mentality," in *Nature, Man and Society in the Twelfth Century: Essays on New*

Theological Perspectives in the Latin West, ed. and trans. Lester Little and Jerome Taylor (Toronto: University of Toronto Press, 1997), 99–145.

CHAPTER 5

86. The idea that a new relic had been stolen: See Patrick J. Geary, *Furta sacra: Thefts of Relics in the Central Middle Ages*, rev. ed. (Princeton: Princeton University Press, 1990).
86. "in a loud voice": Adémar de Chabannes, *Chronique*, trans. Yves Chauvin and Georges Pon (Turnhout: Brepols, 2003), Book 3, p. 273.
90. newer texts . . . juxtaposed with earlier layers of chant: See David Hiley, "The Music of Prose Offices in Honour of English Saints," *Plainsong and Medieval Music* 10 (2001): 23–37.
91. Example 5.3: N. De Goede, *The Utrecht Prosarium* (Amsterdam: Vereniging voor Nederlandse Muziekgeschiedenis, 1965), 111.
92. cannot be reconstructed, although attempts to do so have been numerous: *Performing Medieval Narrative*, ed. Evelyn Birge Vitz et al. (Cambridge, and Rochester, NY: D. S. Brewer, 2005).
94. new and better ways to instruct the children in their care: See Susan Boynton, "Training for the Liturgy as a Form of Monastic Education," in George Ferzoco and Carolyn Muessig, eds., *Medieval Monastic Education* (London: Leicester University Press, 2000), 7–20.
96. ut (C), re (D), mi (E): See Dolores Pesce, "Guido d'Arezzo, 'Ut Queant Laxis,' and Musical Understanding," in Russell Eugene Murray, Susan Forscher Weiss, and Cynthia J. Cyrus, eds., *Music Education in the Middle Ages and the Renaissance* (Bloomington: Indiana University Press, 2010), 25–36.
97. "harmonize in their dissonance": Guido of Arezzo, *Micrologus*, in *Hucbald, Guido, and John on Music: Three Medieval Treatises*, ed. Claude V. Palisca, trans. Warren Babb (New Haven: Yale University Press, 1978), 77.
97. "everywhere throughout the town": Wulfstan of Winchester, *Narratio metrica de S. Swithuno*, cited in Michael Lapidge, *The Cult of St. Swithun* (Oxford: Oxford University Press, 2003), 387.
98. troper of Winchester Cathedral . . . a significant body of polyphonic works: On the monophonic tropes of Winchester, see especially Alejandro Planchart, *The Repertory of Tropes of Winchester* (Princeton: Princeton University Press, 1977).
98. expansion of . . . earlier practices that developed in the eleventh century: See especially the introduction to Susan Rankin, ed., *The Winchester Troper* (London: Stainer and Bell, 2007).
98. eleventh century, when some scribes began to notate polyphonic works: See Peter Williams, "The Meaning of 'Organum': Some Case Studies," *Plainsong and Medieval Music* 10 (2001): 103–20.
99. Example 5.5: Rankin, *Winchester Troper*, 67.
99. write down polyphonic practices rather than being content only to improvise: See Wulf Arlt, "Stylistic Layers in Eleventh-Century Polyphony: How Can the Continental Sources Contribute to Our Understanding of the Winchester Organa?" in Susan Rankin and David Hiley, eds., *Music in the Medieval English Liturgy* (Oxford: Oxford University Press, 1993), 101–41.
100. constant exchange . . . during this period: Joan Malcolm, "Epistola Joannis Cottonis ad Fulgentium episcopum," *Musica Disciplina* 47 (1993): 159–69, suggests that John may have been the cantor at St. Maximin in Trier.
100. "So let him . . . compose a song": John, *On Music*, in *Hucbald, Guido, and John on Music*, ed. Palisca, trans. Warren Babb, chap. 1, p. 104.
102. "See to it . . . anyone composing thus": John, *On Music*, chap. 22, p. 146. 102. Example 5.6: Palisca, ed., *Hucbald, Guido, and John on Music*, trans. Babb, 145.

CHAPTER 6

104. "Lord of his fatherland, Le Mans!": Michel Huglo and George W. Hopkins, "A Lament for William the Conqueror," *Musical Times* 108 (1967): 124–25.
104. Bayeux Tapestry . . . created in the late eleventh century: Howard Bloch, *A Needle in the Right Hand of God: The Norman Conquest of 1066 and the Making and Meaning of the Bayeux Tapestry* (New York: Random House, 2006),

uses the mysteries of the embroidery as an introduction to the times.

105. Example 6.1: Archibald T. Davison and Willi Apel, eds., *Historical Anthology of Music, Oriental, Medieval, and Renaissance Music*, Rev. ed. (Cambridge: Harvard University Press, 1968), 18a.

106. Monasteries . . . in charge of book production, including notational systems: The shift is explained clearly and simply in Christopher de Hamel, *Scribes and Illuminators* (Toronto: University of Toronto Press, 1992), 4–7.

107. In Glastonbury . . . imposed by the Normans: See David Hiley, "Thurstan of Caen and Plainchant at Glastonbury: Musicological Reflections on the Norman Conquest," *Proceedings of the British Academy* 72 (1986): 57–90.

108. Example 6.2: Nicole Sevestre, *"Jerusalem Mirabilis,"* in *Jerusalem, Rome, Constantinople: l'image et le mythe de la ville au Moyen Age*, ed. Daniel Poirion (Paris: Presses de l'Université de Paris-Sorbonne, 1968), 4.

108. "blowing trumpets . . . marching barefooted": Raymond d'Aguilers, *Historia Francorum Qui Ceperunt Iherusalem*, trans. John Hugh Hill and Laurita L. Hill (Philadelphia: American Philosophical Society, 1968), 123. According to d'Aguilers, the crusaders sang "Haec dies qui fecit Dominus" at the close of their day of slaughter and triumph and chanted the Office of Easter (128).

109. Example 6.3: Davison and Apel, *Historical Anthology of Music, Oriental, Medieval, and Renaissance Music*, 18a.

109. the Seventh Crusade had failed . . . 1271: The numbering of the crusades accounts for only some of the many wars fought during this period.

110. Cluniac monks . . . liturgical and musical practices: See, for example, Susan Boynton, "Medieval Musical Education as Seen through Sources Outside the Realm of Music Theory," in Murray, Weiss, and Cyrus, *Music Education in the Middle Ages and the Renaissance*, 52–62.

111. "strengthened them still more": For further discussion of the Office at Cluny, see David Hiley, "The Office of the Transfiguration by Peter the Venerable," in Bryan Gillingham and Paul Merkeley, eds., *Chant and Its Peripheries: Essays in Honor of Terence Bailey* (Ottawa: Institute of Mediaeval Music, 1998), 224–37; and, for study of another Office, Ruth Steiner, "The Music for a Cluny Office of Saint Benedict," in Timothy G. Verdon, ed., *Monasticism and the Arts* (Syracuse, NY: Syracuse University Press, 1984), 81–113.

111. proclaimed in such architectural decorations: See Charles E. Scillia, "Meaning and the Cluny Capitals: Music as Metaphor," *Gesta* 27 (1988): 133–48.

113. cutting edge of musical developments in the twelfth century: On text-music relationships in the repertory, see Rachel Golden Carlson, "Two Paths to Daniel's Mountain: Poetic-Musical Unity in Aquitanian *Versus*," *Journal of Musicology* 23 (2006): 620–46.

113. But score notation, too, is problematic . . . relationships between the voices at cadences: An overview of the notational problems and identification of the nine strophic works in the Aquitanian repertory that use successive notation is found in Sarah Fuller, "Hidden Polyphony: A Reappraisal," *Journal of the American Musicological Society* 24 (1971): 169–92.

113. Example 6.4: Sarah Ann Fuller, *Aquitanian of the Eleventh and Twelfth Centuries*, vol. 3 (Ann Arbor, MI: University Microfilms International, 1976), 2.

115. Muslims, Jews, and Christians—created their own sense of the past: Stefan Schreiner, "In Search of a 'Golden Age': Jews, Christians and Muslims in Mediaeval Spain," *Concilium* 4 (2003): 35–50.

115. Queen Urraca . . . imported chant and liturgy: See Therese Martin, "The Art of a Reigning Queen as Dynastic Propaganda in Twelfth-Century Spain," *Speculum* 80 (2005): 1134–71.

115. But when it was finally written down . . . transformed by Frankish traditions: On the surviving manuscripts, with essays and deluxe images of them, see Susana Zapke, ed., *Hispania Vetus: Musical-Liturgical Manuscripts from Visigothic Origins to the Franco-Roman Transition* (Bilbao: Fundación BBVA, 2007). A color facsimile of the León Antiphoner is available as well: *Liber Antiphonarium de toto anni circulo*, ed. Ismael Fernández de la Cuesta (Madrid: Ministerio de Cultura y Cabildo de la Sancta Iglesia Cathedral de León, 2011).

117. "joy and exultation are sung together": *The Miracles of Saint James*, book 2, trans. Thomas F. Coffey, Linda Kay Davidson, and Maryjane Dunn (New York: Italica Press, 1996), 18–19.
118. *Alma perpetui . . . Ave regina caelorum*: See Susan Rankin, "*Exultent gentes occidentales*: The Compostelan Office of St. James," in José López Caló et al., eds., *El Códice Calixtino y la música de su tiempo* (A Coruña: Fundación Pedro Barrié de la Maza, 2001), 311–30.
118. Example 6.5: Susan Rankin, "*Exultent Gentes Occidentales*: The Compostelan Office of St. James," *El Códice Calixtino y la música de su tiempo*, ed. José López-Calo and Carlos Villanueva A Coruña (Fundación Pedro Barrié de la Maza, 2001), 329.
119. Example 6.6: Paul Helmer, *The Mass of Saint James* (Ottawa, Canada: Institute of Mediaeval Music, 1988), 187.

CHAPTER 7

122. Their story . . . exists in many guises: Mary Shepard, "A Tomb for Abelard and Heloise," *Romance Studies* 25 (2007): 2942, demonstrates how an early nineteenth-century artist reused early tomb fragments and the legends surrounding them to create a monument proclaiming his own artistic identity.
123. the woman was immediately seduced: See the useful introductions to the following English translations: *Abelard and Heloise: The Letters and Other Writings*, trans. William Levitan (Indianapolis: Hackett, 2007); Abelard, *Selected Songs and Poems*, trans. Stanley Lombardo and Barbara Thorburn (Indianapolis: Hackett, 2007); and *Letters of Peter Abelard*, trans. Jan M. Ziolkowski (Washington, DC: Catholic University of America Press, 2008).
123. "not Peter but imperfect Peter": The letter is printed among the letters of Peter Abelard in the *Patrologia Latina*, ed. J. P. Migne, vol. 178, cols. 358–72, quotation at 371–72.
124. Example 7.1: Chrysogonus Waddell, ed. *Hymn Collections from the Paraclete, Introduction and Commentary* (Trappist, Kentucky: Gethsemani Abbey, 1989), 50–51.
124. The Easter sequence *Epithalamica . . .* attributed to Abelard: The strong reasons for the attribution to Abelard are reviewed in Chrysoganus Waddell, "*Epithalamica:* An Easter Sequence by Peter Abelard," *Musical Quarterly* 72 (1986): 238–71, at 239–42.
125. Example 7.2: Waddell, "*Epithalamica*: An Easter Sequence," 248–53.
126. several possible sets of meanings, some sexual, some courtly, some religious: See Don A. Monson, "The Intertextuality of Love," chap. 3 of his *Andreas Capellanus, Scholasticism, and the Courtly Tradition* (Washington, DC: Catholic University of America Press, 2005), 86–121.
128. "which makes a man shine with so many virtues": Andreas Capellanus, *The Art of Courtly Love*, trans. John Jay Perry (New York: Columbia University Press, 1990), book I, 31.
128. "never loving any man in her heart": Ibid., book 3, 201.
129. none of it dates from the twelfth century: See Joan Tasker Grimbert, "Diminishing the Trobairitz, Excluding the Women Trouvères," *Tenso: Bulletin of the Société Guilhem IX* 14 (1999): 23–38. In fact, most surviving medieval songs are anonymous, and it is often difficult to say who and how many people are responsible for them.
129. more than half of the poems . . . arguments of one sort or another: see Michel-André Bossy and Nancy A. Jones, "Gender and Compilational Patterns in Troubadour Lyric: The Case of Manuscript N," *French Forum* 2 (1996): 261–80.
129. Example 7.3: *The Medieval Lyric: Anthology I* (NEH and Mount Holyoke College, 2001), 94–95.
130. The genre of the song . . . the style of the melody: See Elizabeth Aubrey, "Genre as a Determinant of Melody in the Songs of the Troubadours and the Trouvères," in William D. Paden, ed., *Medieval Lyric: Genres in Historical Content* (Urbana: University of Illinois Press, 2000), 273–96.
130. Example 7.4: *The Medieval Lyric: Anthology I* (NEH and Mount Holyoke College, 2001), 51–53.
131. a sense of community among the artists: See Don A. Monson, "The Troubadours at

Play: Irony, Parody and Burlesque," in Simon Gaunt and Sarah Kay, eds., *The Troubadours: An Introduction* (Cambridge: Cambridge University Press, 1999), 197–211.

131. Example 7.5: *The Medieval Lyric: Anthology I*, 77–78.

135. "any skill or the practice of some discipline": Hugh of St. Victor, *On the Moral Ark of Noah*, in *Selected Spiritual Writings*, trans. by a Religious of CSMV (London: Faber and Faber, 1962), 45.

136. A religious reformer . . . probably in 1146: See Margot E. Fassler, "Who Was Adam of St. Victor? The Evidence of the Sequence Manuscripts," *Journal of the American Musicological Society* 37 (1984): 233–69; and *Gothic Song: Victorine Sequences and Augustinian Reform in Twelfth-Century Paris*, 2nd ed. (Notre Dame, IN: University of Notre Dame Press, 2011).

136. Example 7.6: Fassler, *Gothic Song*, 421.

137. The nuns who copied Hildegard's works . . . in the later Middle Ages: See Cynthia J. Cyrus, *The Scribes for Women's Convents in Late Medieval Germany* (Toronto: University of Toronto Press, 2009).

138. taught her and members of her community how to notate music: See Margot Fassler, "Volmar, Hildegard, and St. Matthias," in Judith Peraino, ed., *Medieval Music in Practice: Studies in Honor of Richard Crocker* (Middleton, WI: American Institute of Musicology, 2013), 85–110.

138. "all the meanings I had heard before": Hildegard of Bingen, *Scivias*, trans. Mother Columba Hart and Jane Bishop (New York: Paulist Press, 1990), book 3, vision 13, p. 525.

139. the region of Germany around Bingen . . . twelfth-century illuminated manuscripts: See Margot Fassler, "Composer and Dramatist: 'Melodious Singing and the Freshness of Remorse,'" in Barbara Newman, ed., *Voice of the Living Light: Hildegard of Bingen and Her World* (Berkeley: University of California Press, 1998), 149–75.

140. Example 7.8: Fassler, "Composer and Dramatist: 'Melodious Singing and the Freshness of Remorse,'" 167.

141. "shadow over the falling flower": Hildegard of Bingen, *The Play of the Virtues*, in Peter Dronke, ed. and trans., *Nine Medieval Latin Plays* (Cambridge: Cambridge University Press, 1994), 160–81, at 169.

141. for the nuns to be free to sing and pray as they chose: Compare two views of this phenomenon, one in music and one in architecture: Heather Josselyn-Cranson, "'Moderate psallendo': Musical Participation in Worship among Gilbertine Nuns," *Plainsong and Medieval Music* 16 (2007): 173–86; and Loraine N. Simmons, "The Abbey Church at Fontevraud in the Later Twelfth Century: Anxiety, Authority and Architecture in the Female Spiritual Life," *Gesta* 31 (1992): 99–107.

PART 3

144. instrumental dance music from 1250 to 1430: Timothy McGee, *Medieval Instrumental Dances* (Indianapolis: University of Indiana Press, 1989); Joan Rimmer, "Medieval Instrumental Dance Music," *Music and Letters* 72 (1991): 61–68.

145. ecclesiastical schools . . . drew students from throughout Europe: See John Baldwin, *Paris, 1200* (Stanford, CA: Stanford University Press, 2010).

145. Music did not play a major role . . . Boethius was still taught: See Joseph Dyer, "Speculative 'Musica' and the Medieval University of Paris," *Music and Letters* 90/2 (2009): 177–204; and his "The Place of *Musica* in Medieval Classifications of Knowledge," *Journal of Musicology* 24 (2007): 3–71.

146. following the model . . . set forth by Aristotle: See Alex J. Novikoff, "Toward a Cultural History of Scholastic Disputation," *American Historical Review* 117 (2012): 331–64.

146. musical repertories . . . rooted to the places in which they were made: See John Haines and Patricia de Witt, "Johannes de Grocheio and Aristotelian Natural Philosophy," *Early Music History* 27 (2008): 47–98; and Jean A. Givens, *Observation and Image-Making in Gothic Art* (New York: Cambridge University Press, 2005).

CHAPTER 8

147. "universal noise of song": James Joseph Walch, quoting Carlyle, in *The Thirteenth: Greatest of Centuries* (New York: [Fordham

Univ. Pr., Mullen,] 1952). For the medieval source of this theme from the troubadour Raimon Vidal (fl. 1200), see Elizabeth Aubrey, "Genre as a Determinant of Melody in the Songs of the Troubadours and Trouvères," in *Medieval Lyric: Genres in Historical Context*, ed. William Paden (Urbana: University of Illinois Press, 2000), 273–96, at 278. Aubrey includes the original Old Occitan and her English translation.

149. a saint who was larger than life: See Rosalind B. Brooke, *The Image of St. Francis: Responses to Sainthood in the Thirteenth Century* (Cambridge: Cambridge University Press, 2006), esp. 160–63.

150. "to do something that will recall the memory of the child who was born in Bethlehem": Thomas of Celano, *First Life of St. Francis* (London: Methuen, 1908), 83–86.

150. "My sisters, the swallows": Thomas of Celano, *First Life of St. Francis*, 30:59.

151. Laude also offered . . . expanded in the fourteenth century: See Cyrilla Barr, "From *devozione* to *rappresentazione*: Dramatic Elements in the Holy Week Laude of Assisi," in Konrad Eisenbichler, ed., *Crossing the Boundaries: Christian Piety and the Arts in Italian Medieval and Renaissance Confraternities* (Kalamazoo, MI: Medieval Institute Publications, 1991), 11–32.

151. vernacular religious song . . . composed and notated in the fourteenth century: See Peter Loewen, "Francis the Musician and the Mission of the *joculatores Domini* in Medieval German Lands," *Franciscan Studies* 60 (2002): 251–90.

151. Example 8.1: Hans Tischler, ed., *The Earliest Laude: The Cortona Hymnal* (Ottawa: Institute of Medieval Music, 2002).

152. town-gown friction that sometimes resulted in violence: See Thomas B. Payne, "'Aurelianis civitas': Student Unrest in Medieval France and a Conductus by Philip the Chancellor," *Speculum* 75 (2000): 589–614.

153. manuscript includes . . . some 24 song fragments at the end: Carol Symes, "The Appearance of Early Vernacular Plays: Forms, Functions, and the Future of Medieval Theater," *Speculum* 77 (2002): 778–831, demonstrates the thin line between what is a play and what is not recognized as a play (but may be!).

154. Example 8.2: *Carmina Burana. Gesamtausgabe der Mittelalterlichen Melodien mit den, Dazugehorigen Texten* (München: Heimeran, 1979), 45.

156. Example 8.3a and b: Michael Korth, ed. *Carmina Burana: lateinisch-deutsch : Gesamtausgabe der mittelalterlichen Melodien mit den dazugehörigen Texten.* Transcribed with commentary René Clemencic; text commentary by Ulrich Müller ; trans. René Clemencic und Michael Korth. (München: Heimeran, 1979), 131.

157. Example 8.4a: Carmina Burana. Gesamtausgabe der Mittelalterlichen Melodien mit den, Dazugehorigen Texten (Munchen: Heimeran, 1979).

157. Example 8.4b: *Danielis ludus: The Play of Daniel: A Thirteenth-Century Musical Drama*, edited for modern performance by Noah Greenberg; based on the transcription from British Museum Egerton 2615 by Rembert Weakland (New York: Oxford University Press, 1959), 22.

158. Many trouvère poems . . . some may be ascribable to women: See Eglal Doss-Ginby et al., ed. and trans., *Songs of the Women Trouvères* (New Haven: Yale University Press, 2001).

158. "I do not scorn the devices of the trouvères": *Les Miracles de Notre Dame par Gautier de Coinci*, ed. V. Frederic Koenig (Paris: Librairie Minard, 1961), vol. 2, miracle 11, lines 2310–17, p. 93.

159. Trouvère songs exist in many guises: See Elizabeth Aubrey, "Reconsidering 'High Style' and 'Low Style' in Medieval Song," *Journal of Music Theory* 52 (2008): 75–122.

159. medieval song . . . lives of women real and imagined: See John Haines, *Medieval Song in Romance Languages* (Cambridge: Cambridge University Press, 2010), esp. ch. 3, "Love Song."

159: Example 8.5: Friedrich Gennrich, ed., *Troubadours, Trouvères, Minne- and Meistersinger* (Cologne: Arno Volk, 1960), 38.

160. Some of this commentary was local . . . some of it was learned: See Jennifer Saltzstein, "Relocating the Thirteenth-Century Refrain: Intertextuality, Authority and Origins, "*Journal of the Royal Musical Association* 135 (2010): 245–79.

161. jongleurs wrote plays . . . to keep spirits high: See Carole Symes, *A Common Stage: Theater and Public Life in Medieval Arras* (Ithaca, NY: Cornell University Press, 2007).
162. Adam's output was collected: For the "collected works" of Adam de la Halle as found in Paris, BN fr. 25566, see Sylvia Huot, *From Song to Book: The Poetics of Writing in Old French Lyric and Lyrical Narrative Poetry* (Ithaca, NY: Cornell University Press, 1987), 64–86.
162. Example 8.6: Adam de la Halle, *Oeuvres Completes* (Ridgewood NJ: The Gregg Press, Inc., 1965 [1872]), 347–48.
162. Example 8.7: Adam de La Halle, *The Lyric Works of Adam de la Hale*. Transcribed and edited by Nigel Wilkins. (Dallas: American Institute of Musicology, 1967), 52.
163. *Cantigas de Santa María* . . . the entire thirteenth century: See Martha E. Schaffer, "The 'Evolution' of the *Cantigas de Santa María*: The Relationships between MSS T, F, and E," in Stephen Parkinson, ed., *Cobras e son: Papers on the Text, Music, and Manuscripts of the "Cantigas de Santa María"* (Oxford: Oxford University Press, 2000), 186–213.
164. music and form of the cantigas may show Arabic influence: See Manual Pedro Ferreira, "Rondeaux and Virelais: The Music of Andalus and the *Cantigas de Santa María*," *Plainsong and Medieval Music* 13 (2004): 127–40. Ferreira studies possible survivals of these forms found today in northern Africa.
165. Example 8.8: Higinio Anglés, trans. and ed., *La Musica de las Cantigas de Santa Maria del Rey Alfonso El Sabio* (Barcelona, Duputacion Provincial de Barcelona, 1943), 158.
166. the stream that moved the mill wheel: From Bertran Carbonel (fl. 1252–1265), "A cobla without a melody is like a mill that has no water . . . ," identified, translated, and discussed in Elizabeth Aubrey, "Genre as a Determinant of Melody," 273–74, and note.

CHAPTER 9

168. a sacrament which the Albigensians denied: See Damian J. Smith, *Crusade, Heresy and Inquisition in the Lands of the Crown of Aragon (c. 1167–1276)* (Boston: Brill, 2010).
169. notational understanding that made the rhythmic modes possible: See Fassler, *Gothic Song*, 141.
169. conditioned by teaching found in the schools: See Dorit E. Tanay, *Noting Music, Marking Culture: The Intellectual Context of Rhythmic Notation, 1250–1400* (Holzgerlingen: Hänssler, 1999), esp. 17–47; and John Haines and Patricia DeWitt, "Johannes de Grocheio and Aristotelian Natural Philosophy," *Early Music History* 27 (2008): 47–98.
172. Marie d'Oignies . . . mystical devotion to the Eucharist: See Annecke B. Mulder-Bakker, ed., *Mary of Oignies: Mother of Salvation* (Turnhout: Brepols, 2006).
174. parallels between St. Thomas's Eucharistic thought and the texts . . . to establish his authorship: See Barbara R. Walters et al., *The Feast of Corpus Christi* (University Park: Pennsylvania State University Press, 2006).
175. Musical developments . . . required training in the schools to be mastered: See Guillaume Gross, "Organum at Notre Dame in the Twelfth and Thirteenth Centuries: Rhetoric and Music," *Plainsong and Medieval Music* 15 (2006): 87–108.
175. we can assume that theoretical treatises . . . St. Ursula at the Sorbonne: See Richard and Mary Rouse, "The Early Library of the Sorbonne," in *Authentic Witnesses: Approaches to Medieval Texts and Manuscripts* (Notre Dame, IN: University of Notre Dame Press, 1991), 370–72.
176. In this part of the portal . . . native Chartrain: See Kathryn Horste, "'A Child Is Born': The Iconography of the Portail Ste.-Anne at Paris," *Art Bulletin* 69 (1987): 187–210.
176. The singers of the most complex repertory . . . sixteen choristers hired each year: See Craig Wright, *Music and Ceremony at Notre Dame of Paris* (Cambridge: Cambridge University Press, 1989), 24–27. Wright's book provides evidence for now-standard identifications of Albertus, Léonin, and Pérotin.
179. Some scholars think . . . for his conductus texts: see Wright, *Music and Ceremony*; and Thomas B. Payne, "Aurelianis civitas: Student Unrest in Medieval France and a Conductus by Philip the Chancellor," *Speculum* 75 (2000): 589–614. For pieces now attributed to Philip

besides conductus, see Philip the Chancellor, *Motets and Prosulas*, ed. Thomas B. Payne (Middleton, WI: AR Editions, 2011).

179. adept at performing both monophonic and polyphonic repertories: See Susan Rankin, "Some Medieval Songs," *Early Music* 31 (2003): 331–44.

183. an authoritative new edition of the *Magnus liber organi*: See Mark Everist, "From Paris to St. Andrews: The Origins of W_1,"*Journal of the American Musicological Society* 43 (1990): 1–42. Transcriptions with invaluable notes in *Magnus Liber Organi: Parisian Liturgical Polyphony from the 12th and 13th Centuries*, Edward Roesner, gen. ed., 7 vols., with editorial work by Mark Everist, Edward Roesner, Rebecca Baltzer, and Thomas Payne.

183. The most recent theory . . . his new royal chapel, the Sainte Chapelle, in 1248: see Barbara *Haggh Huglo* and Michel *Huglo*, "Magnus liber, maius munus: Origine et destinée du manuscrit F," *Revue de musicologie* 90 (2004): 193–230. On how and why King Louis IX became a saint, see M. Cecilia Gaposchkin, *The Making of Saint Louis: Kingship, Sanctity, and Crusade in the Later Middle Ages* (Ithaca, NY: Cornell University Press, 2008).

183. Each genre has its own relationship . . . notational characteristics unique to it: See Edward Roesner, "Codex Calixtinus and the Magnus Liber Organi: Some Preliminary Observations," in José López-Calo and Carlos Villanueva, eds., *El Códice Calixtino y la música de su tiempo* (A Coruña: Fundación Pedro Barrié de la Maza, 2001), 135–61.

183. *copulae* . . . on a variety of pitch levels: See Jeremy Yudkin, "The Anonymous of St. Emmeram and Anonymous IV on the Copula," *Musical Quarterly* 70 (1984): 1–22.

185. Example 9.3: Edward H. Roesner, ed., *Magnus Liber Organi* (Les Remparts, Monaco: Editions de L'ouiseau-Lyre, 1993).

187. perfection of the number three foundational to the system: For contemporary discussion of the perfection of the Trinity and the importance of proportion, see Bonaventure (1221–1274), *The Mind's Road to God*, trans. George Boas (New York: Liberal Arts Press, 1953), esp. book 2, 18–21.

188. The best way to study the motet . . . several of its settings: See Alejandro Enrique Planchart, "The *Flower's Children*," *Journal of Musicological Research* 17 (2003): 303–48.

188. The possibilities for glossing . . . humor and irony: See David Rothenberg, "The Marian Symbolism of Spring, ca. 1200–ca. 1500: Two Case Studies," *Journal of the American Musicological Society* 59 (2006): 319–98.

189. Example 9.4: Yvonne Rokseth, ed., "Plus bele que flors," in *Polyphonies du XIIIe Siecle* (Paris: Editions de l'Oiseau Lyre, 1936), 46.

PART 4

196. great strides in understanding the mechanisms of the natural world: See John E. Murdoch, "*Subtilitates anglicanae* in Fourteenth-Century Paris: John of Mirecourt and Peter Ceffons," in M. P. Cosman and B. Chandler, eds., *Machaut's World: Science and Art in the Fourteenth Century* (New York: New York Academy of Sciences, 1978), 52–55.

CHAPTER 10

198. "diverses chançons and diverses motés": Catherine Jean Parsoneault, "The Montpellier Codex: Royal Influence and Musical Taste in Late Thirteenth-Century Paris" (Ph.D. dissertation, University of Texas, Austin, 2001), 158. The citation comes from the *Grandes chroniques de France*, the French translation of the original Latin version made by the thirteenth-century chronicler Guillaume de Nangis.

199. an activity that might distract them from more dangerous possibilities: See Christopher Page, *Voices and Instruments of the Middle Ages: Instrumental Practice and Songs in France, 1100–1300* (Berkeley: University of California Press, 1986), esp. 50–84.

199. Pierre, who was summarily hanged: See William C. Jordan, "The Struggle for Influence at the Court of Philip III: Pierre de la Broce and the French Aristocracy," *French Historical Studies* 24 (2001): 439–68.

201. characteristics associated with motets in the Petronian style: see Gisèle Clément-Dumas and Isabelle Fabre, "Saint Étienne et l'Amant Courtois: Jeux sur la figure du martyr

dans le motet *S'Amours*," in *Lingua Mea Calamus Scribae: Mélanges offerts à Madame Marie-Noël Colette*, ed. Daniel Saulnier et al., *Etudes gregoriennes* 26 (2009): 63–87.

201. Example 10.1: Yvonne Rokseth, ed., *Polyphonies du XIIIe siècle; le manuscrit H 196 de la Faculté de médecine de Montpellier* (Paris: Éditions de l'Oiseau lyre/Louis B. M. Dyer, 1936), 77.

202. Example 10.2: Rokseth, *Polyphonies du XIIIe siècle*, 223.

203. "they could contain an infinite populace": Jean de Jandun, quoted in Erik Inglis, "Gothic Architecture and a Scholastic: Jean de Jandun's 'Tractatus de laudibus Parisius' (1323)," *Gesta* 42 (2003): 68. Although Sainte Chapelle survives, the complex built by Philip the Fair does not.

205. the moment when Lady Fortune's wheel turned: See Edward Roesner, "Labouring in the Midst of Wolves: Reading a Group of 'Fauvel' Motets," *Early Music History* 22 (2003): 169–245.

205. soundscape of early-fourteenth-century Paris: See Emma Dillon, *The Sense of Sound: Musical Meaning in France, 1260–1330* (New York: Oxford University Press, 2012).

205. The brilliant intertextuality . . . beginning with the first folio: See Roesner, "Labouring," 201–12; and Emma Dillon, *Medieval Music-Making and the "Roman de Fauvel"* (Cambridge: Cambridge University Press, 2002). The four main text scribes have been identified by Susan Rankin, "The Divine Truth of Scripture: Chant in the 'Roman de Fauvel,'" *Journal of the American Musicological Society* 47 (1994): 205.

207. the musicians express their own hopes for change: As Isidore of Seville explained in his *De ecclesiasticis officiis*, 72 is a mystical number; there are 72 books of the canonical Bible; Moses chose 72 priests; Jesus sent 72 disciples to preach; and 72 tongues were spread throughout the world. Roesner, "Labouring," 213.

207. Example 10.3: Leo Schrade, ed., *The Roman de Fauvel; The works of Philippe de Vitry; French Cycles of the Ordinarium Missae* [Polyphonic Music of the Fourteenth Century, Vol. I] (Munich: Editions de l'Oiseau-Lyre, 1956), 4.

208. the hamlet that gave him his name (Vitry-en-Artois): See Anne Walters Robertson, "Which Vitry? The Witness of the Trinity Motet from the *Roman de Fauvel*," in Delores Pesce, ed., *Hearing the Motet: Essays on the Motet of the Middle Ages and Renaissance* (Oxford: Oxford University Press, 1997), 52–81, at 75; and Margaret Bent, "Polyphony of Texts and Music in the Fourteenth-Century Motet: *Tribum que non abhorruit/Quoniam secta latronum/Merito hec patimur* and Its Quotations," ibid., 82–103.

208. allow us to reconstruct a fairly full biography: See Lawrence Gushee, "Jehan des Murs and His Milieu," in Frank Hentschel, ed., *Musik und die Geschichte der Philosophie und Naturwissenschaften im Mittelalter* (Leiden: Brill, 1998), 339–71.

209. a precise temporal relationship that used ever-smaller note values: See Bent, "Polyphony of Text and Music," 98; and Andrew Wathey, "The Motets of Philippe de Vitry and the Fourteenth-Century Renaissance," *Early Music History* 12 (1993): 119–50.

212. Example 10.4a: Schrade, *The Roman de Fauvel*, 54.

212. Example 10.4b: Willi Appel, ed., *Corpus of Early Keyboard Music: Keyboard Music of the Fourteenth and Fifteenth Centuries* (American Institute of Musicology, 1963).

216. a good ending for the pilgrim's journey: See Anne Walters Robertson, *Machaut and Reims: Context and Meaning in His Musical Works* (Cambridge: Cambridge University Press, 2002); and Anna Zayaruznaya, "'*She Has a Wheel that Turns . . .*': Crossed and Contradictory Voices in Machaut's Motets," *Early Music History* 28 (2009): 185–240.

216. his own attention to his legacy: See Elizabeth Eva Leach, "Dead Famous: Mourning, Machaut, Music, and Renown in the Chantilly Codex," in Yolanda Plumley and Anne Stone, eds., *A Late Medieval Songbook and Its Context: New Perspectives on the Chantilly Codex* (Bibliothèque du Château de Chantilly, Ms. 564) (Turnhout: Brepols, 2009), 63–93.

216. Example 10.5: Guillaume de Machaut. *The works of Guillaume de Machaut*. Ed. Leo Schrade. [Polyphonic Music of the Fourteenth Century, Vol. II] (Munich : Editions de l'Oiseau-Lyre, 1956), 137.

217. Example 10.6: Daniel Leech-Wilkinson, *Machaut's Mass: An Introduction* (Oxford: Clarendon Press, 1990), 186.

218. could bring wholeness to the soul: See Gur Zak, *Petrarch's Humanism and the Care of the Self* (Cambridge: Cambridge University Press, 2010).
220. Example 10.7: Gordon K. Greene, ed., *Polyphonic Music of the Fourteenth Century*, vol. 19 (Les Remparts, Monaco: Editions de l'Oiseau-Lyre, 1981–82), 65.
220. in ways that only they could understand: See Elizabeth Eva Leach, "Nature's Forge and Mechanical Reproduction: Reading, Writing, and Performing Song," in Mary Carruthers, ed., *Rhetoric Beyond Words: Delight and Persuasion in the Arts of the Middle Ages* (Cambridge: Cambridge University Press, 2010), 72–95.
221. the last major French composer to do so: See David Maw, "Meter and Word Setting: Revising Machaut's Monophonic Virelais," *Current Musicology* 74 (2002), 69–102.

CHAPTER 11

224. Marchetto had contact with learned French theorists and musicians: See Carla Vivarelli, "'*Di una pretesa scuola napoletana*': Sowing the Seeds of the Ars Nova at the Court of Robert of Anjou," *Journal of Musicology* 24 (2007): 272–96.
225. crucial not to superimpose . . . thirteenth and fourteenth centuries: A brief overview of the "singer's rules" for the use of accidentals is found in Lucy E. Cross, "Musica Ficta," in Ross W. Duffin, ed., *A Performer's Guide to Medieval Music* (Bloomington: Indiana University Press, 2000), 496–509.
225. motion involving chromaticism: Marchetto's *Lucidarium* has been edited and translated into English by Jan Herlinger (Chicago: University of Chicago Press, 1985), with a very useful introduction and notes.
226. Example 11.1: Richard H. Hoppin, *Medieval Music: A Norton Introduction to Music History*, example XVIII-2. Copyright © 1978 by W. W. Norton & Company, Inc. Used by permission of W. W. Norton & Company, Inc.
226. the Feast of the Annunciation, March 25, 1305: See Eleanora M. Beck, *Giotto's Harmony: Music and Art in Padua at the Crossroads of the Renaissance* (Florence: European Press Academic Publishing, 2005); and Anne Walters Robertson, "Remembering the *Annunciation* in Medieval Polyphony, *Speculum* 70 (1995): 275–304.
227. 45 motets, 38 of which survive only in Trecento manuscripts: See Michael Cuthbert, "Tipping the Iceberg: Missing Italian Polyphony from the Age of Schism," *Musica Disciplina* 54 (2009): 39–75, at 47, with updates since supplied by the author.
227. Rossi Codex . . . even greater collection: See Vatican City, Biblioteca Apostolica Vaticana, Rossi 215 ("Codex Rossi") and Ostiglia, Opera Pia G. Greggiati, Biblioteca Musicale, s.s. ("Ostiglia fragment").
227. the rise of opera in the seventeenth century: See Brooks Toliver, "Improvisation in the Madrigals of the Rossi Codex," *Acta Musicologica* 64 (1992): 165–76.
228. Example 11.2: Nino Pirrotta, ed., *The Music of Fourteenth-Century Italy* (American Institute of Musicology, 1960), 21.
229. the pieces they worked from: See John Nádas, "The Squarcialupi Codex: An Edition of Trecento Songs, c. 1410–1415," in Alberto Gallo, ed., *Il Codice Squarcialupi: MS Mediceo Palatino 87, Biblioteca Medicea Laurenziana di Firenze* (Florence, 1992), 87–126.
233. "a branch over Francesco's head": From Giovanni Gherardi, *Il Paradiso degli Alberti* (c. 1425); cited in F. Alberto Gallo, *Music of the Middle Ages*, trans. Karen Eales (Cambridge: Cambridge University Press, 1985), 2: 135.
233. "Landini cadence" . . . into polyphonic pieces: See Michael Long, "Landini's Musical Patrimony: A Reassessment of Some Compositional Conventions in Trecento Polyphony," *Journal of the American Musicological Society* 40 (1987): 31–52.
233. Example 11.3: Leo Schrade, ed. *The Works of Francesco Landini* [Polyphonic Music of the Fourteenth Century, Vol. 4] (Munich: Editions de l'Oiseau-Lyre, 1958), 80.
234. most skilled musicians were also editors: See Blake McDowell Wilson, *Singing Poetry in Renaissance Florence: The "Cantasi Come" Tradition (1375–1550)* (Florence: Olschki, 2009); and Elena Abramov-van Rijk, *Parlar Cantando: The Practice of Reciting Verses in Italy from 1300–1600* (Bern: Peter Lang, 2009).
234. Example 11.4: Jamieson B. Hurry, *Sumer is icumen in*, 2nd ed. (London: Novello, 1914), 32.

235. spilling over to around 1420: See Michael Scott Cuthbert and Elizabeth Nyikos, "Style, Locality, and the Trecento Gloria: New Sources and a Reexamination," *Acta Musicologica* 82 (2010): 185–212.

236. Example 11.5: Kurt von Fischer and Alberto Gallo, eds., *Polymusic of the Fourteenth Century*, vol. 13, *Italian Sacred and Ceremonial Music* (Monaco: Oiseau-Lyre, 1987), 104–05.

236. dramatic ceremonies of their "deaths": See David Cressy, "Book Burning in Tudor and Stuart England," *Sixteenth Century Journal* 36 (2005): 359–74.

237. libraries of recusant Catholic families . . . the sacraments and the chant: See Nancy Pollard Brown, "*Paperchase*: The Dissemination of Catholic Texts in Elizabethan England," *English Manuscript Studies, 1100–1700*, vol. 1 (1989): 120–43; and E. J. Dobson and F. Ll. Harrison, eds., *Medieval English Songs* (Cambridge: Cambridge University Press, 1979).

238. Example 11.6a: Richard H. Hoppin, *Anthology of Medieval Music* (New York: Norton, 1978), 108.

238. Example 11.6b: E. J. Dobson and F. L. Harrison, *Medieval English Songs* (Cambridge: Cambridge University Press, 1979), 269.

238. Example 11.6c: Dobson and Harrison, *Medieval English* Songs, 270.

239. "ending on 5ths and octaves": Johannes *Boen, Musica*, ed. W. Frobenius (Stuttgart, 1971), esp. 76. For further discussion of Boen and comparison with other contemporary "listeners," see Sarah Fuller, "'*Delectabatur in hoc auris*': Some Fourteenth-Century Perspectives on Aural Perception," *Musical Quarterly* 82 (1998): 466–81.

240. Example 11.7: Anon., From the catilena Christi messis in E. H. Sanders, "Cantilena and Discant in Fourteenth-Century England," *Musica Disciplina* 19 (1965): 11.

240. *cantilena* . . . notated in score: See Julie E. Cumming, "Motet and Cantilena," in Duffin, *A Performer's Guide to Medieval Music*, 52–82, at 66; and Peter Lefferts, *The Motet in England in the Fourteenth Century* (Ann Arbor: UMI Research Press, 1986).

240. he had imposed upon its leaders: See Ernest Sanders, "English Polyphony in the Morgan Library Manuscript," *Music and Letters* 61 (1980): 172–76.

241. Example 11.8: Ursula Günther, ed., *The Motets of the Manuscripts Chantilly* (American Institute of Musicology, 1965).

242. Example 11.9: Andrew Hughes and Margaret Bent, eds., *The Old Hall Manuscript*, CMM 46–1, pt. 1 (American Institute of Musicology, 1968), 94–95.

242. polyphonic settings of these texts: See Andrew Kirkman, *The Cultural Life of the Early Polyphonic Mass: Medieval Context to Modern Revival* (Cambridge: Cambridge University Press, 2010), 170–75.

244. in the Lowlands . . . out of thin air: Reinhard Strohm, "The Ars Nova Fragments of Gent," *Tijdschrift van de Vereniging voor Nederlandse Muziekgeschiedenis* 34 (1984): 109–31.

CHAPTER 12

248. four-string vielles . . . several percussion instruments: On the use and non-use of instruments in performance, see Anthony Rowland-Jones, "Iconography in the History of the Recorder up to c. 1430: Part 1," *Early Music* 33 (2005): 557–74; Christopher Page, *Voices and Instruments of the Middle Ages* (Berkeley: University of California Press, 1986); Charles Brewer, "Non-Liturgical Monophony: Latin," in Duffin, *A Performer's Guide to Medieval Music*, 115–21; Howard Mayer Brown and Stanley Sadie, eds., *Performance Practice: Music before 1600* (New York: Norton, 1989); and Tess Knighton and David Fallows, eds., *A Companion to Medieval and Renaissance Music* (New York: Schirmer Books, 1992).

248. much as country fiddle players do today . . . a sense of what the most sophisticated German minstrel music sounded like: See Maricarmen Gómez, "Minstrel Schools in the Late Middle Ages," trans. Barbara Haggh, *Early Music* 18 (1990): 212–16; Paul Bracken, "The Myth of the Medieval Minstrel: An Interdisciplinary Approach to Performers and the *Chansonnier* Repertory," *Viator* 33 (2002): 100–116; and Maria Dobozy, *Re-Membering the Present: The Medieval German Poet-Minstrel in Cultural Context* (Turnhout: Brepols, 2005).

248. "the whole feminine sex in his poems": Albert von Strassburg (1303–1359), translated by Barbara Newman in *Frauenlob's Song of Songs: A Medieval German Poet and His Masterpiece* (University Park: Pennsylvania State University Press, 2006), 43.

248. some sort of improvised polyphonic elaboration: See Lorenz Welker, "Some Aspects of the Notation and Performance of German Song around 1400," trans. Barbara Haggh, *Early Music* 18 (1990): 235–46.

249. "my Beloved is mine": Quoted in Newman, *Frauenlob's Song of Songs*, 23; original German on p. 22.

249. "works on it as best he can": Quoted in Newman, *Frauenlob's Song of Songs*, 209 (from strophe 17 of the *Marienleich*).

249. the art of making contrafacta was finely honed: See Horst Brunner and Karl-Günther Hartmann, eds., *Spruchsang: Die Melodien der Sangspruchdichter des 12. bis 15 Jahrhunderts* (Kassel: Bärenreiter, 2010).

250. Example 12.1: Karl Stackmann and Karl Bertau, eds., Frauenlob (Heinrich von Meissen) Leichs, Sangsprüche, Liede, (Gottingen: Vandenhoeck & Ruprecht, 1981), 258.

250. Example 12.2: Hoppin, *Anthology of Medieval Music*, 317.

251. approach that *transcends iconographic stereotypes:* See Jeffery F. Hamburger and Susan Marti, eds., *Crown and Veil: Female Monasticism from the Fifth to the Fifteenth Centuries*, trans. Dietlinde Hamburger, foreword by Caroline Walker Bynum (New York: Cambridge University Press, 2008).

251. *Every verse has an initial . . . added by the nuns:* See Jeffery F. Hamburger, ed., *Leaves from Paradise: The Cult of John the Evangelist at the Dominican Convent of Paradies bei Soest* (Cambridge: Harvard University Press, 2008).

254. "moderated with discretion": Cited in Anne Bagnall Yardley, *Performing Piety: Musical Culture in Medieval English Nunneries* (New York: Palgrave, 2006), 215. See also E. A. Jones and Alexandra Walsham, eds., *Syon Abbey and Its Books: Reading, Writing, and Religion, c. 1400–1700* (Woodbridge: Boydell, 2010); articles by Katherine Zieman, Margot Fassler, Elizabeth Schirmer, and Steven Justice, in Linda Olson and Kathryn Kerby-Fulton, eds., *Voices in Dialogue: Reading Women in the Middle Ages* (Notre Dame, IN: University of Notre Dame Press, 2005); and Rebecca A. Baltzer, "The Little Office of the Virgin and Mary's Role at Paris," in Margot Fassler and Rebecca A. Baltzer, *The Divine Office in the Latin Middle Ages* (Oxford: Oxford University Press: 2000), 463–84.

254. granddaughter would serve as abbess: See Anne Bagnall Yardley, "'Ful weel she soong the service dyvyne': The Cloistered Musician in the Middle Ages," in Jane Bowers and Judith Tick, eds., *Women Making Music: The Western Art Tradition, 1150–1950* (Urbana: University of Illinois Press, 1986), 15–38; and Wesley D. Jordan, "Four Twelfth-Century Musico-Liturgical Manuscripts from the Cistercian Monastery of Las Huelgas, Burgos," *Manuscripta* 37 (1993): 21–70.

255. "these songs have been written here": Montserrat, Biblioteca del Monasterio MS 1, f. 22r (trans. Peter Jeffery).

255. accompaniment by drums . . . (. . . their reputations): See Mauricio Molina, *Frame Drums in the Medieval Iberian Peninsula* (Kassel: Reichenberger, 2010).

256. Example 12.3: Kurt von Fischer, ed. *Polyphonic Music of the Fourteenth Century*, French Sacred Music, vol. XXIIIB (Monaco: Editions de L'Oiseau-Lyre, 1959).

258. closer to early systems of sound: See Richard Widdess, *The Rāgas of Early Indian Music: Modes, Melodies, and Musical Notations from the Gupta Period to c. 1250* (New York: Oxford University Press, 1995).

CREDITS

MUSICAL EXAMPLES

4 and 5 Anonymous, *Ave Maris Stella, O Maria Due Maire*, *The Medieval Lyric: Anthology I* (NEH and Mount Holyoke College, 2001), p. 24. Reprinted with permission. **129** Comtessa de Dia, *A chantar m'er*, *The Medieval Lyric: Anthology* I (NEH and Mount Holyoke College, 2001), pp. 94–95. Reprinted with permission. **130** Marcabru, *L'autrier jost' una sebissa*, *The Medieval Lyric: Anthology* I (NEH and Mount Holyoke College, 2001), pp. 51–53. Reprinted with permission. **131** Guiraut de Bornelh, *Reis glorios*, *The Medieval Lyric: Anthology* I (NEH and Mount Holyoke College, 2001), pp. 77–78. Reprinted with permission. **171** Anonymous, *Salve Regina*, *Liber Usualis*, Benedictines of the Solesmes Monastery, New edition (1997), p. 276. Reprinted with permission of Abbaye Saint-Pierre. **189** Anonymous, Yvonne Rokseth (ed.),"Plus bele que flors" in *Polyphonies du XIIIe Siecle* (Paris: Editions de l'Oiseau Lyre, 1936), III, p. 46. Reprinted by permission of Éditions de l'Oiseau-Lyre. **216** Guillaume de Machaut, *The Works of Guillaume de Machaut*, ed. Leo Schrade, *Polyphonic Music of the Fourteenth Century*, Vol. II (Munich: Editions de l'Oiseau-Lyre, 1956), p. 137. Reprinted by permission of Éditions de l'Oiseau-Lyre. **226** "French and Italian 'manners' of reading semibreves," from *Medieval Music: A Norton Introduction to Music History*, by Richard H. Hoppin, example XVIII-2. Copyright © 1978 by W. W. Norton & Company, Inc. Used by permission of W. W. Norton & Company, Inc. **240** Anonymous, From the *cantilena Christi messis*, E. H. Sanders, "Cantilena and Discant in 14th-Century England," *Musica Disciplina* 19 (1965): 11. Reproduced with permission. **242** Richard Queldryk, *The Old Hall Manuscript*, ed. Andrew Hughes and Margaret Bent, CMM 46–1, pt. 1 (American Institute of Musicology, 1968), pp. 94–95. Reproduced with permission. **250** Frauenlob (Heinrich von Meissen) Leichs, *Sangsprüche, Liede*, ed. Karl Stackmann and Karl Bertau (Vandenhoeck & Ruprecht, 1981), p. 258. Reprinted with permission. **256** Anonymous, Laudemus Virginem, from the *Llibre Vermill*, in *Polyphonic Music of the Fourteenth Century*, ed. Kurt von Fischer. French Sacred Music, vol. XXIIIB. Reprinted by permission of Éditions de l'Oiseau-Lyre. **A7** Anonymous, *Graduale Triplex*, Abbey of St. Peter of Solesmes Monks, 196–97. Reprinted with permission of Abbaye Saint-Pierre. **A19** Charles M. Atkinson, *The Critical Nexus: Tone-System, Mode, and Notation in Early Medieval*

Music (Oxford: Oxford University Press, 2009). **A21** "The Psalm Tones," from *Medieval Music: A Norton Introduction to Music History* by Richard H. Hoppin, p. 82. Copyright © 1978 by W. W. Norton & Company, Inc. Used by permission of W. W. Norton & Company, Inc. **A22** Peter Jeffery, Medieval poems for memorizing the psalm tones. Reprinted with permission.

PHOTOGRAPHS

6–7 Reproduced from the original held by the Department of Special Collections of the Hesburgh Libraries of Notre Dame. **22** © Oxbow Books; **31** Foto Marburg /Art Resource, NY; **33** HIP/Art Resource, NY. **39** Stiftsbibliothek St. Gallen Abbey Library of St Gall, Cod. Sang 390, 13; **47** Stiftsbibliothek St. Gallen Abbey Library of St Gall, Cod. Sang 359, 107; **50** Bibliothèques-Médiathèques de Metz/ Département Patrimoine. **57** © The Trustees of the British Museum/Art Resource, NY; **61** Val Thoermer/Agefotostock; **62** Courtesy of Peter Jeffery; **68** Stiftsbibliothek St. Gallen Abbey Library of St Gall, Cod. Sang 159, 6. **85** V&A Images, London/Art Resource, NY; **87** bpk, Berlin/Kunstgewerbemuseum, Staatliche Museen/Saturia Linke/Art Resource, NY; **88** Charroux-La_tour_Charlemagne 2011: en.wikipedia.org/wiki/Public_domain. **93** Henri de Feraudy.**105** Erich Lessing/Art Resource, NY; **111** Giraudon/The Bridgeman Art Library; **112**: Henri de Feraudy; **116** Album / Art Resource, NY. **127** Henri de Feraudy; **132** Universal Images Group/Art Resource, NY; **134** Henri de Feraudy; **135** Scala/White Images/Art Resource, NY; **138** Erich Lessing/ Art Resource, NY. **149** Alfredo Dagli Orti/The Art Archive at Art Resource, NY; **155** Bayerische Staatsbibliothek; **161** Bibliotheque des Arts Decoratifs, Paris, France/Archives Charmet/ The Bridgeman Art Library; **164** Album/Art Resource, NY. **173** © Bodleian Library, University of Oxford; **177** © 2008 Holly Hayes/ Art History Images. All rights reserved; **178** Anthony Scibilia/Art Resource, NY; **184** Biblioteca Medicea Laurenziana, TECA Digitale. **200** From Bibliothèque interuniversitaire de Montpellier.BU de médecine, © BIU/IRHT (CNRS); **206** Bibliotheque Nationale de France; **219** Vanni/Art Resource, NY. **226** Cameraphoto Arte, Venice/Art Resource, NY; **230** Bibliotheque Nationale de France; **232** Lebrecht Music & Arts; **237** International Photobank/Alamy. **247** Henri de Feraudy; **252** © Universitäts- und Landesbibliothek Düsseldorf, urn:nbn:de:hbz:061:1-39664; **256** HIP/Art Resource, NY

INDEX

Note: Page numbers in *italics* indicate illustrations or musical examples.